Politics in France and Europe

EUROPE IN TRANSITION: THE NYU EUROPEAN STUDIES SERIES

The Marshall Plan: Fifty Years After
Edited by Martin Schain

Europe at the Polls: The European Elections of 1999
Edited by Pascal Perrineau, Gérard Grunberg, and Colette Ysmal

Unions, Immigration, and Internationalization: New Challenges and Changing Coalitions in the United States and France
By Leah Haus

Shadows over Europe: The Development and Impact of the Extreme Right in Western Europe
Edited by Martin Schain, Aristide Zolberg, and Patrick Hossay

Defending Europe: The EU, NATO and the Quest for European Autonomy
Edited by Joylon Howorth and John T.S. Keeler

The Lega Nord and Contemporary Politics in Italy
By Thomas W. Gold

Germans or Foreigners? Attitudes toward Ethnic Minorities in Post-Reunification Germany
Edited by Richard Alba and Peter Schmidt

Germany on the Road to Normalcy? Politics and Policies of the First Red-Green Federal Government
Edited by Werner Reutter

The Politics of Language: Essays on Languages, State and Society
Edited by Tony Judt and Denis Lacorne

Realigning Interests: Crisis and Credibility in European Monetary Integration
By Michele Chang

The Impact of Radical Right-wing Parties in West European Democracies
By Michelle Hale Williams

European Foreign Policy Making Toward the Mediterranean
By Federica Bicchi

Sexual Equality in an Integrated Europe: Virtual Equality
By R. Amy Elman

Migration and Activism in Europe since 1945
Edited by Wendy Pojmann

Politics in France and Europe
Edited by Pascal Perrineau and Luc Rouban

Politics in France and Europe

Edited by
Pascal Perrineau and Luc Rouban

palgrave
macmillan

First published in 2009 by
PALGRAVE MACMILLAN®
in the United States—a division of St. Martin's Press LLC,
175 Fifth Avenue, New York, NY 10010.

Where this book is distributed in the UK, Europe and the rest of the world, this is by Palgrave Macmillan, a division of Macmillan Publishers Limited, registered in England, company number 785998, of Houndmills, Basingstoke, Hampshire RG21 6XS.

Palgrave Macmillan is the global academic imprint of the above companies and has companies and representatives throughout the world.

ISBN: 978–0–230–61480–2

Library of Congress Cataloging-in-Publication Data

Politique en France et en Europe. English.
Politics in France and Europe / edited by Pascal Perrineau and Luc Rouban.
p. cm.—(Europe in transition)
ISBN 978–0–230–61480–2 (alk. paper)
1. France--Politics and government—21st century. 2. Europe—Politics and government—21st century. 3. Comparative politics. I. Perrineau, Pascal. II. Rouban, Luc. III. Title.

JN2594.2.P64613 2009
320.94—dc22 2009012780

A catalogue record of the book is available from the British Library.

Design by Newgen Imaging Systems (P) Ltd., Chennai, India.

First edition: December 2009

10 9 8 7 6 5 4 3 2 1

Printed in the United States of America.

Contents

Figures and Tables

Figures

Tables

Contributors

Daniel Boy, Research Director, Cevipof, Sciences Po, Paris
Jean-Marie Donegani, Cevipof, Senior Research Professor, Sciences Po, Paris
Emiliano Grossman, Senior Research Fellow, Sciences Po, Paris
Guy Groux, Research Director, CNRS, Cevipof, Sciences Po, Paris
Florence Haegel, Research Director, Sciences Po, Paris
Nonna Mayer, Research Director, CNRS, Sciences Po, Paris
Arnaud Mercier, Political Scientist, Professor of Information and Communications Sciences at the University of Metz,
Janine Mossuz-Lavau, Research Director, CNRS, Cevipof, Sciences Po, Paris
Anne Muxel, Research Director, CNRS, Cevipof, Sciences Po, Paris
Pascal Perrineau, Senior Research Professor, Cevipof, Sciences Po, Paris
Henri Rey, Research Director, Cevipof, Sciences Po, Paris
Luc Rouban, Research Director, CNRS, Cevipof, Sciences Po, Paris
Etienne Schweisguth, Research Director, CNRS, Sciences Po, Paris

Introduction

Pascal Perrineau and Luc Rouban

The contributors to this book have been guided by two main concerns. The first was to offer students, as well as general readers with an interest in politics, a rigorous analysis of a number of aspects of French and European political life. The following chapters are required reading for students taking the international program on political and social sciences at Science Po's Centre for Political Research (CEVIPOF), which has been running since 1998. In making our selection of themes, we have inevitably failed to include analyses of every aspect of political life. Given the current state of research findings, it is questionable whether such an exhaustive study would even be feasible. In any event, we consider, rightly or wrongly, that the topics selected have allowed us to go to the heart of the current crisis of political representation, to the extent that they all either contribute to the crisis or are symptomatic of it.

Our second concern was to review the situation in France in the light of Jean-Marie Le Pen's success in the first round of the 2002 presidential election, as well as the "no" vote in the referendum on the European Constitutional Treaty in 2005. Recent political debates, including discussions provoked by the 2007 presidential elections—whether they have centered on participatory democracy, the "liberal rupture" or giving preferential treatment to French people when recruiting—have regularly referred to the need to redefine the relationship between citizens and elected officials. The following questions also needed to be addressed: Does French politics have any special defining characteristics and if so, what are they? In what ways are the French different? Will European integration eventually result in the disappearance of such differences, or will distinct national identities survive? Furthermore, certain commonly held views which can be uncritically accepted by some politicians—regarding levels of xenophobia, acceptance of liberalism, or interest in politics, for example—need to be evaluated and, on occasions, challenged. In the course of this overview we will also be led to speculate on—inter alia—the likelihood of France following a Scandinavian style social democratic model or a British-style social liberal model, the electoral future of extremist politics in France, and the future development of the French trade unionism.

Two complementary preoccupations run through the book: first evaluating what distinguishes France from its European neighbors, and second assessing the degree of political homogeneity in Europe.

The reader should not expect to be provided with a theory, or a doctrine, or definitive arguments regarding politics in France and Europe. None of the contributors to this collection has written the kind of academic article which takes a partisan view. Although theory has not been neglected, we have preferred to focus our attention on reliable empirical arguments. The reader has thus been provided with a collection of essays which, though inevitably provisional and incomplete, give an overview of what political science can tell us about political values, actors, and choices. Most of our empirical data was provided by the first two waves of the European Social Survey (ESS), a survey of unprecedented scope whose methodological rigor earned it, in 2005, one of the most prestigious academic awards in Europe, the *Descartes Prize*.[1]

We have restricted the scope of our study to a number of European countries of comparable size which are, however, representative of a variety of institutional systems: centralized states, such as France, have been studied as well as federal states, such as Germany, or highly regionalized countries, such as Spain and Italy.[2] We were also careful to make a selection of European countries which were representative, in terms of religious tradition, geographical zones, and political cultures.

These were the limits we imposed on ourselves before embarking on this probabilistic and relativistic political science project.

Notes

We would like to express our gratitude to Henri Rey for his support in helping to bring this project to fruition.

1. Details of the basic data, methodology, questionnaires, and organization of the ESS surveys are available on the following Web site: http://www.europeansocialsurvey.org. Our authors used either the first wave (2003 results, available at the end of 2004) or the second wave (2004 results, available at the end of 2005), depending on their requirements and the contents of the modules in question. The surveys involved conducting face to face interviews of randomly chosen individuals. The size of the samples varied from country to country: the largest was 2,900, the smallest 1,500. When comparing countries, the results were weighted to take into account the distribution of age groups (Dweight variable).
2. Although the largest European countries are all discussed in each chapter of the book, there is a certain amount of variation from chapter to chapter in the countries covered, depending on each author's focus, and the nature of the available data. In the tables accompanying the text the following abbreviations are used: Germany (GE), Belgium (BE), Denmark (DK), Spain (SP), France (FR), the United Kingdom (UK), Greece (GR), Italy (IT), the Netherlands (NL), Poland (PL), Portugal (PT), and Sweden (SW).

CHAPTER 1

The Crisis in Political Representation

Pascal Perrineau

In order to evaluate how democracy is developing in Europe today, the extent of the current crisis itself needs to be measured and in particular the critical condition of representative democracy. We will compare the current crisis with similar situations in the past where representative democracy has been under attack before moving on to identify the causes of the present crisis. Finally, we will seek to present a true picture of emerging democratic practices and suggest a number of measures or approaches that might contribute to a revival in democratic participation.[1]

Democracy in Crisis: The Symptoms

The Rising Number of Abstentions and of Blank or Invalid Votes

In many European countries, and even—and sometimes especially—those where the right to vote freely was only recently obtained (some Central and Eastern European countries), abstention, and the casting of invalid votes as a form of protest have been on the increase.

In France also, with its long democratic tradition, rates of abstention in local, national, and European elections have all hit record highs over the past fifteen years. In the most recent European elections, held in June 2009, there was a sharp drop in voter turnout in most of the twenty-five EU Member States: 59.4% of French electors abstained, and 57% of European voters turned their backs on the ballot box compared to only 37% in 1979 when the first European elections by direct universal suffrage were held. Analysis of this rise in abstention rates reveals two broad categories of non-voter.

On the one hand, what we are witnessing might be called abstention born of indifference which concerns citizens who are far removed from the political system, are often little educated and are socially disadvantaged. In France, for example, 63% of French voters with no educational qualifications abstained during the June 2009 European election. Their abstention reflects the social and cultural distance which separates them from a political system which, in their eyes is reserved for "people at the top of the social scale." This type of abstention characterized by a very strong sociological component is not on the increase.

On the other hand, we are witnessing the development of a type of abstention as protest from educated, younger citizens from the middle or even upper social classes who are sometimes highly politicized. These people do not recognize themselves in the existing political system and their abstention reflects their disagreement with and protest at representative democracy, the party system, and politicians. This type of abstention is constantly increasing in European democracies. Rather than simply abstaining some of these voters actually go to the polling booth and cast a blank or invalid vote as a sign of their discontentment with official political representation. For example, in the first round of the 2002 presidential election, nearly 1 million French voters cast a vote of this type even though the choice of candidates had never been so diverse (16 candidates). This new way of using the vote is clearly emerging among voters using abstention as protest. This type of vote no longer indicates a steadfast political choice, is less openly promoted and more spasmodic, Actually casting a valid vote has now become just one means amongst many of being involved in political life. It is used only episodically and can be rejected in favor of other modes of participation and notably through political protest such as demonstrations, petitions, occupation of buildings, violence, and so forth.

The Collapse of Political Commitment

To different extents, European systems are experiencing a strong fall-off in numbers within the political parties and trade unions that often for many decades have been expressing the political and social demands of the population. Both parties and trade unions are increasingly becoming "professional" organizations that are not always fuelled by "social demand." In many countries, less than 5% of the population is actively involved in a political party as the results of the 2003 *European Social Survey* show (table 1.1). In such a situation, the representative role of the parties becomes rather weak and this phenomenon only reinforces the distance between political representation and the supposedly represented citizens. Party membership rates are often very low and their image among the population, as regularly measured by opinion polls, often varies between mediocre and catastrophic. This has created a serious crisis for democracy as citizens' needs are no longer clearly "articulated" and the political system therefore finds it difficult to read and to hear these needs. There is thus a certain amount of tension between the low level of involvement in the parties on the one hand and an ongoing affirmed interest in political questions on the other hand (with the exception of the two democracies in Southern Europe: Spain and Italy), as shown by table 1.1. There is therefore a real gap between political supply and demand.

Table 1.1 Active involvement in a political party and interest in politics in Europe in 2003 (%)*

	GE	*SP*	*FR*	*UK*	*IT*	*NL*	*PL*	*SW*
Active involvement in a political party	6	4	3	4	6	6	2	9
Strong interest in politics	63	21	40	52	33	66	40	58

Note: * For this table and for the following two tables, scales from the ESS survey coded from 0 to 10 were used by carrying out a division into three classes: from 0 to 3, levels of interest, confidence and satisfaction are considered to be weak; from 4 to 6, they are considered to be moderate or mixed; from 7 to 10, they are considered to be strong.

The Deteriorating Image of the Political Class and of Political Organizations

Unlike the continued interest in politics which has not disintegrated when observed over a long period of time, the image of political practitioners and institutions has greatly deteriorated in most cases. First, there is a strong feeling that a rupture between representatives and those they represent has taken root. Only a minority of European populations feel they are well represented by politicians. This unease with representation is often accompanied by the feeling that the political class is corrupt. A majority of the European public believe that politicians are "quite corrupt." This of course brings about a strong feeling of defiance and even a rejection of politics which is seen as something to be wary of. This distrust (or at best lukewarm confidence) is a serious problem in a democratic society where confidence should be one of the mainsprings. It should not be forgotten that the notion of confidence was one of the founding elements of the representative system from the beginning of 1789. This is evidenced by the writings of the Abbé Sieyès and in the debates of the constituent Assembly: "voters will place their confidence in those who are more able than themselves to perceive the general interest," writes Sieyès.[2] Today, the depth of the crisis in confidence may well breathe new political life into political movements which have little to do with pluralist democracy (left and right-wing extremisms, neo-populism, etc.). In many European societies, this crisis in confidence is expressed through an extensive "fragmentation of the practice of voting." Rather than voting, citizens are more and more often looking for other means to express their political opinions thus nourishing protest movements of many different kinds.

Generally speaking, in Europe the majority of the population has only an average level of confidence in the political class. Apart from the Netherlands and Sweden, the minority that has little confidence in them is perceptibly larger than the small minority that has a strong level of confidence in them (table 1.2).

A Withdrawal to the Private Sphere

In his book, *Shifting Involvements: Private Interest and Public Action,*[3] Albert O. Hirschman shows how democratic societies go through cyclical alternations between phases of strong attachment to public activity and phases of detachment from public activity accompanied by a withdrawal to "private happiness."

Table 1.2 Level of confidence in the political class in Europe in 2003 (%)

	GE	*SP*	*FR*	*UK*	*IT*	*NL*	*PL*	*SW*
Strong level of confidence	17	17	18	22	18	42	7	37
Average level of confidence	51	46	50	50	51	46	45	48
Low level of confidence	32	38	32	28	31	12	48	15

This might be applied to a number of European societies where, throughout the 1970s and until the beginning of the 1980s, there was great belief in the virtues of public activity and its ability to change things. This was followed by a sense of profound disillusionment at different periods during the 1990s that was accompanied by a withdrawal to the private. In this type of climate, democracy is no longer an object of strong attachment and interest in the public sphere declines. This phase of retreat from public affairs has shown signs of lessening here and there leaving room for a return to public activity but this is generally through protest. This is what the French sociologist, Jean-Louis Missika, pointed to as being the beginning of a cycle of "negative politicisation" where citizens return to politics and to public activity but mainly through protest.[4] The major and sometimes violent demonstrations surrounding anti-globalization themes which have shaken a great number of European countries in recent years (Seattle in 1999, Genoa in 2001, Florence in 2002, Barcelona in 2005) are symptomatic of this new form of politicization which is not always easy to integrate into the classic democratic system.

Currently, we are witnessing multiple signs of a crisis in representative democracy, of its fragility and also of a search for alternatives. However, before examining this phenomenon, it would be useful to put the extent of this crisis into perspective with regard to historical precedents.

Is the Crisis in Representative Democracy New?

This is not the first time that democracy—particularly in its representative form—has been contested in Europe.

On many occasions, democracy has been subjected to the bitter criticism of political extremisms. By way of example, in the inter-war period, the extreme-right nourished itself on the weaknesses of parliamentary democracy. The weak German Weimar Republic, the fragility and uncertainty of Italian democracy, and the confused Spanish Republic all fell into the jaws of an Extreme-Right that had nothing but the greatest scorn for the subtle mechanisms of representative democracy. The Extreme-Left and its condemnation of "parliamentary stupidity" contributed to the weakening of pluralist democracy in 1968 and throughout the years that followed. It promoted a belief in the supposed virtues of direct action and (even possibly terrorism). Italy, Germany, and to a lesser degree France, all suffered during these "dark years." Finally, Communist discourse denouncing the limits and deadlocks of "formal democracy" and praising the charms of "real democracy" which always ended in the dictatorship of a single party should also be mentioned. Thus, from the end of the nineteenth to the beginning of the twenty-first century, democracy was constantly contested and sometimes threatened by the champions of authoritarianism or the high priests of an unattainable "popular democracy."

Other criticisms of representative democracy and its limits include technocratic and self-management discourse which come together in their common belief in the ability of society to govern itself by resorting to the use of experts or "representatives of civil society." In the 1950s and 1960s, discourse on the "the end of politics" and on the ability of societies to govern themselves through the use of technocrats flourished in western democracies.[5] All of these theses that are found in the works of James Burnham,[6] or indeed John Kenneth Galbraith,[7] advocate "the Management Age" and revive Saint-Simon's old dream of substituting "the administration of things for the government of men."[8] This discourse was particularly attractive to right-wing governments in many European countries where recourse to technocracy contributed to delegitimating classic representative democracy. On the left, the discourse on self-management was the jewel of this "technocratic" culture at the end of the 1960s and beginning of the 1970s. A whole section of the European Left praised the charms of self-management, the ability of society to organize itself and the salvatory recourse to "civil society" which possessed none of the evils of "political society."[9]

Thus, representative democracy has repeatedly been contested and sometimes even threatened. However, today, the crisis in democracy—whose symptoms include low electoral turnout, a lack of interest in political life, little involvement of citizens, declining levels of respect for parties and politicians, and a tendency to elect managers rather than leaders—has intensified as a result of globalization and because of the fact that values relative to traditional rights and liberties seem to be eroding. Added to this, the development of democracy in certain countries that have only recently become democratic remains fragile and uncertain. For example, Poland is the country with the lowest proportion of citizens who are happy with the way in which democracy functions. However, there are also strong levels of dissatisfaction in countries with a long democratic tradition such as France and Britain. The peaceful democracies of Northern Europe (the Netherlands and Sweden) are the only ones to show a relatively high level of satisfaction. In many countries and notably in Italy, the symptoms of a malfunction in democracy have been apparent for almost 20 years (table 1.3). However, the scope, depth, and durability of the crisis in democracy are in many ways new.

Table 1.3 Satisfaction with how democracy functions in Europe in 2003 (%)

	GE	*SP*	*FR*	*UK*	*IT*	*NL*	*PL*	*SW*
Greatly satisfied	36	37	29	30	24	42	15	50
Moderately satisfied	30	40	30	33	40	38	29	27
Dissatisfied	35	23	41	38	36	20	56	22

Causes of the Crisis in Democracy

This current crisis has a variety of causes which are political, economic, social, and cultural in nature.

The Political Causes

In many countries, the bisecular referents of the Left and the Right that gave meaning to politics are in a state of crisis. All European societies are marked by a profound movement toward individualism and a distancing from traditional collective allegiances. This movement affects the durability of political choices anchored in strong feelings of belonging to either the left or the right. In 1990, while reflecting on "civil desertion," the French philosopher, Marcel Gauchet, observed that we are moving toward "an individualism of disunity and disengagement, where the demand for authenticity is at odds with involvement in the collective."[10] This movement toward disunity is perceptible at three levels.

From an ideological point of view, the old Right-Left cleavage which structured political choices and orientations for decades is undergoing a profound crisis. A majority of European citizens continue to feel that they belong either to the left or the right but these categories are not necessarily deemed useful today for a clear understanding of the positions adopted by parties and politicians on the major issues (Europe, globalization, international policy, etc.). On many themes, the traditional collectives of ideological belonging are experiencing a real crisis of identity. This is an understandable phenomenon among the electorate especially at a time when, within the European Parliament itself, the two main components of the European Left (ESP) and the Right (EPP) have agreed to alternate the presidency of the parliament.

From a social point of view, the traditional opposition between left and right was underpinned by a strong social bipolarity during the postwar decades. However, the classic patterns of the class struggle and the unequivocal social pyramid were replaced by a number of cleavages which cut across the social divide. These included security and insecurity of employment, households with one salary as opposed to households with two salaries and different access for different people to the resources of the Welfare State. This process of differentiation was accompanied by a strong increase in numbers among the salaried middle classes (mid-level and senior executives) who, for the first time, in many countries were now more numerous than the working class sections of the active population. This large "central cluster" brought about a veritable "middling" of European societies but also a breakdown in "social representation" around which political representation was organized.

For example, the process of "gentrification" that the European Left is experiencing has greatly contributed to making the cleavages between Left and Right less distinct. As Pierre Rosanvallon remarked in *Le Peuple introuvable*,[11] in a society that is not very readable in sociological terms and less cleavaged ideologically, representative procedures lose their explicit appeal.

Another obvious feature of the Left-Right divide was the presence of political cleavages in given geographical areas. The Left and Right often became entrenched in particular areas. Although this is still somewhat the case, these areas are now changing and becoming defined along different lines as a result of accelerated internal migration. Changes in productive capacity, the spread of urbanization, the redefining of particular areas, and the multiple usage the places themselves are now put to have all contributed to producing a permanently mobile society characterized by constant movement. This has meant that these territories which have become more fragmented and abstract no longer carry strong and permanent political identities as they used to.

This shifting of the geographical, social, and ideological bedrocks of political representation has provoked a profound unease with democracy. This is expressed with particular virulence when Europe as an issue is on the political agenda. Europe cuts across the traditional left-right divisions exploding them as it does so. It has taken root more within a system of cultural opposition (with respect to the future of Europe, openness to others, confidence in change, connections with the state, etc.), than within a class based socioeconomic cleavage.

Finally, Europe which is more of a project and a permanent invention than a territory with limited borders, has broken up not only the old territorial positions of the left and right but also the idea of the nation-state as the only platform where political conflicts can be expressed and made explicit. The challenge of Europe has accentuated the process whereby the traditional ideological, social, and territorial bases of politics are coming apart. This process is at work throughout European societies and political systems. This undoing of links between the explicitly political and the society which gave meaning to the political system is also revealed by the relative dilution of existing political cultures. The internal heterogeneity of the latter is being reinforced and at the same time the differences between opposing major parties is lessening. The right-wing is experiencing a profound fracture with the classic right and the extreme-right moving further and further apart.[12] The left-wing cluster has been fragmented into several cultures in which the degree of "cultural liberalism" or the desire for vigorous reform of the economic structures varies greatly.[13] In an interview given to the newspaper, *Le Monde*, the socialist leader of the Spanish government makes this diversity among the left in Europe apparent:

> I believe that, above all, the modern left must build a new stage in democracy. Society, politics, culture, education, research, economic power, the family, all must be democratised. [...] Democracy is the natural tendency of the left, but the left of the second half of the 20th century has centred its project on the economy and the public state sector. It has forgotten society and the functioning of democracy [...]. It is more effective to design programmes for positive discrimination, for example, to ensure there are more women scientists than to increase taxes or introduce a 35-hour working week.[14]

Left-wing thinking has been exposed to economic liberalism and the opening up of the economy to the strong forces of internationalization. Right-wing thinking no longer denies the benefit of the state and social welfare.

These developments in the political cultures of the Left and the Right are expressed through the rapprochement between the economic and social programs of the two political families. This has had the effect of blurring the distinctions between them and making them less readable for ordinary citizens.

Another political factor in the crisis in democracy is the archaic nature of certain organizations and the political messages they carry. The parties within the European political system date back to the end of the nineteenth century and the beginning of the twentieth century, a period during which the shape of the "*parti de cadre*" and the "*parti de masse*" was structured. These parties are often based on the bureaucratic or client-based model. They tend to be very hierarchical and not very strong on internal democracy. They are often quite out of touch with the type of party younger generations want to see. Young people tend to be more interested in less hierarchical organizations where participation is valued. They also tend to favor occasional or temporary organizations such as Act Up, Les Restos du cœur (meals for the homeless), Amnesty International, and so on. On the whole, they are deserting the political parties and a great many of them are to be found in more flexible organizations characterized by a "moral political activism." These include humanitarian organizations, organizations for the defense of minorities, anti-globalization movements, and so on. Furthermore, political parties tend not to be very representative of social diversity within the population. Being representative is not only a quantitative problem (members/voters ratio), it is also a demographic and social problem. Most of the time, there are too few women, too few young people and too few people from working class or immigrant backgrounds in the parties themselves. They remain essentially bourgeois or middle class and do not address themselves sufficiently to the population as a whole.

Economic and Social Causes

The economic crisis and the process of globalization have considerably reduced the room to maneuver of national political power. And yet, political life is mainly expressed on "national stages" which may then seem to be "shadow theatres" in the eyes of much of the electorate who believe that anything that is truly important is being dealt with elsewhere. The surprising abstention rate recorded in the most recent European elections may be connected to the fact that many voters find it difficult to understand the pertinence of a "national stage" where the most important part of the "drama" of the elections takes place whereas the questions and solutions raised during the electoral campaigns are usually dealt with far beyond the national level.[15] This gap between what national politics can actually supply and the demands made on it which are much less national in nature contributes to highlighting the crisis in democracy and the need to invent a veritable supranational level.

This feeling that the problems and possible solutions to them are not being dealt with at the level they ought to be is particularly strong when the questions posed are about Europe, globalization, or indeed international issues. This has given rise to a whole new social and cultural cleavage between people with a higher level of education on the one hand and people with a lower level of education on the other. The former tend to be more pro-European, more tolerant, and more open to globalization while the latter tend to be concerned about the opening up of European societies and are often tempted by the rejection of "others" and of Europe. In France, this cleavage expressed itself vigorously for the first time during the French referendum on the Maastricht treaty in 1992. At that time, France was more or less divided in two with the "yes" vote obtaining a very small majority and the "no" vote more than 49% of votes cast. As the geographer Jacques Lévy wrote about the "yes" coalition:

> It would be incorrect to refer to the yes vote as being an alliance of the rich and even less so as being an electorate structured by the right-wing. There are clearly two independent strands at work here, one structured by money and the other by education, and it is the latter of these, leaning to the left which was most active.[16]

The "yes" vote was dominant in areas marked by strong social innovation and in urban areas making up a "veritable European Hanseatic League."[17] Jacques Lévy adds:

> Culture and education, cities and towns, Europe: these are not chance encounters, each of these terms goes together. Each of them constitutes a metaphor for the others. When joined together they provide at least the beginning of an idea for how individuals might develop socially within society. They provide a way to prevent a withdrawal into small ghettoised communities and to encourage people to live fully within the world at all its different levels. In this way educated and urbanised individuals are delivering a message which goes beyond just the European question thus heralding new types of political discourse and action.

Rather than the traditional social cleavages, it is this cultural or educational cleavage, this way of seeing the world, society and the future which give meaning to this cleavage on Europe, globalization and more broadly speaking "global issues." This is the cleavage which is constantly at work in the political and social life of European countries. The debates on the General Agreement on Tariffs and Trade (GATT) and on the World Trade Organization (WTO), European elections, cleavages on the intervention in Kosovo, questions surrounding the introduction of the Euro, debates on the war in Afghanistan, and of course the controversy surrounding the European constitutional Treaty regularly cause it to resurface.[18]

Cultural Causes

The crisis in the major messianic ideologies and particularly in Marxism as a reference, which have been apparent since the end of the 1970s and which were confirmed by the collapse of the Communist camp at the end of the 1980s, left part of the European left-wing electorate orphaned. The discovery in the 1970s by the public at large that the Communist utopia hid nothing but a vulgar totalitarianism (what some what called the "Soljenitsyn effect") brought about the collapse of the Communist idol and the organizations related to it (decline of the French and Italian communist parties and of other Extreme-Left organizations in Europe). These ideologies therefore no longer provided a stomping ground for people who had been "disappointed" by the economic and social crisis or the "losers" of globalization. These are the people who, on the other hand, have frequently swelled the ranks of those who use abstention to express their discontent and who have turned to protest-fuelled populism.

Finally, improvements in the average level of education within European societies and the subsequent increase in demands made on politics have been expressed by what political scientists in the English-speaking world have called a phenomenon of "cognitive mobilisation." These politically active citizens do not necessarily recognize themselves in the classic channels of representative democracy. These are citizens who are "critical"[19] demanding, not necessarily pacified by the end of the major ideological conflicts and who have new demands to make of democracy.

The New Demands on Democracy

Having observed what seems to be coming undone in the political life of European democracies, the next step is to envisage what kind of new political arena is in the process of taking shape.

Indeed, behind this attitude to representative democracy where a great deal of distrust, withdrawal, and protest together with a crisis in long-lasting loyalty can be observed, the emergence of a new, ever-more critical citizen can be glimpsed. In a major international survey on the attitudes of citizens in democratic regimes, a team of political scientists led by Pippa Norris[20] established that as democratic values progress across the globe, the level of confidence in democratic institutions is waning. This erosion of confidence coupled with the rise of what Pippa Norris calls a "growing cynicism" toward democratic governments, has brought about a deterioration in classic democratic participation (electoral turnout, party activism, civil engagement). At the same time, this relative alienation from the democratic regime has encouraged the rise of a type of "protest politics" (extremist movements, protest activism, urban unrest) and has contributed to damaging attitudes toward common law and a sense of the general interest. In the "leisure society" as depicted by the sociologist Joffre Dumazedier as early as the end of the 1950s,[21] the devaluing of work and the new individualism have fed off each other and produced a new *homo socius*. He said of *homo socius* that "it is to be feared that [the latter] will consider his involvement in leisure groups to be his essential and indeed his only involvement in society," thus allowing a gap between the democratic ideal and a reality marked more by "cyncism," disenchantment and critical distance to take hold in many democracies. This distancing may well contribute to the destabilization of democratic regimes which, according to this theory, only have skeptical support among public opinion. However, it can also breathe new life into democracy by encouraging reflection on reforms designed to dynamize representative democracy and develop direct participative democracy. This of course is provided that participative democracy is something more than "a desire to see protest integrated into decision-making," as Marcel Gauchet[22] says, and that in the same spirit, the manifestation of this is not elevated to a kind of right to veto by the minority. Such a risk does exist in some "protest movements" at work in our societies which are influenced by a neo-left-wing which the sociologist Jean-Pierre Le Goff qualifies as being "born of the meeting between traditional forms of extremism and the radicalisation of individualism."[23] It is imperative therefore to remain vigilant and to avoid all discourse about the inevitable decline of democracy. There is clearly a need to focus on what might arise from existing representative democracy and contribute to the renewal of democracy in general. In a piece of research carried out at the end of the 1990s and the beginning of the 2000s, on the attitudes of citizens to democracy, a team of Cevipof researchers[24] showed how citizens today remain attached to the central institutions of representative democracy: the act of voting and Parliament. The real unrest arises in relation to the people who incarnate and who run these institutions on a daily basis: the politicians and political parties. At the same time, a strong desire for more direct democracy and more participation through referenda or protest can be observed. A type of antagonism between representative democracy and participative democracy might have been feared particularly when this takes the form of protest (the use of demonstrations for example). This, however, is not the case: citizens see participation through protest as going hand in hand with more conventional involvement in democracy such as voting, party membership, and so on. This is a sign that protest-driven modes of action have become normalized and routine. Based on an analysis of the social movements and collective mobilizations of the past few years, this research confirms the links between representative and participative democracy, at the very least in terms of citizen representations and practices. One might even say there is a "new type of democratic action: an in-between type of democracy, an intermediary type of democracy which is to be found somewhere between classic representative democracy and the more mythical direct democracy."

This same in-between idea is present today in the notion of "electronic democracy." Certainly, Internet can not provide an answer through technology to a crisis in politics. "Electronic democracy" can not be thought of as a substitute for traditional democratic mediation but rather as a tool amongst others for the revitalization of the public sphere—a public sphere where new modes of deliberation are being born. The Cevipof research shows how the public sphere within European democracies which are currently undergoing a profound questioning of themselves has managed to generate a whole series of new practices. These bypass classic modes of parliamentary representation to invent mechanisms which mean that citizens can both express their interests and have their own expertise taken into account. New forms of deliberative democracy have emerged, developed and have sometimes become institutionalized. These include consensus conferences, focus groups, deliberative surveys, citizen juries, neighborhood committees, etc. Thus, in the same way that a body which is unwell produces anti-bodies, the disenchanted democracy of the turn of this twenty-first century has invented new practices. On the margins of a representative democracy which has become somewhat weakened, there is an attempt to ensure that collective deliberation be concerned with real objects and not with mythologies. Disenchantment with democracy is perhaps the price to pay for the establishment of a more prosaic and more substantial form of democracy.

Notes

1. An earlier, different version of this chapter was published in Perrineau, 2005b.
2. From a speech of September 7, 1789 on the royal veto.
3. Hirschman, 1982.
4. Missika, 1992.
5. Birnbaum, 1975.
6. Burnham, 1945.
7. Galbraith, 1967.
8. The doctrine of Claude Henri de Rouvray de Saint-Simon (1760–1825), which created a sort of cult of scientists, is explained in different works: *L'industrie* (1816–1817), *La politique* (1819), *Du système industriel* (1822), *Cathéchisme des industriels* (1823–1824).
9. Rosanvallon, 1976; Julliard, 1977.
10. Gauchet, 1990.
11. Rosanvallon, 1998.
12. Grunberg and Schweisguth, 1997a.
13. Hastings and Strudel, 2000.
14. Le Monde, 2004.
15. Delwit and Poirier, 2005.
16. Lévy, 1993.
17. The Hanseatic League was an alliance of towns that developed in medieval Europe. It brought together German towns and merchants in the Netherlands, in England, and in the Baltic Basin. Within the monarchical Europe of the time, it was democratically managed by a Diet made up of representatives of the member towns whose number reached 85 at the end of the fourteenth century.
18. Perrineau, 2005a.
19. Norris, 1999.
20. Norris, 1999.
21. Dumazedier, 1962.
22. Gauchet, 2003.
23. Le Goff, 2003.
24. Perrineau, 2003.

CHAPTER 2

Political Values and Attitudes in Europe

Etienne Schweisguth

At a time when all the major ideologies are in decline, one might wonder whether the political leanings of voters continue to be influenced by values per se or whether these leanings are merely the result of choices made by voters in relation to a certain number of concrete issues. It might indeed be argued that this is not a real debate and that the issues—such as abortion, immigration, social laws, and so on—are always, more or less linked to values. The real question is rather whether the choices made by citizens on various political and social problems are structured by a global and coherent ideology or whether these choices are largely independent of each other and fall outside a global ideological framework.

In Europe today, there are three major sets of values which account for the way in which voters make political choices and position themselves on the Left-Right axis. The first of these is the religious set of values. Irreligion is a factor which is frequently found among left-wing voters whereas religious belief and observance frequently characterize voting to the Right of the political spectrum. The second is the economic and social set of values. Belief in the virtues of state intervention to ensure the greatest level of equality in living conditions incites individuals to vote Left whereas belief in the virtues of free enterprise as a way of ensuring the interests of all tends to incite a right-wing vote. The third set of values concerns humanist and universal values. Those who adhere to the values of tolerance and individual fulfillment are inclined to vote to the Left whereas ethnocentric and rigorist values favor right-wing and indeed Extreme-Right-wing voting.

Social Change and Changes in Values in Europe

Since the end of the Second World War, European societies have undergone considerable upheavals which have entailed significant changes in their value systems. They have become urbanized which has led to a weakening of the weight of traditions. Social behavior used to be controlled locally by neighbors in the village or small town but this has now disappeared and been replaced by the anonymity of large towns and cities which in turn facilitates the transgression of norms. This has also meant that norms and traditions can be more easily called into question and even modified. Standards of living have considerably improved which in turn has encouraged the spread of hedonistic values. Improvements in standards of living have also resulted not in a suppression but in an easing of frustrations and tensions linked to the harshness of the material conditions of existence. The result has been a lesser tendency to opt for extreme solutions or to direct aggressive sentiment toward various scapegoats. The enormous efforts made by European societies to generalize secondary level education and to develop higher education has followed the same course. A higher standard of education has meant a better understanding of social mechanisms, a greater sense of cultural relativism, a lessening of tendencies toward simplistic explanations and a greater aptitude for tolerance. It has also fostered a greater capacity for independent thinking and, therefore, a greater tendency to call values based on tradition into question.

The term "individualism" is often evoked to characterize the value systems of contemporary European societies. However, it is in fact an ambiguous term which is often used pejoratively. It is used to designate an attitude which consists of subordinating the general interest to one's own particular interest. In this sense, it is almost a synonym of the pseudo-scientific term of egotism. It then becomes merely the contemporary form of a recurrent discourse on moral decadence. This type of discourse can be found just as easily in the nineteenth century as in the Middle Ages and even in Judaic, Greek or Roman antiquity.

Others, on the other hand, try to offer more neutral definitions of the term, the details of which are not needed here. To put it simply, it can be argued that the major value of the Age is quite simply the individual human being. What counts today is the life of the individual, including individual security, fulfillment, and physical and moral well-being. Saying this in no way implies that the dominant value today is for individuals to take themselves as an end in themselves and to subordinate the well-being of others for their own well-being. Within the value systems of our time, it is the *individual in general* who constitutes the cardinal value.[1] Our institutions are founded on the principle according to which the basic aim of social organization is to ensure as good a life as possible for all individual human beings. Such a concept is based on the idea that the seminal principle which must guide us is the principle of what is good for individuals rather than a principle decreed by a transcendent divine or social entity with its own aims to which human aims would be subordinate. It is based on the idea that the groups to which the individual belongs such as the nation or the family for example, have value indeed but only in as much as they contribute to the well-being of the individuals. Finally, it is based on the idea that it is indeed worthwhile to be concerned for others, but not on the idea that concern for others should totally disqualify regard for oneself.

The emergence of such a moral conception has obviously caused upheaval for previous value systems based on the devaluing of desires and impulses, unconditional submission to established authority—notably religious—and on an ascetic moral code of abnegation and dedication to the good of collective entities such as the family or the nation.

Religious Values

Religious Observance and the Right-wing Vote

Opinion poll results constantly show that a strong level of religious observance is closely co-related to right-wing voting (see table 2.1).

The reasons for this narrow link between religious practice and right-wing voting can partly be explained by history. In Catholic countries, the democratic movement came up against the resistance of the Church which had strong ties with monarchist regimes or, later, with certain dictatorships as was the case in Spain and in Portugal.

These regimes supported the Church and guaranteed it an important social role especially in education. For its part, the Church legitimized the regime and used all the weight of the religious message to justify the established order. Early on in European history, the Catholic Church abandoned the subversive character of original Christianity establishing itself firmly on the side of political power and developing a way of functioning and an organizational structure which was hierarchical in nature.

In Protestant countries, on the other hand, the Reform was based on the principle of the free right of believers to have direct access to sacred texts, on the principle of a free examination of conscience and against the principle of the authority of the Church over individual consciences. Protestantism turned each believer into an autonomous religious actor thus finding itself on the same wavelength as the democratic movement which aimed to make each individual a political actor. The Protestant churches did not, therefore, oppose the introduction of democracy and did not appear to be deployed on the side of conservative forces.

The second reason accounts for the influence of the religious variable on political orientation: religious belief brings meaning to the lives of believers. Belief in another life which will compensate for the miseries of this world and the belief in a good God whose existence gives meaning to the misfortunes of this world allows believers to find a meaning for the order of existing things. Religious observers therefore frequently find themselves on the side of those who consider that the existing social order is, if not good, then at least just and

Table 2.1 Polled respondents who attend a religious service at least once a month according to their position on the Right/Left axis (%)

	GE	*SP*	*FR*	*UK*	*IT*	*NL*	*PL*	*SW*
Left	16	18	10	16	40	14	66	8
Neither Left nor Right	22	30	11	17	48	18	77	12
Right	24	48	24	22	43	29	83	13
Average	*20*	*29*	*14*	*19*	*44*	*21*	*76*	*11*

Table 2.2 Polled respondents who completely agree with the following proposition: "Homosexuals must have the right to live their lives as they wish," according to their position on the Right/Left axis (%)

	GE	*SP*	*FR*	*UK*	*IT*	*NL*	*PL*	*SW*
Left	39	44	58	26	36	55	9	33
Neither Left nor Right	23	33	49	18	23	42	9	23
Right	18	23	41	12	25	35	8	25
Average	*28*	*36*	*50*	*18*	*28*	*43*	*9*	*28*

in a certain way "normal." Conversely, irreligion is more linked to the idea that evil in the world is of social origin and that the aim of all human action is to improve society. Finally, the sense of religious belonging is linked to religious dogma on moral issues. The issues of abortion, divorce, and homosexuality have been, and in certain countries continue to be, issues which oppose the political Left and Right (see table 2.2).

Several countries such as Germany or Italy have or have had a Christian-Democrat party for a long time. In France, at the turn of the twentieth century, the conflict between clerics and secular forces which was essentially about the relationship between religion and schools was one of great intensity and strong feelings. This question of links between religion and schools remains a sensitive issue in certain countries. In Germany, the question of the presence of religious symbols in the classroom arose recently. In France, the question of religion in private schools has given rise to the largest mass demonstrations over the past quarter of a century. This is because in France, most private schools are religious and therefore the law on secularism does not apply to them.

Nowadays, conflicts related to religion are usually linked to moral issues. Divorce is not allowed or is very difficult to obtain in certain countries such as Italy. Poland, Germany, Italy, and Ireland have very restrictive legislation on abortion. There also exist significant differences with regard to the rights of homosexuals. Certain countries authorize homosexual marriage or allow homosexual couples to adopt children. Opinions on morals are not only at the basis of political cleavages within the different countries of the European Union, they are also a source of tension between the countries of the Union. Countries which are more advanced on moral issues sometimes find themselves at odds with the positions of countries where the religious tradition is stronger. In 2004, when the European Commission was being staffed, its President had to renounce on appointing a commissioner whose conservative position on questions related to the family and to homosexuality had shocked public opinion in the more advanced countries.

The Decline of Institutional Christianity

The political importance of the religious cleavage is nonetheless decreasing for one major reason: the decline of the major institutional religions in Europe. This decline concerns all countries or at the very least those in Western Europe for which solid statistics over long time periods are available.[2] It might be premature to say that this is an irreversible phenomenon, but it is at the very least a long-term one. It corresponds to a mechanism for change by virtue of generational renewal. One constant result from opinion polls shows that older people tend to practice religion more than younger people do. Such a result can be interpreted in two different ways. The first would be that the fact that older people are more religious is related to the cycle of life phenomenon: the nearer one gets to death the more one might feel the need to become religious in order to better ensure one's place in the afterlife. If this hypothesis is correct, then one could expect those young people who don't practice much to become more religious as they grow older. The other hypothesis is that religious practice is not linked to age but to a generational phenomenon. Young people practice less than their elders not because they are young but because they belong to more recent generations where the rate of religious observance is weak. All the surveys of the past several decades show without any doubt that the second hypothesis is the correct one. For people born during a given period the rate of religious practice remains stable over time: it does not increase with age. Studies have shown that the rate of religious practice for people born in the same year remains more or less the same at the age of 25 and 40 years later when they are 65. The difference in level of religious practice according to age observed in the surveys does not suggest a change in religious practice due to aging but simply that former generations practiced more than recent ones.[3] A word should be said here about a theme frequently evoked by the media: the supposed return of religion.

The first thing to specify here is that this analysis concerns Europe and not all countries on the planet. Different economic, social, and political conditions foster different changes in religious practice. It makes no more sense to talk about a global change in beliefs than, for example, to talk about a global change in obesity.

Second, to understand the significance of current religious change, it is essential to look at the reasons for the decline of the major religious institutions. There seem to be two major factors to account for the decline of institutional Christianity: on the one hand, advances made by science; on the other hand, the development of a hedonistic ethic which is in contradiction with traditional religious ethics.

The decline of institutional Christianity is undoubtedly linked to the development of scientific knowledge. However, it should be noted immediately that this does not mean that the progress of science has brought about an increase in rationalism among Europeans. Since the sixteenth century, scientific discoveries have eroded the likelihood of the Christian account of our origins. We know today that the planet Earth is not in the centre of the world but that it is only a miniscule part of a gigantic universe. We know that the world was not created 4,000 years before the birth of Christ but that it is 15 billion years old. We know that man was not created in one go but that he is the result of millions of years of animal evolution. All of this knowledge which is part of the average European's baggage has eroded the credibility of the Christian account of our origins and has reduced its significance to that of an allegorical account. However, this knowledge does not mean that our contemporaries have become scientists, positivists, or rationalists. It certainly does not constitute an obstacle to belief in the supernatural. On the contrary—and this is what is true in the "return of the religious" theme—current surveys do indeed record an increase in religious belief such as belief in God and in reincarnation[4] particularly amongst young people. It would be a mistake to believe that this is a return in force of traditional Christianity and that the churches will be filled again as if religion was necessarily always identical to itself. The phenomenon we are witnessing today has nothing to do with a return of the old forms of religion. What is being practiced today is what the sociologists call "religion à la carte." Believers take a belief from one religion, a second belief from another and, for example, a third from one of the new systems of belief which refer to *chakras*, to karma, to waves and to energy. What we are witnessing today is the emergence of a new type of religiousness with varied and diffuse content. We do not yet know whether it will become institutionalized or not and if so in what way.

The second factor to have contributed to the decline of institutional Christianity is the incompatibility of the latter with the new hedonistic values, notably in terms of sexuality, which have been developing since the end of the Second World War. Even if the Protestant churches have shown themselves to be more flexible than the Catholic Church, Christianity remains nonetheless founded on dogmas which know no other form of sexual legitimacy than heterosexuality within the framework of marriage. It also continues to transmit an austere moral code which denies pleasure. Its attempts to adapt are generally inadequate and too late for the Churches to find themselves in touch with modern times. Conversely, by not referring to any dogma or prescription on this question, the new forms of religiousness provide an adequate framework for those who recognize themselves in one form or another of belief in the supernatural but who consider Christian dogma on morals to be obsolete.

Economic and Social Values

The cleavage on economic and social questions was born in the nineteenth century at the same time as the development of industrialization. During the first half of the twentieth century and subsequently in the first decades after the war, it became the dominant political cleavage in many countries to the extent that it has sometimes been considered as the only explanation for the political Left/Right cleavage.

It took different forms in different countries. In the German, Scandinavian, and British social democracies it accompanied and intensified conflicts between the unions and management. In France, which is characterized by a strong tradition of state intervention, the Left was distinguished from the Right by a strong state presence.

But the cleavage also included a certain number of common elements. The ideal on the Left was to create equality in living conditions whereas the ideal on the Right stressed the necessary respect of individual liberty of which the USSR offered a counter example. The cleavage consisted of two productive forces: work and capital. It was also often seen as an opposition between social groups or classes. Thus, the British left-wing party was called Labor—the Workers' Party. The French Socialist Party was originally called the French Section of the Workers' International (SFIO). In the northern countries, the conservative parties were designated by the term "bourgeois" parties.

The Shift on the Left toward Economic Liberalism

The cleavage on economic and social problems became dominant during the second half of the twentieth century, albeit at different paces and with different modalities depending on the country concerned. In all countries, a shift toward greater forms of economic liberalism was to become apparent (see table 2.3). The 1959 *Bad Godesberg* congress became a symbol of this change. During the congress, the German social-democrats officially proclaimed their break with Marxism which until then had been their theoretical reference.

In 1976, the Swedish social-democrats underwent similar change. They presented themselves at the general election with a program which provided for the appropriation of corporate capital by the unions which was nothing else but a form of nationalization. Their electorate did not follow them on this and, as has rarely been the case in Sweden, they lost the election. Since that episode, they have abandoned any project aiming to modify the ownership of capital. And although the tradition of the Welfare State remains very strong in Sweden, the country has recently managed to considerably reduce the number of civil servants it employs and the costs related to state operations.

In Great Britain, under the auspices of Margaret Thatcher, the Conservative Party undertook a liberal revolution in 1979 by engaging in full combat with the trade unions. They emerged as the victors of the conflict with a heavy price to pay in social terms. When Tony Blair's Labour Party came to power in 1997, after 18 years of conservative government, he took up the reins of Thatcher's legacy and freed himself from the guardianship role of the unions which, until then had weighed on the way in which the party functioned and on its decision-making process.

In France, the arrival of the Left in power in 1981 marked a break not with capitalism but with the anti-capitalist ideology of the traditional Left.

Table 2.3 Polled respondents who completely agree or more or less agree with the proposition that: "The less the state intervenes in the economy, the better it is for the country," according to their position on the Right/Left axis

	GE	*SP*	*FR*	*UK*	*IT*	*NL*	*PL*	*SW*
Left	35	30	25	25	31	14	25	13
Neither Left nor Right	51	28	31	27	35	19	25	22
Right	57	17	32	36	26	19	29	36
Average	46	27	29	29	32	17	26	23

Although the French Socialist Party had explicitly and officially taken on the aim not of reforming capitalism but of abolishing it and although it considered the "supposed economic realities" to be nothing else than "the mask of conservative ideology," it rallied rapidly to the market economy and between 1997 and 2002 proceeded with several privatizations.

In Italy, from the 1970s on, the powerful Communist Party engaged in the search for a "historic compromise" which ended in an alliance including Communists and the inheritors of the Christian-Democrats. In Spain and Portugal, the Left, which was leaving the clandestine years of Franco and Salazar's dictatorship behind, fully recognized the principle of the market economy from the outset.

From the Class Struggle to Solidarity

It is a delicate task to formulate an explanation for these changes which started well before the signing of the European Single Act in 1986. It is possible that the counter-example of the USSR played an important role here. It is also very likely that the vigorous economic growth of the thirty-year period following the Second World War which drove standards of living and of education upward also played a capital role in turning voters away from extreme solutions. The development of social mobility certainly weakened the tendency to see society as an implacable antagonism between social classes. Contrary to popular belief, the second half of the twentieth century was a period of great social mobility. This social mobility supplied the numbers which caused an increase in the proportion of middle and upper level social categories. In France, for example the number of middle range or upper level employees went from 8% in 1954 to 31% in 1995. The probability for the son of a manual worker to become a middle or senior executive rose from 10% in 1953 to 29% in 1993. There is no homogenous social origin in the category of senior executives: in 1993, 39% of this category had a father who was a manual or non-manual worker. The idea which is very predominant in France at the moment that "the social elevator is stuck," reveals the psychological reality of aspiration to success at school and socially. It shows a feeling of social marginalization among those who fail in their education at a time when educational success is more and more a factor in social success and when, in reality, the proportion of people who leave the educational system without any diploma has never been so low. It also reveals the disenchantment of a generation which has realized that the development of higher education has resulted in a devaluing of degrees and that the mere fact of holding a degree is no longer an automatic open sesame for social success. On the other hand, it in no way reveals the statistical reality of a society where upward social mobility is said to have disappeared.

What the different countries which make up Europe have in common is that they have moved away from visions of society in terms of social classes in conflict toward the idea of a society made up of individuals all of whom have the right to seek success through talent and merit. The same countries have also all developed the idea of the right of each individual to assistance from society in times of need and of social handicap. Although there are so many complaints about the lack of solidarity in our societies today, this is not because this particular value is disappearing as believed by some people with a certain amount of nostalgia for more rural societies. In fact, a kind of institutional solidarity as demonstrated through the role of the state and through the work of humanitarian and charitable organizations has substituted itself for the interpersonal, familial, and neighborly solidarity which characterized the more rural societies of the past.

It would appear that increasing importance is attached to this value today. The reference to solidarity as a principle of social protection applicable to all individuals is new in European countries. Whereas it is not featured either in any Constitution or in any Declaration of Rights, it is present for the first time in the Charter on rights in the draft European Constitution and will perhaps become an official principle of European societies if ever the draft is officially adopted.

Universal Values

The third major set of values to have an important effect on electoral behavior is linked to a new political issue which began to appear in Europe in the 1980s: immigration. Favorable attitudes to immigration tend to foster a left-wing vote (see table 2.4). A hostile attitude to immigration is naturally a factor in the vote for xenophobic Extreme-Right-wing parties. It is also a factor in the vote for Center-Right parties whom many voters see as being less lax on this issue than the Left.

This new political phenomenon is sometimes too rapidly interpreted in a falsely obvious way: the rise in xenophobic parties quite simply reflects the rise in xenophobia as a reaction to the increase of immigration. In fact, such an interpretation merges two levels of reality and of analysis which on the contrary should be distinguished: the appearance of new issues and political parties on the one hand and the change in value systems on the other.

Neither immigration nor xenophobia is a new phenomenon. Furthermore, immigration does not necessarily result in the emergence of xenophobic parties and reciprocally these parties can emerge outside a context of immigration. For example, France experienced significant Italian immigration at the beginning of the twentieth century. This did not bring about the birth of a new

Table 2.4 Polled respondents in favor of authorizing the immigration of large numbers of people with different ethnic origins from those found in the host country, according to their position on the Right/Left axis (%)

	GE	*SP*	*FR*	*UK*	*IT*	*NL*	*PL*	*SW*
Left	70	58	66	61	75	71	56	88
Neither Left nor Right	55	52	46	49	57	53	54	78
Right	44	40	48	44	61	52	55	81
Average	*56*	*52*	*55*	*50*	*64*	*58*	*55*	*83*

political party but it did reveal the presence of a deep-rooted xenophobia which expressed itself in the scorn and insults it heaped on the Italian immigrants and their children and even by a few massacres of Italians by local French populations. On the contrary, in the 1930s, Germany witnessed the emergence of a racist party without significant immigration to the country. The combination of economic depression and the national humiliation caused by Germany's defeat in the First World War were responsible for the success of the Nazi party which drew strength from preexisting anti-Semitism.

Indeed, during the second half of the twentieth century there was no linear development of xenophobia similar to the rise and fall of mercury levels in a thermometer in Europe. There were two changes with contradictory effects. The first of these began immediately after the Second World War and continues today: it consists of a dramatic rise in humanist and universal values. The second began in the 1980s when immigration began to become a political issue.

The Rise in Universal Values

We have seen that the change in values spectacularly affected private life by making individual fulfillment a cardinal value. There is another change in values which, though less immediately visible, is nonetheless hugely important in understanding political behavior. This is the change which has taken place in the egalitarian or hierarchical conception of individual values. It is this change which the notion of universal values refers to and which will be explained below.

Like any system of social representation, the European system of representation and values is based on a certain number of conceptions. These conceptions are implicit more often than not but are nonetheless very present. One of these conceptions is the system of representation according to which certain individuals or groups may be of greater or lesser worth than others. Such an idea can be expressed directly. This is the case for example, with this respondent who says the following within the framework of a non-directive interview:

> I'm a quiet, well-behaved sort of man. When people... when I like people, I'd give them the shirt off my back, even if it was an Algerian, a Black or something like that. If the guy is worth it, I'd give him the shirt off my back. But if he's worthless, I wouldn't have anything more to do with him!

It is also the case in this quote from the French nineteenth-century writer, Gustave Flaubert, in his novel, *L'Éducation sentimentale*, where the author describes his hero who is about to board a boat. He is looking at a scene which, in his eyes, is distressing where the sailors are making the final preparations before departure:

> He was sickened by the baseness of the figures, the stupidity of their exchanges, their imbecile satisfaction sweating on their foreheads! However, his awareness of being more worthy than these men relieved his fatigue at watching them.

This way of denying all value to another using the noun "worth" or the verb "to be worthy" is rarely heard nowadays. To our ears it sounds very poor indeed and particularly in educated circles. It is no longer done to declare brutally and openly that somebody has no value or that human beings are of unequal value.

However, there are many linguistic procedures available to make either a favorable or unfavorable judgment on the value of an individual. Apart from the rich and colorful vocabulary of sexual, scatological or mental insults, the metaphors most frequently used are related to verticality, classification and grading, "to be on top," "to be the first" means having great worth; "to be on the bottom" or "to be the last" means having little or no worth. The use of terms such as "superior" or "inferior" is undoubtedly one of the simplest ways to make a direct judgment on the overall value of an individual or a group. If someone took the risk of saying, straight out, that one race is superior to another or that men are superior to women, that individual would certainly provoke a scandal but would also supply the proof, if it were needed, that used in such a way, the meaning of the terms "inferior" and "superior" is immediately understandable.

Nowadays, the tendency is to minimize or to euphemize any expression of the devaluation of individuals. We know that an individual suffers when devalued. Even though it has not been written down anywhere, increasingly the norm is to avoid inflicting hurt on someone else by devaluing them in so far as this is possible. Generally speaking, it can be said that the hierarchical conception of the value of individuals is decreasing in European societies.

The idea that all human beings carry a minimum amount of value which must be respected reveals itself in several ways. First, in the idea that individuals who are victims of a social handicap are not simply responsible for their failure because of a lack of merit or value but that they have a right to the solidarity of the society they live in. Second, in the fact that the death penalty has been abolished in all European countries on the basis of the principle that all men, even criminals nonetheless carry a minimum of value and human dignity.

The other major principle to be adopted by all European countries is that the value of an individual human being may depend on what he or she does but not ever on what he or she is. The official principle in European societies is that of the *a priori* equal value of all human beings whatever their nationality, ethnic origin, age or sex might be. Neither is there any question of judging the value of an individual on the basis of belonging to a group the individual has not chosen. In this sense, the official value system of European societies can be said to be universal as it poses the equal value of all individual human beings as a universal principle.

The fact that these values make up the official value system in European societies does not mean that these values are dominant in the sense that they are massively adhered to and practiced. We know that in practical terms European citizens frequently contravene the principle of the equal value of women and men or the equal value of nationals and foreigners. The equality in principle between the sexes is far from being expressed in all countries as equality in domestic work, in income or in responsibilities. The official antiracism of our value systems does not prevent discrimination in housing, employment or in the expression of prejudice.

However, all indications are that universal values are in progress amongst Europeans. Three major factors are undoubtedly responsible for this.

The first is the shock caused by the revelation after the Second World War of the crimes committed by the Nazis in the name of racism. Until then, it was not reprehensible to affirm the superiority of Whites over other races or to consider Jews to be human beings who are not completely the same as other human beings.

The second factor, already mentioned above, is the improvement in living standards and health and welfare systems which has weakened societal frustrations and reduced people's tendency to designate a scapegoat. It is not difficult to imagine what the social and political consequences might be in many European countries were they to witness strong immigration and an economic situation similar to the great depression of the 1930s.

The third factor is the considerable development in levels of education which European societies have experienced. Opinion polls show in fact that the level of education is the factor which best explains adherence to universal values.[5] The number of people with a secondary education continues to grow and in many European countries the majority of young people have completed secondary school. Teachers and the media broadcast the antiracist message which is relayed by the middle and upper classes. Antiracism has become the norm among the educated population which, as a rule, tends to impose its norms on the rest of the population.

A new ideology seems to be taking shape in Europe based on recognition of the dignity and value of every human being. One of the most surprising results of Cevipof surveys among the French population, is the revelation that public opinion on the death penalty is one of the variables which best predicts attitudes to the building of Europe. In 2002, when asked if they would regret if the European Union were abandoned, only 26% of people in favor of reestablishing the death penalty answered that they would regret it. Amongst respondents hostile to the reestablishment of the death penalty, this proportion is as high as 70%.[6] This correlation between attitudes to Europe and opinion on the death penalty is not due to level of education. The same correlation can be found amongst people with equal levels of education. In the same way, attitudes to immigrants are very strongly linked both to attitudes to Europe and to opinions on the death penalty.

These results seem to show that attitudes to the death penalty, to immigrants and to Europe are all universal values and that the cement which links them is the principle of recognition of the intrinsic value of every human being. To refuse xenophobia is to affirm the principle according to which the value of a human being does not depend on ethnic, racial, or national origin. To oppose the death penalty is to believe that even a criminal holds some human value which must be respected. To be in favor of the European Union is to consider that the inhabitants of all other European countries are not part of a humanity which is different or inferior to our own and that we can form a community with them.

The Emergence of Immigration as a Political Issue

From the 1980s onward, the presence of immigrant populations of non-European origin began to become more visible in European societies. Until then, European countries had mostly hosted foreign workers, i.e. adult males who lived without family in hostels or shanty towns. Their arrival in the country was sometimes organized to satisfy the need for industrial labor. They were often the object of fear or of scorn but they represented neither a social problem nor a political issue. The situation changed when their families began to arrive and they started to live with them and to be present in the public arena, i.e. to occupy housing, to use public transport and to use the schools. The cohabitation of immigrants and nationals in the same places then provoked tension due, on the one hand, to different customs and, on the other, to the delinquency and lack of civic behavior on the part of a small minority of the immigrant population. The unstoppable mechanism of xenophobia, based on a tendency to see others as radically different and to attribute the rightly or wrongly perceived faults of the few to the whole group,[7] was then set in motion. Thus, while the norm condemning xenophobia was gaining ground in society, xenophobia which had previously concerned faraway and somewhat abstract populations found a new application in the concrete presence of immigrants in the public arena. It would be foolish to try to deny the reality of the many xenophobic reactions to the presence of immigrants. But it would also be a mistake not to see that the value systems in European countries have considerably evolved during the second half of the twentieth century in their representation of the equality of value and dignity among all groups of human beings.

As a new social problem, immigration has become a political issue and has played a part in the appearance of various xenophobic parties in France, Switzerland, the Netherlands, Belgium, Denmark, and Austria. The emergence of these parties has changed the political landscape at the same time as bearing witness to the changes which had already taken place in the values which the major government parties used as a reference point. One of the factors which paved the way for the emergence of these parties was the way in which Right of center parties had evolved. They had followed the same direction as society as a whole and had become less nationalist and less ethno-centric than before. This caused a split between moderate and Extreme-Right parties. When an alliance takes place between these two forces in a given country it tends to provoke tensions and the reprobation of other European countries. Furthermore, if a certain section of the electorate, particularly within the working class, chooses to vote in function of the immigration issue this is partly because they feel that there is no real difference between the major parties with regard to economic and social problems, which previously accounted for the dominant political cleavage.

A Political Landscape with No Dominant Cleavage

There is very little correlation between these three sets of values—religious, economic, and social and universal. Contrary to what is often believed, a strong religious sentiment does not imply adherence to xenophobic values but on the contrary constitutes a barrier to such values because of the stress placed by Christianity nowadays on the value of each individual and the respect due to him or her. In the same way, adherence to universal values does not necessarily go hand in hand with hostility to economic liberalism. On this point, there even exists an internal contradiction within each voter which is inherent to social position. An higher social position favors both adherence to universal values that are strongly linked to a good level of education and conservative positions on economic and social issues. Conversely, members of the working class do not adhere much to universal values and because of their less satisfactory social situation tend to support measures favorable to the delivery of health and welfare services and the protection of buying power generally proposed by the political Left. All voters therefore have reasons both to vote Left and to vote Right.

The decline of the economic and social cleavage showed itself in the decline of class voting where in former times the working class voted Left and the well-off voted Right. An increasing number of voters feel closer to the Left on some points and closer to the Right on other points. The tendency of voters to identify with the Left or the Right or indeed with a particular political party has necessarily been weakened as a result of this. This is confirmed by long-term opinion polls in the vast majority of European countries (Schweisguth, 2002) and is reflected in the range of political parties on offer. The content of political discourse on the part of candidates for election is tending to become more and more similar and electoral campaigns are more and more characterized by personalization. A new form of politics is perhaps emerging in Europe, which in certain countries such as France, seems to be becoming more like American politics.

Notes

1. Schweisguth, 1995.
2. The case of Islam will not be dealt with here. Muslims, who represent only about 3% of the European population, tend to be under-represented in opinion polls. There is therefore a lack of sufficiently solid data for a precise diagnostic to be made. What can be said is that available indications do not in any way confirm the hypothesis of a rise in religious belief among the immigrant population from Muslim countries. Although it tends to be spectacular and a source of potential violence, the fundamentalist phenomenon concerns only a tiny minority of European Muslims and is

not part of any statistical study. Politically, Muslims seem more inclined to favor left-wing parties than "home-grown" nationals from the countries they live in.

3. Schweisguth, 1998.
4. Lambert, 2002.
5. Schweisguth, 1998.
6. Grunberg and Schweisguth, 2003.
7. Tajfel, 1978.

CHAPTER 3

Religion and Politics

Jean-Marie Donegani

Europe is the only continent to have been wholly Christianized. The Gospels began to be preached in the second century, they reached the former territories of the Roman Empire in the sixth century, and the rest of Europe was converted during the ninth and tenth centuries. Nevertheless, after an initial period of unity, the history of the continent was marked by a number of splits, starting with the schism between the Western and Orthodox churches in the eleventh century, followed by the Muslim conquest of the Balkans in the fifteenth century and the Reformation in the sixteenth century. The impact of these ruptures was still being felt across Europe centuries later, notably in the conflicts which have punctuated Irish history since the beginning of the last century, as well as the wars in Eastern Europe and Bosnia and Herzegovina which followed the disintegration of the communist bloc. In other words, far from being a unifying force, Europe's religious baggage has been a constant source of divisiveness, manifesting itself not only in tension between nations, but also in relations between Church and State, and in the attitudes and behavior of various European populations. From this point of view, France occupies a particular place. France's revolution—the first great revolution of the eighteenth century—led to the substantial modification of the alliance between the Catholic Church and the State, and provided a model of the secularization of politics which was subsequently adopted in other countries. For so long the *fille ainée de l'Eglise* ("the Catholic Church's eldest daughter"), France is today the European country which has gone furthest in escaping the grip of religion, followed slowly but surely by its European neighbors, and setting the tone for the future of religion in Europe.[1]

The secularization of Europe has played itself out in a number of quite distinct religious contexts: the Catholic countries (France, Italy, Spain, Portugal, Austria, Belgium, and Ireland), the Protestant countries (Sweden, Denmark, and Finland), mixed countries (Germany, the Netherlands, the United

Kingdom), as well as the mainly Orthodox countries of the East of Europe. Despite these national differences, all these countries have experienced a shift from the sacrality of the past to present day secularity. This process began with the establishment of freedom of conscience and the abrogation of denominational discrimination, after which the role of the state was confined to the maintenance of civil order, and no longer included protecting the unity of the faith. This reduction of the role of the state had the effect of destroying the identification of a society with a single religion and the secularization process was completed by the Church's loss of its prerogatives in public life, when religious and administrative acts were disassociated.

Nevertheless, the secularization of Europe has been by no means uniform. Some countries—like the Netherlands—recognized religion and institutionalized it using a pluralist model, other countries—such as Germany—accord churches the status of corporations in public law, while in England, for example, a special link between the Crown and the Established Church has been maintained. In France, on the other hand, in 1905 legislation was passed establishing strict separation between state and church. In Europe today there are therefore a variety of systems for managing the relationship between religion and politics. The first model is that of a state religion, like Anglicanism in England or Lutheranism in the Netherlands; in the second model the State, using concordats, grants the church the prerogative to participate to varying extents in certain areas of public life, as is the case in Spain, Italy, Portugal, and the French departments of Alsace and Moselle; other countries accord a special status to the church, like Germany, where a religious tax is levied, or Ireland, where the constitution is placed under the sign of the Holy Trinity and responsibility for education and the health and social services are given over to the church; lastly there are countries where there is a separation of church and state. This separation may be complete, as in France, where state interference in church matters and church interference in politics is forbidden, or less strict as in Belgium, where there is a tradition of denominational schools, media, and trade unions operating alongside secular equivalents. In all of these countries, with the exception of France, religious education is part of the national school curriculum and many state universities have departments of theology.

As mentioned above, all European countries, irrespective of the status given to churches, are experiencing a process of secularization and a consequent decline in the importance of religion. Despite the appearance of new religious movements and sects, the increasing popularity of charismatic movements and evangelical churches within Christianity, and sporadic evidence of a "return to the sacred"—leading some observers to theorize a global desecularization movement[2]—one survey after another confirms the declining importance of Europe's religious heritage. This is in contrast with opposite trends in the rest of the world. Moreover, throughout Europe the degree of individuals' religious integration and their political orientation seem to be linked. These two phenomena need to be closely examined in order for the relationship between religion and politics to be better understood.

Secularization, which will be discussed in greater detail below, manifests itself first in the decline in churchgoing and the number of believers, especially among the young, and second, more generally, in the privatization of religion. This phenomenon has a fundamental political significance in that it marks the victory of the liberal conception of the relationship of religion and politics, namely that religion should remain a private matter which has no place in public life, and is not under the control of any single religious authority. Secularization is therefore a multidimensional process, which results in religious change being considered in the light of its political consequences.

Furthermore, it is a fact—confirmed by every relevant survey undertaken in the last forty years—that the more frequently and intensely an individual practices their religion, the more likely they are to hold conservative political views. This applies to individuals of all faiths. The link between religious integration and political orientation is all the more remarkable, given not only the decline in religious conformism, orthodoxy and orthopraxy, but also, and more significantly, in light of the fact that an institution as historically intransigent as the Catholic Church, which had refused any compromise with the values of post-revolutionary bourgeois liberal French society, operated its *aggiornamento* at the last council and accepted two of the main articles of faith of modern politics, namely the separation of secular and religious power and freedom of religion. The first French sociologists to highlight the relationship between religious integration and right-wing political views offered a socio-historical explanation: they argued that the link between political conservatism and Catholicism could be explained by the fact that the Church proposed an alternative and opposing model to the model which came out of the French Revolution. The counter-model supplied by the Church was organic and hierarchical, and was inspired by the norms which governed its own internal functioning.[3] Research has shown this explanation to be unsatisfactory: a correlation between religious integration and right-wing political values is also present among members of Orthodox and Protestant churches.[4] This indicates that it is necessary to go further and question the political significance of not only religious integration, but also of religious gestures in the strict sense of the term.

We will therefore first examine the classic relationship between religious integration and political orientation. Given that, as we have just indicated, the secularization of religious conduct and attitudes has political implications, we will then examine the contemporary evolution of European religious attitudes, and finally the significance of this evolution from a political point of view.

Religious Integration and Political Attitudes

The relationship an individual has with politics can be measured using three types of indicator. The first is politicization, which indicates the amount of interest an individual has in politics and the place it occupies in their life. It is known that there is a relation between the extent to which an individual is likely to be involved in politics and their educational level, and that those on the Left are more interested in politics than those on the Right. In fact, unlike the political Right, the Left values conflict and adapts itself more easily to political reality, which is by its very nature a source of division and opposition between individuals and groups. The second indicator is concerned with attitudes toward types of otherness, in particular foreigners, as well as attitudes concerning family and sexual ethics. Xenophobia is known to be linked to both an individual's level of education (the less educated they are, the more likely they are to be xenophobic) and their political orientation (a right-wing individual is likely to be more xenophobic than a left-wing individual). Moreover, a focus on so-called family values and moralistic attitudes has historically been characteristic of the Right, people of the Left being more individualistic and having liberal cultural values. The third indicator is of course political orientation per se, namely the propensity to vote for or support a left- or right-wing candidate.

Turning to the link between religion and politics, it can be said that as a rule the more religiously integrated an individual is, the more likely they are to have conservative political attitudes. This holds true for voting behavior as well as for political values regarding, for example, an individual's attitude to foreigners, or their sexual or family ethics. As regards politicization, on the other hand, it appears that the level of religious integration is less important than the cultural environment or national traditions, which demonstrates the limitations of positing a simple link between the intensity of religious feeling and political attitudes.

Politicization

If a comprehensive indicator of politicization is constructed, using a variety of questions—about level of interest in politics, whether an individual discusses politics with their friends, and the subjective importance they attach to politics—it can be observed that the level of politicization tends to depend first on educational level and then on the cultural context, religious integration per se having no impact on politicization.[5] Catholic countries are always less politicized than Protestant ones.

In Europe as a whole 45% of individuals are highly politicized. This figure drops to between 26% and 40% for Catholic countries like Spain, Italy, Portugal, France, and Ireland, whereas in Protestant countries, such as the United Kingdom, Denmark, the Netherlands, and Germany, the percentage of politicized individuals is always higher (between 50% and 68%), see table 3.1.

These differences can certainly be attributed to cultural context; the inhabitants of countries where Protestantism took root have always been encouraged to learn to read and write in order to give them access to the Bible. Protestantism also encourages discussion, introducing people to public debate, which today forms an integral part of the national culture of countries where Protestantism has historically been strong. Politicization is therefore linked to national culture, rather than an individual's religious belief, as demonstrated by the fact that in Protestant countries there is no perceptible difference between the levels of politicization of Catholics and Protestants.

Table 3.1 High level of politicization by religious attitude and country (%)

	W-GE	*DK*	*SP*	*FR*	*UK*	*IR*	*IT*	*NL*	*PT*	*Overall*
Regularly practicing Catholics	67	—	23	57	58	38	32	66	28	41
Irregularly practicing Catholics	66	—	26	38	34	40	27	60	25	36
Non-practicing Catholics	63	—	27	36	63	39	35	54	36	40
Regularly practicing Protestants	67	63	—	—	57	38	17	73	—	61
Irregularly practicing Protestants	73	56	—	—	60	—	—	79	—	65
Non-practicing Protestants	67	54	—	—	51	—	—	47	—	58
No religion	71	64	30	35	42	50	39	65	42	44
Overall	68	57	26	38	50	38	33	65	33	45

Note: The countries are indicated in the table using the following abbreviations: East Germany (E-G); West Germany (W-G); Belgium (BE); Denmark (DK); Spain (SP); France (FR); United Kingdom (UK); Ireland (IR); Italy (IT); Netherlands (NL); Portugal (PT).

Source: ISSP Survey, 1998.

If we examine the level of religious integration across denominations, it becomes apparent that the frequency with which an individual makes an act of worship has no bearing on their level of politicization. In Spain, which is the least politicized of the countries under consideration, the frequency of church attendance by Catholics[6] has no bearing on the level of politicization: 23% of regular churchgoers, 26% of irregular churchgoers and 27% of non-practicing Catholics are politicized.

In Germany, which is the most politicized country, the frequency of church-going of both Catholics and Protestants has no bearing on levels of politicization: 67% of Catholics who attend church regularly, 63% of non-churchgoing Catholics, 67% of Protestants who attend church regularly and 67% of non-churchgoing Protestants are politicized. It would therefore seem to be the national cultural context that has the most impact on a country's overall levels of politicization, rather than its religious composition.

Xenophobia and Permissiveness

An initial indication of a given population's attitude toward foreigners may be provided by answers to the following question, regarding discrimination in favor of one's own nationals: "When jobs are scarce, employers when recruiting should give preference to . . . ," followed by the nationality of the interviewee. 61% of Europeans support discrimination in favor of individuals of their own nationality. In Protestant countries this preference is less pronounced, and there is no significant difference between Protestants and Catholics in this regard: in the United Kingdom, job discrimination in favor of one's own nationals meets with the approval of 45% of Protestants who attend church regularly and 43% of Catholics who attend church regularly. In the Netherlands 40% of

Table 3.2 Proportion of Europeans supporting job discrimination in favor of nationals by religious attitude (%)

	W-GE	*DK*	*SP*	*FR*	*UK*	*IR*	*IT*	*NL*	*PT*	*Overall*
Regularly Practicing Catholics	60	—	77	70	43	70	73	41	86	70
Irregularly Practicing Catholics	65	—	81	72	70	73	77	40	68	73
Non-practicing Catholics	60	—	76	66	25	68	72	21	68	67
Regularly Practicing Protestants	61	47	—	—	45	63	65	40	—	52
Irregularly Practicing Protestants	59	61	—	—	55	—	—	28	—	58
Non-practicing Protestants	50	53	—	—	57	—	—	42	—	54
No religion	51	28	69	51	49	36	66	32	86	53
Overall	57	52	76	61	49	68	72	34	86	61

Source: ISSP Survey, 1998.

regular Protestant churchgoers and 41% of regular Catholic churchgoers take a similar view on this question. In Catholic countries this kind of preferential treatment for one's own countrymen and women is more pronounced—ranging from 66% to 90%—but, given the low numbers of Protestants in France, Italy, Spain and Portugal, it is not possible to compare the attitudes of Protestants and Catholics in these countries. So once again we have an indication that the national cultural context has a more decisive influence than the level of religious integration (table 3.2).

Nevertheless, the most interesting observation to be made concerns the results obtained when different indicators are used. Whereas this kind of preference for one's nationals was expressed by 61% of Europeans surveyed, this figure rose to 63% for churchgoers who were not members of a denominational organization and dropped to 48% of churchgoers who were members of such an organization. This indicates that religious integration takes different forms, and that there is a difference between integration through churchgoing and integration through active involvement in a church organization. The difference is not to be found in the degree of religious integration—religious activists attend church as regularly as churchgoers who are not members of a religious organization—but in the orientation of the religious integration itself. This is an essential element in the analysis of the relationship between religion and politics which we will come back to later.

An individual's attitude toward foreigners can also be measured using another, more discriminating indicator. Here a scale of xenophobia is established using questions regarding categories of people who the interviewee would not like to have as a neighbor: people of a different race, Muslims, foreign workers, Jews and Hindus. Whereas belief that employment discrimination in favor of one's own compatriots is quite widespread in Europe, xenophobia is much less so: only 25% of interviewees expressed a desire not to have as a neighbor someone belonging to one or more of the above categories of people (see table 3.3).

Here the most influential factors are educational background and age: 19% of 18 to 29-year-olds and 33% of those aged 60 and above are xenophobic; 15% of those who were still in education at the age of twenty, compared to 30% of those who left school at 15, were xenophobic. By factoring in these

Table 3.3 Xenophobic people in Western Europe (excluding at least one category of foreigners) by religious attitude and country (%)

	W-GE	*DK*	*SP*	*FR*	*UK*	*IR*	*IT*	*NL*	*PT*	*Overall*
Regularly practicing Catholics	34	—	19	24	15	18	27	27	35	26
Irregularly practicing Catholics	33	—	15	31	25	15	26	27	40	27
Non-practicing Catholics	31	—	16	26	18	25	26	17	25	24
Regularly practicing Protestants	34	22	—	—	22	13	5	29	—	26
Irregularly practicing Protestants	31	19	—	—	23	—	—	26	—	27
Non-practicing Protestants	28	22	—	—	26	—	—	18	—	26
No religion	30	9	18	19	21	11	23	18	32	22
Overall	31	22	17	23	22	18	26	21	32	25

Source: ISSP Survey, 1998.

variables the effect of religious belief becomes clearer. It can be observed that, while for the 18–29 age group the more religious individuals tend to be less xenophobic than those who are less religious, for the over-60s the reverse is the case: the relatively religious are more xenophobic than the less religious. This leads us to draw the conclusion that religious integration can take on a variety of forms and be greatly influenced by the way an individual has been socialized. The oldest interviewees were undoubtedly integrated into a conservative religion which was relatively intolerant of otherness, whereas the youngest interviewees have been brought up in a religion more open to and accepting of difference.

Finally to add another dimension to this analysis of the link between socio-political attitudes and religious integration, we can consider the question of sexual permissiveness. It is well known that religions have traditionally paid a great deal of attention to questions of sexual morality, and been deeply concerned about the preservation of the family. Surveys carried out across Europe confirm this: the countries where levels of church attendance are highest are also those where there is less sexual permissiveness, with the exception of Spain, which has high levels of both permissiveness and church attendance. The key point to be noted is the central importance of national cultures, since Protestant countries are more permissive than Catholic ones. In stark contrast to the previous results regarding politicization, however, in countries with relatively large Catholic and Protestant populations there is a significant difference between Protestants and Catholics, the latter being consistently less permissive than the former. This is a symptom of the different relationships these churches have with modernity. After the Reformation established individualism and secularism in the West, these two ideologies came to become two of the defining features of modern culture. Meanwhile, Catholicism parted company with modernity—at least until the last council/—in its fierce opposition to individual freedom and moral relativism.

Political Orientation

By way of concluding this first part of our survey, it is necessary to turn our attention to the perceptible links between religious integration and political orientation. Here things seem more straightforward: the more an individual practices their faith, the more likely they are to vote for a right-wing candidate. In all the countries under consideration, with the exception of the United Kingdom, a deep commitment to Christianity, indicated by frequency of church attendance, goes hand in hand with right-wing political views.[7] In the United Kingdom the relationship between churchgoing and voting behavior is rather different: since the tendency for churchgoers to be further to the Right than non-churchgoers only holds true for Catholics. In fact Anglicans always tend to be more conservative than Catholics; this is equally true for both churchgoers and non-churchgoers. The differences between Protestants and Catholics in this regard vary from country to country, Protestants tending to be more right wing than Catholics in the Netherlands whereas the opposite is the case in Germany (table 3.4).

We have seen, therefore, that differences in levels of politicization or attitudes toward discrimination in favor of one's compatriots are due to different national contexts rather than religious integration per se, since in Protestant countries the data for Catholics and Protestants are very similar, and variations in regularity of churchgoing have little impact on the results. Above all it is apparent, from the differences in levels of xenophobia between young and old people, and the differing attitudes toward discrimination in favor of one's own compatriots among militant churchgoers and non-militant churchgoers, that the relationship between religious integration and political attitudes is far from straightforward. Relations between political attitudes and religious attitudes appear to change, depending on which indicator is used. This means that religious integration is itself capable of assuming an "orientation" in the same way as political integration does. The similarity of the links between religious practice and voting conservatively for Catholics, Protestants and even Orthodox Christians—as with the contrast between militant and non-militant churchgoers mentioned above—provides sufficient indication that there are, not only regarding religious integration but also certain gestures

Table 3.4 Proportion of right-wing individuals by degree of religious integration in Western Europe (%)

	E-GE	*W-GE*	*DK*	*SP*	*FR*	*UK*	*IR*	*IT*	*NL*	*PT*
Practicing Catholics	40	61	—	45	48	29	67	37	61	33
Non-practicing Catholics	56	24	—	33	27	16	43	25	45	20
Practicing Protestants	58	42	53	—	—	45	65	—	74	—
Non-practicing Protestants	39	26	34	—	33	46	60	—	44	—
No religion	21	17	27	24	10	31	20	10	33	15
Overall	28	30	35	36	22	36	58	29	42	25

Source: ISSP survey, 1998.

chosen to express it, political implications which refer to underlying attitudes that determine both a political practice and a religious practice. The results of a survey, conducted in Grenoble and the surrounding area, of individuals who attended Sunday mass provided support for this hypothesis. While churchgoers in these parishes tend to be relatively right wing, this orientation becomes less pronounced for those individuals who engage in private Bible study, and even less common for churchgoers who actively participate in the liturgies. Indeed, in the latter group left-wing individuals are in the majority.[8] Here, our concern is not with the intensity of religious integration, as is the case when regular churchgoers are compared with irregular churchgoers or non-churchgoers. It is rather a matter of the orientation of the religious integration itself. Religious gestures are loaded with political meaning, and the choice of a particular form of religious expression may reveal certain political attitudes. This is because these ways of expressing oneself can indicate either independence and individual liberty or submission and allegiance. Furthermore it is well known that the Left and Right have very different ideas about liberty and authority. We cannot offer an analysis of what determines the meaning of the relationship, but it is clear that a relationship between certain kinds of religious expression and certain political orientations exists. That is why, in an investigation of the links between religion and politics in Europe, it is absolutely necessary to examine the religious attitudes themselves before speculating on their political significance.

Attitudes to Religion in Contemporary Europe

It should be noted from the outset that in Europe religion is in decline. Between 1981 and 1999 all available indicators registered a fall in religiosity, whether they were in the form of objective data—such as the number of Catholics (49% in 1999, down from 55% in 1981) or Protestants (21% down from 30%) as well as church attendance (30% down from 36%)—or subjective replies to questions concerning levels of trust in the Church (43% down from 51% having "a great deal of trust" or "a certain amount of trust"), belief in God (68% down from 74%), or the fact of considering oneself religious (56% down from 62%) (see table 3.5).[9]

A comparison of the data for 18 to 29 year olds and the over 60s reveals that all the indicators without exception, and for every country and religious denomination, are lower for the younger age group. This provides support for the thesis that the whole of Europe is undergoing a process of secularization, although there are of course significant differences between the most religious countries, such as Italy, to the least religious, like France. Nevertheless, secularization marks less a decline in religiosity than its transformation. This transformation has two aspects: attachment to a highly influential institutional religion has been largely replaced by an individualized religiosity which imposes no sanctions and obligations; and a logic of objective belonging has been replaced by a logic of subjective identification.

Table 3.5 Attitudes to religion in Western Europe (%)

	W-GE	*BE*	*DK*	*SP*	*FR*	*UK*	*IR*	*IT*	*NL*	*9 countries 1999*	*9 countries 1981*
Religious person	52	62	71	56	44	37	71	83	63	56	62
Religion provides comfort	45	47	30	49	32	33	80	68	44	45	48
Religious background	76	63	88	82	57	82	90	82	46	75	85
Catholic background	32	55	1	81	53	13	87	81	24	49	55
Protestant background	40	3	87	0	2	51	2	0	17	21	30
Performs act of worship once a week	30	28	12	36	12	19	67	53	26	30	36
Prays to a personal God once a week	34	35	20	39	19	27	68	61	34	36	—
A lot or a certain amount of trust in Churches	37	42	55	41	44	33	52	66	29	43	51
Churches can provide answers to spiritual needs	52	46	40	48	51	47	57	66	37	52	44
to moral problems and needs	45	32	16	33	33	26	27	55	29	38	36
to family problems	36	29	12	29	26	23	25	43	24	31	34
to social problems	29	24	9	23	20	21	24	38	29	26	28
Belief in God	62	66	62	81	56	51	93	88	60	68	74
Belief in a personal God	34	29	24	46	21	28	63	70	23	38	30

Source: ISSP survey, 1999.

Disinstutionalization and Pluralism

The weakening of systems of religious control first manifested itself in the disinstitutionalization of religion, that is, the separation of religion as subjectively experienced and religion as regulated by an institution which dictates the truths to be believed and the virtues to be practiced. There are always more individuals who regard themselves as being religious than individuals who go to church at least once a month (table 3.5). The discrepancy between these figures amounts to 11% on average in the Lutheran countries (Sweden, Finland, and Denmark), 25% in the mixed-religion countries (Germany, Netherlands, and the United Kingdom), and 30% in the Catholic countries.[10] The rate of churchgoing in France is lower than in any other European country: 12% of French people attend a church service at least once a month (this figure rises to 34% for the over 60s and falls to 8% for 18 to 29 year olds).

The significance of this decline in churchgoing was already clear from the results of a 1985 survey, where French interviewees were asked: "For you, what does being a Christian entail?"[11] The religious practice in equal last position—with involvement in Catholic movements—was "attending church," with 8% of replies. The most commonly chosen response was "helping needy people you know" (47%), followed by "having a closely-knit family" (39%), "giving your children a religious education" (27%), and "praying, thinking about God" (24%). These results indicate that the importance attached to objective gestures prioritized by institutionalized religion has decreased, while religious meaning is increasingly located in the private sphere, and is considered to be a personal matter.

In the light of the above, it is no longer possible to regard religious integration as a univocal continuum, since the very effect of disinstitutionalization has been to separate the various traditional components of integration. For example, although only 39% of young Dutch people are members of a church, fully 82% of them pray (this was revealed by the 1999 *Valeurs* survey). Furthermore those who pray tend to do so in a way which fails to fit the description of prayer in traditional Christian spirituality; prayer becomes a form of psychological introspection which makes no claims to have a transcendent dimension.[12]

The disinstitutionalization of religiosity is also reflected in people's attitudes to churches. The general falling away of trust in religious institutions between 1980 and 1999 has already been noted. It must be stressed, however, that individuals still consider churches to be trustworthy, at least as regards the guidance they give on spiritual and, to a lesser extent, moral matters. There is a lack of trust, however, in their ability to offer solutions to problems related to family and social life (table 3.5). When the churches' claim to regulate society and the lives of individuals is brought into question it is a sure sign that a general secularization of that society is underway. The disinstutionalization of religiosity is a reaction against integralism, understood as the kind of religious system which, by imposing it conception of ethical social values and sexual behavior, exercises a controlling influence on all areas of people's lives.

This disinstitutionalization of religiosity is likely to lead to a pluralization of identities. Although there is a lack of comparative surveys which have investigated this question, it has been shown that in France a given religious reference can lead to radically different value systems and conceptions of the world.[13] Most religious references do not require an institutional grounding, which enables us to speak, after Michel de Certeau, of the dissemination of the Christian body, wandering, floating, and of the availability of religious signs for aesthetic interpretation and private appropriation.[14]

Subjectivism and Relativism

Religion appears increasingly to be experienced as a personal and private matter, beyond the sway of institutionalized religion. This subjectivism in no way indicates a lack of interest in religion: a survey conducted in France, the most secularized country in Europe, revealed that only 18% of those interviewed agreed with the proposition "Religious faith no longer means anything to me," while 67% believed that "religion can help people to bear life's hardships."[15] Although the rise of subjectivism does not necessarily indicate a decline in interest in religion, it does lead to a new à la carte system in which individuals, when creating their vision of the world, can choose from a variety of religious options, free from pressure to show loyalty or conform to certain beliefs or practices. In the past belief systems were backed up by the threat of social sanctions for those who transgressed. This is no longer the case, and religious groups are less easily identifiable, since religious groups are themselves less subject to institutional regulation. We are now also witnessing a decline in the notion of heterodoxy.

The rise of subjectivism is evidenced by the fact that 71% of French people are of the opinion that "it is for each individual to define their religious beliefs, independently of Churches." Furthermore, 83% of them claim that, when faced with major life decisions, they listen above all to their own consciences (1% are guided primarily by the stance of their church).[16] Subjectivism also has an impact on religious beliefs. Although belief in God is shared by a majority of Europeans (68%), only 38% believe, in accordance with Christian tradition, in the existence of a personal God. Unsurprisingly, the more believers there are in a country, the higher the percentage of believers in a personal God (table 3.5). In Ireland, where 93% of the population believes in God, almost two thirds of individuals believe in a personal God, whereas in France, where 56% believe in God, only 21% believe in a personal God. In this subjectivist culture, it becomes possible to select one's beliefs and mix and match them without considering dogmatic consistency; more and more people, for example, claim to believe in both the Resurrection and reincarnation. The choice and adaptation of beliefs are governed by a logic of psychological security, more than any need for dogmatic consistency. Religion is called upon to provide support in the here and now, and the question of the ultimate ends is put to one side while we seek the immediate benefits to be derived from taking care of ourselves. The notion of sin loses its eschatological significance and now merely refers snags in our relationships with others, ourselves, and God. Furthermore, churches appear to be depositories of religious meanings where anyone is free to come and construct, independently and in any way they see fit, the belief system which works best for them. The European survey reveals that far more people believe in God (68%) and consider themselves to be religious (56%) than go to church (30%), providing further confirmation for the thesis that individuals have a preference for à la carte religion, where the subject is sovereign. Alongside subjectivism, a belief in relativism—which regards truth as being relative to the individual who experiences it—is becoming increasingly widespread. Such an attitude leads all religions to be regarded as possessing an equivalent alethic charge, each individual being at liberty to embrace one "truth" and turn their back on another. The European study showed that very few individuals, especially among the younger generations, believe that one religion has a monopoly on truth (table 3.6).[17]

We can once again observe a difference between Catholic and Protestant countries, the former being always less relativistic than the latter, but only for the oldest category of individuals. Young people, whether they are Protestant or Catholic, almost all have a relativist outlook. Today in France only 4% of 18–29-year-olds agree with the proposition that the truth is present in only one religion; in 1952 45% of the 20 to 34 age group shared this point of view. Even

Table 3.6 Attitudes to religious truth in Western Europe (%)

	W-GE		*DK*		*SP*		*FR*		*UK*		*IR*		*IT*		*NL*	
	1	*2*	*1*	*2*	*1*	*2*	*1*	*2*	*1*	*2*	*1*	*2*	*1*	*2*	*1*	*2*
Religions contain very little truth	16	10	24	15	26	8	23	18	19	7	7	8	8	8	13	12
There are fundamental truths in many religions	59	63	63	53	49	32	46	55	58	71	74	46	63	46	59	59
Only one religion contains any truth	4	13	7	12	14	44	4	10	4	7	6	34	17	34	9	9

Notes: 1: 18–29-year-olds; 2: 60-year-olds and more.
Source: ISSP Survey, 1998.

allowing for the fact that the age groupings used in these two studies were not identical, the contrast between the results is striking and gives a clear indication of the rise of relativist and pluralist conceptions of religiosity over the past half century.

It is necessary to make clear that the rise of relativism is less a sign of a general lack of interest in religious truth than a consequence of the rise of subjectivism and pluralism. In a culture where religious pluralism is a given and a subjectivist view of religious conviction holds sway, people have difficulty believing that any given religious viewpoint has a monopoly on the truth. In a survey of 12 to 15 year olds carried out in France a number of years ago, 66% of interviewees replied in the negative to the question "Is there a religion which is truer than any other?" When, in a follow-up question, individuals were asked to give the reason for their choice, most replied that they gave this answer not "because religions all say the same things," nor "because they are all false," but "because it is a matter of individual choice," indicating the fundamental link between subjectivism and relativism.

It can also be observed that belief is increasingly formulated in terms of possibility or probability. Belief in God is generally expressed as a probability, interviewees being more likely to opt for "God probably exists" rather than "God certainly exists." This attitude is consistent with contemporary forms of belief, which accord legitimacy to personal choice and disassociate religious faith from any desire to make a reasoned defense of a particular religion. There is no requirement to attempt to convince others of the validity of one's beliefs, as it is up to each individual to decide for themselves which beliefs satisfy them.

We can conclude here that traditional religious world views are being reconstructed within the context of advanced modernity. Even though certain beliefs, such as the existence of God, are widely held, they have different meanings for different individuals. The validity of a system based on an obligation to follow religious dictates is losing ground. Individuals now make a subjective selection of the beliefs and practices which they feel achieve the best fit with their evolving identity and world view. Orthopraxy, as well as orthodoxy, is in decline. Over the last twenty years, the majority of Christian faiths have fewer and fewer adherents, particularly among young people. The only belief which is increasingly held by members of the younger generation is belief in life after death. Nevertheless, this is not an exclusively Christian belief and is less an expression of religious dogma than a subjective affirmation regarding the pursuit of happiness, which is understood to continue after death. In fact more people believe in Heaven than Hell (38% and 25% of Europeans, respectively), and the category of young people for whom belief in life after death is on the increase are also the least religious. Therefore a new belief system is in place in which individuals' relationships with religiosity are pluralized, subjectivized, and deregulated. We will now analyze the political significance of this shift.

The Political Significance of Changing Attitudes to Religion

We will now shift over attention away from the link between political orientation and religious integration to the meaning of the trends related to changing relationships with religion, mentioned above. The evolutions in religious belief outlined above are typical of secularized societies, characterized by the privatization and disinstitutionalization of religion. Even in those European countries where secularism is not official state doctrine, and where there continue to be links between religious and political institutions, secularist ideology has so impregnated the way moral standards are viewed that individuals can decide to accept or reject them. They are free to select from the stock of religious options available and construct—free of sanction or obligation—value systems and codes of behavior which exist beyond institutional regulation. The deregulation of belief—which is widespread—is the clearest indication of the secularization of European societies, a secularization which distinguishes them from other countries. Even countries like Ireland, in Western Europe, and Poland, in Eastern Europe, have been affected by this seemingly irresistible secularizing wave, which is characteristic of liberal industrial societies, where the autonomy of the subject and the market model are the dominant ideologies. It would be mistaken to see religious change in European societies simply in terms of the erosion of Christian values; its relationship with other aspects of mores and mentalities should not be overlooked. Religious changes have a specifically political dimension insofar as, by demonstrating the triumph of secularization, they imply a conception of the subject and of social order which has close links with theories of liberalism and democracy.

Secularization and Politics

Secularization theory is the sociological theory which best describes the status of religion in the majority of Western countries (those which can be characterized as economically developed liberal democracies).

Secularization describes the outcome of a historical process in which more and more areas of human thought and activity have detached themselves from the influence of religious institutions. In the history of the West first art, then the law, science, politics and most recently morality have severed their links with their religious and sacred roots. Secularization goes hand in hand with modernity, which has led religion to become just one sector of society, rather than having a direct involvement in—and giving meaning to—every area of social life. This ideology of separation was vigorously criticized by the Catholic magisterium, which opposed the society that was established in the period following the Lumières and the French Revolution. The ideology of separatism and compartmentalization—which underpins secularization—supposes that social life is made up of several autonomous sectors, each distinct from the others, each with their own way of reasoning, values, behaviors, and, above all, institutions. The most important separation is not, however, a separation between institutions, but the separation between the public and private spheres. Heavily influenced by liberalism, the secular conception of religion restricts it to the private sphere, and makes it the responsibility of each individual to regulate their own religious life. Individuals are guided by their conscience and are under no obligation to obey the dictates of any external authority. People make up their own mind on religious matters, free from the intervention of Church or state. The separation of public and private spheres therefore goes much deeper than the judicial separation of religious and political institutions. The public/private split is a cultural and mental process which has its origins in the birth of modernity, the promotion of individual autonomy, and the invention of a subject defined without reference to membership of a larger body. This separation laid the foundations for the development of cultural and religious pluralism, and the establishment of tolerance as a key value: the State is the guarantor of public order and the free circulation of competing values, which individuals are free to accept and reject as a matter of personal conscience. Thus, secularization does not lead to the elimination of religion, rather to its institutional marginalization, disinstitutionalization, and privatization. Religion, while it has not been eliminated from social life altogether, has lost its unifying power and its ability to influence the way people behave. It is just one kind of activity and social sector among many others, and no longer constitutes a register which is the all-encompassing source of meaning.

It is easy to understand how the contemporary changes in religious expression and identifications described above can be interpreted politically. These religious changes all represent an abandonment of systems of domination, an affirmation of the autonomy of individuals from institutional diktats, and a belief in the primacy of the wishes of individuals. These values are echoed in the evolution of modern politics, which has seen the primacy of natural order and tradition be replaced by a belief in the fundamental right of individual autonomy. Voluntarism is at the very core of modern theories of power and social cohesion. The origins of this movement can be traced as far back as Scotism which posits, unlike Thomism, that God's will is not governed by necessity and that the essential cannot preexist will. Subsequently it is on this base—of the primacy of will—that the subject is theorized in the field of the philosophy of knowledge by Descartes and Kant, in political philosophy in the artificialism and contractualism of Hobbes and Locke, and in the field of the philosophy of history, with the Hegelian assimilation of the empire of the spirit and the empire of the will.[18]

Nevertheless, it is clear that the implications of this reversal are most keenly felt in the inner life of individuals, leading to the relationship between politics and religion being defined by liberal thought. Separated at the institutional level, politics and religion take on a social dimension, since they are reconciled within the consciences of individuals. Separatist ideology only makes sense where it leaves the individual free to make choices based on what they consider to be plausible, desirable, and true. For Constant, there is a part of human existence which necessarily remains individual and independent of any external sovereignty. The authority of the state does not extend to matters of personal conscience. Each individual is free to make their own decisions about truth and form their own opinions. Moreover, by the same token, religious freedom is a primary requirement of political freedom, since individuals' political opinions, like their religious beliefs, are a matter for their consciences alone.[19] Similarly, for Tocqueville, religion regulates politics not by exerting any direct influence on the government, but rather through its influence on moral values and standards. Christianity and democracy harmonize through beliefs not institutions, by opening the individual to alterity and tempering the tendency for modern politics to descend into despotism. The democratic ethos and the Christian ethos overlap insofar as religious belief both enlarges and directs desire. Historically, the elective affinity between Christianity and democracy, identified by Tocqueville, has often been hidden by the existence of alliances between government and religious institutions, and an authoritarian strain running through religion. This affinity only becomes apparent when religion and politics are separated at an institutional level, allowing them to be reconciled within the conscience of each individual.[20] If transformations in contemporary belief are reinterpreted in the light of this intuition, made by liberal scholars, the traditional problematic of relations between religion and politics will clearly have to be thoroughly revised.

Polytheism or Monotheism of Values

The link between political orientation and the practice of a religion still exists but has grown weaker, as obligations become less binding and "believing without belonging" becomes more widespread.[21] Nowadays, the dominant trend in Europe is the rise of individualism which, as is well known, influences both political and religious attitudes. Paradoxically, contemporary views of religion—influenced by subjectivism and relativism—have led the strict division between religion and politics—an article of faith for liberals—to be increasingly porous. In fact, the separation between religion and politics, which was the battleground for the struggle between hard line Catholicism and modern liberalism, has been subsumed by the division between the public and private spheres. Now that it is generally accepted that determining what is good, true and fair is between an individual and their conscience, deciding which values are religious and which are political is also a personal choice, making it difficult to go beyond an individual's account of their own beliefs and give them an objective definition. For example, a majority of young people in France today consider peace to be a religious value,[22] and that words like "love," "justice," "liberty" and "truth" have a religious sense.[23]

In the light of the above, we can put forward the hypothesis that the guiding principles of contemporary societies are axiological: we adhere to values which constitute a new "sacred trust," understood as the values we hold most dear and which are both intangible and unquestionable. Yves Lambert has offered a precise definition of this contemporary axiology.[24] It is not an ideology because it offers neither a model of society nor a particular view of history. It may also be distinguished from both religion—since it is not heteronomous and chooses not to address questions about the afterlife and salvation—and ethics, as it eludes rational systemization. According to Lambert, we can now characterize the dominant axiology of European liberal societies as a "monotheism of values," since:

> A number of fundamental values [. . .] have established themselves in such a way that conflictual pluralism is underpinned by and unquestioning of these core values, which are axiological in nature [. . .]; given the irreductibility of different ideological, philosophical and religious frames of reference, this minimum common core can only be composed of values, which form the basis for social exchange.[25]

Contemporary axiology may be considered to encompass pluralist democracy, human rights, non-violent conflict resolution, religious indifferentism—according to which all religions are equally valid -, tolerance, peace and freedom of conscience. The results of the surveys just mentioned underline the difficulty of defining this axiology as either political or religious since paradoxically, and in a way the first theorists of secularization failed to anticipate, the individualization of belief has resulted not in a narrowing but a widening of the field of religious meanings.

We can follow Durkheim's characterization of modernity as a process which leads to the shrinking of the religious field, providing that religion is understood as institutional religion. As religion ceases to be a source of our societies' standards and common values, it takes on a new life as a resource which can be freely accessed and used in the construction of individual value systems. While Durkheim saw secularization as a movement which led to the autonomization of individual consciences and freed individuals from the grip of religion, Weber had a less optimistic view of this phenomenon. He saw modernity as giving rise to a system of "polytheism of values" based on the separation of the various sources of authority. This phenomenon was, however, problematic for Weber, because no criterion used in one field of practice or knowledge could be applied to govern or regulate another field. Specialization creates knowledge ghettos and leads to relativism, but also to endless heated debates which go unresolved in the absence of any unifying authority able to intervene and offer a universally acceptable judgment. In his opinion, the polytheism of values entails an immanent law of permanent struggle within the framework of this separation between economics, politics, religion, art, and sciences. Any value which is dominant in one sector is liable to be challenged by another value which comes from another sector, and all values are accepted only by those who hold them, making conflict resolution impossible.

Although contemporary theories tend to confirm Weber's predictions concerning the rise of relativism, two elements mean his conclusions regarding the spreading war between conflicting points of view need to be nuanced.

First, despite the individualization of belief, the existence of a stock of commonly held values, shared by the vast majority of individuals, allows a "monotheism of values" to be posited. These values, which are considered to be inviolable, constitute a core of fundamental belief and relate to the very conditions of belief themselves. What is considered sacred is the establishment and protection of the preconditions that give individuals the freedom to believe what they like. 'The sacred' involves giving access to individual sovereignty of belief within a system of pluralization of beliefs. Although pluralism implies a level of decisionism—according to which it is up to each individual to decide what is true and what is good—since this decisionism operates in a highly relativistic context it does not lead to the war which Weber spied upon the horizon of modernity. Since each truth is one individual's truth, having no special claims to challenge the sovereignty of other individuals' right to choose, decisionism lacks the warlike quality which Weber ascribed to it. It is merely the consequence of the affirmation of the prevalence of the private sphere and the sovereignty of individual conscience.

A second fact needs to be taken into consideration, namely that the separation of spheres of activity and knowledge, which Weber believed would lead to a "war of the gods," has actually been subsumed by the separation of between the public and private spheres. This separation does not give rise to conflict because it establishes the sovereignty of individual conscience, which is universally recognized in both the political and religious spheres. The sacred, which is inviolable and unchallengeable, is no longer strictly speaking a certain set of values or collection of truths, but refers to the conditions which enable truth to be accessed, hence guaranteeing the legitimate plurality of values. It is therefore this subsumption of all separations by the separation between private and public which explains why, in the final analysis, relativism and decisionism do not result in the war of the gods.

* * *

After the above analysis, three remarks need to be made. First, regarding the link between religious integration and political orientation, it should be noted that while the differences between the attitudes of Protestants and Catholics are progressively disappearing, Protestants as a group are still more secularized than Catholics, indicating how the attitudes of Catholics may well change in the future. Second, both Protestant and Catholic religious integration, achieved in particular by regular churchgoing, engenders more conservative political attitudes than non-integration. In every European country non-religious individuals tend to be more left wing, permissive and anti-authoritarian than their religious compatriots. Nevertheless, the symbolic systems of non-religious people should not be framed in terms of a lack, or an absence. These systems are just as structured as religious systems and, in the majority of European countries, receive support from non-religious organizations that provide non-religious people with meaning. In Europe there is, therefore, a clear division between religious and non-religious people as regards attachment to not only ethical principles and family values, but also to otherness and abnormality. Finally the orientation as well as the intensity of religious integration must be taken into consideration, as religious gestures themselves reveal attitudes toward authority and freedom which are related to the political dimension of the systems of attitudes.

Evidence of the impact of disinstitutionalization, deregulation, subjectivism, and pragmatism on European religious systems indicates that the level of secularization in Europe is higher than anywhere else in the world. These secular conceptions of religion—as a source of meaning having, however, no claims on imposing its values on either believers or non-believers—and churches—as institutions which are custodians of a stock of significations which can be accessed by any individual but which lack any coercive power—could lead to a system where indifferentism is replaced by indifference. The long term decline of religious indicators lends support to this hypothesis. Religion, as a source of meaning, has come to obey the logic of personal utility. Given that, we can wonder if the still perceptible links between religious and political preferences are not destined to become even weaker, giving rise to a loose conglomeration of value systems characterized by the pursuit of earthly fulfillment and the embrace of an afterlife, stripped of its more dramatic features. In the future, religion could well bear only a vague resemblance to traditional religions in the past, with Christianity being defined as a kind of transcendental humanism susceptible to being freely interpreted and reinterpreted by the faithful, unloosed from the moorings of tradition. The *mondanization* of religion, characteristic of the process of secularization, leads to a problem of interpretation. One can either conclude that the vast majority of individuals are imperceptibly moving toward an abandonment of Christianity, or alternatively that future generations—seeking a religious system in greater harmony with the constituent elements of ultramodernity—will be drawn toward a new kind of religious system.

Notes

1. Rémond, 1998.
2. Berger, 2001.
3. Michelat and Simon, 1977.
4. According to the 1992 Eurobarometer Survey, which covered the twelve member states of the European Union, the following percentages of practicing and non-practicing Christians defined themselves as left wing: practicing Catholics 30%,

non-practicing Catholics 41%; practicing Protestants 23%, non-practicing Protestants 28%; practicing members of the Orthodox Church: 21%, non-practicing members of the Orthodox Church: 34% (Talin, 1999).

5. All data comes from the 1990 European Values survey. Cf. Bréchon, 1996, whose analysis we draw on for tables 3.1, 3.2 and 3.3.
6. There are too few Protestants in Spain to enable reliable percentages to be established.
7. Statistics provided by the 1998 ISSP survey, as analyzed by Bréchon, 2002a.
8. Bréchon and Denni, 1983.
9. This data comes from the 1981 "Values" survey 1981 and the 1999 ISSP survey. Cf. Lambert, 2002.
10. The median of individuals who consider themselves to be religious is 63% in the Catholic countries, 50% in the "mixed" countries and 54% in the Lutheran countries.
11. Sofres-La Croix Survey, April 1985.
12. Janssen and Prins, 2000.
13. Donegani, 1993.
14. de Certeau, 1987.
15. The CSA-Le Monde-La Vie-L'Actualité religieuse Survey in *Le Monde-Forum des communautés chrétiennes,* January 1994.
16. Ibid.
17. This data comes from the 1998 ISSP survey. Cf. Bréchon, 2001.
18. Donegani and Sadoun, 1994, pp. 116–122.
19. Constant, 1957, pp.1215–1231.
20. Tocqueville, 1981, pp. 391–401.
21. The expression "Believing without Belonging" was used by Grace Davis to describe the relationship that the English in particular, and Europeans in general, now have with religion. See Davie, 1990.
22. When asked "Would you say that "peace" is a religious value?," 55% of 15–20-year-olds replied "yes" and 43% replied "no" (CSA-Phosphore Survey, May-June 1994).
23. *Faits et opinions,* Bayard Presse survey of 12- to 15-year-olds, June 1980.
24. Lambert, 1990.
25. Lambert, 1990, p. 94.

CHAPTER 4

Gender and Politics

Janine Mossuz-Lavau

In former times, this chapter might have been entitled, "Women and Politics" or even" Sex and Politics." Not so very long ago, this is how work produced by political science on how French women voted and on questions of eligibility among them was designated. However, times have changed. The notion of gender which was used firstly in the English-speaking world is now present throughout the human sciences in France. It is an extremely useful notion as it allows a distinction to be made between social and biological sex. The latter, defined as the configuration of the genital organs, is not susceptible to radical change. On the other hand, gender, i.e. that which corresponds to the position of a sex from a sociological point of view and from the point of view of its history, is in a constant state of change as determined by whatever affects its position in society. This includes education, work, social representation, "mentalities" as they are often called, and the extent to which a woman can or cannot do as she wishes with her own body. Furthermore, gender only has meaning within a comparison or a confrontation between men and women. Women are no longer seen to be an isolated category, a minor tribe that is not really part of the community and as if the discrimination they suffer could not be reduced without taking the other component part—men—into consideration. Gender is a new instrument which avoids the essentialism often brought about as a result of taking only the biological into account and including masculine domination or at the very least the comparison or relationship with men in any analysis. The term gender was popularized among American psychologists and researchers in 1968 by Robert Stoller's book, *Sex and Gender.*[1] It was taken up again by the British sociologist, Ann Oakley, who published *Sex, Gender and Society* in 1972.[2] In France, the sociologists were the first to use it at the end of the 1980s and then female historians (specializing in the history of women) in the second half of the 1990s[3] and finally political scientists. Examples include, *Genre et Politique*[4] and the colloquium organized by the *Association Française de Science Politique, Genre et politique*, in Paris in May 2002.[5]

Three main themes will be covered in this chapter: taking an interest in politics, becoming involved in political activity, and being the object of a (public) policy. In other words, gender in relation to political behavior, (and in particular the vote), to eligibility and to public policy.

Taking an Interest in Politics

In France, women were given access to citizenship later than in the majority of other European countries. They obtained the right to vote by a decree issued on the April 21, 1944, a long time after Finnish women (1906), Norwegian women (1913), Danish women (1915), German women (1918), Austrian women (1918), Dutch women (1919), Swedish women (1921), British women (1928), and Spanish women (1931).

When French women first started to exercise their right to vote, they didn't do it in quite the same way as men did. There were three stages of development. The first, which continued up to the end of the 1960s, was a period of learning. Women abstained more than men and they voted much less than men for candidates on the political Left. One example of this was in 1965 during the second round of the presidential election which saw General de Gaulle and François Mitterrand competing against each other. Only 39% of women voters supported the latter as against 51% of male voters. A second stage began in the 1970s. This was the period of "lift-off" during which time, little by little, women went to the ballot box as much as men did and this is also when the gap in the left-wing vote decreased (dropping under 10 points). Finally, the period of autonomy arrived for which one key date should be retained: the 1986 national elections. For the first time, while maintaining their turnout rate, women voters voted to the Left of the political spectrum as much as men did. This would continue to be the case throughout the following decades. Moreover, these women sometimes even convinced their male counterparts to vote Left as well. In 1988, more women than men voted for left-wing candidates in the first round of the presidential election. Given that the electoral behavior of both sexes seems identical, one might wonder why autonomy is mentioned at all. The answer is that there are several reasons to do so. First, because on several occasions women expressed a marked preference for socialists and ecologists in the first round of a ballot. This preference for ecologist candidates was not to last but the attraction to the Left did. But more importantly, as early as the beginning of the 1980s, women refused to join sides with the *Front National* and this continues to be the case today (table 4.1).

On the evening of April 21, 2002, France found itself in an unprecedented situation: for the first time since the beginning of election by universal suffrage a right-wing and an Extreme-Right-wing candidate topped the polls making it through to the second round. This was not in any way the responsibility of women voters. If they alone had voted, Jacques Chirac would have come first

Table 4.1 Male and female votes in the first round of the 2002 presidential election (%)

	Total	*Men*	*Women*
Arlette Laguiller	6	5	7
Daniel Glückstein	0	1	0
Olivier Besancenot	4	4	5
Robert Hue	3	4	3
Lionel Jospin	16	16	16
Christiane Taubira	2	2	2
Noël Mamère	5	6	5
Corinne Lepage	2	2	2
Jean-Pierre Chevènement	5	6	5
François Bayrou	7	6	8
Christine Boutin	1	1	2
Jacques Chirac	19	17	22
Alain Madelin	4	4	4
Jean Saint-Josse	4	6	3
Jean-Marie Le Pen	17	20	14
Bruno Mégret	2	2	2

Source: French Electoral Panel, Cevipof, CIDSP, CECOP, 2002.

(with 22% of their votes), followed by Lionel Jospin (16%), Jean-Marie Le Pen would only have got 14% of their votes.

If men, on the contrary had been the only ones to vote, the leader of the *Front National* would have come first (20% of votes), Jacques Chirac second (17%) and Lionel Jospin third (16%).

This reticence of women toward the Extreme-Right is not proper to France alone. Pretty much everywhere in Europe and particularly in Switzerland, Norway, Austria, Denmark, and Italy, "the populist parties of the radical Right attract a markedly higher proportion of male than female voters."[6] By way of example, in Switzerland in 2003, the *Union Démocratique du Centre* obtained 32% of male votes as opposed to only 23% of female votes. Doubtless, the warrior character of these parties and their sometimes violent way of doing politics dissuades the female electorate from supporting them. We know that in France, the *Front National*'s program itself contributes to this distancing: by attacking the gains made by women over the past decades (the right to do as they want with their own bodies, the right to work), by wanting to revoke legislation on abortion and because they want to send mothers back to the home, Jean-Marie Le Pen's party is far from being on the same wavelength as women and their aspirations.

French women do not only concur with European women on their attitude to the Extreme-Right. In several countries, they are also in harmony with many of them vis-à-vis their position to the Left of the political spectrum (table 4.2).

Thus, in Germany, in Britain, in the Netherlands and in Sweden, slightly more women than men situate themselves to the Left on the classic Left-Right scale. It is only in Spain, Italy and Poland, all of which are countries which have been particularly marked by Catholicism, that they are less likely to make

Table 4.2 Position on the Left-Right scale according to gender in eight European countries

		Left	*Centre*	*Right*	*No Answer*	*Total*
GE	Men	34	34	25	6	100% (1404)
	Women	37	36	18	9	100% (1515)
SP	Men	40	27	17	16	100% (818)
	Women	35	24	19	22	100% (910)
FR	Men	39	26	30	5	100% (705)
	Women	40	25	27	8	100 % (799)
UK	Men	21	38	34	7	100% (997)
	Women	23	41	22	13	100% (1054)
IT	Men	35	20	29	17	100 % (541)
	Women	28	21	24	27	100% (665)
NL	Men	27	21	49	2	100% (1081)
	Women	30	29	34	6	100% (1282)
PL	Men	29	29	29	13	100% (1034)
	Women	23	31	25	22	100% (1077)
SW	Men	37	19	40	4	100% (1014)
	Women	40	23	30	7	100 % (981)

such a choice. Moreover, in these three cases they are characterized by a strong propensity (in comparison to their masculine counterparts) not (to know or want) to position themselves in these terms. Thus, in Italy, 27% of women do not even answer this question as against 16% of men.

The developments observed in France clearly correspond to a process which had already begun in a large part of Europe and notably in Northern Europe which has always been a pioneer in terms of women's rights.

Do these changes mean that in France firstly and also in those European countries where comparison is possible, women are now as actively involved in politics as men are?

This objective has not yet been attained or in any case not completely. In France, electoral turnout is almost the same, although a slight gap was observed in 2002 (29% of women and 26% of men abstained from the first round of the presidential election). In table 4.3, the gap seems bigger. It is possible that the

Table 4.3 Male and female electoral turnout in the last national election in eight European countries (%)

	GE	*SP*	*FR*	*UK*	*IT*	*NL*	*PL*	*SW*
Men	77	71	77	66	87	82	64	81
Women	79	73	72	68	83	80	59	82

Table 4.4 Strong politicization according to gender in eight European countries (%)

	GE	*SP*	*FR*	*UK*	*IT*	*NL*	*PL*	*SW*
Men	53	21	34	34	32	50	37	37
Women	42	12	22	23	20	37	19	34

crisis in representation and the discrediting of political elites weigh even more heavily among female than among male voters.

However, in Germany, Spain, Sweden, and the United Kingdom, more women than men voted in the last national election to take place in their country. A slight female deficit can be observed in Italy, the Netherlands and Poland.

It is clear therefore that women voters have decided to exercise their right to vote. There are a few exceptions to this, notably amongst older sections of the population where women were socialized without having the right to vote, or where they did have the right to vote but society had not yet admitted that women now had a role to play in a domain until then reserved for men alone. We know that older women are markedly less likely to have educational qualifications than men of the same age, which tends not to predispose them to being interested in politics. Although patterns of electoral turnout are less and less likely to distinguish men from women, this does not mean that the latter are as interested in politics as men are. This poses a question which arises in all European countries. The number of women to appear politicized is still lower, including in northern countries, even if the gap there is less significant than elsewhere, as the case of Sweden shows for example (table 4.4).

The 2003 European survey facilitated the building of an index of politicization.[7] In France, only 22% of women (as against 34% of men) show themselves to be "strongly" politicized. Although they are less "strongly politicized" than their male counterparts, German, Dutch, and Swedish women are distinctly more involved in politics than women in other countries with Spanish women coming last preceded by Italian and Polish women, bringing us back to the scenario already observed.

Indeed, in all the countries observed, women declare more than men that politics is "often" too complicated: in France, this percentage reaches 51% (35% of men), in Britain (50% as against 30%), in Poland (52% as against 35%), and in Spain (48% as against 36%). In Germany, Sweden and to a lesser extent in the Netherlands, fewer women hold this view. It should be noted that amongst all European women, it is Swedish women who most often have university level degrees and who are most often of no religion.

In the countries mentioned above, there is a tendency among women to admit to a feeling of incompetence which is imposed on them by a society which has not yet totally admitted that they have taken politics on board. They perhaps do not yet feel sufficiently legitimate in this domain finding it more difficult than men to present themselves as people interested in politics. This is in spite of the fact that the number of men with higher level qualifications is only marginally higher than the number of women and in France and Spain the figure is lower. When women remain at home this is accentuated. A survey carried out in France in 1978, shows that when women work outside the home they tend to develop more politicized behavior and are more oriented to the political Left.[8] According to the European survey, Sweden is where the lowest number of women remain at home (11%) and Spain is where the highest number of women remain at home (60%).

In the French case, any examination of how the political evolvement of women is related to changes which have occurred in their economic, social and cultural position must take their new political autonomy and how it is linked to their personal autonomy into account. Three major features should be highlighted.

Firstly, women started going to university in great numbers. For a long time, they enrolled in courses of short duration only as they were destined above all to become wives and mothers. In 1950, there were only 44,000 women at university out of a total of 125,000 students. In 1971, there were more women than men in higher education. We know that interest in politics increases with level of education. Consequently, these women no longer had a reason to abstain from voting and it is not by chance that the few differences recorded in electoral turnout occur among the older population where the gap in level of education is highest. In the first round of the 2002 presidential election, among people with no university level education, 22% of men and 31% of women abstained, whereas the figures among people with higher education were respectively 20% and 21%.

A second factor comes into play to explain the political changes presented above: the massive entrance of women into the labor market and notably as paid employees. In 1954, they made up 35% of the active population, today they make up 47%. As has been said above, from 1978, it was observed that work influenced the behavior of female voters making them both more politicized and more inclined to vote Left. This link has been confirmed on numerous occasions. Thus, during the presidential election of 1995, the work effect once again played a huge role. According to IFOP, in the first round, 40% of active women voted for left-wing candidates as compared to 28% of women at home.

A third factor explains this new situation: the way in which French women relate to religion, which is also undergoing huge change. In 1952, at the start of our reference period, 52% of women as against 29% of men declared that they went to mass every Sunday.[9] The gap between the two has greatly decreased since the 1990s: 11% of women and 9% of men attend a religious service at least once a week. We know that religious observance—and today even irregular observance—is strongly linked to a classic right-wing vote. In the first round of the 2002 presidential election, Jacques Chirac obtained one of his best scores (31%) from women who practiced a religion both regularly and irregularly as against 20% from female non-observers and 11% from those with no religion. Fewer the women present in church, the more they are likely to vote to the Left of the political spectrum.

The effects of these three factors (education, work, disaffection with religion), all entail a stronger level of politicization and a distinct preference for the Left. These two factors are strong enough to compensate for the age factor which works the other way around (among voters of 60 and over, in the first round of the 2002 election, 35% of women chose Jacques Chirac, as against 14% to 15% of voters less than 46 and 21% of 46–59-year-olds).

For young French women, age means belonging to a certain generation and the luck of being born at a time when equality of treatment between men and women was beginning to develop. For older women, it means the misfortune of having grown up and spent part of their lives in a condition which diminished access to education, employment, professions requiring a qualification, and to a whole universe which doubtless creates more interest in collective life than the daily accomplishment of domestic and child-rearing tasks.

Some women are not satisfied with being interested in politics and voting. They also want to act, "to make a career of politics." However, although with regard to the first point they have indeed become fully fledged citizens and the balance sheet is "positive overall," the same can not be said for their actual chances of being elected. There are of course important variations in this depending on the country.

Becoming Actively Involved in Politics

Very quickly, in all the countries concerned here, many women were not content merely to go and put a voting slip into a ballot box from time to time. Some of them wanted to become actors in the political game. They joined parties, they intended to become candidates and they wanted to be elected. And this is where the difficulties began. For within the masculine bastions which the political parties are, they were not always welcomed with open arms. Given that a job given to a woman is necessarily a job taken away from a man who, "has not shown himself to be unworthy," there were many obstacles to overcome.

In France, the obstacles are still there even though the situation has changed compared to what it was initially. In 1946, the proportion of women in the National Assembly was 6%. This figure decreased after a few years and notably with the establishment of the Fifth Republic and Gaullism (2% from 1958 to 1973). There was a slight rise after that. On the evening of the 1993 general election that proportion reached 6% and after the early election in 1997 a record was reached with 11%. This figure can be explained by the decision of

Lionel Jospin, the then leader of the Socialist Party (PS), that 30 % of constituencies be reserved for women and in actual fact 28% of them were. In the corridors of the PS, men predicted that the party would lose the election because of this and that in any case, there wouldn't be enough female candidates. This proved to be entirely false as the Left won the election and that in almost 40% of "reserved" constituencies, there was not one but two or three women who wanted to be candidates.[10] In 2002, in spite of the so-called law on parity—which I will return to later—only 12% of National Assembly Deputies were women. In 2007, this figure reached 18.5%.

These results place France at the back of the line in Europe as far as female representation in what are called the "lower" Houses (or single Houses in countries which, unlike France, do not have a Senate or its equivalent) are concerned. As of July 31, 2006, France was far behind Sweden, (45% of elected representatives), Norway (38%), Finland (37%), Denmark (37%), the Netherlands (37%), Spain (36%), Belgium (35%), Austria (34%), Germany (32%), Switzerland (25%), Portugal (21%) and the United Kingdom (20%). France has been "passed out" by countries which were ranked behind it for a long time: Italy which now has 17 % of women in its lower House, and Greece (13%). Ireland also has 13 %.

The Northern countries, where elected female representatives are numerous have been pioneers from the start. Thus in Sweden, in 1964, there were 13% of women in the *Riksdag* (or single House), and in 1979, there were 28%. Similarly, in Norway the figures went from 8% in 1965 in the *Storting* to 26% in 1981.[11] The situation in Spain must be looked at in the context of the end of dictatorship in 1975. This freed political forces desperate for liberty, equality and innovation which were particularly favorable to the promotion of women even if it took a little time for female political elites to appear.[12] The other democracies followed suit as they were also aware that they could no longer ignore this "other half of humanity" who were rushing to break open the doors of the political arena. They were carried along in this by the left-wing parties who have almost always been more daring on this issue, particularly the Communist parties, but also very often, the Socialist parties. The political Left, which presents itself as being engaged in a fight against inequality and injustice, was sensitive to the position of women, sometimes described as "internal immigrants," and to the demands of feminist organizations earlier than the Right was. It therefore opened the doors of politics a little wider to those who in turn wanted part of the action. In some respects it set an example. Looking back to the beginning of the 1990s, Conservative parties in the Northern area were by then sending as many women to parliament as the left-wing parties were. However, in the rest of Europe, this example has not yet been sufficiently followed. In France, on the evening of the 1981 general election, there were 9% of women in the Communist group, 7% in the *PS-Mouvement* group of the radical Left (MRG), as against 2%, in the *Union pour la démocratie française* (UDF) and 4% in the *Rassemblement pour la République* (RPR). Similar configurations can be observed in Italy, Portugal and to a lesser extent (as the gaps are not very significant), in Britain, Spain, Ireland, Greece, Switzerland, and the Netherlands.[13]

Coming back to the situation in France, during the 2002 general election the Union pour un mouvement populaire (UMP) presented a little less than 20% of female candidates, while the Socialist Party presented 36%. It wasn't yet parity but a greater effort toward achieving this had been made. The latest example available: following the 2008 local elections in towns with over 100,000 inhabitants, 18.7% of left-wing mayors are women as against 4.9% only for right-wing mayors.[14]

Paradoxically, women are present in French governments in greater proportions than in parliament. Here again, progress is quite slow and on several occasions has ended up creating situations which may seem paradoxical. As Geneviève Fraisse wrote, "women govern but they do not represent."[15] Moreover, this paradox goes back to older times. In 1936, Léon Blum appointed three women as under-secretaries of state to the *Front Populaire* government who were neither eligible for election not voters themselves. It was not until 1947 that a woman, Germaine Poinso-Chapuis, became a fully fledged minister. Under the Fifth Republic, it was not until the presidency of Valéry Giscard d'Estaing (1974) that women became a little more visible at the executive level. He created the post of Secretary of State for the Female Condition, appointed Simone Veil as Minister for Health (asking her to present a bill for the legalization of abortion) and had a total of four women (one Minister and three Secretaries of State) in a team of 38 people, equaling 10% which was a record in comparison with previous periods. In 1981, in the first government formed by Pierre Mauroy, there were six women, equaling 14%, a percentage which was scaled down to 10% when the Right came back into power in 1986 with the Chirac government. Things improved when the Left won the election in 1988: 13% of Rocard's second government were female. In May 1991, France had a female Prime Minister for the first time (Édith Cresson) and 15% of her government were women (17 % in the government formed by Pierre Bérégovoy in April 1992). There was a feeling that a record had been broken after the May 1995 election which brought Jacques Chirac to the Presidency of the Republic. The Prime Minister, Alain Juppé, brought twelve women into the government team of 42 people (28%). But the upturn did not last. A few months later, in November, the so-called "juppettes" episode occurred. In order to form his second government which he wanted to draw closer together, Alain Juppé fired eight of them and the figure fell back down to 12 % of women (of whom only one had the rank of Minister). In 1997, when Lionel Jospin became Prime Minister after the early general election and until 2002, women were given better representation in government, with close to 30% of posts depending on how these were shuffled up. After the political earthquake of the April 21, 2002, (when Jean Marie Le Pen made it through to the second round of the presidential election) and the ensuing general election, the Right came back into power and women were a little less present: the Raffarin government included 26% of women and they made up 19% of the De Villepin team. In 2007, after the election of Nicolas Sarkozy, the Fillon government included 33% of women in keeping with the president's concern to project an image of open-mindedness and diversity.

At the end of the " *fait du prince* " (the decision to appoint women to power taken by the president alone), as it was called, the situation is that for the past two decades, the proportion of women in executive functions has been higher than at the National Assembly or the Senate where in 1998 they reached 6% with great difficulty. Nonetheless, it has to be accepted that even during those years—before the so-called law on parity was introduced—women were better represented at local level and in the European Parliament. In 1995, the municipal councils were made up of 21% of women, the delegation sent to the European Parliament after the 1994 election 30%, and in 1998, the regional councils contained 26% of women. However, the situation was not as favorable in the Conseil Général (Council of a French department) (5% of women) or among mayors (8% in 1995). It was therefore deemed necessary to envisage the introduction of restrictive measures so that the parties would consent to better ensuring access for women to the political arena. This brings us to the third aspect of this relationship between gender and politics. This concerns public policies "aimed at" women and which modify not only the ways in which political posts are attributed but also, more generally, the position of women in the country as a whole, in a way which is sometimes different from what can be observed elsewhere.

Being a Policy Goal

In Western Europe, the second half of the twentieth century was characterized, amongst other things, by the strong presence of public policy in moral issues. This had a direct effect on women as they were at last granted the right (having fought long and hard to obtain it), to do as they wished with their own bodies. In France for example, many years later than in other European countries, laws were passed authorizing contraception (Neuwirth Law of 1967), then abortion (the 1975 Veil law) and also a real repression of rape (1980), which until then had been considered more as an attack on the honor of the family than as a crime against an individual. Other laws were adopted on family, professional equality (1983 and 2001) and, in the area of education great advances were made with co-education in schools. Finally, with regard to the exercise of citizenship, France was the first country to pass a law on what is known in France as parity. This law ordered that henceforth, for most elections taking place within the national territory as many female as male candidates would have to be presented. For a long time, the term "the French exception" had been used to designate this denial of democracy which the absence of women in elected assemblies constituted. With the introduction of this law, "the exception" now designated a novel and daring attitude. How were these procedures set up and what conclusions can be drawn about them today?

At the end of the 1970s and during the 1980s, thinking on this issue was mostly in terms of quotas. In 1982, there had been an amendment to a law requiring that lists for municipal elections should not include more than 75% of candidates of the same sex. However, the Constitutional Council annulled the amendment, arguing that citizens could not be divided into "categories."

Moreover, some women were not prepared to fight for this, as they found it humiliating that at the end of the day, 53% of the electorate were only granted one quarter of the candidacies.[16] In 1992, the demands changed. The idea of parity was in effect "launched" by the publication of a book by Françoise Gaspard, Claude Servan-Schreiber and Anne Le Gall, at the Seuil publishing house, entitled *Au pouvoir citoyennes: liberté, égalité, parité*, which called for parity to be explicitly present in the law in the following form: "Elected assemblies, both at territorial and national levels, will be composed of an equal number of women and men."

The promoters of parity received support from European decision-making bodies which were more advanced than France in this area. As early as November 1989, a seminar on "democracy with equal representation" had been held in Strasbourg at the initiative of the Council of Europe. In November 1992, at the request of the Commission of the European Communities the first *European Summit on Women in Power* was held in Athens. It brought together female Ministers or former Ministers and adopted a charter pronouncing that "equality of women and men imposes parity in the representation and the administration of Nations."

In France, women's associations were created to defend the idea of parity. Others which had already existed for a long time also made this combat their own. At their initiative, the "Manifesto of 577 for democracy with equal representation" (signed by 289 women and 288 men) was published in *Le Monde* on November 19, 1993. The figure of 577 was chosen to evoke the number of deputies with seats in the National Assembly. In 1996, another manifesto relaunched the debate. This was the "Manifesto of ten for parity," published in the *Express* and signed by ten women, all of whom were former Ministers or holders of senior posts, from both the Left and the Right ranging from Simone Veil to Édith Cresson.

However, in the meantime one party from the left-wing political class had reacted to the calls for parity. Several bills had been submitted to Parliament as early as 1994 notably calling for the inclusion of parity in the constitution. Moreover, in 1994, during the European elections, six lists reflected parity or were close to it: this was the case for the Socialist Party (which was the first to state its intentions on this), the Communist Party, the *Mouvement des citoyens*, (a left-wing party), *Les Verts*, *Lutte ouvrière* (Trotsyist Communist party led by Arlette Laguiller), and also for the "small" list formed by Christian Cotten. During the 1995 presidential election, the role of women in political decision-making bodies became an election campaign theme for the first time. The principle candidates were questioned by the promoters of parity and had to take a stand on the issue and make certain promises. Jacques Chirac, who was elected on the May 7, kept one of his and created the *Observatoire de la parité*, the Parity Watchdog, by a decree issued on October 18, 1995. It was designed to report to the Prime Minister and was composed of personalities chosen for their ability in the subject. It was placed under the responsibility of a female spokesperson, Roselyne Bachelot-Narquin, a Deputy from the Maine-et-Loire region. It was charged with producing analyses and making concrete proposals concerning the position of women. The "Political Parity" commission jointly headed by Roselyne Bachelot-Narquin and Gisèle Halimi, drafted a single report which was submitted to the Prime Minister on December 11 1996. A debate without vote was held on March 11 1997 at the National Assembly during which Alain Juppé, the then Prime Minister made a declaration which fell far short of the expectations of supporters of parity:

> I am in favour of modifying our Constitution on a temporary basis, for ten years for example, so as to enable the law to develop incentives to encourage female candidacies in elections where lists of candidates are presented. These are the only ones for whom this type of thinking is appropriate."[17]

This was never enacted as Jacques Chirac announced the dissolution of the National Assembly on April 21, 1997. At the end of the early election, the Left had won and there was no longer any question of "encouragement of female candidacies," at the very least in official speeches, but rather of parity. The new Prime Minister, Lionel Jospin, faithful in this respect to his campaign promises, announced a change to the Constitution to that effect on June 19, 1997, during his declaration of general policy at the National Assembly: "French women must be allowed to engage in public life without obstacle [. . .]. A revision of the Constitution will be proposed to include the objective of achieving parity between women and men."[18] These were not just words. A year later (June 17, 1998), the president of the Republic, Jacques Chirac, signed a constitutional bill "relative to equality between men and women."

This step toward parity aroused bitter debate within the political class, within the Left and more especially among feminists. Although these debates are no longer relevant today, it is nonetheless worth mentioning them: there was concern about universalism being called into question, about the risk of creating separate communities, about the danger represented by the supposed differentialist component of parity, about a possible infringement of the voter's freedom of choice, and so on.[19] However, the bill was nonetheless submitted to Parliament. Finally, after a lot of shuttling back and forth between the Assembly and the Senate an agreement was reached. Parliament was brought together in congress at Versailles on June 28, 1999 to modify two articles in the Constitution. To Article 3 it added: "The law supports equal access for women and men to electoral mandates and elective functions," and to Article 4 on political parties: "They shall contribute to the execution of the principle set out in the last paragraph of Article 3 under the conditions determined by the law."

It then became necessary to vote in new texts for the organization of elections according to the principle of parity. This was done one year after the modification of the Constitution. Law No 2000-493 was promulgated on June 6, 2000.[20] It made provision for alternating parity[21] for single round elections such as European or Senate elections which are by PR; parity by groups of six for two-round elections such as municipal elections (in areas with 3,500 inhabitants and more) and regional elections (these were subsequently modified when the Right returned to power and the 2004 regional elections also respected the principle of alternating parity). These were effective constraints to the extent that lists which were not drawn up on this basis were quite simply not registered. On the other hand, for general elections, the system was only designed as an incentive. Parties which did not present 50% of female candidates were given less public finance. They were therefore completely free to decide to designate as many men as they wanted and receive less money if they so wished. The law was modified in January 2007. Provision was made for alternating parity in the municipal elections already covered by the law and heavier financial penalties for general elections which did not respect the law.

Cantonal and Senate elections, elections by majority vote and municipal elections in towns with fewer than 3,500 inhabitants were not subject to the law. However, these areas were not completely cast aside, as Article 16 specifies that "an evaluative report of the present law will be presented by the government to the Parliament in 2002, and after that, every three years. This report shall also include a detailed study of progress made in the feminization of cantonal elections, of the senatorial and municipal elections not covered by the law, of deliberative bodies, of inter-communal structures and of local executives." The evaluation was to be carried out by the *Observatoire de la parité*. One of the objectives was to determine whether it had a knock-on effect on procedures which were not under its jurisdiction or if, on the contrary, it had only been very narrowly applied. We shall turn now to look at elections which have taken place since the law was introduced.

Since the adoption of the so-called law on parity, (the term itself is not used in the text), several elections have taken place in France, seven of which were subject to the parity rule: the 2001 and 2008 municipal elections, several senatorial elections, the 2002 and 2007 general elections, the 2004 regional elections and the 2004 European election.[22]

When the final results of the 2001 municipal elections came in, 47% of town councilors in areas of 3,500 inhabitants or more were female. These were the only constituencies to be covered by the law. Thirty per cent of councilors in constituencies with less than 3,500 inhabitants were female, giving a total of 33% of women elected to the municipal councils of the country as a whole. It can therefore be considered that there was indeed a knock-on effect in the smaller constituencies not subject to the law as in 1995 only 21% of local councilors were female. In 2008, the local elections granted access to local power to the 48.5% of elected female councilors.

Several senatorial elections have taken place since 2001 and each time one third of the seats are up for election or indeed reelection. Two changes marked these elections. Firstly, the July 10 2000 law imposed the proportional representation system on constituencies electing three or four Senators (as against five until then). Elsewhere, the law of June 6, 2000 imposed alternating parity on these list systems. Departments with election by majority vote were not covered by the law. It is evident that the proportion of female candidates varied according to what type of voting system was used. In 2001, in departments with PR, 45% of candidates were women, and in the others 2%. Furthermore, a number of outgoing Senators wanting to ensure their reelection, got around the spirit of the law in a certain sense by presenting dissident lists. They knew that if they were in third position behind a man at the head of the list and then a woman necessarily in second place, they ran the risk of not being reelected. They therefore composed their own list placing themselves at the top of it. As of October 2008, a total of 21,9% of senators are female.

The 2004 regional elections conformed to what was expected of them, as on the evening of March 28, 48% of the councilors were women. On June 13, 2004, 44% of the deputies in the French delegation to the European Parliament were women.

The main problem was the 2002 general elections which only returned 12% of women to the National Assembly. The smaller parties played the game of parity but the larger ones such as the UMP and the Socialist Party chose financial penalties over the feminization of their representation. Thus, the UMP, which presented less than 20% of women, registered an annual loss throughout its term of office of a little more than 4 million euros. For its part, the Socialist Party with 36% of female candidates lost over 1 million euros per year of public finance. Some progress was made in 2007 and 18.5% of Deputies are now female.

The cantonal elections not covered by the law took place at the same time as the regional elections: only 11% of elected councilors were women. The local executives also remained predominantly masculine: 1% of mayors were women, 5% of presidents of Public Establishments for Inter-communal cooperation (EPCI) are women and there was a single female regional president (though 36% of regional executives were women). In 2008, 13% of councilors in French departments are women as are 8.5% of mayors in towns with 3,500 inhabitants or more.

It is clear, therefore that the public policies put in place were not crowned with unbridled success. They were successful for local and European elections but this success was thwarted by the refusal of certain parties to feminize their representation thus limiting access for women to Parliament itself and to real legislative power. In the absence of constraints, it is difficult indeed to ensure that a party from the political class makes any kind of real progress in this respect. For the 2007 general election, the Socialist Party announced the figure of 50% of female candidates (not necessarily in winnable constituencies), the UMP announced 30%. For the moment therefore, the hour has not yet come for a National Assembly with equal representation in France.

Other European countries have adopted or are attempting to adopt restrictive measures. In 1994, Belgium passed a law "aiming to promote a balanced share between men and women on lists of candidacies for election."[23] This law made provision that an electoral list could only include a maximum of two-thirds of candidates of the same sex (for all elections both national and local). But as nothing was specified about the roles women should occupy, they were all too often relegated to the end of the lists and after the general election of 1999, only 23% of elected representatives were women (whereas

39% of the candidates were female). In 2002, Belgium therefore decided to establish parity for candidacies, and ordained that the first two candidates on each list had to be of a different sex. Nothing was indicated for the rest of the list.

Italy and Portugal also attempted to improve their female representation but have not yet managed to establish a restrictive system. In 1993, Italy adopted a law which ordained that for local and provincial elections no more than three-quarters of candidates could be of the same sex in areas with fewer than 15,000 inhabitants and no more than two-thirds in other areas. Furthermore, for general elections, one quarter of the deputies had to be elected by PR, on a list which respected alternating parity. The law was applied in 1994 and then cancelled in 1995 by the Constitutional Court. However, a constitutional revision took place in 2003 which committed the Republic to "promoting parity between men and women using adequate measures to do so." A 2004 law ordained that one third of candidates in a general election had to be women. But it was designed only to incite, not to enforce and parties who didn't respect it merely had to pay a financial penalty. It nonetheless brought about a sizeable increase in the number of female deputies. In Portugal, a revision of the Constitution in 1997 was intended to promote equality between men and women in political rights. But here again, laws for the concrete application of this objective have not yet seen the light of day.

In other countries and particularly those with a strong level of female representation (in the North and in Germany notably), the parties themselves decided to establish quotas.

In France, in any case, it can be objectively stated that the idea of taking gender into account in public policy is making progress. However, tensions continue to exist between new and old models. Not all of society is prepared to follow in the footsteps of those who support a new concept of the female population characterized by its ability for autonomy and its advances toward more real rights similar to those of men. A frame of reference for equality which implies action against the types of discrimination women are still exposed to has come into being opposite a frame of reference based on complementarity (or on the natural order) corresponding to an ideology based more on the family. In France and beyond, in a number of other countries, it seems as if the first of these frameworks is in the process of carrying the day although further measures will be needed to ensure its victory. For some people this calls for one last question to be asked: is there not a risk that the fact of taking gender into account in public policy, the establishment of specific measures and treating women as a particular group needing special protective measures and measures to help them catch up, will "ghettoize" this population? This question must surely be answered in the negative. The policies adopted for the moment have overall had a positive impact ensuring more freedom and a greater degree of equality for the "second sex." In any case, on several occasions, France has created ministerial structures in order to facilitate the "feminizing of the state." The state secretariat for the Feminine Condition of 1974 was succeeded by a National Delegation for the Feminine Condition, a state secretariat, and a

Ministry of State and then in 1981, François Mitterrand created a Ministry of State for women' rights that became a fully fledged Ministry in 1985. The body responsible for women's rights then became a state secretariat again for a long number of years and then a Ministry of State in 2002. In 2005, Catherine Vautrin was appointed minister of state for Social Cohesion and Parity.[24] Since 2007, this kind of Ministerial post has disappeared.

There has been undeniable progress in the slow progression of women toward taking political power. Moreover, this has been acquired as a result of the new autonomy women have gained. It remains to be seen whether this will one day be recognized by the election of a "female head of state," to take up the expression used by André Fontaine.[25] There is no shortage of precedents for this in Europe. As early as 1980, Vigdís Finnbogadóttir became president of the Republic of Iceland. Today, Mary McAleese is president of Ireland and Micheline Calmy-Rey president of the Helvetic Confederation (Switzerland). Tarja Halonen is president of Finland and Angela Merkel German chancellor. Other countries throughout the world (such as Chili or Liberia) have also promoted women to the highest level (today there are 15 women presidents of the Republic or Heads of government). There is no reason why France should not innovate in this respect one day, even if the experience attempted in 2007 with the candidacy of Ségolène Royale for the French presidency failed.

Notes

1. Stoller, 1968.
2. Oakley, 1972.
3. Thébaud, 1998.
4. Ballmer-Cao et al., 2000.
5. Bard, Baudelot, and Mossuz-Lavau, 2004.
6. Betz, 2004, p. 173.
7. The index of politicization is calculated on the basis of three variables: the expression of a strong interest in politics, the consideration that politics is important in life and the fact of talking about politics frequently with friends and family. This index was recoded in two modalities (strong politicization and weak politicization).
8. Mossuz-Lavau and Sineau, 1983.
9. According to IFOP surveys.
10. Bataille and Gaspard, 1999.
11. Mossuz-Lavau and Sineau, 1984.
12. The composition of José Luis Rodriguez Zapatero's 2004 government should also be noted as "proof" of modernity.
13. Mossuz-Lavau and Sineau, 1984.
14. Figures provided by the *Observatoire de la parité.*
15. *Libération*, September 13, 1995.
16. Mossuz-Lavau, 2005.
17. Journal officiel, Débats parlementaires, 12 March 1997.
18. *Le Monde*, June 21 1997.
19. Mossuz-Lavau, 1998.
20. *Journal officiel* of June 7.

21. This term refers to the fact that each electoral list alternates between men and women systematically so that if the first candidate is a man the second will be a woman, etc.
22. Zimmermann, 2005.
23. Pereira, 2003.
24. Achin and Lévque, 2006.
25. *Le Monde*, October 25, 2006.

CHAPTER 5

Young People and Politics

Anne Muxel

Throughout Europe the level of political participation among young people is a cause for concern: when compared with previous generations contemporary European youth are found accused of lacking moral fiber and political commitment. Young people are regularly described as being less reliable and less politically involved citizens than their elders. The attitude of young people toward politics is constantly debated, often giving rise to pessimistic predictions about the future health of Western democracies. The steady increase in electoral abstentionism and the decline in identification with political parties are regarded as being symptomatic of disillusionment with political representation which, though present in all age groups of society, is particularly acute among the younger generations. How do things really stand? What kind of relationship with politics do today's young people have? Are they less politicized than their elders? Do they have the same political culture and references as earlier generations, or are they politicized using new models and forms of expression which have redefined contemporary citizenship?

In order to address these questions, we need to isolate the effects of age, in the sense of position in the life cycle, the effects of the period, namely the effect of the historical and political context on individuals of all ages, and finally generational effects, which refer to the specific attitudes and political behavior of young people today. This chapter seeks to examine the similarities and differences between younger generations and their elders, and establish the salient characteristics of the ways they relate to politics.

Young People and Politics: Between Heritage and Experimentation

Measuring the effects of age is more difficult than might be supposed, and analyzing the evolution of political phenomena within generational dynamics gives rise to a number of difficulties.[1] When young people's replies to survey questions are compared to those of their elders, how can we establish whether the differences observed are due to different stages in the life cycle or whether they are indicative of real and lasting transformations in opinions and values between generations? This question can only be answered by analyzing data by cohorts, relying on a series of surveys which use the same measurement indicators and are spread out over time, thus enabling the replies of individuals of the same age, collected at different times, to be compared. The definition and delimitation of generations presents another major obstacle, raising questions about the conditions of each generation's production and specificity.[2] Once again, longitudinal studies and observations made over an extended period are needed if such problems are to be addressed in a rigorous way. Nevertheless, the presence of these obstacles should not lead to the abandonment of all attempts to measure the effects of age on political attitudes and behaviors. Several major studies have already identified the role and place of changes in values in generational renewal, for example, to the drop in the level of religious integration, an affirmation of cultural liberalism and universal values, as well as a widening of participation in protest movements. The differences between the attitudes typical of the young and their elders are less to do with effects of age as such, understood in both its biological and social senses, than generational effects.[3] Therefore in this chapter we will take differences between age groups as usually being indicative of generational differences.

At both social and individual levels, each new generation negotiates its political heritage, which is informed by a history, a political culture, and specific national characteristics, and marks every generation as continuing or modifying a political community grounded in attachments and experiences. Each individual's heritage is also made up of choices, attitudes, and behaviors formed within and outside the family context. In this way each new generation participates to a greater or lesser extent in the reproduction of the existing political system and sets up the conditions for the emergence of political renewal and change.

Young people need to both identify with their elders and to innovate, and their relationships with politics emerge out of the tension between inherited values and experimentation. Heritage not only follows the logic of identification and reveals traces of established reference points, but also acknowledges a transmission of political values and hence intergenerational continuity. Experimentation, on the other hand, introduces the possibility of a break with the past. Knowledge as well as political practices is molded by each different generation and individual. This interaction between heritage and experimentation gives rise to apprenticeships which allow opinions and electoral and party choices to be articulated. The historical and political conjuncture, as well as the specificity of national cultures which are the contexts for all political socialization, also play a role in the development of a young person's engagement with politics.

The Continuing Centrality of the Role of the Family

Despite the decline of the traditional family, the increasing diversity of types of family in society, and less fixed models of parental identification, the transmission of political values from parents to children still continues to operate. In families, political and religious convictions are more likely to be passed down intact from one generation to the next than certain other values, such as moral values or values associated with particular lifestyles. This transmission operates more effectively when parental preferences are clear and homogenous.[4] Some families are in a better position than others to organize a transmission, and political socialization is by no means always a straightforward process. Individuals can construct their political values by opposition to, or as a reaction to, those of their family, as well as under the influence of references which are not specifically political. Families provide, or fail to provide, children with their first points of reference and, in so doing, play a crucial role in the formation of subsequent political choices. This may appear paradoxical, given the individualization of family life,[5] and the relatively serious current crisis in political representation.[6] Nevertheless, it is undoubtedly the case that the values which are most likely to be handed down intact from one generation to the next are political ones.

In France, the Left-Right divide continues to structure ideological allegiances. About half of young French people (49%) acknowledge that they have the same (left or right wing) political affiliation as their parents. If we add the 22% of individuals who regard themselves as apolitical—having neither left- or right-wing leanings—in common with their parents before them, it would seem that almost three quarters of young people (71%) can be considered as having inherited their parents' political orientation.[7]

On a European level these figures vary considerably, but overall other young Europeans seem less likely to inherit their parents' left- or right-wing political affiliations than young French people. Only a third of young Europeans (33%), in a sample drawn from eight EU member countries, stated that they had the same left- or right-wing political orientation as their parents, while just less than half of them (47%) regarded themselves as being neither left nor right wing, in common with their parents. Therefore about seven out of ten of the young people questioned (70%) classified themselves in a way which indicated continuity of political orientation between generations.[8]

In all the countries in the survey, a close correlation between the levels of politicization of parents and children can be observed. The higher the level of political awareness of parents, the more politicized their children are. By the same token, parents who are less politicized appear to have children who share their lack of political awareness.

Children who have grown up in a politically aware family environment tend to have a more positive view of politics. 80% of them stated that they were interested in politics (compared to 14% of those whose parents were relatively politically unaware), and 29% said that they supported a political party (7% was the equivalent figure for those individuals whose parents were relatively unpoliticized). They are generally more positive about the effectiveness of government policies (40% compared to 16%), and also have more faith in political institutions (21% have confidence in them compared to only 9% of individuals whose parents are relatively politically unaware).

The family environment creates a range of political values which result in individuals being predisposed to behave in particular ways. Thus 83% of children of politically aware parents choose to exercise their right to vote (compared to 37% of those whose parents are relatively politically unaware). Parental influence also has an impact on non-conventional political participation: 36% of young people whose parents are politicized have participated in a demonstration, compared to 7% of those whose family environment failed to politicize them.

Young people's attitudes and political behavior appear to vary according to both the ideological orientation of their parents, and their political affiliation. The political profile of the young people who have inherited their parents' left- or right-wing views is unlike that of those individuals who do not share their parents' ideological orientation. Members of the former group have relatively well thought out political views and adopt clear political stances, whereas the latter group are more indifferent about and less interested and involved in politics. Thus 52% of young people who have inherited their parents' right-wing political convictions and 57% of those who have inherited their parents' left-wing values claim to be interested in politics. On the other hand, only 25% of those young people who share their parents' lack of commitment to either the political Left or Right considered themselves to be interested in politics. Young people who have inherited a commitment to the Right or the Left, on the other hand, are more likely to be politically involved: of young people who regard themselves as having the same political orientation as their parents, 75% of those on the Right and 74% of those on the Left participate in elections, compared to 50% of those who, like their parents, are committed neither to the Left nor the Right. Those who have inherited left-wing views are far more likely to be involved in some form of political protest than young people who share their parents' commitment to the Right: 40% of them have participated in a demonstration, compared with 17% of those who have inherited right-wing views and 19% of the whole sample (see table 5.1). Left leaning youth tend to be more anti-establishment and have more faith in the usefulness of being

Table 5.1 Parental political orientation and relationship to politics (%)

	Right Wing	*Left Wing*	*Neither Left nor Right*	*Overall*
Very interested in politics	52	57	25	37
Close to a political party	37	31	8	17
Has voted	75	74	50	59
Has participated in a political demonstration	17	40	10	19
Belongs to an association	54	56	42	48
Regards political action as very effective	30	38	19	25
Has a lot of confidence in political institutions	26	16	11	14

Source: Euyoupart 2004.

politically active, whereas right-leaning youth protest less and have more faith in political institutions.

Although self-positioning in relation to the Left-Right political divide tends to be passed down from one generation to the next, children do not necessarily support the same party, share the same values, and have the same way of interpreting politics, or vote in the same way as their parents. Furthermore, as the political landscape changes, so do notions of what constitutes "left" and "right," and over a generation the key issues and priorities for both the Right and the Left can evolve. Above all we can observe that today there is a general weakening of identification with politics, both in terms of party affiliation and ideology. In France, although the Left-Right divide still structures the way many social and political issues are debated, and continues to influence voter behavior, the division is becoming increasingly blurred. According to the second set of results provided by the French political barometer of September 2006, as many as 34% of French people, rising to 39% for the 18–30 age group, would not define themselves as either left or right wing. This lack of a clear division between Left and Right is not confined to France: more than half (55%) of the young Europeans aged between 15 and 25 who participated in the Euyoupart survey of eight European countries defined themselves as neither left nor right wing.[9]

The Way Young People Experience Politics

The overall political context of Europe has been radically modified. Numerous reference points and models have all but disappeared. Young people are faced with the malfunctioning of political systems in which affiliations and identifications are more random and less clearly stated. Only half of the citizens of EU countries claim to be close to a political party (50%, and only 41% of 18 to 24-year-olds).[10] A growing number of individuals, when making political choices, especially at election time, use criteria which have less to do with commitment to or support for particular values or candidates than a desire to oppose or distance themselves from a particular political stance. Electoral voting behavior, in particular, is greatly influenced by this kind of "negative politicisation," though the consequences and impact of this phenomenon on different generations vary greatly.

Members of most adult age groups, particularly those which include the parents of today's youth, began formulating their views in a world where ideological labels, the division between the Left and the Right, and the definition of competing international power blocs were all well established. Today's young people live in a very different world: political experimentation is the order of the day. Older generations, though they also choose to involve themselves in more autonomous and spontaneously political initiatives, still recollect traditional forms of political activism and allegiance, whereas today's young form their political views without the aid of clearly established reference points. Their political socialization is more experimental and less structured by party or trade union politics, and tends to focus on mobilizations around quite specific issues and debates. Moreover, it is increasingly difficult to differentiate between left- and right-wing political values. Human rights, solidarity, democracy, the market economy, tackling unemployment, or rising crime are now all recurrent mobilizing themes in the political discourse of the majority of French political parties.

Today's young people are living through a period of transition which requires them to engage with several sets of references and a number of political cultures. A wide variety of parameters and perspectives are available to help young people decipher the increasingly complex social and political environments in which they find themselves. They are more knowledgeable about politics than they are sometimes given credit for, but have difficulty translating their inherited values and political experience into support for a particular political party or candidate in an election. These kinds of choices are particularly difficult in a world where political landscapes change quickly and there is a general and long-standing crisis of political representation.

Young People's Attitudes toward Politics

Young French people are particularly critical of politicians and have little trust in those who govern them. Dissatisfaction with political representatives can be detected in citizens of all ages, but the symptoms are particularly acute among the young. In France, 84% of 18 to 24 year olds question the honesty of politicians, compared to 52% of over 65s.[11] Suspicion of politicians is felt by young people of all social classes and educational levels, and extends throughout all age groups in French society. There is also a perceived disconnection between those who govern and ordinary citizens, who as a consequence feel increasingly resentful. Although the French seem only marginally less interested in politics than they were in the past (today 45% of them claim to be very or quite interested, compared to 46% in 1978), increasing numbers of them believe that politicians do not care about their problems (74% in 2000 compared to 59% in 1978).[12]

In France, although the general level of interest in politics has remained relatively stable in recent years, certain significant generational changes may be noted. Although the educational level of the most highly educated young people has risen—which one would expect to have a positive effect on overall levels of interest in politics—levels of interest in politics have in fact dropped, constituting a reversal of the former trend. While in 1978 68% of holders of the baccalaureate aged under 40 claimed to be very or quite interested in politics, by 2000 this figure had dropped to 41%. Nevertheless, students are still more politicized than uneducated young people. Qualifications make a big difference: 52% of students claim to be very or reasonably interested in politics, compared to 22% of people without qualifications.[13] Two thirds of young people (67%) believe that politicians do not care very much or do not care at all about the people they represent.[14]

Attachment to Democratic Procedures

It would hardly be surprising if this crisis in political representation were accompanied by calls for change to the procedures of representative democracy, in particular those related to the voting system and political parties. The growing lack of confidence in politicians and governments could be thought to undermine the legitimacy of political institutions themselves, particularly in the eyes of young people. In fact, this is absolutely not the case. When questioned just before the first round of the 2007 Presidential election, 64% of young people aged between 18 and 24 declared themselves satisfied with the way democracy functions in their country.[15] Therefore, a relative disconnection exists between the feeling of being cut off from and suspicious of politicians and a continuing attachment to the institutions of representative democracy, such as party political and voting systems. About half of French people of all age groups consider the presence of political parties to be extremely or very important for the functioning of a democracy. Young people clearly consider voting to be important. They attach only marginally less importance to it than their older compatriots do. The young may not always exercise their right to vote, but that does not mean that they do not regard voting as being useful: more than three quarters (77%) of 18 to 24 year olds consider it to be very or extremely important.

Examined at a European level, political attitudes of the young and the less young are more an expression of national differences and specificities rather than differences between generations (see table 5.2). The views of young Europeans tend to magnify the characteristic features of their elders' attitudes toward institutions and political organizations, and to political life in general.

Although young people certainly do seem a little less interested in politics than their elders, in many countries these differences are only slight. Support for political parties seems to have dropped: with the exception of young Swedes, young people are less and less likely to identify with a political party than the rest of the adult population. Support for political parties

Table 5.2 Relationship to politics

	GE	*SP*	*FR*	*UK*	*IT*	*NL*	*PL*	*SW*
Very or quite interested in politics								
18–30–year-olds	51	20	31	46	23	65	30	55
Overall	64	21	40	52	33	66	40	57
Gap	–13	–1	–9	–6	–10	–1	–10	–2
Often thinks that politics is too complicated								
18–30–year-olds	29	38	43	43	37	30	43	34
Overall	26	43	44	41	40	32	44	27
Gap	+3	–5	–1	+2	+3	–2	–1	+7
Does not trust political representatives								
18–30-year-olds	33	46	27	22	29	10	49	13
Overall	32	38	32	28	31	12	48	15
Gap	+1	+8	–5	–6	–2	–2	+1	–2
Feels close to a political party								
18–30-year-olds	34	35	37	33	37	49	16	70
Overall	48	50	50	48	45	58	29	69
Gap	–15	–15	–13	–15	–15	–9	–13	+1

Source: ESS survey, 2003.

was, on average, 10 points lower for the young Europeans surveyed than for their elders. Although it is certainly the case that the younger generation feels estranged from political parties, there is—perhaps surprisingly—a degree of similarity between young people and the adult population as a whole regarding "feeling competent to make political judgments." Paradoxically, in most countries more young people feel "politically competent" than members of older age groups. Levels of lack of trust in politicians are in many cases comparable, and the variations observed are more attributable to different national contexts than to inter-generational differences.

There are, however, some striking differences between the countries in the survey, reminding us of the influence that historical and national contexts can exert on individuals' attitudes to politics. A clear division can be made between the countries of Northern Europe and Southern Europe, linked to those specific features of their respective religions—Protestantism in the North and Catholicism in the South—which have greatly influenced the development of their political cultures. In Northern European countries citizens are more politicized and involved in politics. In the countries of Southern Europe citizens are relatively detached from the world of politics. So the level of interest in politics is well above average in the Netherlands, Sweden, and Germany, and relatively low in Spain and Italy. France is in an intermediate position, and its levels of politicization are not particularly high. Four out of ten French people (40%) and three out of ten young French people (31%) claim to be interested in politics, leaving a large majority who are relatively uninterested. The feeling of being politically competent is more widespread in Germany, the Netherlands, and Sweden, countries where political and civic education are particularly well developed, not only as part of a child's schooling but also within various branches of their adult education systems. Once more the highest levels of trust in political representatives are to be found in the Netherlands and Sweden. Young citizens and their elders were the most mistrustful of politicians in Spain and in Poland, which has gone through a series of political crises in recent years. As regards French levels of mistrust of political representatives they are, once more, close to Europeans averages. Finally, identification with political parties is generally more common in countries whose levels of politicization, political competence, and political self-confidence are highest. In the Netherlands and most strikingly in Sweden larger majorities of citizens claim to feel close to a political party (58% and 69% respectively). Moreover in Sweden this figure is not lower for younger generations. Within Europe Sweden presents an exceptional case: seven out of ten young Swedes claim to feel close to a political party. Only just over a third of young French people share this feeling (37%).

Social and Political Splits within French Youth

This overview of the relationship of the younger generations to the principles and apparatuses of democratic regimes needs to be nuanced. There is a clear division between young people with and without educational qualifications.

The most highly educated members of the younger generations, though highly critical of politics, are deeply attached to representative democracy. Their internalization of universalist values, with which they interpret political issues, compensates for their skepticism of politics, and underpins their unwavering attachment to the current system of representation. As for less educated young people, although they more readily embrace universalist values than older people with the same level of educational qualifications, their universalist beliefs are not sufficiently strong to compensate for their relative rejection of politics. Their trust in representative democracy has been more seriously undermined, and their estrangement from politics extends to a weakening of their belief in democracy itself. When compared to their more highly educated contemporaries, they are less likely to be involved in any kind of civic participation, such as voting and political protest, and more likely to view in a favorable light the kind of authoritarian regimes which rely on charismatic personal leadership and are based on limiting the power of democratically elected bodies, such as Parliament. The danger of an increasing democratic deficit is greatest among this category of the young. Whereas more than three quarters (79%) of the most highly qualified young people are opposed to this kind of authoritarian regime, this figure drops to 49% for those who did not obtain the baccalaureate.

Similar trends were identified by the Euyoupart survey. More than a third of the sample had pronounced authoritarian tendencies (36%), and this figure was even higher for poorly qualified young people.[16]

We can therefore observe two co-existing trends which create tension, and the risk of widening intragenerational divisions: on the one hand, among the most highly educated young people, a strengthening identification with democracy, underpinned by values of tolerance and openness and, on the other, a questioning of the principles of representative democracy by their less educated peers. This split can already be observed in both political behaviors and choices.

Political Choices and Their Electoral Consequences

Young French people constitute approximately 14% of the total electorate, and can therefore bring a real influence to bear on the decision-making process which establishes the political, and hence economic and social, direction of the country. Their votes can determine who wins an election. Politicians are acutely aware of the importance of the youth vote, which they carefully court during election campaigns.

Although young people attach a lot of importance to their right to vote, it is a right they do not always choose to exercise. On average, they are less likely to participate in elections than their elders, either by not registering or not voting. 5 to 6% of French people are not registered on the electoral roll. The proportion of unregistered young people, though difficult to accurately quantify, is undoubtedly considerably higher than this, despite the 1997 decree making registration at 18 years of age automatic. The parameters linked to conditions of social integration are decisive. Unqualified working class urban youth, who experience difficulties integrating into society, are least likely to be registered to vote.

In France, although abstentionism at legislative, municipal and in particular European elections is higher among young voters than in the electorate at large, Presidential elections succeed in mobilizing the younger sections of the electorate: their level of participation in these elections does not differ significantly from that of other classes of voter.

In the first rounds of the 1981 and 1988 Presidential elections youth abstentionism was no higher than for the rest of the electorate. This was also the case in 1995 (24% of 18 to 24 year olds abstained, compared to 21% of the electorate as a whole). In 2002, however, more young people stayed at home on polling day, and the increase in abstentionism was greater among 18 to 24 year olds than among the rest of the electorate (there was a 10 point drop in turnout for young people between 1995 and 2002, compared to 7 points for their elders). In fact, one young person out of three did not vote (34% of 18–24-year-olds and 32% of 25–30-year-olds, compared to 28% of the electorate as a whole).

The fact that there were a large number of candidates was regarded as positive by one in two young electors (49% compared with 38% of all French electors). Nevertheless, this did nothing to mitigate either the deepening crisis of political representation or young people's dissatisfaction with the choice of candidates they had been given.[17] There was a high turnout for the 2007 Presidential election among all voter age groups, including the young, although youth abstention was still slightly higher than abstention among the population as a whole (18% and 16%, respectively, for the first round of voting).

With the exception of presidential elections, young people are much less likely to vote than their elders by an average margin of 10 percentage points: in the March 2004 regional elections 52% of 18 to 24 year olds abstained, compared to 38% of the electorate as a whole; in the June 2004 European elections, 60% of 18 to 24-year-olds and 71% of 24 to 35–year-olds abstained, compared to 56% of all registered voters; finally, 43% of 18 to 24-year-old French people failed to vote in the referendum on the European Constitution, compared to 31% of the electorate as a whole. The results for Europe as a whole revealed youth abstentionism to be higher by a similar proportion: in the 2004 European elections 67% of 18 to 24-year-olds did not vote, compared to 54% of the total European electorate.

There can be no single reason for electoral abstentionism, particularly youth abstentionism, as it is the result of a combination of individual circumstances, sociological factors, and political explanations. In fact, an individual's engagement with politics during their youth takes place in the context of a period of transition and identity construction. This particular stage of the process of political socialization is to a large extent subject to the conditions for acquisition of adult status and social roles. The idea of a moratorium—coming from the Latin *morituri*, signifying the granting of a delay—captures the nature of this process quite well. Today young people tend to take longer to settle into a career; they get married and start a family when they are nearer thirty than twenty; they also leave the parental home later. The decision to delay becoming a fully independent adult have an impact on political attitudes and behavior. We can see that young people start voting later. The specific nature of the electoral moratorium of the young can be explained by the fact that, at that age, life is experienced with a particular intensity, and that individuals are confronted with many difficult choices and situations which have to be negotiated.[18] The period of time between a right being acquired, at the age of 18, and that right actually being exercised constitutes a period of adjustment and negotiation of one's identity, where values and knowledge, including political views, hitherto largely acquired within the family, are called into question by the young adult.

Depending on biographical circumstances and job history, this moratorium can vary in duration, and a decision not to vote can be interpreted in various ways. Young unemployed people are always less likely to vote, and their abstentionism is closely related to sociological factors connected to their situation. The level of political integration of secondary school and university students, on the other hand, always seems higher, even if they are increasingly erratic in their electoral participation, depending on both their objective availability, and their feelings about politics at the time. The effects of the political conjuncture can accentuate or modulate the level of abstentionism. Reasons for non-voting are increasingly linked to politics, and the difficulty young people have identifying with the stances of French political parties.

Political abstentionism, whether motivated by a lack of identification, a desire to protest about the options made available to the voter, or the expression of dissatisfaction, has increased in recent years, especially among the young. Young people tend to be "floating voters," and at election time many only decide who to vote for at the last minute. This lack of commitment to one party or candidate represents a general trend among French voters of all ages, not just the young. For the first round of the 1988 Presidential election, 18% of electors claimed to only have decided for whom to vote in the last few weeks of the campaign. Some even made their choice on election day. In 2002, the proportion of late deciders rose to 42%. On April 22, 2007, the day of the first round of the Presidential election, many young people were still relatively undecided about how to cast their votes, despite a highly politicized atmosphere. Almost a third of them (31%) claimed to have made their choice of candidate on the day itself (compared with 22% of the population as a whole).[19]

The decision to vote, or not vote, appears to be influenced by a number of factors which are increasingly difficult to predict or control. The electoral behavior of young voters is highly volatile when compared to that of their parents' generation. Analysis of voter participation in European elections throughout the EU reveals significant differences in voting behavior between young voters and their elders (see table 5.3). While 60% of voters aged 55 and over voted in the same way as they had in previous elections, this was the case for only 35% of 18 to 24-year-olds and 48% of 25 to 34-year-olds. The level of indecision of young voters is high: while 15% of voters aged 55 and over made up their mind about who to vote for in the last few days of the election campaign, or indeed on election day itself, twice as many 18 to 24 year olds (31%)

Table 5.3 Voting and abstention in the 2004 European elections (%)

	Voted		*Did Not vote*	
	Has always voted in this way	*Decided within days of the election or on election day itself*	*Never votes*	*Decided within days of the election or on election day itself*
18–24	35	31	30	39
25–39	48	23	21	31
40–54	51	17	16	37
55 and over	60	15	18	32
Overall	52	19	21	38

Source: Post-2004 European elections survey, *Flash Eurobaromètre*, 162, carried out by EOS Gallup Europe, June 2004.

made their decision during the same period. The younger generations decide how to vote and express themselves politically in different ways from their parents. This represents a major evolution in electoral behavior and democratic expression.

In France, in the course of the last few elections, the voting behavior of young people has lost its specificity and has come to more closely resemble that of older voters. It has evolved in line with changes in government and has gradually come to resemble more closely the voting behavior of the French population as a whole.

In the 2002 Presidential elections the choices of young electors were similar to those made by their older compatriots.[20] In the first round, the electorate sanctioned the outgoing President and Prime Minister. A considerably lower percentage of young people voted for Jacques Chirac than in 1995 (13% of 18 to 24-year-olds in the first round in 2002, compared to 19% in 1995). In 2002 the Chirac vote among young electors was much lower than for the electorate as a whole (20%). On April 21, 2002, Lionel Jospin also captured less of the youth vote than he had in the first round in 1995 (13% compared to 21% seven years earlier). He also performed less well among young voters than among the electorate as a whole, 16% of who voted for him. Fairly substantial numbers of young electors, in common with the electorate as a whole, voted for extremist candidates of the Left (14%) and the Right (17%). Almost one young elector in three cast a protest vote. The Far Left, in particular Olivier Besancenot, attracted a lot of young voters, both students and non-students (14% of the youth vote went to a Far Left candidate, compared to 10% for the electorate as a whole, 7% of young people voted for Olivier Besancenot, compared to 4% of the total electorate). The 2007 Presidential election saw a drop in the number of protest votes, and a revival in electoral fortunes of the two main parties of government, the UMP, and the PS. Young voters actively participated in this return to a broadly two party system. In the first round 10% of them voted for a candidate from the non-PS Left, a similar proportion to that of the electorate as a whole (11%). In the second round, they voted in greater numbers for Ségolène Royal than for Nicolas Sarkozy (55% to 32%). Between 1995 and 2002 there had already been a decrease in the proportion of the youth vote which went to Jean-Marie Le Pen (18% of 18 to 24 year olds in the first round in 1995—which was 3 points higher than for the electorate as a whole-compared to 13% in 2002—which was four points lower than for the electorate as a whole), and in 2007 the Front National's share of the youth vote dropped again, and more dramatically, to 5%, 4 percentage points lower than for the electorate as a whole. The likelihood of a young person voting for the Front National varies according to their level of social integration and, in particular, their educational qualifications: 22% of 18 to 30 year olds who did not have the baccalaureate, compared to 9% of all young electors, voted for Jean-Marie Le Pen in the first round of the Presidential election, while only 3% of students voted for him. These figures confirm that the electoral base for the Front National and its leader among young voters is largely made up of individuals who have already started work, usually in a job which requires few qualifications and offers low job security and social status. In 2002, the same division was already apparent: Jean-Marie Le Pen attracted a much higher proportion of the votes of young people who had left school without a baccalaureate than those who were still in higher education (29% and 8%, respectively).

In 2002, as in 2007, young students and graduates tended to vote for left-wing candidates, in particular the socialist candidate: 63% of students voted for Ségolène Royal (compared to 37% who voted for Nicolas Sarkozy).

The young French electorate should not be regarded as a homogenous bloc, either socially or politically. Although the current social and political malaise and a tendency to be pessimistic affect the whole of society, and the desire to protest is widespread among the young, different categories of young people are affected differently and do not translate these widely shared feelings into the same electoral choices.

Analysis of the voting behavior and electoral participation of European youth reveals both significant national specificities and inter-generational differences.

European young people are more likely than their elders to identify themselves as left wing, and to vote for a moderate left-wing party or candidate (see table 5.4). A gap of around ten points separates French youth from the rest of the population on these two points. A large part of European young people, therefore, vote for a left-wing party or candidate.

Although considerable numbers of young people acknowledge that a good citizen should vote, the percentage of those who hold this belief is lower than in the population at large. Finally, in all the countries in the survey the percentage of young people who voted was lower than for the population as a whole. In some cases the differences between levels of participation between younger and older people were particularly significant: in Spain and in the United Kingdom, for example, only 45% of young people voted (compared to 72% and 67% of the national electorate, respectively). In France, on the other hand, although there was a gap between voter participation of young people and their elders (-17), a clear majority of 18 to 30 year old French people did turn out to vote on election day (58%).

Table 5.4 Political choices and electoral voting behavior

	GE	*SP*	*FR*	*UK*	*IT*	*NL*	*PL*	*SW*
Self-positioning on the left								
18–30 year olds	69	79	68	46	56	47	49	60
Overall	62	67	58	44	54	42	49	53
Gap	+7	+12	+10	+2	+2	+5	—	+7
Importance of voting to be considered a good citizen								
18–30 year olds	64	41	77	54	61	72	65	83
Overall	73	55	83	67	72	75	73	85
Gap	–9	–14	–6	–13	–11	–3	–8	–2
Voted in the last national elections								
18–30 years old	65	45	58	45	71	74	48	77
Overall	78	72	75	67	85	81	62	82
Gap	–13	–27	–17	–22	–14	–7	–14	–5
Voted for the moderate left in the last elections								
18–30 years old	61	49	69	77	30	42	61	57
Overall	54	50	58	70	33	39	69	57
Gap	+7	–1	+11	+7	–3	+3	–8	—

Source: ESS 2003.

The left-wing orientation of younger generations is strongest in France and Spain, and to a lesser extent in Germany and Sweden. Spain comes out at the top of these rankings: almost eight out of ten young Spaniards have left-wing sympathies (79%).

The country with the highest proportion of young people who associate voting with good citizenship is Sweden. 83% of young Swedes believe that for an individual to be regarded as a good citizen, it is important that they vote. France was in second position in this ranking, with a score of 77%.

In Spain, on the other hand, much less importance is attached to exercising one's right to vote in elections. Only 55% of Spaniards, and 41% of young Spaniards, believe that a good citizen is under an obligation to vote.

Finally, Poland and the United Kingdom had the lowest levels of voter turnout in their last parliamentary elections. In the Netherlands, Sweden, Germany, and Italy, on the other hand, among young voters as well as the electorate as a whole voter turnout was relatively high. Voter participation of young French people, though not as high as this latter group, did not sink to Spanish or British levels, which are the lowest in this sample.

Involvement in Politics and Forms of Participatory Protest

Membership of political parties and trade unions has dropped significantly over the last two decades. In many countries, less than 5 or 6 per cent of the population belong to a party or a union. While twenty years ago in France a quarter of the working population were unionized, this figure has now dropped to 8%, and rates of membership for young employees are even lower. The number of party activists has always been relatively low (around 4 to 5% in France), and the proportion of young activists is even lower (between 1% and 2%). The fall in membership of these organizations has been accompanied by the gradual disappearance from the political landscape of the symbolically important figure of the political activist, who had been particularly key figure in left wing organizations.[21] Young people today have a generally negative view of political activists, who are less successful than in the past at recruiting young members. The declining fortunes of political parties and trade unions may be contrasted with the rise of socially or politically committed organizations. Such groups, which help the socially marginalized, such as the homeless, the unemployed and immigrants without proper identity or working papers, and lobby the authorities on human rights or humanitarian issues, are more likely to attract the attention and gain the trust of young people. Associations find it easier than political parties to efficiently run the kind of results-oriented projects which appeal to today's young people. It should be noted, however, that despite the sympathy associations generate among the young, such positive feelings translate into actual support and, in particular, long term activism in only a small minority of cases.

A crisis in representative politics has resulted in more calls for direct democracy, and greater involvement in protest campaigns by citizens. These trends are particularly clear among the younger generations.

Voting, although still regarded as useful and effective by the young, is no longer considered to be the sole way of expressing oneself democratically. Young people seek other forms of participation; new forms of civic involvement and expression of political awareness are emerging, and protest is increasingly seen as being legitimate.

Non-conventional political participation is on the increase in all European countries. While only 17% of Europeans participated in two or more protests in 1981, by 1999 this figure had risen to 28%.[22] This is predominantly a generational phenomenon: members of the older generations are unlikely to be involved in protests, baby boomers more likely, and those who are reaching their majority today more likely still: increasing involvement in protest is a continuing trend. In France, one in two young people has taken part in a street demonstration. Between the two rounds of the 2002 presidential election, a quarter of young French people took to the streets to demonstrate against the presence of Jean-Marie Le Pen in the second round (25% compared to 9% of the adult population as a whole).[23] With the individualization of practices and norms, the range and diversity of political behaviors has decreased. In this new context, political protest has become more common and has as a consequence acquired greater legitimacy. The redefinition of political participation is particularly clear among the younger generations. In France, the younger a citizen is, the more importance they are likely to attach to political demonstration: 68% of 18 to 24 year olds compared to 48% of the over 65s consider that in a democracy it is extremely or very important for people to demonstrate. One out of two young people (51%) who consider voting to be a fundamental feature of a properly functioning democracy also believe that demonstrations are extremely or very important. Only a third of the over 50s (34%) attach the same degree of importance to these two forms of democratic expression.[24]

Through involvement in protest, young people genuinely embrace political activism.[25] The wide variety of issues which give rise to their collective mobilization show that, far from being indifferent or solely preoccupied with their own problems, young people take an interest in many matters which have to do with the functioning and organization of society. There are many ways of getting involved: antiracism initiatives, support for immigrant communities—in particular immigrants without the proper identity or working papers—and demonstrations against the Front National, for example. Young people often take the lead in organizing protests. In France, for over twenty years, *lycée*, and university students have joined together to oppose various attempts by left- and right-wing governments to reform the school system and employment policy. On every occasion the government has been forced to back down. Conventional participation—voting—and non-conventional participation—demonstrating—are not rival options but closely linked and often complement each other.

The development of non-conventional participation in European societies, often in the form of protest movements, should not be considered as the rise of a form of political participation that sets itself as an alternative to electoral participation. Particularly when participatory democracy takes on a strong protest element, it could be thought of as an adversary of representative democracy. This does not seem to be the case: the more citizens value conventional participation, the more they also regard participating in protests as important.

In 1999, almost one in three Europeans (30%) took part in one or more protests, but with significant differences between the results from country to country.

The increasing involvement in protest movements by younger generations of Europeans manifests itself differently in different parts of Europe. The biggest differences between the youngest groups and the rest of the population (+7 and +8 points) can be observed in the southern European countries of France, Italy, and Spain, as well as in Germany (see table 5.5). France and Spain, in particular, stand out as the countries where young people demonstrate the most. A quarter of young Spaniards and a quarter of young French people claimed to have taken part in a demonstration in the previous twelve months. Elsewhere in Europe, the culture of protest is much weaker, even—in the Netherlands and Poland—almost absent and young people's involvement in protest, such as it is, is scarcely distinguishable from that of the rest of the population.

The other forms of participation or political involvement are more or less equally engaged in by young people and their elders. Only a minority of young people are active in party organizations or associations, in proportions which are not much lower than their elders. The likelihood of a young person joining a political group is highest in Sweden, the United Kingdom, and Germany. In France the probability is lower: only 13% of young French people say that they can see themselves participating in a group of this kind. Membership of associations is generally quite low. In the United Kingdom, Italy, and Poland very few individuals are actively involved in an association. French levels of involvement in associations are similar to those in Germany, Spain, and the Netherlands.

Table 5.5 Involvement in politics and forms of political participation

	GE	*SP*	*FR*	*UK*	*IT*	*NL*	*PL*	*SW*
Has taken part in a demonstration in the previous twelve months								
18–30 years old	18	25	25	6	18	3	2	8
Overall	11	17	18	4	11	3	1	6
Gap	+7	+8	+7	+2	+7	—	+1	+2
Would consider joining a political group								
18–30 years old	28	12	13	30	14	21	21	36
Overall	28	12	15	27	16	20	19	34
Gap	—	+2	–2	+3	–2	+2	+2	+2
Is or has been a member of an association								
18–30 years old	16	19	16	6	9	18	6	22
Overall	18	16	18	9	8	23	6	25
Gap	–2	–3	–2	–3	–2	–5	—	–3
Has signed a petition in the previous twelve months								
18–30 years old	31	33	40	43	15	22	8	45
Overall	32	24	35	40	17	23	7	41
Gap	+1	+9	+5	+3	–2	–1	–1	+4

Source: ESS Survey, 2003.

Young people are more likely to sign petitions and boycott certain products. Young Swedes sign more petitions than anyone else (45%). In the United Kingdom and France significant numbers of young people make this type of political gesture (43% and 40%, respectively). In Poland, on the other hand, the corresponding figure is 8%. Finally, French people are more likely to boycott products than their European neighbors: 30% of young French participants in the survey claimed to have boycotted a product or products in the previous twelve months. Young Swedes make the most use of product boycotts (39%), while young Italians and Poles are the least likely to use this method of expressing themselves politically (both 5%).

* * *

To conclude this comparative study of young people's attitudes to politics in France and Europe and the evolutions in their political participation, certain instances of continuity and change between generations can be identified. Examples of continuity would be the decisive influence on individuals of the political orientation of their families, a certain similarity between the political attitudes of young people and their elders, and a fairly constant level of politicization. Other attitudes that cross the generation gap include suspicion of the political class, as well as an enduring attachment to the values and procedures of representative democracy. As regards changes, we can note a significant decrease in identification with political parties, a less straightforward attitude to voting, a greater number of voters who do not always vote for the same party, and finally a greater propensity to protest, in particular by participating in political demonstrations.

Young people cannot be treated as a homogenous group. Political divisions are perpetuated by differentiated social experiences, divisions between individuals with different educational backgrounds, and the different entry points into the job market open to young people. These divisions create groups who exhibit different voting behaviors and ways of participating in politics.

In the European political landscape, young French people are both similar to and different from their neighbors. Their level of politicization is not very high when compared to that of young Northern Europeans. On the other hand, they are relatively willing to engage in protest, and develop ways of expressing themselves politically that are more characteristic of Southern European countries.

Notes

1. Drouin, 1995; Percheron, 1985.
2. Percheron, 1991; Crête and Favre, 1989; Manheim, 1990; Nora, 1992.
3. Dalton and Kuechler, 1990; Inglehart, 1990; Topf, 1995.
4. Percheron, 1993.
5. De Singly, 1996.
6. Perrineau, 2003.
7. Muxel, 2001.
8. The Euyoupart Survey, financed by the European Commission in 2004, of the political participation of young people aged 15 to 25 (N = 8 000), which used interviews with young people from eight countries (France, Germany, Great Britain, Italy, Finland, Austria, Slovakia, Estonia).
9. Ibid.
10. Post-2004 European Elections Survey, *Eurobarometers*, The European Commission, July 2004.
11. Enquête Démocratie 2000, Cevipof.
12. Cevipof-Sofres postelection surveys.
13. Baromètre Politique Français, Vague 1, Cevipof, 2006.
14. Panel électoral Français, 2007, Cevipof.
15. Idem.
16. Grunberg and Muxel, 2002.
17. Panel électoral français, Cevipof, CIDSP, CECOP, 2002.
18. Muxel, 2001.
19. Panel électoral Français, Cevipof, 2007.
20. Muxel, 2002; Tournier, 2004.
21. Ion, Franguiadakis, and Viot, 2005.
22. Bréchon, 2005.
23. Muxel, 2002.
24. Grunberg and Muxel, 2002.
25. Becquet and de Linares, 2005.

CHAPTER 6

Interest Groups in France and Europe

Emiliano Grossman

Relations between state and society in Europe tend to vary greatly and are often based on compromises negotiated over centuries that have evolved only slowly over time. This is why the very foundations of modern democracies in Europe often reflect particular attitudes of the state toward organized economic and societal interests—attitudes which in many cases continue to exist today. The compromises negotiated are therefore the fruit of the specific history of each country which explains why there is such a great variety of models throughout Europe.

Added to this, relations between state and society may also vary from one sector to another within the same country. Certain sectors, such as agriculture for example are historically characterized by a strong level of cooperation between sectoral interest groups and public authorities. On the other hand, in many other political domains, relations between stakeholders and the public authorities have been quite difficult and sometimes stormy throughout Europe as is the case with environmental policy for example.

This chapter will explore this duality and will start by proposing a certain number of definitions. The perspective will be to analyze interest-group politics and the focus will be on the way in which relations between these organizations and the state are organized. Issues relative to the corruption of elected representatives or civil servants by economic actors will be left aside. As a study of interest groups this chapter does not focus on corruption or any other kind of illegal practices, but provides an account of the immense variety of these relations—most of which are "legal"—and of their political importance.

Nor does a study of interest groups exclude social movements or "social movement organisations." However, more attention will be paid to relations with public authorities rather than to the emergence of groups or movements. In other words, the focus will be on social movements and other societal organizations only insofar as they attempt to influence public authorities and organize themselves to participate in—and have an impact on—political processes. From this perspective, the differences between interest groups and social movements are drastically reduced. The choice of strategies is indeed constrained by the type of resources available, but, as we shall see, strategies tend to converge.

There exist many different mixes of strategies depending on the types of state-society relations in a given case as will be demonstrated by the examples of six member states—Germany, Italy, The Netherlands, Poland, Spain, Sweden, and the United Kingdom.

In order to account for the variety of actors, strategies and contexts, the historical models of relations between state and organized interests and others will first be presented. The way in which these models account for how these relations are played out in several EU member states will then be discussed. Finally, the focus will be on the way in which the European Union further complicates the debate by providing an interface between interest groups and fully fledged public authorities, thus bringing its weight to bear on relations between state and organized interests at national level.

Relations between State and Society

The pluralist and neo-corporatist models are undoubtedly the best known of the many models of state-society relations in Europe. It is often considered difficult to place France within this dichotomic classification. These models vary with regard to the role of the state, the ability of economic and societal interests to organize and mobilize and in function of types of cooperation between the state and these interests. Each of these models provides information both on the dominant strategies of the interest groups and social movements and on the attitude of the state toward these actors.

The models must be seen as ideal-types. They all derive from types of relations which exist or have existed in reality, but this does not mean that each country can be placed into one single category. Depending on the case, these ideal-types can provide an understanding of how a public policy or a policy network functions.[1]

An important distinction should be made between attitudes adopted toward intermediary bodies. Historically, two traditions can be distinguished: one openly publicizes its hostility toward them while the other adopts a more pragmatic position. This tension polarized the attitudes adopted by different governments toward intermediary bodies of all kinds very early on. In France, for example, there is a tradition of strong hostility to intermediary bodies, in opposition to other traditions where compromise has entailed either that competition is regulated between groups, or that the more important groups are integrated into the political process. Three models may be distinguished here: pluralism, neo-corporatism and "Statism."

Pluralism

Pluralism, as the first "school" is called, was born in the United States. The majority of contemporary actors recognize Arthur Bentley as the founding father of pluralism in the study of interest groups. Following the example of Jordan and Richardson,[2] the term Bentleyism is often used rather than pluralism. However, it was after the publication of *The Governmental Process* in 1951 by David Truman[3] that the pluralist approach really took off. For at least two decades, this would be the main axis of all political theory and the influence of this school remains perceptible and highly significant today. It continues, notably, to be dominant in the analysis of interest groups.[4] In its postwar version, pluralism in the United States was composed primarily of a vision of society based on groups. This society then functioned according to a mechanism of checks and balances. According to this vision, both partisan competition and the state are clearly subordinate to competition between groups.

Groups are the result of our primary socialization and as such are a component of our personality and identity.[5] Truman, who was close to liberal sociology, believed that an individual can belong to different groups at the same time and can mobilize successively in the name of different causes. In other words, one cleavage does not dominate over another. The social cleavage is therefore just one among many and is in no way predominant. All cleavages are equal to each other and it is impossible to establish a hierarchy among them. Bentley himself summarizes the essence of pluralism in the following way: "All phenomena of government are phenomena of groups pressing one another and pushing out new groups and group representatives (the organs of government) to mediate the adjustments." Hence, "when the groups are adequately stated, everything is stated."[6]

Groups are selfish and incapable of thinking of the public good. They pursue their own aims exclusively even to the detriment of other groups within the limits of legality. This does not mean that the public good is out of reach: it is achieved as a result of competition between groups and therefore results from the action of an "invisible social hand."

This is where the second central idea of pluralism comes into play: checks and balances. By definition, political power is scattered in a modern democratic society and the lasting domination of one group is prevented by the permanent emergence of new counter-powers, i.e. groups who are opposed to the dominant group. There are always a large number of groups in existence who are ready to mobilize as soon as one of their interests is seriously threatened. So-called "latent" or non-institutionalized groups will organize as soon as the pursuit of happiness and well-being of one group interferes with their ability to do the same. This checks and balances mechanism therefore acts like an invisible hand which pushes toward the general interest or rather toward the satisfaction of the greatest number while at the same time ensuring the protection of minorities.

This vision of social regulation carried out by a mechanism similar to the market, competition between groups, has important consequences for the vision of the political. Ideally, the state merely records the power struggle between interest groups. Governmental decisions then become simply the "result of the effective access of various interests" to government agencies.[7] In other words, political processes are about producing laws. And these laws reward the most successful interest groups.[8] From the 1970s, in response to criticisms developed in the next section, certain authors supported or called for a more active state. This state would be responsible for ensuring balance thus facilitating access to the state by relatively underprivileged groups. This would notably counteract the supposed excessive weight of groups representing economic interests.

Beyond a rather reductive vision of the state even in its renewed version, politics is relegated to a place of secondary importance. From this perspective, partisan competition or elections become secondary elements. Politicians are above all targets for the interest groups as they depend on them to finance their electoral campaigns. Therefore, according to this economic vision of politics, electoral victory is above all the product of the means invested in the electoral campaign. In other words, political parties and politicians have no autonomy and no ideology which allows the pluralist theory to turn a blind eye on all the objects of political sociology.

This world vision was criticized both for its cynical evaluation of politicians but above all for its optimism concerning the result of competition between interest groups. Charles Wright Mills probably wrote one of the most hard-hitting criticisms by confronting the model with the reality in the United States.[9] This inaugurated a long tradition of criticism of the political system in the US exemplified among contemporary critics of the George W. Bush administration.

Neo-corporatism

Unlike pluralism, neo-corporatism made changes to the economic environment one of its main explanatory variables. From the middle of the 1970s, a new way of thinking about the representation of sectoral interests developed following the rediscovery of corporatism. It coincided with and was fed by a more general reflection on the evolution of national economic systems. It was inspired by previous reflection on intermediary bodies as mediators in social conflict and government policy.[10] Neo-corporatism as an analytical approach came about because it proved impossible to explain systems of interest intermediation only on the basis of competition between interest groups.[11]

Neo-corporatism (or societal corporatism) should above all be understood as a response to the growth of demands made on the state and the resulting increase in responsibility for the latter. A second driving force of neo-corporatism was the increasing interdependence between states in the context of the growing liberalization of trade in the postwar period. Employees were given a greater sense of responsibility by neo-corporatism as it gave to them the right to have their voice heard both on economic policy and on how the national revenue was shared out.

Like pluralism, neo-corporatism was far from constituting a unified and coherent theory. However, from the outset, it did constitute an answer to the international economic problems which arose during the 1970s according to the supporters of this trend:

> To an important degree, corporatist concertation in the 1970s must be understood as a sometimes desperate turn to domestic, political and institutional resources in a search for solutions to what really were international problems.[12]

In the original ideal-type developed by Schmitter, neo-corporatism is a system for the representation of interests in which individuals are part of a limited number of organizations of which membership is mandatory. These groups are organized hierarchically and differentiated by economic sector. Finally, they are recognized and sometimes created by the state which gives them a monopoly over representation of their specific sector in exchange for a certain amount of control over the selection process of leaders and the formulation of political demands.

Some groups are necessarily stronger than others and can even obtain control of a sector belonging to the public authorities—the "capture" of a political domain which the pluralists were so afraid of.[13] The large groups based on social class tend to become rather bureaucratic and to develop a more or less efficient infrastructure together with specific knowledge of the political domains which concern them. They also tend to control the interests within their sector in such a way that they acquire the powers of a de facto government in these domains.

In contrast to pluralist approaches, all cleavages are not equal: social cleavages are the most central. Claus Offe,[14] for example, distinguishes between "market participants" and policy takers.[15] The first category includes "class based" organizations which represent either the supply or the demand side of the labor, goods, or services markets, that is, employers and trade unions but also investors, consumers, savers, and so on. These organizations act as pressure groups to improve their relative market share. In spite of their positions of relative power or weakness they are in a position to influence government policy and to have a more or less destabilizing effect on the political, social, and economic order. This ability to destabilize ensures them a decidedly more predominant role compared to other groups.

Those organizations belonging to the second group suffer the effects of these politics. They are part of a "political market" which does not have a direct impact on the stability of the political order. Regional governments in Germany, the association of mayors in France, but also taxpayers and student associations or automobile clubs are all part of this category.

The state can delegate political power in both cases but it does so for very different reasons:

> For working class organizations, what is to be achieved is restraint, discipline and responsibility, and the greater predictability of conflict behaviour that

> results from bureaucratization. In the case of ordinary pluralist interest groups, which are granted a public law status and the right to "self-administration," the dominant motive is the delegation, devolution and transfer of political issues and demands into an arena in which they do not directly affect the stability of (central) government and the cohesion of its supporting party or party coalition, but, on the contrary, help to reduce the "overloaded" agenda.[16]

It should be specified that the first case retains all the attention in the literature, whereas the second is ultimately closer to former types of corporations or medieval guilds. It is also true that this type of delegation exists in societies like France, which in other respects are very far from the neo-corporatist model. Orders of physicians, solicitors, or accountants can also be seen as slightly anachronistic structures which have survived partly thanks to the permanent nature of the corporatist interests which were at the origin of their foundation and partly thanks to the functional interest which they continue to represent today as outlined by Offe.

Statism

This model can not really be called a model at all. It is based on the French experience and on the experience of a small number of other European countries. Although it has given rise to an ideal-type of state-society relations which has often been used in comparative literature under various names,[17] it is not a model in the normative sense of the word in the same way that the other two models are.

As its name indicates, the main initiative here comes from the state which can choose to consult the interest groups, but which is also free to reverse its decisions or indeed not to take the positions of the stakeholders consulted into account. It is characterized, depending on the case, by a dominant administrative elite or by policy networks which have infiltrated large sections of the administration.

In theory, interest groups do not actively participate in the political process and are even held apart from it. When public authorities do consult them, this is often done to legitimize their actions in the eyes of public opinion rather than to obtain the agreement of a particular section of society or to harness the expertise available within the sector.

Interest groups are somewhat powerless vis-à-vis this attitude, particularly because they characteristically tend to be fragmented and are not always fully representative. These two factors, on the one hand, and the wariness of public authorities toward them on the other, prevent any real organizational development of interest groups. This in turn, reinforces the public authorities in their refusal to integrate the interest groups in the decision-making process. In this context, competition between interest groups and notably between unions has proved to be an additional source of weakness and has prevented any institutionalization of relations with public authorities. This weakness also characterizes economic interest groups, who, because of their proximity to certain

Table 6.1 Models of state-society relations

Model	Role of the State or of Public Authorities	Interest groups/Social movement organisations	List of main types of action	Resources available	«Typical» public policy
Statist	Strong State: puts a brake on the development of organized civil society	Weak: fragmented and often little organized, Competition	→ Conflict/ Confrontation/ Social mobilization («the street»)	→ Ability to mobilize/ Media networking	*Dirigiste* distributive policy
			→ Informal/Collusion/ Clientelism	→ Old boy networks/ Capture/Financial resources	Policies for the allocation of resources/public markets
Pluralist	Regulatory State: in principle low profile «recorder of claims», but also a duty to «balance», (see Neo-pluralism) delegations/ independent agencies	Average: strong degree of professionalization, «services» for members, strong competition between IGs	→ Lobbying & expertise	Experts/expertise → Knowledge Financial resources	«Reglementary» policies/ Independent agencies
Neo-corporatist	Mediatory State: Strong presence, tripartite negotiations and/or delegation controlled by the State or the Law, attribution of public status	Strong: very organized, centralized, hierarchically organized, public status, monopoly of representation, small number of organizations by sector	→ Negotiation (class-based organizations)	→ Ability to mobilize, representivity, control over members	Distributive policies
			→ Policy takers	→ Knowledge, expertise, effectiveness	Reglementary policies by «sector» (e.g., Associations of doctors, lawyers, etc.)

sectors of the administration are often reduced to playing the role of mere reporters of the state's industrial policies.

This weakness necessarily limits the means of action. As far as the economic interest groups are concerned, the scope of their action is essentially limited to informal contacts. With regard to public interest groups, social movements, consumer groups, or unions, the absence of these networks limits the amount of possible contact with public authorities. This brings about a greater tendency toward social conflict, demonstrations, or the occupation of factories or government agencies. This kind of strategy, at best, puts a brake on ongoing projects but rarely exerts any kind of positive influence. To a certain extent, these political configurations are the result of the type of public policy issues proper to an interventionist state. With the precise intention of developing the national economy together with a desire for social harmony, the allocation of resources is conceived of in very centralized terms leaving little space for concertation with the social partners or consultation with representatives from the economic and social sectors concerned.

There are many pitfalls present in this model resulting from the marked imbalance in favor of the state. State clientelism and corporatism emerge as the two greatest dangers. This model is a hybrid one and must therefore be dealt with carefully and all the more so as it is in the process of disappearing in the countries of interest to us here. In its "purist" version, it is none other than a type of pluralism weakened by the power of the state (see table 6.1).

The Models in Practice in France and in Europe

The models described above all have a heuristic value in the contemporary world, though their explanatory power should not be overestimated. It is true that these models tell us nothing about political behavior or the forms which political engagement takes. While the models do point in certain directions, it is nonetheless necessary to see to what extent the cases under study here corroborate these directions or not.

We will therefore look at six states grouping them together according to type of state-society relations.

Sweden, the Netherlands, Germany: The Neo-corporatist Galaxy

These three countries can be classed in the same group, even though each of them represents a very different experience. First, in one of the founding works, Peter Katzenstein[18] stated that arrangements of the neo-corporatist type were above all proper to "small" countries. According to him, countries such as Sweden, Austria, the Netherlands, or Belgium are naturally turned toward the outside. Because of this, they are particularly sensitive to the problems of competition. Under these conditions, social harmony and wage moderations become objects of priority.

In spite of its very solid export capacity, Germany is not in this situation. According to this logic, it is not surprising that in spite of the "consensual" nature of its democracy,[19] Germany is at best a hybrid model. The German political scientist, Martin Sebaldt expressed this very well with the expression "organised pluralism."[20] The best known component of this model is undoubtedly "parity," which grants permanent seats on company boards to employees. However, this participation in company management is far removed from neo-corporatist arrangements which institutionalize participation in the economic government of the country.

What is certain is that from the point of view of political commitment, Germany is different from the other two neo-corporatist countries in the sample. Whereas neo-corporatism is supposed to ensure social harmony, participation rates in demonstrations or in illegal activities are clearly stronger in Germany than in the other two countries (table 6.2).

This confirms the hybrid character of the German model. Sweden and the Netherlands, on the contrary, are among the countries with the lowest rates for these two indicators. Furthermore, these countries are still experiencing very strong rates of unionization (table 6.3). It is true that both of them have always been placed in the category of neo-corporatist countries. Sweden is often considered to be one of the cases closest to the ideal-type developed by Schmitter.[21]

Table 6.2 Individual political activity over the past twelve months according to country

	SW	*FR*	*UK*	*GE*	*SP*	*NL*	*IT*	*PL*	*Ave.**
Contacted a politician	16	18	18	13	12	14	12	10	14.7
Worked within a political party	5	5	3	4	6	3	3	3	4.2
Signed a petition	41	35	40	31	24	23	17	7	25.8
Participated in an authorised demonstration	6	18	4	11	18	3	11	1	9.4
Boycotted certain products	33	27	26	26	8	10	8	4	17.4
Gave money to a party	7	3	8	9	5	8	3	9	6.8
Participated in illegal protest actions	1	3	1	1	2	0	2	0	1.3

Note: * Average (Europe of 25).

Source: ESS survey 2003.

Table 6.3 Membership of organizations (%)

	GE	*SP*	*FR*	*UK*	*IT*	*NL*	*PL*	*SW*	*Ave.**
Unions	14	6	9	16	9	22	6	56	17.7
Parties	3	3	2	3	3	5	2	8	3.7
Churches, religious organizations	19	6	5	14	5	26	3	15	12.9
Humanitarian organizations	6	4	6	4	4	8	1	14	5.8
Environmental or pacifist organizations	6	2	5	3	20	1	6	7	6.8
Other	38	70	57	38	73	26	88	26	56.9

Note: *Average (Europe of 25).

Source: ESS survey 2003.

The Saltsjöbaden agreements in 1938 introduced a mechanism for the resolution of social conflicts by closely associating employers and the confederation of unions, *LO*, with the political process through several thousand advisory councils. Negotiations on salaries and wages are centralized and in exchange for security of employment and a favorable division of national revenue, Swedish employees accept high levels of flexibility in working hours and jobs, together with somewhat restrictive employment policies for the unemployed.

The system worked well as long as economic growth prevailed. It entered into a state of crisis several times during the 1970s but it was above all during the 1990s that it began to be more and more contested to the point that systematic consultation was finally abandoned.[22] Contestation also arose because the social cleavage was no longer the only or indeed the most structuring cleavage. Since the 1970s, environmentalist and feminist groups had been protesting against a system where there was no place for them. Although unionization remains important, participation in humanitarian organizations or those with other vocations has also become very significant.

The Netherlands has often been considered to be the exception which proves the rule. Unlike the other neo-corporatist countries, it experienced persistent unemployment and an unfavorable economic climate in the early 1980s. The 1983 Wassenaar agreements inaugurated a new period and there was even talk of a "Dutch miracle." The agreement revitalized the neo-corporatist institutions but placed the objective of wage adjustment at centre stage in exchange for security of employment. Dutch "competitive corporatism" is therefore very different from the Swedish system. The Dutch model is strongly contested by some because of its tendency to aggravate social inequalities with the emergence of the working poor phenomenon.[23] To this can be added the current questioning of Dutch "consensualism" that is incarnated notably by the electoral success of the Pim Fortuyn list and the assassination of its leader. Even if these events have not had a direct effect on state-society relations, corporatism—even "competitive" corporatism—needs a wide social foundation. In a context of increasing intolerance and xenophobia this foundation may well become no longer evident.

Statism: France, Italy, Spain

Terms such as Statism or interventionism are above all attempts to give a name to a case which in many ways is particular to France. France does indeed resemble other Southern European countries. And yet, Italy and Spain present far more hybrid cases.

As with Sweden and Austria for neo-corporatism, France incarnates (better than any other country) the idea of a strong state which shapes relations with civil society as it pleases and makes most of the decisions in all domains. However, it is also true that this "model" has without doubt been the most contested during the last two decades.

It is not possible of course to establish a perfect relationship between territorial organization and the structure of organized interests. Furthermore, it would appear that strongly centralized states are not conducive to the development of representative structures such as trade unions or others capable of rivaling the state. France, which is usually described as "weakly corporatist,"[24] has a very fragmented trade union structure with a rate of union membership far lower than in other countries (see table 6.3). Moreover, these unions tend to be very polarized politically and in the past, have rarely managed to achieve unity of action in a given area of conflict. On the contrary, the major social movements in May 1968 or in the winter of 1995 took place somewhat in isolation from the major unions and indeed even sometimes against them.

At the same time, France today has a very vibrant associative community,[25] which slightly contradicts classic theses on the demobilizing effects of French interventionism. However, in terms of interest groups, the ambiguous relations between political and economic elites remain one of the central characteristics of the French system of interest intermediation. Today, these relations are under question and even if it is still useful to distinguish a specifically French model,[26] relations between groups and the state are changing under the joint influence of European integration, globalization, and state reform.[27]

In the other Southern Europe countries, different systems have been characterized as Statist, even though in the case of Spain, Portugal, and Greece this type of Statism is above all the effect of a tardy transition from an authoritarian to a democratic regime. Italy is often compared to France despite the fact that most observers agree that Statism is coming to an end in Italy. Indeed, it disappeared progressively throughout the 1980s and 1990s. Like France, Italy has always been classed in the category of "weakly corporatist" states, with relatively low rates of unionization, ideologically polarized and disunited unions, and decentralized wage negotiations. At the same time, the Italian case might seem particularly interesting to the extent that since 1993, there have been some attempts to develop concertation, although they have not lasted over time.

Italy is frequently associated with "clientelism." Partisan fragmentation may well be the reason for the relative proximity between interest groups and political parties. In turn, the "partytocracy" ensures that groups have access to critical resources within the state and their effective capture of whole sections of public policy at the expense of the general interest. This is just a brief description of the characteristics of the Italian intermediation system. In practical terms, clientelism is thought to have originated as a result of the inability of modernizing and centralizing elites to integrate sub-national and heterogeneous elites into the modernization project, which very frequently—in Southern Europe—was inspired by the French case. Here, as elsewhere, European integration has played a key role in the reorganization of interest groups.[28] The perspective of entering the economic and monetary Union was also at the origin of negotiations at the national level including with the main trade unions and the *Confindustria* (the employers' organization) for the first time in Italian history. Although the results of these negotiations were unequal and the attitudes of the main actors unstable,[29] this episode clearly breaks with the historic relations between state and society and calls clientelist structures into question wherever they continue to exist.

The Italian experience is repeated in other southern states including Spain.[30] It goes without saying that the problem of clientelism is not strictly limited to those countries. There are many examples to indicate that such relations also exist north of the Alps and the Pyrenees. However, the phenomenon seems to have been more significant in these countries.

Overall, the three cases—France, Italy, and Spain—confirm table 6.1. An omnipresent state entails the demobilization of civil society, which tends not to be very involved in the unions, parties, or other political organizations (see table 6.3).

It is no surprise either that the highest levels of participation in demonstrations and in illegal protest activity are found in these three countries (table 6.2). Given that it is difficult for civil society to participate cooperatively in the elaboration of public policy, protest is a necessary and frequent strategy.

In Search of Pluralism in Europe: The United Kingdom?

Whereas pluralism continues to constitute the most important school in terms of political analysis, pluralist intermediation systems are historically rare in Europe. Although the United Kingdom is often described as the European example of "pluralism," it nevertheless has had a rather eventful history as far as relations between the state and interest groups are concerned. All those who have tried to retrace the history of these relations in the postwar period concede that the United Kingdom was undoubtedly closer to the U.S. pluralist model than any other country in Europe. At the same time, all Labor governments in the immediate postwar period saw neo-corporatism as a way to better organize the market. At most, it could be said that this resolve was weaker in the United Kingdom than in the continental countries, but it certainly did exist.

Thus, a chronological approach is necessary for a clear understanding of the British case. At first sight, the United Kingdom might seem to be predestined to neo-corporatism because of its very unified trade union movement within the framework of the Trade Union Congress (TUC), which is a particularly resourceful organization. In the immediate postwar period, the government took on responsibility for the functioning of the economy. It also committed itself to the building of the Welfare State. However, the strength of the union movement was not matched by employer organizations which remained scattered in several different organizations.[31]

In certain sectors, neo-corporatist type arrangements can be found in the United Kingdom. As in most other postwar European countries, this is the case for agriculture notably. However, the symbol of "UK-style corporatism" is without any doubt the *National Economic Development Council* (NEDC) which was created in 1962. It was intended to discuss the major economic problems and to develop solutions to them but it never attained a level of authority comparable to that of the Austrian "Chambers" or even the Dutch Economic and Social Council. One observer of the period described the system of representation for British interests as "pluralist with corporatist tendencies."[32]

The 1960s saw the emergence of new political issues such as equal opportunities, the right to abortion, disarmament and the protection of the environment. The appearance of these issues caused a renewal of political competition which, although it wasn't proper to the United Kingdom alone, contributed to the gradual relativisation of social cleavages and the decline of the unions. The most spectacular example of these new movements was undoubtedly the Royal Society for the Protection of Birds. Its membership increased ten-fold between 1971 and 2000 making it the largest British society today with over one million members. An even more striking example is Greenpeace which went from 10,000 members in 1980 to more than 400,000 in 1992.

When Margaret Thatcher arrived in power in 1979, the rupture with corporatist endeavors was confirmed. Criticism of the overburdening of the state was matched by political criticism of the supposed bypassing of democratic institutions and the increasing ungovernability resulting from this. Thatcher then severely limited contacts with unions, as well as with employer organizations such as the Confederation of British Industry (CBI). She relied more on think-tanks with similar positions to those of the new Right, such as the *Institute of Directors*. In this respect, Thatcher undoubtedly provides a unique example of the reaffirmation of governmental authority among the postwar democratic and industrialized countries.

The Labour Party's return to power in 1997 did not undo what Thatcher had accomplished. None of the reforms to union law which had been bitterly fought by the Labour Party during the 1980s were called into question. With regard to other interest groups, the government has shown itself to be very open but, according to certain observers, in such a way that their influence will continue to be minimal.

Thus, the British case bears certain classic pluralist features but this is the result of a history which is far from unilinear. Pluralism is therefore not an intrinsic characteristic of the Anglo-Saxon world but rather, as far as the United Kingdom is concerned, a recent creation with discordant points. This is also confirmed by a rate of unionization which remains significant in spite of a palpable decrease since the 1970s. Furthermore, the low level of participation in demonstrations indicates that there exist other ways to weigh on political decision-making in Britain.

Searching for Civil Society in Eastern Europe

Philippe Schmitter and Jürgen Grote[33] have assimilated some of the social pacts concluded in countries which have only recently joined the EU to neo-corporatist type structures. The data are still preliminary and must be approached with caution. The rare analyses available[34] tend to be very skeptical about the success and the truly neo-corporatist nature of these institutions. They suggest that, given the weakness of union organizations, the trilateral agreements concluded during the 1990s were essentially made at the expense of the workers in order to impose cuts to the social budget and the liberalization of labor law. At best, the authors add, these institutions have allowed workers to better accept their own marginalization.

In any case, interest groups are still in the process of emerging and there is therefore not yet enough hindsight for an overall picture of these groups in Central and Eastern Europe to be drawn. Two contradictory tendencies can nonetheless be seen. On the one hand, in many cases, the transitions have been introduced by more or less formal organizations which have emerged either as an alternative to existing organizations or by drawing on existing organizations to turn them into vectors for political protest. In some cases, the influence of these organizations has lasted beyond the process of democratic transition and has laid the foundations of a new civil society.[35] On the other hand, the fact that the Unions were tightly linked to the communist system has permanently discredited these organizations, which today are struggling to emerge as political actors. The data on membership mentioned in table 6.3 are very clear on this. Employers seem to have succeeded in equipping themselves with long-lasting organizational structures. This is often done at the instigation and with the support of U.S. or Western European organizations, foundations, or interest groups.

Finally, we are also witnessing the emergence in strength of sectoral groups in the political life of these countries. Agriculture probably provides the best example of this. Agrarian parties have begun to appear in several countries and, as in the case of Poland, sometimes play a role of paramount importance in the political life of the country. In Poland again, the strong electoral presence of the Family League is also worth noting. In some ways, it can be expected that these "sectoral parties" will disappear as democracy and the partisan system further consolidate. However, the continuing existence of *Chasse Pêche Nature Traditions* (CPNT) in the French political landscape is a reminder that such phenomena are not necessarily linked to the establishment of democracy or to economic development.

Moreover, individual political activity remains very weak, according to all indicators. With time, the practice of liberal democracy should give rise to rates of individual activity more comparable with those in the other countries considered here, which, it should be recalled, also vary greatly.

Tests and Challenges: Toward What Kind of Relationship between State and Society?

It is obvious that relations between state and society are undergoing profound transformations. These transformations are taking place on three different levels: at the level of the relationship between individuals and the state; the transformation of the state itself; and finally, the challenge posed by the emergence of a multilevel political system. The real question concerns the adaptability of the different systems in the light of these challenges. It remains to be seen who is more likely to have to change and what type of relation between the state and society seems most solid when faced with these challenges. Any attempt to answer this will necessarily be preliminary and incomplete. We will now have a quick look at the different challenges before examining their effects on the different type of relations between state and society.

Individuals, Politics, and the State

A first series of changes which constitutes a major challenge, concerns the relationship between individuals and the state and more broadly speaking attitudes toward authority in general. Indeed, as certain surveys on changes in values show,[36] the citizens of liberal democracies have less and less confidence in politicians and in political parties. It is nonetheless true that, at the same time, support for democracy has remained constant and has even increased. Generally speaking, individuals are less and less inclined to accept the vote as the only form of political participation.[37] It is above all the emergence of so-called post-materialist values from the 1970s onward that has contributed to a weakening of the social cleavage and which has been accompanied by the emergence of new societal demands concerning the environment, women's rights, or human rights.[38]

The different models are unequally equipped to deal with these new demands. The pluralist model seems to be the best prepared, but the other two seem to be less well-armed. As it happens and as mentioned above, the United Kingdom has undergone profound transformation for multiple reasons.

For Statist and neo-corporatist models, it is quite certain that the questioning of the role of the state and of the unions or parties has had more serious consequences. Protest has certainly undermined the success of the neo-corporatist model and has contributed to its being called into question. With the Statist model, this protest has clearly contributed -and continues to contribute—to opening up the political process to new actors. This is very evident in France[39] and also elsewhere.

The Rise of the Regulatory State

In parallel to this, transformations within the state represent another major challenge. Repeated economic crises and the end of the "*Trente glorieuses*" may explain the rise of the Regulatory State.[40] This can be understood as a state which progressively abandons the modes of classic regulation, signaled by public property, taxation, expenditure, and redistribution. The Regulatory State contents itself with organizing exchanges between individuals and other societal actors by fixing the rules. In this respect, it is the product of transformations in the vision of the state and of the decreasing prerogatives of the state. One of the paradoxes of this type of state is that its "weakness" has been accompanied by a rising level of reglementary or legislative activity: there are "freer markets [and] more rules."[41]

In this context, the state is being compelled more and more to build partnerships with interest groups far removed from the hierarchical relations that are so characteristic of most countries in Southern Europe. It is this change and the emergence of a strong level of diversity in forms of sectoral joint management between public and private actors which are described by the terms "governance"[42] or "regulation."[43]

The consequences of this are of primary importance for the neo-corporatist models whose legitimacy is above all based on the principle of redistribution.

And yet, the "Dutch miracle" and the social pacts of the 1990s show that there is no functional link between neo-corporatism and redistribution. To put it simply, the decline of distributive policies has contributed to the transformation of these systems. Generally speaking, the changing attitude of the state has entailed an increasing level of participation from sectoral interests in political processes, in all models, as demonstrated by all of the countries studied here.

European Integration

Finally, European integration represents a challenge in many ways for national systems of intermediation. European integration has developed supranational forms of government. In doing this, it has provoked and sometimes encouraged the emergence of more and more significant European lobbying. This "European model" alone represents a permanent challenge for the member states, depending on their closeness to or divergence from the national system. Brussels today has become a place where demands abound from economic interest groups mostly but also from associations or NGOs defending a great diversity of causes. According to some analysts,[44] this model is above all pluralist and, in this respect, represents a danger for neo-corporatist regimes. Indeed, much more even than in the most pluralist member states, the European Union is home to an abundance of lobbies, interest groups, lobbying consultancies, representative structures and other forms of non-partisan representation. What is certain is that the emergence of a European political system is not without consequences for relations between state and society at a national level. In many cases, the need to ensure a presence in Brussels has resulted in in-depth restructuring of national representative structures.

The "Europeanization" of interest groups seems to be one of the most important factors of change. This change is following a similar path to the one taken by the other two factors in that greater representation of sectoral interests and greater competition between them can be observed. Henceforth, national public authorities encourage national groups to reinforce their presence in Brussels.[45] Because of the lessons learnt, this Europeanization has without any doubt had repercussions on the national scene where political power is often shared among many levels.

The effects are varied and it would be incorrect to predict that they will follow one single direction.[46] Nonetheless, in spite of divergent opinions,[47] one has to observe that the European political system favors representation of the pluralist type. The United Kingdom therefore finds itself in a favorable position without any doubt[48] although other countries are doing their best to catch up.

The Regulation of Lobbying

One fundamental issue in a period when lobbying as a means to influence political choices has become commonplace is how to regulate it. The issue of regulation is not about corruption. In spite of perceptible differences in the definition of misdemeanors and all forms of corruption, this is nonetheless well defined throughout the member states of the European Union.

The multiplication of contacts between professional representatives of societal interests and administrative personnel or elected representatives has created new issues. The participation of professional lobbyists in political processes poses problems for equality of access by all sectors of society or, at the very least, the problem of more difficult access for particular sectors. Moreover, the question of the honesty of representatives in their dealings with interest groups is also posed. For this reason, in the late 1990s, the European Commission encouraged industry to equip itself with a code of conduct, which was then used as an example for a code imposed by the European Parliament on requesting a laisser-passer for access to the Parliament. Furthermore, the Commission has sought to make the consultation of civil society systematic notably through the setting up of a portal called Your Voice in 2003.

At the national level, a number of different solutions have been found, most often with the establishment of mandatory directories of interest groups in Parliament, as in Germany. In Quebec, a specific institution has been created, the "*Commissaire au lobbyisme*," whose mission is to monitor and also to inform public opinion.[49]

Even in France, a debate has been launched with the proposal of the "Grosskost-Beaudouin" resolution at the National Assembly, aiming to create a register of lobbyists. Although the proposal seems to have little chance of succeeding in the immediate future, it has nonetheless launched an important debate, and the interest it has aroused suggests that a wider discussion on the regulation of lobbies has been started as, furthermore, many of the practioners themselves are keen to see.

* * *

All these factors of change seem to lead to greater participation of interest groups in the elaboration of public policies. This seems to favor the pluralist "model," even though it is also possible that a great variety of hybrid models are emerging.

The changes currently taking place have destabilized often very old political compromises. The crystallization, the stabilization, and indeed the institutionalization of new models will probably take time and developments will have to be monitored. It is probable that the preliminary conclusion here, a tendency toward more pluralism, will be confirmed by ongoing transformations, but political science is hardly a predictive discipline and endeavors of this type fail far too often for them to be worth making.

Notes

1. Le Galès and Thatcher, 1995; Marsh and Rhodes, 1992.
2. Jordan and Richardson, 1979.

3. Truman, 1951.
4. Vogel, 1996a.
5. Truman, 1951, pp. 17–24.
6. Quoted in Jordan and Richardson, 1979, p. 3.
7. Truman 1951, p. 507.
8. Dunleavy and O'Leary, 1987, p. 43.
9. Mills, 1956.
10. Manoilescu, 1934.
11. Schmitter, 1974.
12. Schmitter and Streeck, 1991, p. 143.
13. Stigler, 1971.
14. Offe, 1981.
15. Literally, taker or sufferer of policies, i.e., an actor who is not sufficiently powerful to have a say in the choice of policies and who therefore suffers these decisions.
16. Offe, 1981, p. 140.
17. For a recent version, cf. Schmidt, 2002.
18. Katzenstein, 1985.
19. Lijphart, 1999.
20. Sebaldt, 1997.
21. Schmitter, 1974.
22. Blom-Hansen, 2000.
23. Visser, 1998.
24. Lehmbruch, 1982.
25. Barthélémy, 2000.
26. Schmidt, 2002 and 2003.
27. Grossman and Saurugger, 2004.
28. Constantelos 2004.
29. Vatta, 2001.
30. Hopkin and Mastropaolo, 2001.
31. Coxall, 2001, p. 20.
32. Shonfield, 1994.
33. Schmitter and Grote, 1997.
34. Ost, 2000; Pérez-Solorzano, 2001.
35. See, e.g., Fink-Hafner, 1998.
36. Bréchon and Tchernia, 2000.
37. Grunberg and Mayer, 2003.
38. Norris, 2002.
39. Grossman and Saurugger, 2004.
40. Majone, 1996.
41. Vogel, 1996b.
42. Le Galès, 2004.
43. Commaille and Jobert, 1999.
44. Schmitter and Streeck, 1991.
45. Schmidt, 1996 and 1999.
46. Risse and Cowles, 2001.
47. Falkner, 1997.
48. Grossman, 2003.
49. See extracts from national regulations in Grossman, 2005.

CHAPTER 7

Trade Unions and Politics

Guy Groux

For a long time, French trade unionism constituted a clear illustration of what has been dubbed the "French exception." This is no longer the case. The fact remains that the actions of French trade unions seem paradoxical to many foreign observers. In today's Europe French trade unions are unique. They retain the ability to mobilize large-scale protests movements and regularly force the cancellation of government reform packages. Most trade union movements in the European Union no longer have this kind of power to mobilize, or if they do, they choose not to exercise it. In the last decade or so there have been numerous instances of the French trade union movement demonstrating its capacity for mobilization—including street demonstrations and strikes—from the December 1995 movement to more recent conflicts over pensions and employment contracts for young workers.[1] French unions' ability to organize large scale mass protest, demonstrations and strikes has created the impression that the French trade union movement wields more power than unions elsewhere. In fact, the French trade unions are weak, certainly much weaker than many of their European counterparts. How can this paradox be explained? It seems that the ability to mobilize, engage in conflict and protest can be reconciled with a greatly weakened trade union movement. Indeed, these two phenomena might actually reinforce each other. In fact the weakness of the French trade union movement is due to its internal divisions, deep divisions which have their roots in the history of the workers movement and which, at least for the moment, show no signs of healing.

Weaknesses and Divisions within the French Trade Union Movement

France has, and by a considerable margin, the lowest rates of union membership of any European or OECD country. In 2003 the total membership of all French trade union organizations amounted to 8% of the national workforce, compared to 78% in Sweden, 34% in Italy, 29% in the United Kingdom, 23% in Germany, 22% in the Netherlands, and 16% in Spain.[2] Another striking statistic concerns the large, even dramatic, drop in union membership in France, compared to other countries. Between 1970 and 2003 it fell by 47%. In Europe levels of union membership evolved in a variety of ways. The only other European country which experienced a large decrease in union membership over the same period was the United Kingdom[3] where, despite the hostility toward the TUC shown by governments under Margaret Thatcher throughout the 1980s, the proportional drop in union membership (35%) was not as great as in France.[4]

Chronic Decline in Union Membership

If we look beyond the figures relating to the overall drop in trade union membership, other more detailed statistics provide us with a clearer picture of the state of trade unionism in France. We can first mention the oft-cited argument that relations between employees and trade unions have clearly been affected by the lack of job security and the flexibilization of the job market. Indeed, according to several major surveys, including the European Social Survey (ESS), France has the highest percentage of employees who say that they do not have a secure job, especially in the private sector. The French figure is 51%, compared to 45% in Germany, 35% in the Netherlands, 34% in Spain, 32% in the United Kingdom, and 29% in Sweden. Nevertheless, the estrangement between French workers and the trade union movement is not only the result of recent developments in the job market—lower job security, flexibilization—but a long-standing state of affairs borne of factors that predate the immediate social context. The French trade union movement has never been able to establish a strong power base or enjoy high membership, except for short highly exceptional periods (the Popular Front, the period around Liberation). Such observations regarding the fragility of French trade unionism—which have been made by scholars researching all periods of the history of unions in France[5]—apply equally to the present, as the results of the European Social Survey confirm. The proportion of French employees who have never been a member of a trade union is higher than anywhere else in Europe: 75%, compared to 14% in Sweden, 56% in the United Kingdom, and 62% in Germany.

Consequently, the relationship between French workers and trade union organizations cannot be explained solely by reference to the job market, levels of unemployment, and the flexibility measures which have been introduced into many companies, particularly in the private sector. Certainly, the above factors are important when considering this phenomenon, but it would be wrong to focus too closely on problems connected to the economic conjuncture. There are other, more fundamental explanations for the chronic weakness of the French trade union movement, which are related to its historic development and in particular its long-standing and deep-seated internal divisions. In many opinion polls, French employees cite these internal divisions as one of the main reasons for their disillusionment with French trade unionism.

The Primacy of Political Divisions

In fact, splits within the trade union movement have remained deeper and more long-lasting because they are deeply rooted in political divisions which often have an international dimension. Splits within French trade unionism have hardly ever solely been over professional or economic issues. These divisions have usually been caused by the incompatibility of the various political cultures which have exerted a significant long-term influence on French politics and industrial relations. The schisms between the "two CGTs"—the CGT and CGT-FO—occurred at moments of great historical and political change: in the aftermath of the Bolshevik Revolution, at the time of the German-Soviet Pact of 1939, and at the beginning of the Cold War. The only times when these two organizations moved closer together or merged were highly charged politically or historically. This was the case during the Popular Front period, and later during the Resistance, when the two CGTs briefly merged. The divisions which tended to prevail were between on the one hand a reformist secular culture, and on the other the revolutionary political culture which continued to dominate the CGT until well into the 1980s.

Christian trade unionism and its avatars were no exception to the rule. When the French Confederation of Christian Workers (CFTC) was founded in 1919, it was certainly with the intention of supporting the papal encyclical *Rerum novarum* and evangelizing French workers. Nevertheless, the pioneers of Christian trade unionism also sought to combat what they saw as an unhealthy and dangerous trend, namely the growing influence of the Bolshevik Revolution on the French working class. Similarly, the schism between the CFTC and the Confédération française démocratique du travail (CFDT) in 1964 cannot be solely attributed to the decline in religious observance in France or transformations in the industrial world in the 1950s, such as the growing presence of workers from the South and/or former colonies.[6] Neither can the split be explained simply in terms of changes in religious practices in French society, and the consequent undermining of Catholic trade unionism. The issue of secularization certainly was discussed at length at the 1964 Congress, but other divergences played a role in the split: since Liberation the "reconstruction" tendency, which included such activists as Vignaux, Descamps, Maire, Moreau, Kaspar, and others, was pitted against the "old house of Christian trade unionism," for many years dominated by Gaston Tessier and his friends. Differences of opinion on the colonial wars—the Algerian War in particular—also contributed to the split. In fact, in 1964 two different worlds decided to go their separate ways. One grouping consisted of partisans of "reconstruction," whose "social democratic" project was carried forward first by the Parti socialiste unifié (PSU) then the "deuxième gauche." The rest remained loyal to the traditional stance of the CFTC and a certain idea of social Catholicism and its political representation.[7]

Repetitions of these schisms—which in a certain way marked the major turning points in French trade union history—occurred more recently, if on a smaller scale than in the past. The immediate catalyst for the foundation of Solidaires, unitaires, démocratiques (SUD), a movement which broke away from the CFDT, included strikes by postal workers and nurses at the end of the 1980s, but the deeper causes of this split lay in fundamental ideological and political differences between the CFDT and SUD, which manifested themselves in sharply contrasting visions of the way French society needed to be transformed. Similarly, within the teachers' organization—the former Fédération de l'Education Nationale (FEN)—rifts appeared between groups led by militants close to the French Communist Party (PCF) and other groups of more social democratic persuasion. This split led to the formation of the Fédération syndicale unitaire (FSU) and the Syndicat des enseignants (SE), the latter being the leading force within the Union nationale des syndicats autonomes (UNSA) (the National Union of Independent Trade Unions). Basically, the French trade unionism movement continues to be split up into groups with antagonistic political cultures. These divisions may not be as deep as in the past, and it is certainly true that some trade unions such as the CGT have changed, as have relations between "trade unionism" and "politics" (see above), but internal antagonism still remains.

The French trade union movement is therefore characterized by a degree of internal division which is not present in other countries, where unions are often affiliated with a dominant or hegemonic central grouping. This is the case in the United Kingdom, Germany, or the United States. In the same way, the enduring historical divisions between the large confederations—which have provoked the more recent schisms (SUD, the FSU, UNSA . . .)—produce a fragmented movement quite unlike the large groups of organizations found in other countries, groups which are linked to current trends in globalization. Examples of the latter model are Verdi in Germany, Japanese trade unionism, the network of Italian private sector unions, and even—on an international level—the recently founded International Trade Union Confederation (ITUC). The ITUC resulted from the merger of the International Confederation of Free Trade Unions (ICFTU) and the World Confederation of Labour (WCL), and its formation brought a chapter in the history of international trade unionism to a close.[8]

Party—Union Links

Clearly, the causes of the internal divisions within the French trade union movement explain why those divisions are so deep. Equally clearly, the weakness of French trade unions can be explained by the fact that many salaried employees, presented with the spectacle of a disunited movement, decide against joining a union. Trade unions' problems are compounded by the fact that potential recruits regard them as being not only divided, but also too politicized. Indeed the "divisions" and the "politicization" have always been mutually reinforcing, particularly in the past.

Nevertheless, the politicization of the major French trade unions while unquestionable, has also been ambiguous. In view of the history of trade unionism, to say that unions have close links with certain political parties amounts to stating the obvious. For a long time the Leninist theory of the "transmission belt" informed relations between the CGT and the PCF, although for over a decade this has been no longer the case. While the other groups of affiliated unions did not generally follow the CGT-PCF "model," and even opposed it, they have all enjoyed important lasting relationships with one particular political party or another: Force Ouvrière (FO) and the SFIO, the FEN and the PS, the CFDT and the *deuxième gauche* then the PS,[9] the *Confédération générale des cadres* (CGC) and parts of the Gaullist movement, and—as we have seen—the CFTC and the Mouvement des républicains populaires (MRP).

Nevertheless these kinds of relationships between trade unions and political parties are by no means confined to France. Indeed, the links several European and Western trade union bodies enjoy with political parties actually appear to be even closer. In England, the Labour Party grew out of the TUC, and even today its influence within the party is greater than that of any French trade union on a political party. By way of example, the TUC, apart from being an important source of Labour Party funding, controls a third of the votes when the party leader is selected. In Sweden, their welfare state model has relied upon the close alliance between the trade unions—LO—and the Social Democratic Party. The influence German trade unionism exerted on the Sozial-demokratische Partei Deutschlands (SPD) and the role that US trade unions played in the life of the Democratic Party are also well documented.[10] In other countries, there are many other examples of these kinds of links: the relations that exist between French trade unions and political parties are by no means unique. Indeed in some cases they appear to be less close than in other national contexts.

A Long Dominant Factor: Ideology

In fact the specificity of the relationship between French trade unions and politics lies elsewhere. While the kinds of links they have with political parties may be observed in many other national contexts, the same cannot be said for French trade unions' visions of society and in particular their attitudes toward capitalism and the market economy. Most European trade unions, including those with social democratic roots, have long since accepted the principle of needing to work within the market economy. Some have even accepted that its "redistributive" mechanisms are more effective than those which used to operate in the state interventionist economies of Eastern Europe. By contrast, the main French trade unions—the CGT in particular but also the CFDT in the 1970s—operated on two levels: they campaigned on a day-to-day basis for improvements in working conditions in companies and in the market economy in general, while at the same time articulating a revolutionary, anti-capitalist vision for the future.[11] Therefore the engagement of French trade unions with politics is not limited to their direct and immediate relations with political parties. Their "politics" were highly ideological and focused less on cultivating links with political parties than trying to envisage alternatives to the existing social arrangements.[12]

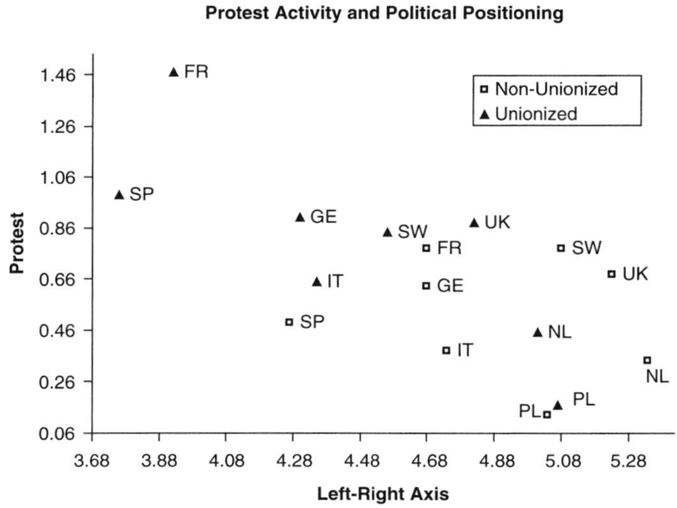

Figure 7.1 Protest activity and position on the political spectrum

The deeply ideological nature of French trade unionism has long been one of its defining characteristics. It explains both the long-established propensity of French trade unions to challenge authority, and their close links with those left wing parties who are critical of capitalism and the market economy. The survival of ideology, as an important part of the cultural and political heritage of trade unionism in France, is all the more striking when we compare the situation in France with other European countries, using data from the European Social Survey. In fact, if we take a protest indicator calculated from four variables—taking part in a demonstration in the previous twelve months, signing a petition, boycott of a product for political reasons, participation in an illegal protest—and map it against positioning on the left-right political spectrum, two observations can be made. First, French trade unions are, and by a wide margin, the most likely to engage in protest activities, and also among the most left wing (in this regard they contrast most sharply with Dutch trade unionists). Second, of all the countries in the survey, the difference between unionized and non-unionized workers is the greatest in France (figure 7.1).

Beyond the Parties: Trade Unionism and The State

Apart from the ideological agenda of French trade unions, which has distinguished them from unions in other European countries, the other unique characteristic of the trade union movement in France has been its close ties with the State, and the high degree of political and legal regulation of French industrial relations. In fact, it is arguable that the nature of relations between trade unions and political parties has ultimately been molded by State interventionism, and by the conception that the unions have had of the State. In this context, "union-party" links were strengthened by the fact that they were "instrumentalised" by the powerful French state. In other words, when we talk about the relationship of trade unions with "politics," the term "politics" encompasses three registers, of which one is dominant: the register of political parties, the register of the legislator, and finally the principal and hegemonic register of the State.

Certainly, in the postwar period many of the countries which now make up the European Union had well developed welfare states and pursued Keynesian policies. This led to agreements between employers and unions being reached which were redistributive in effect.[13] Nevertheless, French industrial relations, as well as being guided by certain welfare state principles inspired by Keynesianism, also displayed characteristics linked to France's specific historical circumstances. One defining characteristic of postwar French industrial relations was the prominent influence which the *Conseil National de la Résistance* (CNR) exerted on the State's social policy.

An Enduring Legacy: The Conseil National de la Résistance

The State's adoption of a central role in the regulation of industrial relations resulted from a set of circumstances which prevailed after the Liberation. The CNR's program was introduced in the mid-1940s with the full support of the two biggest French trade unions—the CGT and the CFTC—and almost all of the political parties represented in the parliament: Gaullists, Socialists, Communists, and Christian Democrats. Indeed, although the coalition of political parties and trade unions was subsequently undermined during the Cold War, one legacy of the CNR—the preeminent role of the State in the development of labor relations—established after the Liberation, was not seriously called into question until the 1980s, and could even be detected in certain measures taken in 1997 and 1998.

Immediately after the Liberation, the State enacted legislation and introduced reforms which prioritized the general interest over the interests of political groups. On September 12, 1944, in a meeting of the CNR at the Palais de Chaillot, General de Gaulle made speech which laid out his conception of what constitutes the public interest.[14] Laws were passed to set up systems of worker representation in firms (staff representatives, works committees, health and safety pension committees); social welfare coverage (sickness benefits, pension schemes)[15]; the fixing by the State of minimum wage rates and the hierarchical classification of workers following collective bargaining negotiations (1945–1950). In the 1960s and 1970s legislation was passed to regulate the following: workers' sharing of company profits; unemployment benefit systems; the creation of unions within private firms; and the consultation of the social partners over working conditions. At the beginning of the 1980s, after the left took power, there was an increase in legislative activity, as laws were passed regarding, inter alia, the following matters: the definition of the obligations of employees regarding collective bargaining; the obligation to consult trade unions when new production technologies were introduced; the right of employees to be consulted about their working conditions; the procedures to be followed by unions and management regarding professional training of employees; the reduction in the length of the working week to 39 hours.

All things considered, the intervention of the State and the application of the law have been varied and far-reaching, extending to all areas of employment negotiations and trade union activity. Consistently high levels of State involvement in major industrial relations reform, underpinned by the legitimacy of a government elected by universal suffrage, is clearly a preeminent characteristic of French industrial relations. Nevertheless, the extent of state intervention in France cannot be wholly explained by the fact that the government has a judicial legitimacy. The presence in France of a large nationalized sector, characterized, from the 1950s until quite recently, by collective bargaining agreements and innovative industrial relations, partly accounts for the high levels of state interventionism.[16] Another factor is cultural: French people across the political spectrum are broadly in favor of the State playing a central role. These convictions are deep and long-standing, and were recently confirmed by opinion polls which revealed that 92% of French people are still in favor of the development of public services.[17]

Another factor, more directly related to the French trade unionism, which helps account for the prominent role of the state in the regulation of industrial relations, is the historic weakness of French trade unions. This weakness has frequently prevented unions from having their demands met, especially at the company level. Changes in the length of the working week provide an illustration of this. In 1977 the CFDT, followed by the CGT in 1978, made the adoption of the 35 hour week a priority. Nevertheless, these demands failed to win sufficient support among the work force and were not met until 1998, and only then as a result of legislation. So the law and State intervention compensate for the weakness of the unions, imposing changes to the social contract which the unions on their own would have failed to obtain.[18] In this context, the law takes precedence over collective bargaining, legislation trumps contractual terms, and political and legal regulations take precedence over both regulations drawn up in the workplace by the social partners, and over "autonomous regulations."[19]

The Mid-1980s: A Turning Point

The historical traditions which underpinned relations between unions and the State, and French industrial relations in general, were increasingly called into question from the middle of the 1980s onward. At the root of this, and the subsequent redefinition of the links between collective bargaining and the law, was the deep political and social crisis of 1983 and 1984. Despite the state's voluntarist policies, unemployment continued to rise and inflation remained high. Public debt was also high, and the balance of trade deficit had, according to many experts, hit record heights. There were divisions within the government of Pierre Mauroy over the social and economic consequences of policies which, inspired by "left-wing Keynesianism," aimed to use redistributive measures to boost salaries and purchasing power, in order to stimulate consumption and so create growth and jobs. Dissenting members of the government argued for certain reforms to be put on hold, and austerity measures were introduced regarding, in particular, pay awards. In July 1984, with the departure of the communist ministers and the arrival of Laurent Fabius as the prime minister, economic and social relations policy took on a new direction. Some commentators were quick to label the new approach "left-wing Barrism," named after Raymond Barre, a former prime minister who favored economic liberalism: the government now appeared to be aiming to "rehabilitate business" and stimulate growth and job creation through encouraging investment rather than increasing purchasing power.[20] The failure of the government policies of the early 1980s led, in the field of labor relations, to the relationship between the law and professional bargaining to be severely called into question, across the political spectrum and by governments, until well into the 1990s.

At the beginning of 1986, the Delebarre law relating to the length of the working week, marked a departure from well-established French tradition. This piece of legislation—unlike the laws passed in 1936, 1968 and 1982—did not impose rules on companies regarding how many hours employees were to work, but rather established a framework for negotiation between the social partners, with a view to passing a collective agreement which would stipulate how the law would be applied. This type of legislation is an incitative law, as opposed to a mandatory law.[21] Shortly afterward, Philippe Séguin, the Employment Minister in the new Chirac government, introduced regulations abolishing the administrative authorization of redundancies which had been in place since the mid-70s. As a concession, works councils were granted new prerogatives, giving them more contractual powers regarding jobs and social benefits linked to job cuts. The long-standing dispensatory agreements relating to night work by women led to Parliament, under the Jospin government, calling into question the law that had hitherto banned such work, and a national collective agreement about professional training inspired the most recent legal provisions in this area, in a law passed by the Raffarin government.

In this general context, the Aubry laws on the 35 hour week may be seen in a particular light. On the one hand, as we have seen, they used the State and legislation to compensate for the weakness of the trade unions, and the unions' inability to enter into negotiations with the employers over the 35 hour week. On the other hand, however, the Aubry laws also reflect perfectly the unprecedented, ambiguous relations which were developing between the law and the social partners. In fact, in order to ensure their own smooth passage, the Aubry laws—inspired by many company-level agreements—called into question several areas of French labor law.[22] In this way, between the first Aubry law and the final piece of legislation, which was passed in 2000, local level agreements contributed to the modification of important parts of labor law, including the status of overtime in the context of the annualization of working hours, the standardization of the minimum wage (SMIC), the representativity of the written agreements relating to company referenda, and the working hours of managers, etc.

Therefore new relationships between legislation and negotiated settlements have been established and have transformed, to varying degrees, traditional relations between trade unions and the State. Today these changes are conspicuous and all the more significant since they do not only result from the State's desire, for various reasons, to play a different role in the regulation of industrial relations. What some have called the "disengagement of the State" is also due to massive changes within business which lead to local level negotiation being preferred to regulation by legislation.

Business, the Individual, and the Market

The French business world is now dominated by two paradigms which give it a more capitalistic nature than it had in the past. On one hand is the individual, on the other the market. This state of affairs fundamentally changes both contractual negotiations and relations between trade unions and the State.

The Individual, or the Fragmentation of Negotiation

In the past, French trade unionism overlooked individual actors. Nevertheless, in three contexts—the management context, the contractual context, and the context of employee demands—the individual is a key player within industrial relations in companies, where the traditional mode of contractual relations between the company and the body of employees as a whole is in decline. This trend was examined as long ago as 1986 by Edmond Maire in an article which stressed the links between individuals and trade union action and went on to discuss business and anti-capitalism.[23] This text was premonitory, and was published at a pivotal moment between the two distinct periods of individualization of the business context which have marked the last thirty years. Indeed, the status of the individual in French companies has experienced major changes over this period, and its registers have been both modified and amplified.

The first phase of individualization policy took place during the 1970s and 1980s. Changes were made in a wide variety of policy areas—the introduction of flexible working hours, the individualization of salaries, the management of employees according to their skills rather than their qualifications—which were part of an overall employer strategy, implemented at local level and endorsed at conferences of the CNPF (the National Council of French Employers). One objective of policy changes of this period was to bypass collective bargaining procedures and avoid the kind of union involvement which could result in industrial conflicts.

The situation changed again in the 1990s, in a paradoxical way. Individualization practices within companies were not necessarily applied outside the contractual and collective sphere. The 70s and 80s were succeeded by a phase where agreements were individualized in a way which departed from traditional industrial relations practices. The individualization of certain kinds of agreement within companies is becoming increasingly widespread. Many agreements concerning the "time savings account" (a mechanism allowing wage-earners to get payment in lieu of holidays not taken), employee savings schemes, vocational training, or certain kinds of social protection are still made using traditional contractual procedures. Nevertheless, in their application agreements are increasingly adapted to individual requirements or requests, and can vary significantly according to individual circumstances.[24] Employees use the agreement in a variable, flexible and non-prescriptive way and the options or the choices defined by the employee—which vary depending on the employee's needs—can influence the final terms of the agreement. As Anne Flautre has shown, with regard to the "time savings account," details of the contents and application of agreements, which were once exclusively in the public sphere, can now originate in the private sphere.[25]

Individualization affects not only the formation of agreements, but also the formulation of demands themselves, which may or may not be related to the evolution of organizations' hierarchical practices. Now, questions of stress and harassment—of all levels of employee including managers[26]—are mentioned in employment agreements and can give rise to workplace disputes. Nevertheless, here again the methods and procedures actually used for dealing with these kinds of disputes are not governed by clauses in the employment contract. On the one hand, negotiations take place within bargaining institutions and established collective bodies (trade unions, companies). They produce rules which are frequently based on common principles. Nevertheless, it is often the case that these common rules, once defined, can only be applied to the employees they cover in particular or "individualized" ways. As one psychiatrist observed, during the 2002 European Week for Health and Safety at Work during which the focus of discussions was stress and stress-related psychosocial risks: "Employees feel that they are all in the same boat, but at the same time extremely isolated."[27] Therefore the paradigm of the individual—as embodied in various managerial, contractual, and industrial dispute practices—has fundamentally modified the links which used to characterize relations between collective bargaining and the law. Such a paradigm leads to specific agreements which are applied in an increasing variety of ways, and give rise to demands which are often related to the subjectivity of employees. This context seems particularly ill-suited to regulation by legislation, since laws seek the objectivation of working conditions, as well as the establishment of practices and methods of application which follow overriding and consistent principles.

The Market or Institutionalized Instability

As well as being undermined by the privatization of collective agreements and certain kinds of industrial dispute resolution, the links between professional negotiation and the law are also affected by the redefinition of the workplace with relation to the production process and the market. In fact, the workplace was governed for an extended period by the particular conditions created by the development of capitalism. Indeed, for many historians, at an early stage in their development capitalist firms went through a major transformation. They changed from being organizations which responded to demand to adopting practices which centered on the "act of production."[28] In this context the producer is the dominant actor and companies begin to operate differently. Entrepreneurs no longer aim to adapt their industrial strategy to the vicissitudes of existing demand, as artisans had done. Their objective became to stimulate and even shape the nature and extent of demand. The advent of Fordism added momentum to this trend. A Fordist factory is a place "where exchanges with the outside are limited and controlled and the states can be predictable in terms of probabilities."[29] The market is characterized by the primacy of production and hence of the producer.[30] In this context, the world of work and the trade unions were at the heart of labor bargaining in companies and the agreements, which were the fruit of these negotiations, were solidly grounded in the law, referring as they did to powerful production collectives and highly standardized salary structures and working conditions. In this sense, for a long time Fordism went hand in hand with Keynesianism.[31]

Today another trend is in the ascendancy, as the results of numerous empirical surveys have shown. Perhaps the most important of these surveys was organized at the end of the 1990s, covering thirty-five employment sectors and involving 60,000 individuals. Commenting on these results, Yves Lichtenberger[32] remarked upon "a shift in the molding of work" before observing:

> Work was previously determined top-down by the operating methods and the technical norms related to conformity with product specifications and processes; it is now more often driven bottom-up by considerations such as client and user requirements and the quality of the services provided.[33]

Naturally, such a switch of perspectives has had an impact on industrial disputes and collective bargaining. It has caused a profound diversification of the structures of business and, once again, a calling into question of the relations between negotiation and the law, and hence a calling into question of the traditional representations of the trade unions in relation to the legislator.

Previously, relations between negotiations and the law were clearer because the contexts within which they operated were stable, long-term and clearly defined, as were the varieties of standardized production which shaped the industrial economy between the 1930s and the mid-1980s. In other words, the existence of such relations grew out of the basic need for stable socio-economic contexts. Nowadays, the threat to such contexts has undermined the political relations which produced the legal or generally applied rules on which company collective agreements were based. The way the Aubry laws on the 35 hour week and the recent Fillon law on collective bargaining have operated demonstrates that legislation is becoming increasingly difficult to apply. Many regulations, when they are actually applied in companies, are of limited effectiveness.[34] Basically, now the context within which labor relations and contractual relations operate has been radically transformed. The rules governing employment relationships and company regulations operate within contexts which are unstable and in a state of flux. Such contexts cannot be adequately regulated by rules which are designed to be fixed, even rigid, and apply over an extended period of time. The impact of new technologies in the workplace, changes in the way work is organized, and the nature of the new skills employees need to master have all contributed to the instability of working practices. Companies today operate within ever shorter cycles of accelerating obsolescence,[35] leading to a rejection of "the main guidelines which were formerly used to govern employment relationships."[36] Now regulations are more hybrid than ever, and terms of employment are increasingly defined by the employment contract, rather than legislation. Another consequence of accelerating change is the emergence of subtle interactions between legislation and local regulations. This entails a radical transformation of relations between collective bargaining agreements, trade unions, the State and the law, and gives company-level negotiations a more central role, which can have problematic consequences.

An Ambivalent Social Context

Both the fixed criteria which applied to former systems of organization and the criteria which standardized working conditions often failed to take account of individual circumstances. Their application has been replaced by local and company level negotiations. Interestingly, although the introduction of widespread company-level collective bargaining arrived later in France than in other European countries, it is now very well established, particularly regarding negotiations over salaries. This has been confirmed by a number of Eurofound and OECD studies. France, in common with the United Kingdom, is the European country where wage negotiations are most likely to held in companies and where negotiations are less coordinated at other levels. In other words France is one of the countries where company negotiations have a high degree of autonomy. According to a 2004 European Commission report on employment negotiations, which established an index of wage bargaining coordination, France obtained the lowest score among EU countries. France's index of 0.12 put it just below the United Kingdom (0.13), and well behind countries such as Germany (0.47), Denmark (0.47), and Belgium (0.61).[37]

Increasingly autonomous company-level negotiations now play a central role, whereas the importance of other kinds of collective bargaining (at sector, branch, and interprofessional levels) and employment law are have declined.[38] What are the consequences of these changes on French trade unionism?

In fact the above changes have resulted in highly ambivalent situations. On the one hand, the decentralization of the French system of collective bargaining has fundamentally modified the relations which traditionally existed between the State and trade unions. In the long run, it may also greatly modify the representations and protest strategies of unions. Being constantly and more directly confronted with company-level problems, unions may abandon some of the ideological preoccupations which dominated their thinking in the past—and still, to a certain extent, survive to this day[39]—and adopt approaches which are more pragmatic and realistic from an economic point of view. If this is the case, and French trade unions become progressively more reformist, they will move closer to those European trade unions—of broadly social democratic persuasion—which comprise the European Trade Union Confederation (ETUC).[40] Indeed, unions like the CFDT are already well placed to make this transition.

On the other hand, the rapid development of company-level negotiations could well constitute a danger for trade unions, whose power is already greatly diminished. We have here a typically French paradox. In fact, as company-level negotiations become increasingly autonomous they are less subject to legal regulation. At the same time the trade unions are weak, and made even more vulnerable by the absence of the legislative protection which they previously enjoyed. The unions no longer have close relations with the State and now that their weakness is no longer compensated for by labor law provisions, they find themselves in difficult bargaining positions in company-level negotiations, particularly in small and medium sized companies but latterly also in large firms.

The current situation is clear: negotiations are less subject to legal regulation but more vulnerable to market forces; the trade union movement is as weak and divided as ever, and the State has, over the last twenty years or more, become less and less involved in the regulation of relations between unions and management. These factors help to explain the why many observers rightly regard industrial relations as being deadlocked, and in crisis. The various analyses offered by union activists, politicians and management—of the representativity of trade unions, the legitimacy of written agreements, or the priority given to collective bargaining by successive major labor law reforms[41]—have so far had little impact on a state of affairs which seems increasingly beyond the control of all parties involved.

Notes

1. Groux and Pernot, 2008.
2. All percentages quoted in this chapter have been rounded up or down to the nearest whole number.
3. Visser, 2006.
4. The French trade unions failed to capitalize on the favorable political climate created by the succession of left wing governments which were in power throughout this period, with the exception of the 1986 to 1988 cohabitation.
5. Julliard, 1988; Lefranc, 1967 inter alia.
6. It should be noted that in the 1960s and in particular the 1970s the CFDT was well-established among skilled workers, many of whom were immigrants who had no affinity with Christian trade unionism (Groux and Mouriaux, 1989).
7. The *Mouvement des républicains populaires* (MRP) was for a long time the political party closest to the CFTC.
8. The ITUC was founded on November 1, 2006 and incorporates the ICFTU—a product of the cold war era—the WCL—which was a branch of the International Trade Union movement, as well as other organizations, hitherto without international affiliation, such as the French CGT.
9. The post-1974 PS, which emerged from the "Assises du socialisme."
10. There are many other examples we could quote. It should be noted, however, that recent research by Jean-Marie Pernot revealed that in many European countries relations between unions and political parties have been in decline, including in

those countries where, historically, such ties have been particularly close (Pernot, 2005, p. 144 onward).

11. Today SUD is attempting—with limited success—to revitalize the revolutionary tradition which, though typical of French trade unionism, is also well established in a number of the Latin countries of Europe.
12. Did other trade unions unconsciously copy the CGT, or did they feel obliged to imitate it, given the context the French trade union movement, in which the CGT long exercised a degree of hegemony? Other French trade unions also attempted to articulate alternative visions of society, although on a modest scale and along more reformist lines. The CGC, for example, introduced the concept of the "économie concertée" and the CFTC proposed reforms which variously drew on principles of subsidiarity, community, or planism.
13. Boyer, 1986.
14. General de Gaulle had this to say about the general interest and the role of the State:

    To sum up the principles which will underlie the policies of France as a nation, we would say that while guaranteeing the maximum amount of liberty for all, and seeking to always nurture the spirit of free enterprise, our country will ensure that private interests always be required to give way to the public interest, that the great sources of common wealth will be exploited and run not for the benefit of a few, but for all, and that the coalitions of interest, which have had so much influence on the lives of individuals and even on State policies, shall be abolished, once and for all. (L'Année Politique, 1944–1945, p. 441)
15. Palier, 2002.
16. Groux, 2000.
17. BVA-Le Figaro-LCI opinion poll.
18. Naturally, as we will see below, this aspect of relations between the law and union demands remains at the heart of debate about industrial relations, despite important transformations in French collective bargaining procedures.
19. Reynaud, 1997; Terssac, 2003.
20. "Vive la crise"—a television program made by, among others Laurent Joffrin and Alain Minc, and presented by Yves Montand—remains particularly representative of the (political and social) atmosphere which prevailed at the time.
21. Amadieu and Groux, 1999.
22. The first law formed the basis for negotiations at a local level over how the law would be applied in companies. In the two years between the first and second pieces of legislation 45,000 company-level agreements were signed.
23. Maire, 1986.
24. See Roblain [2006], regarding the importance of the treatment of individual cases in large organizations such as the French Post Office.
25. Flautre, 2002.
26. See the surveys on stress and harassment of managers carried out by CFDT-Cadres and the CGC.
27. *Le Monde*, October 22, 2002.
28. Verley, 1997.
29. Jocou and Meyer, 1996.
30. It is well known that a Ford client was free to choose the color of his car, providing it was black.
31. Members of the French school of salary regulation have clearly demonstrated this.

32. Lichtenberger, 1998.
33. To client and user may be added other actors such as shareholders, NGOs etc., actors present in the company environment whose actions increasingly influence the content of local collective agreements. In this regard, see the work of the MIT Group (Kochan et al., 1986) and their critique of more classic versions of the theory of professional relations and collective bargaining such as Dunlop's, which assumed the existence of a unionized system. For a pioneering approach to professional relations and the need to produce "common rules" in business, see also the Webbs (Dunlop, 1993; Webb, 1965).
34. It is worth noting, here, that the Fillon law on collective bargaining resulted in fewer legal constraints being imposed on the formulation of agreements within companies.
35. Boissonnat, 1995.
36. Also see Gavini, 1998.
37. This data was cited by Jean-Paul Jacquier, 2006. Also see Jean-Marie Pernot who analyses the development of company-level negotiations in France by focusing on certain trade union strategies of "accompaniment" (Pernot, 2005, p.177).
38. See above re the Fillon law on social dialogue.
39. See figure 7.1.
40. See Richard Hyman's major survey of the evolution of European trade unions (2001).
41. This central role of collective bargaining has been enshrined in EU law since the Maastricht Treaty entered into force, and was reiterated by Jacques Chirac in October 2006, in a speech to the French Economic and Social Council.

CHAPTER 8

The Political and Administrative Elites

Luc Rouban

The question of elites is as old as democracy itself. Can a political system that is dominated by a number of social groups who have privileged access to resources and positions of power be regarded as democratic? The idea that the people's choices are in some way betrayed by those whose job it is to take or implement decisions, namely politicians and civil servants, undermines the legitimacy and the legitimation of governments of whatever political stripe. Debates about political elites always come down to the question of the location of political power, namely who really has their hands on the levers of power? Can we not detect, behind the scenes, the presence of hidden power networks, communities of individuals operating on the basis of mutual friendship, social contacts, and common backgrounds, who set the terms of the democratic debate, either by orienting it in their own interests or reducing it to hollow declarations of principle which have little impact on the real business of government? We can go further and ask what is the point of so-called political competition if, right across the political spectrum, we find the same kinds of people, with the same social and educational backgrounds taking all the important decisions? These questions are being asked throughout Europe, and with increasing urgency, as globalization and the growing power of the financial economy lead to doubts being raised about the effectiveness, even the usefulness of current representation mechanisms.

These dissenting voices have been joined by systematic critiques of the French state, which has for centuries—and through numerous regime changes—remained both the breeding ground for elites and the integrating force of civil society. When critics express misgivings about state elites, already a national sport when France had a monarchy,[1] they draw on a wide variety of sometimes contradictory arguments. Some or all of the following long list of allegations are regularly leveled at French elites: they are all cast in the same mould and live and operate in worlds which are cut off from the broader society, they have no qualms about abandoning public service for senior positions in the private sector, they epitomize a social model in which academic excellence is a prerequisite of upward social mobility, they accumulate privileges which leave them protected from social constraints, their reproduction is unaffected by economic changes, and they control social policy as well as regulating the world of work. The charges made against the elites often contradict themselves: elites are variously accused of being parasites, of having the real power in society, and of being both changeable and unchangeable. Recent surveys have shown that criticism of elites in France has intensified in recent years.[2]

The question of elites had remained closely linked with populism, which denounces the monopolization of power by a minority at the expense of the majority, and defines itself as anti-elitist.[3] Populist discourses have enjoyed increasing prominence since the 1980s with the rise of the Extreme Right, and have been fuelled by a succession of high profile *affaires*—involving irregularities in party financing, local authority housing policy, and misuse of company property in some of France's biggest firms, and so on—which exposed corrupt activities by members of both public and private sector elites. Nevertheless, the real question mark hanging over France's elites has to do with their utility, not just their probity: what useful purpose can these deputies, ministers, high officials and captains of industry be said to serve, especially when many of them have shown themselves to be incompetent? Haven't these forms of social power, which have been in place since the nineteenth century, been rendered obsolete by the rise of globalize information exchange? Indeed, attitudes of French citizens to corruption vary greatly: recent research has shown that many people would be happy to turn a blind eye to a certain amount of greasing of palms.[4]

In France, populism has become a term used to reject out of hand any popular complaint voiced by extremists, to the point where it is used to avoid seriously addressing any demand originating from less privileged sections of society—now including parts of the middle classes—regarding such issues as unemployment, off-shoring, and ethnic tensions. All sections of the media have joined in the widespread condemnation of populism, consolidating the media's role as the arbiter of political debate, and arguably also one of the main pillars of the system of elites.

The discourse about and around the elites is therefore not only concerned with condemning them. It also involves a process of constructing boundaries between those who are regarded as constituting the elites, and those who are not. One of the clearest trends of the last few years, with the increase in the number of elections, has been the absorption of the media into the French elites. Far from indicating a liberalization of public space, the "coziness" of the relationship between the media and political power is evidenced by the fact that in France politicians and journalists move in the same social circles to a degree unheard of in other European democracies, the overlap between these two worlds even resulting in marriages between prominent politicians and journalists.

The anti-elitist discourse, like its mirror image the elitist discourse ("the masses are too stupid to be consulted directly, so referenda are to be avoided"), experienced a revival in the context of debates about European integration, the role of scientific expert opinion in public decision-making, and electoral abstentionism. In 2005 the debate around the treaty establishing a constitution for Europe essentially set two groups in opposition to each other. The first group was made up of those who interpreted a "no" vote as indicative of lack of education and a failure to understand the realities of globalization, the second group saw the defeat of the treaty as a popular victory and a rejection of the machinations of the state and private sector elites, who they accused of using Europe as a stalking horse for their project to liberalize Europe.

The critical views taken of the elites and the people (referred to as "listeners," "citizens," "those who are watching us" etc.), which reduce them to homogenous blocs, reinforces the process of caricaturing one's enemies which is a fundamental part of political life. In France, however, stigmatization is used to the extent that it has replaced proper debate about the ideas enshrined in political programs. Such ideas are no longer discussed but rejected out of hand because they originate from an enemy, judged to be either too elitist or too populist. France, unlike most European countries, therefore still has a categorical vision according to which power networks are structured by debates about ideas, leading inevitably to the rejection of individuals whose ideas are different from one's own. This situation is poles apart from the consensual political culture of Scandinavian-type social democracies, which are so often held up as a model to be imitated.

In every country debate about elites gives rise to questions which concern the way democracy functions: is what is required a change of personnel or a change of decision-making processes? Given that a series of governments have failed to resolve the crisis of confidence in politicians, should the French constitution be changed? Would a new political regime result in a change of the elites? Bloody revolutions in the twentieth century—in Cambodia, China, and Russia—proved this could be done, but only at the cost of millions of lives. Liberal democracies prefer to engineer change by embracing new ideas or reforming their legal systems, rather than replacing individuals. A distinction should, however, be drawn here between individuals and social groups: while the former are generally dispensable, the latter are less so. The change of government in France in 1981 had little effect on the traditional administrative elites, and the Socialist Party, like their RPR predecessors, continued to be heavily reliant on the advice of senior officials.[5]

Another question, typically French given the importance of the Ministry of Education within the French state (half the 2.2 million non-military state employees are teachers), concerns the education and training of future elites. There are whole libraries full of reports and surveys which seek to shed light on the following question: which is preferable, a broad education in the humanities which produces generalists who can turn their hand to anything, or a system which trains specialists to carry out specific functions which have a clear economic utility? Despite well-intentioned attempts to widen access to candidates of all social backgrounds, sociological research shows that a system which produces generalists, such as the one which future politicians and high

Table 8.1 The proportion of salaried employees who have a high level of trust in politicians (%)

	GE	*SP*	*FR*	*UK*	*IT*	*NL*	*PL*	*SW*
Managers	22	27	26	19	17	49	7	51
Intermediary professions	18	20	22	23	29	50	10	49
Workers and salaried employees	14	13	15	20	14	37	6	31

Source: ESS, 2003.

ranking officials now pass through, tends to favor candidates from well-to-do backgrounds whose inter-personal skills can mask a lack of technical competence. Despite this, technocrats are also commonly criticized for being too specialized.

The French context therefore displays the following three characteristics: the involvement of intellectual labor in the construction of political conflicts and social status, the astonishing resilience of France's administrative and political elites, and a volontarist conception of the formation of elites which aims to promote social mobility (part of the state's role is to manufacture social elites). Although this historical model is undeniably strong, it has come under heavy criticism in recent years, indicating a widening gulf between France's political elites and the French people. There seems to be a crisis of confidence in elected officials not only in France but throughout Europe, with the exception of countries like the Netherlands and Sweden. The levels of trust enjoyed by politicians in Germany and Spain, for example, are hardly any different from those found in France, despite the fact that these countries have federal or highly decentralized political systems, which should favor the establishment of new local elites (table 8.1).

Looking for a Definition

The notion of a politico-administrative elite encompasses not only the idea of a more or less integrated social group, and therefore the idea of a ruling class which dominates the whole of society, but also an interaction process which is relatively complex and capable of evolving over time, bringing together two types of actor, politicians, and civil servants, whose resources and ability to act vary at different points in time. As they interact, elites can be exposed to new ideas and practices which help them to adapt to changing circumstances. It was in this way that pre-war French technocrats, organized around the senior branches of the civil service—in particular the Inspection des Finances (the department of the Treasury responsible for auditing public bodies)—were able to promote Keynesian economic theory at a time when it was still little known in either French government circles or academia. If elites wish to survive, they have to evolve, and to do so they need to be capable of taking on board and absorbing new concepts.

We now come to the question of what constitutes an elite. The many definitions which have been proposed[6] are far from satisfactory, either because they fail to draw a clear distinction between elites and the upper classes, or because membership of an elite is determined on a case by case basis depending on particular decision-making powers. The definition of an elite we would propose is a social group which is, over an extended period of time, in a position to draw on a greater variety of resources (economic, cultural, network of contacts, etc.) than other social groups, and is therefore able to impose an institutional and doctrinal order which serves their members' interests, putting them in a position to define, among other things, . . . what constitutes an elite. The institutional order organizes the way careers and promotion prospects in the political and administrative milieus are mapped out. It also allows social practices to be articulated in a way that serves to legitimate the political regime (by emphasizing the scientific nature of the state or the pluralistic nature of decision-making, etc.).[7]

The notion of an elite, therefore, encompasses three main characteristics. First, it describes a collective entity: an elite is not made up of a number of isolated individuals but is a community with particular norms governing recruitment and conceptions of what constitutes excellence. This holds true for political, economic, and artistic elites. It is therefore important not to confuse members of political or administrative elites with the holders of decision-making powers. Groups of experts or civil servants who move in very different circles from members of state elites can, on occasion, influence decision making or even take decisions themselves. Conversely, members of some elites groups—such as British royalty—sometimes have no real power to influence society. In other words, contrary to conventional wisdom, being powerful and being a member of an elite are two quite different things. Furthermore, elites establish themselves over an extended period of time. The French administrative elites were formed over two or three centuries in the corridors of first the scientific "grandes écoles" like the Ecole Polytechnique and, more recently, in schools for high-ranking civil servants and the top business schools. So, in many respects, an elite is an institution, which means that a debate about elites is also a debate about the history of elites.

The second characteristic of the notion of an elite is that it is not an absolute term. There are hierarchies between and within elites: some elites are, so to speak, more elite than others. For example, until recently, within the senior branches of the civil service a hierarchy was respected whereby, after graduation, the top students from the Ecole nationale d'administration (ENA) chose to work in the department of the Treasury responsible for auditing public bodies (L'Inspection des Finances). The next most prestigious posts were at the State Council and the Court of Accounts, followed by posts of civil administrator in the Ministry of Finance. Becoming a prefect, the Fifth Republic's representative of the "power of the State" at a departmental or regional level, was, on the other hand, a job generally reserved for middle-ranking ENA graduates. Within this general hierarchy, other hierarchies were established: senior branches of the civil service contained their own elite circles. A member of the Inspection des Finances who has a brilliant career at the head of a financial group would enjoy more personal prestige than someone who remains an auditor for the whole of their working life, for example. In different social contexts, different criteria are used for measuring success. Subtle details, whose full meaning only an informed insider would appreciate, can make all the difference. This is why most of the constant criticism of the "enarchy" and the power of high-ranking French civil servants often misses its target and raises a smile from those "in the know."

Finally, the third characteristic of elites is that, almost by definition, they are the object of criticism and questioning. From where do they derive their legitimacy? Do these groups represent concentrations of excellence, recognized by those who are excluded from them, or is their reputation simply the result of power struggles and the weight of history? It is equally arguable elites serve a useful function within any given society. Certainly every European country has its own particular system of elites, although a general model with common shared features can be detected. The functions elites fulfill may be complex, and are the result of historic compromises between social groups. During the Third Republic, the political community included many graduates of the Ecole Normale Supérieure and *agrégés de lettres* (the cream of French teachers of literature).[8] Under the Fifth Republic this is no longer the case (members of these groups only constitute 1% of deputies). France's intellectual and literary elites are no doubt considered less qualified to supervise the modernization of the French economy than individuals from the business world or the senior ranks of the civil service. Whatever elements come together in the definition of elites, their legitimacy is always liable to be under attack since they have to be in a position to defend their privileged status and develop strategies which enable them to remain at the heart of decision-making processes. There is no such thing as a "natural elite": for elites to survive for any length of time they have to be constantly engaged in struggles to win public recognition and fight off the challenges of competitors.

Classic Explicatory Models of Elites and their Limitations

Debate about elites in France centers around two well-established schools of thought. The first, which we can call the oligarchic model, holds that modern societies have produced elites who, out of economic and social necessity, unite to form a ruling class. This analysis was systematically developed by Charles Wright Mills in his study of American elites,[9] in which he argues that those who occupy the command posts in the military, the federal government and major corporations share a similar background, know each other, mix socially, and constitute a power network where each individual in the course of their career contributes to the overall power of the group. This school of thought, which was heavily influenced by Marxism, includes the work of Pierre Bourdieu, who showed that the homogeneity of the ruling class develops within the context of a common culture.[10] Apart from its critique of the liberal model, this school of thought is characterized by the fact that it focuses on the functional role of elites, which tend to perpetuate themselves, adapting to the changing environment by multiplying their avatars.

This thesis is undeniably central to left-wing anti-liberal critiques of globalization. It also echoes clearly in the rhetoric of opposition to privatization programs and to the 1995 "Juppé plan" to revise public sector pension schemes. Defenders of French-style systems of public services, in which a vast public sector is largely protected from market forces, have consistently argued that the new power elite, constituted by the leaders of the financial and banking sectors, are in the process of displacing the administrative elites, hence narrowing the scope, and undermining the effectiveness of political decision-making. These trends are seen as consolidating the victory of the "*pensée unique*," according to which reform of the state is synonymous with cutting public spending and adapting to the logic of international finance.

The second school of thought proposes a pluralist model, an example of which can be found in the work of the American political scientist Robert Dahl.[11] Dahl's studies of the city of Newhaven showed that the city's various elite groups, far from agreeing on common strategies, were engaged in competition to define which policies should be adopted on a municipal level. Economic and political elites struggle to defend the interests of their respective constituencies. Pluralists focus on the processes of interaction between elites which determine the way political life is organized.

This school of thought informs recent theses regarding the rise of a kind of "governance" which would undermine the power of the nation state. Governance emerges from the interaction of the growing number of actors involved in the decision-making process: private companies, associations, and, of course, European and international bodies, which play an ever greater role in the formation of public policy. Under these circumstances, the state's monopoly is broken and it becomes just one actor among many. The authority of state elites is challenged by competing elites from the world of business or from the European Union, for example. Within this context, globalization is understood as a process of opening-up to the world, entailing a thorough reorganization of national elites, who must now strike compromises with new competitors. Elites may even have to adopt ways of thinking or cultures—such as management culture—that are far more well-established in business schools and in the universities of the English-speaking world than at ENA.

Neither of these two bodies of theory adequately explain the current evolution of elites. The pluralistic model is open to criticism for its failure to adequately consider the importance of the weight of history. Indeed the systems which produce national elites have been operating for decades, even centuries. Enabling graduates of ENA in France or Oxford in the United Kingdom to tackle the challenges created by globalization really only requires their training programs to be modified. Such curriculum changes will have little or no impact on the social profile of these elites, though. It is also worth re-iterating that social structures are highly resilient: in France it is not uncommon for a high-ranking civil servant to marry the son or daughter of a senior executive in the private sector. It is therefore necessary to take into account generational differences and the impact of intermarriage. Elites are not self-regenerating closed groups. Furthermore, claims by theorists of governance regarding the nation state's former monopoly on power are overstated. When the Third Republic was in its republican heyday the state already had to contend with powerful forces of opposition, such as the Catholic Church, and it was also weakened by internal rival networks, like the Freemasons.

The oligarchic model can also be criticized, on the grounds that elite membership profiles change over time. For example, from the eighteenth century onward membership of the wealth-based state elites was no longer the preserve of great landowners. Today, recent advances in technology have helped to break the state administration's monopoly on information. The Internet, in particular, has become a forum for the free circulation of non-official information and discourses, undermining the impact of efforts to reduce the press and other printed media into propagandists for the "*pensée unique*" in all its forms.

We can therefore suggest that a *system of elites* does exist, and that its make-up is complex and reliant on achieving a delicate balance between its various components. The system of elites is the product of alliances between groups whose strategies are susceptible to change. It is an evolving structure which nevertheless has the power to limit internal competition to manageable levels. No social group is either perfectly integrated, nor in position of omniscience and omnipotence. No elite group can afford to take its position for granted, and every group which wants to exert influence has to fight its corner.

The role of politics can be understood in this context. Far from being a mere by-product of social developments beyond its control, politics can have an impact, either by promoting certain values or facilitating the political participation of hitherto marginalized groups, as well as by attempting—if not always successfully—to create new alliances. In 1981 the Left came to power relying on the support of civil servants and espousing a secular philosophy of the civil service. In the 1990s, the Socialist Party worked closely with private enterprise toward the goal of European integration, in spite of the fact that employers had been openly critical of some policies of the left-wing government.

Moreover, the fact that there is no simple correlation between the social composition of elites and economic policy may be explained by the existence of internal power struggles within elite alliances. For example, an empirical study of presidential and prime ministerial advisors showed that the proportion of advisors with upper class backgrounds was 73% under the last Mauroy government, compared to 75% when Fabius was prime minister. So although Fabius's policies were far more liberal than those of his predecessor, the profile of his ministerial team was not significantly more "bourgeois." On the other hand, the corresponding figures for Raymond Barre's last government and Jacques Chirac's 1974 government were 79% and 63% respectively.[12]

The Construction of the French Model

Analysis of elite models in Europe must consider how they have developed over time. Manifesting themselves in both social structures and political representations, national models display relatively unchanging characteristics. Three factors need to be taken into consideration.

The particularity of the French system is the dominant presence of the state, which has built a system of elites as a way of constructing its own modernity on a solid social base. The modern state began to establish itself in the sixteenth century, in response to the problems of a fragmented society largely made up of *corps* and corporations. The struggle against feudalism and the affirmation of the state's central—even monopolistic—role are at the heart of this process. This history tends to position the state in opposition to civil society, and portrays the administration as being privileged and liable to operate in an overly authoritarian fashion.[13]

Faced with this construction of the state, different social strategies emerged. In France, administrative posts were occupied by the nobility. The system of *offices*, purchased at the royal treasury and often hereditary, allowed members of the wealthy merchant classes to become part of the nobility and so come into competition with the established aristocracy. The constitution of this *noblesse de robe* completed the separation between the political and administrative spheres. Under Louis XV, the parliamentary magistrates were locked in a ruthless struggle against the power of the king, blocking reforms and setting themselves up as the legitimate representatives and protectors of the nation against the abuses of the monarchy.[14] In other words, the field of state power was the object of fierce internal competition. In Great Britain, on the other hand, the nobility occupied posts in local government and business.

During the nineteenth century, the establishment of a centralized civil service made up of professionals recruited by competitive examination served two purposes: to isolate the political forces that were competing with the monarchy and later the republic and, in particular, local government, and to confer legitimacy on the civil service by branding it as an agent of upward social mobility for the lower classes. This explains why in France today joining the civil service is still regarded as a way of taking a step up socially.

A third factor is related to political philosophy. In all European countries there is tension between social representation and political representation, which manifests itself in the struggle between society's "natural" elites (the institutionalized pressure groups, the professions) and "artificial" elites (elected representatives in democratic regimes). In fact, two contrasting ideas of who are the best guarantors of state legitimacy emerge. On the one hand, there is the "organic" idea, which regards the communities or professional corporations as the expression of the nation as a whole. This was the position of the French parliaments of the Ancien Regime but it was also the position of those who proclaimed since the early years of the Third Republic on the basis of a solidarist philosophy that the public service has to be regarded as the guarantor of national solidarity, enabling public control of networks of services. The genius of French elites has been to manage to present themselves as the natural expression of an immanent and eternal state. This doctrine was re-enforced by Gaullism. The other, opposing, position is based on the liberal idea that elected representatives are there to protect the general interest, in much the same way as a professional person acts in their client's interests. These representatives of the people can be voted out of their job, unlike civil servants, and are more independent of power struggles within society. The political elite emerges after a period of deliberation followed by an election, but also after genuine political activity. In such a system, elected representatives are obliged to establish their legitimacy. The systems of elites and democratic systems are therefore linked, even if most European countries follow a mixed model which can reflect the prominent roles played by the state (as in France), the business world (as in Great Britain), or religious communities (as in the Netherlands). The preservation of the institution of the monarchy has also enabled several countries to identify and to control the "organic" part of political life.

This balance between the two poles of the theory of representation depends on two variables which are in fact veritable anthropological structures. The first is religion and the second is the nature of relations between state and society.

In Catholic countries, the structure of power is alternately populist (this was the case at the time of the French Revolution, but also during the Fascist period in Italy) and hierarchic (for a long period a democratic system where only payers of a poll tax could vote prevailed, consolidating the power of the notables). We can therefore understand why the systems of *grandes écoles* and civil service corps—which operate in Spain as well as France—are particularly resilient, combining as they do the idea of a meritocracy open to all with the idea of a social order which sanctions a natural hierarchy. Protestant countries, on the other hand, develop the theory of a contract and the notion of community. Political and administrative elites are held accountable for both their results and their moral conduct. Scandals like the "affaire Gaymard," which involved a French minister arguing that, as a servant of the state, he was perfectly entitled to enjoy certain privileges—in this case receiving a rent allowance of 14,000 euros a month, in addition to being provided with a flat which went with his job –, happen far less frequently in a Protestant countries. In Sweden, if the slightest suspicion arose that an official was taking advantage of his or her position for material gain, however modest, he or she would be expected to resign immediately. The idea of community, on the other hand, based on the complete religious and cultural freedom of the individual, leads to positive discrimination policies being implemented. Such policies aim to achieve a balanced ethnic, religious, and social mix within the elites, which ideally should reflect the composition of society in all its diversity.

Furthermore, relations between the state and society explain why political power and public action are interpreted differently from one country to the next. In France a corporate logic is applied: active support for those in power brings collective privileges. This idea is at the heart of decentralization. The fact that the state is the principal social integrating force and that civil servants are representatives of the state explains the French public law tradition as well as the existence of a special administrative legal system under the supervision of the State Council. So, in France the work of the political classes involves both the distribution of corporatist advantages and the promotion of national-republican integration. This takes us back to the volontarist conception of political power, according to which the role of the political authorities is to impose policy on forces in society which are stubbornly protective of their autonomy. In Great Britain and the Scandinavian countries, on the other hand, politics is principally about obtaining the consent of the people. The role of the state is to arbitrate between rival interest groups in society. The administration works in the public interest, not the *Rechtsstaat*: civil servants work for the government and not the state; the common law is widely used and management culture replaces the culture of public law.

Relations between the Political and Administrative Worlds: The Specificities of the French Model

The weight of history and the way various social forces interact means that any analysis of relations between the administrative and political worlds centers on three main questions.

The first is concerned with the way the state apparatus is organized. In France, as in Spain, corporatism has been a major influence, unlike in the Netherlands or Denmark, where the way civil servants are recruited and managed resembles private sector practices. Access to the highest ranks of the French civil service is therefore very limited, and depends on passing the entrance exams for the *grandes écoles*, ENA, or the Ecole Polytechnique. High levels of cross-generational continuity are present: 40% of senior civil servants have a family member who is a state employee. This proportion is significantly higher for the great state corps (*les grands corps de l'Etat*). Within the hierarchical structure of these corps the clearest social division is between the great administrative corps (the General Inspection of Finances, the Council of State, the Court of Accounts, the diplomatic corps) and the great technical corps (state engineers of bridges and roads, state engineers of the mines, state armament engineers), the latter, like scientific branches of the educational system, being more welcoming to middle class individuals. The continuing power of the great corps of the state in French society, which has survived numerous transitions between political systems and changeovers of political power between parties, is based on strong internal organization, including a specific professional culture known as the "*esprit de corps*,"[15] and the support they can give to their members' careers. The French administrative elite is made up of two groups; the members of the grand corps, and those high-ranking officials who belong to other corps, including civil administrators (*les administrateurs civils*).[16] The latter group of officials are far more vulnerable to political pressure as well as the politicization of managerial posts in ministries, which has been on the increase since the late 1970s.

Different countries have different conceptions of the role of the civil service. In France, from the nineteenth century onward, senior civil servants have been actively engaged in modernizing industry and banking. French administrative elites are deeply involved in the modernization of society and the intellectual field. This may be contrasted with Germany, where universities play a bigger role, and Great Britain, where the modernizing influence of the business sector is greater than in France. The establishment of a republican regime in France, inspired by a positivist vision, consolidated the French model. The creation of Sciences Po in 1871 and ENA in 1945 were very much a part of the republican project of creating modernist elites, open to the contemporary world. Republican elitism flourished in the corporatist environment of the *grandes écoles*. This explains why the public management reform process initiated by the President Sarkozy since 2007 is largely in the hands of the traditional administrative elites, i.e. the *grands corps* and particularly the General Inspection of Finances which have detected in this reform the way to secure their domination over the state apparatus.[17]

The French conception of the role of senior civil servants has had two main consequences. First, up until the 1990s many high-ranking civil servants saw it as part of their role to participate in the modernization of private industry or, at least, regarded going to work for a private company as a natural career move. *Pantouflage*—where a civil servant leaves the public sector either permanently, or for a limited period before returning to his or her original post—is common practice. By the middle of the first decade of the twenty-first century, half the members of the General Inspection of Finances had left their corps for industry or the financial sector. Another consequence of the French system is the rivalry it produces in the intellectual field between senior civil servants and academics. France is one of the few countries where senior officials write books or go on have careers in prestigious institutions like the Académie Française. On average, one in four members of the State Council have taught in a university or at Sciences Po, and one in five are published authors.

These differences also have an impact on the conception of how policy is implemented. In France, elites in both the public and private sectors cultivate a model which is composed of two elements: the prestige associated with belonging to a certain group, and "individual heroism," which celebrates the cult of the individual "exploit" and of the "great man." Teamwork, transparency and the importance attached to overall performance are values which are less to the fore in France than in Germany or Great Britain. At the European level, their national culture has enabled the French to have a lot of influence on large, long term projects and strategic planning. On the other hand, French elite culture is less well suited to the daily monitoring of issues, the use of expert advisors, and communicating with civil society, although latterly French civil servants have become more open to input from pressure groups.

Under the Fifth Republic the political system established between 1958 and 1981 allowed a great deal of overlap between its political and administrative elites.[18] With just two exceptions (François Mitterrand and Nicolas Sarkozy), every French president under the present regime has been a civil servant, as have 15 out of 19 prime ministers. In the 1970s, around 40% of deputies were also civil servants and the offices of ministerial advisors played a crucial role in the development of administrative and political careers. Between 1958 and 1974, almost half of government ministers had previously been on the personal staff of a minister, and a significant proportion of them were not even elected representatives (these individuals are known as *ministres techniciens*). The lack of separation between administrative and political elites has led to talk of the takeover of political life by the civil service.[19]

Furthermore, alliances were struck between the state apparatus and the business world. This practice began during the Fourth Republic with the advent of the first five year plans. Private companies were happy to offer senior posts to high-ranking civil servants who could tap into networks of influence and make use of their wide range of contacts. The existence of a large industrial and financial public sector also constituted a buffer zone where civil servants from the central administration could find employment. Until 1981, almost a third of ministers were able to walk out of their jobs straight onto a seat on the board of a big public or private company.

All things considered, before the privatizations of the 1990s, the French elite system was particularly concentrated and the legal system within which French elites operated made it easy for civil servants to have a career in politics. This state of affairs contrasted sharply with the British system, which required the resignation of any civil servant who wished to stand for political office. Moreover, between 1958 and 1981 there was no changeover of political power between parties, which enabled networks of influence to flourish relatively undisturbed. Finally the practice of *cumul des mandats*—simultaneously holding several political posts at various levels of government—which would not be allowed in Germany, for example, enables members of national political elites to fall back on local or regional careers and at the same time gives them privileged access to other senior state officials.

Homogenous Elites?

The homogeneity of state elites in different countries can be measured by applying three separate criteria. First, available career paths can be examined. In some countries it is possible to switch between careers in politics and the civil service. France falls into this category, as does the Netherlands, where three quarters of ministers have had a previous career in the civil service, or worked for parliament. Similarly in Germany over a third of politicians have previously had jobs in the civil service. The German elite is dominated by lawyers: an average of 40% of parliamentarians and 60% of ministers have a legal background.

In a second group of countries the two career paths rarely cross. This is the case in Italy, where the two recruitment processes are quite distinct. As a consequence former civil servants make up barely 5% of deputies. A similar percentage of MPs fall into this category in Britain, where there is a strict requirement for civil servants to be politically neutral.

A second criterion which can be applied relates to social origins. In several European countries (Italy, the Netherlands, and Sweden) the middle classes are well represented in the civil service, whereas the German, French, and British civil services tend to recruit a high proportion of upper middle class individuals for their senior posts.[20] As for the working classes, they are generally underrepresented, rarely accounting for more than 8%–9% of senior civil servants, except in Finland and Sweden (about 17%).

As a general rule members of the lower chambers of parliaments tend to come from more modest backgrounds, although there are exceptions. The British

House of Commons, for example, contains a hard core of privilege: more than a third of MPs are Oxbridge graduates, and 40% have received a public school education, a figure which is considerably higher for the Conservative contingent, of whom about 10% went to Eton.[21] The positive effect of this separation of political and administrative career paths is somewhat cancelled out by this system of social selection. In France, the "executive" nature of the Fifth Republic is strengthened by the disproportionate numbers of members of the social elites in the upper echelons of the civil service. French deputies, on the other hand, tend to have more modest origins, only around a third of them coming from upper or upper-middle class families.

The third criterion concerns the social representativity of the civil service and members of the political class, which in France is generally very low. For example, despite pressure from the European Union, gender parity is far from being achieved. In Europe, there are very few women occupying senior civil service posts: 12% in France and Great Britain, 15% in Spain, and 20% in Italy (although it should be noted that comparisons between national hierarchies are particularly difficult). There has, however, been a big improvement in recent decades: the proportion of female senior officials in administrative headquarters has risen from 2% in 1982 to 14% in 2003. Legislation has been passed to address the lack of gender parity in French politics, but with women still only constituting 12% of members of the French national assembly, France continues to lag well behind many of its European neighbors in this regard.[22]

Although the question of underrepresentation of ethnic minorities in the French civil service has also been raised, French law forbids comparative research in this area. The only available data relate to the geographical origins of a citizen's parents. In 2003, just over 2% of category A male civil servants had one or more parents from the Maghreb. It has been established that French people "of foreign origin" under the age of 30, including university graduates, are under-represented in the civil service.[23] This would suggest that "positive discrimination" programs, such as those put in place by institutions which train future elites, like Sciences Po and some of the top business schools, will not on their own be sufficient to eradicate unequal representation of French nationals whose parents were born outside France.

All things considered, the political and administrative elites of Scandinavian countries are most representative of the various groups which constitute their societies, including the middle classes. Citizens of these countries also have the highest levels of political participation.

The New Alliance or the Fragmentation of the Elites

Since the 1980s, there have been shifts of alliances within all the countries of Europe, including France. In the 1960s, alliances between politicians and senior civil servants led to citizens and private enterprises being governed by technocrats, all in the name of the modernization of European societies. In the 1980s and 1990s, rising unemployment and successive economic crises led to this technocratic model being called into question. The internal functioning of the Welfare State came under heavy criticism, and neo-liberal theories focused on the unaccountability of the higher echelons of the civil service. Public services had to be brought under control and in Great Britain radical reform of the State re-established the primacy of politics. Henceforth, in order to meet the new challenges posed by globalization, elected representatives formed alliances with private sector businessmen. Several businessmen even became directly involved in politics. From that time onward businessmen and private enterprise acquired a new legitimacy, even among intellectuals who had been heavily critical of them in the past. The same period witnessed the emergence of new models of social success, personified by such figures as Margaret Thatcher, Silvio Berlusconi, and Bernard Tapie. Business schools began to provide competition not only for universities but also for the *grandes écoles*. Attacks by politicians on the civil service were rarely supported by the public, except in Portugal, Greece, and Italy, whose civil services were undermined by lack of funding and widespread corruption. Privatizations, the requirement that parts of the civil service compete with the private sector, and the liberalization of network services under orders from Brussels were all imposed in the name of financial profitability, and not as the result of any dissatisfaction with the systems in place being expressed by citizens or consumers. The industrial and financial branches of the public sector disappeared, and with them the most powerful bastions of the trade union movements which, in France in particular, sought to defend social benefits. The legitimacy of the elites and technocratic expertise were also called into question by associations and sections of the media. The development of new environmental policies and a series of public health fiascos (the infected blood scandal, the "mad cow disease" crisis, the mishandling of the 2003 heat wave, etc.) threw light on the connections between politicians and private interests, leaving the political elites open to accusations of being guilty of casualness and incompetence. The political elites became more vulnerable, and consequently keener to protect themselves. They have sought to do this by monitoring the civil service more closely and hence controlling the way policy is applied.[24]

This shift in alliances is linked with the fragmentation of the system of elites: the influence of public and private sector pressure groups is on the increase, the European Union plays the bogeyman (in Great Britain) or provider of alibis (in France), and in the context of decentralization or "devolution" new elites emerge at local and regional levels. Confronted by these centrifugal forces, political elites are forced to devise new tactics, such as the creation of local personality cults (the "entrepreneurial mayor"), using the media to bypass party selection of candidates for political office, and building teams of ministerial advisors who combine expertise and party loyalty.[25] Paradoxically, this system where competing elites struggle for influence means that, at least in France, the state remains the main actor in political life and the location of political power.

What are the main effects of these changes on the French system of elites? The first thing to note is the evolution in the way *pantouflage* works. Members of the administrative elites are still to be found heading large private companies. In 2006 the chairmen and managing directors of the CAC 40 companies included ten ENA graduates and sixteen former students of the Ecole Polytechnique. Nevertheless, the practice of *pantouflage* has become more difficult for younger members of the elites since large private companies now develop human resources policies which create career paths for their employees, hence facilitating internal recruitment of top managers. High ranking civil servants who move over to the private sector tend to be offered less senior posts such as assistant departmental director, and are rarely offered the job of managing director or CEO. These civil servants are often given a trial period to prove themselves, and the rate of subsequent return to the civil service is rising. After an increase in the number of departures of senior civil servants for the private sector between 1980 and 1990, often motivated by the fact that career prospects for civil servants who were not sympathetic to the current left-wing administration were limited, there was a reduction in *pantouflage* between 1990 and 2000: the number of departures for the private sector from the General Inspection of Finances dropped from 93 (in the 1990s) to 59 (in the 2000s) (compared to 83 between 1958 and 1981), and from 53 to 32 for the Council of State (compared to just 16 between 1958 and 1981). The typical profile of a *pantoufleur* also changed: they tended to leave the civil service younger, relatively early in their careers, and offer their resignation before departing, since they had no plans to return to the civil service.[26] Career strategies changed and the *grandes écoles* started to offer a wide range of new courses, in an effort to attract students from the social elites. In France the social elites began to study business in ever greater numbers, and now consider a wider range of career options than in the past. Since the 1990s, around 20% of ENA students have been business school graduates, compared to less than 2% in the 1980s.

A second consequence of shifting alliances in the system of elites has been the politicization of the civil service. Throughout Europe, there is greater political control of appointments to the senior civil service: this phenomenon has been noted in Germany, Spain, France, Italy, and Great Britain.[27] The politicization of the senior ranks of the civil service can be explained by the fact that political leaders, who are operating in an environment where the business of government is more complex and difficult, need to have allies who can ease the passage of their policies. Elected representatives are suspicious of the "neutral" competence of career civil servants who are liable to block their projects. The contractualization of senior posts, decentralization, and the introduction of performance evaluation systems only serve to facilitate this politicization. In France the numbers of ministerial staff who came from the senior branches of the civil service declined from 34% between 1958 and 1974 to 16% between 1984 and 2002. Senior civil servants who were retained as close ministerial advisors were often individuals whose political sympathies were clearly with the government. In that respect the change of government in 1981 marked a watershed in how relations between the civil service and the political world were perceived. The rate of political appointments suddenly increased. While only three prefects were replaced between January and March 1959 at the time of the setting up of the Fifth Republic, 55 departmental prefects and 10 regional prefects were replaced between May and July 1981. Since then this phenomenon has continued, although it has been more pronounced under some governments than others. Between May and July 2002, 45 prefects were replaced and 23 between June and September 2007.

The "strategic" politicization of the senior ranks of civil services is a phenomenon which has been observed in most European countries: individuals occupying the top jobs not only have expertise relating to the sector in which they work, but they are also sympathetic to the government's objectives. So, at the same time as the fragmentation of the elites across the social field occurs, we can observe a process of internal differentiation taking place. There is a clear distinction between political decision-making circles, populated by elected representatives and senior civil servants, where policy is hammered out, and the milieu occupied by professional managers, whose role it is to implement decisions following public management guidelines. The manageralization of the state has therefore often caused splits within the senior civil service, resulting in the reaffirmation of the hierarchical superiority of the political over the administrative.[28]

At the very time when the European political elites were coming under particularly heavy criticism, they managed to increase their control over senior ranks of their civil services either by imposing the norms of New Public Management on them, or recruiting managers directly from the private sector (in Great Britain, both methods have been used). The opening of senior posts in the civil service to outside competition from the private and political sectors can be also observed in France although it operates much more on a political basis. *Tour exterieur* practices (which allow civil servants to be recruited without requiring them to pass a competitive entrance examination) permit careers in the highest echelons of the civil service to be open to politically loyal former ministerial staff and ex-deputies. In this way, the proportion of external recruits to the State Council has risen from 36% between 1958 and 1981 to 47% between 1991 and 2007. In 2006, legislation was passed to facilitate *tour exterieur* recruitment to the Court of Accounts. In France, being actively involved in politics can still a key to social upward mobility.

The civil service, as well as undergoing politicization, has been the target of attacks from the political Right that led, among other changes, to the reform and delocalization of ENA. The real importance of this measure was its symbolism; a signal was sent out that senior civil servants would henceforth be treated with suspicion. These changes were also reflected in the composition of governments. While 54% of the members of Lionel Jospin's government were civil servants and 30% *enarques* (formers students of ENA), no more than 48% of Jean-Pierre Raffarin's ministers were civil servants and only 18% *enarques*. On the other hand 28 full and junior ministers are local councilors, of whom a majority are either chairpersons of private companies or lawyers. With the De Villepin government this trend continued: no more than 40% of its members were civil servants and 22% *enarques*, most of whom were assigned to junior ministries. In 2007, under the Fillon government, 46% of the ministers and state secretaries are former civil servants and only 13% are *enarques*. Moreover,

Table 8.2 The proportion of citizens who trust the integrity of public officials (%)

	GE	*SP*	*FR*	*UK*	*NL*	*PL*	*SW*
Trust	44	45	55	26	41	35	41
Do not trust	20	23	20	27	21	25	18
Neither one nor the other	36	32	25	48	38	40	44

Source: ESS, 2004.

a careful analysis shows that most of these civil servants have served just a few years within state or local administrations and that most of their professional life has been devoted to politics. In some ways, this harks back to the situation before the Second World War, when many members of the political community were professional people or career politicians.

Finally, although it is still true to say that there are a lot of civil servants in French politics (41% of deputies elected in 2007 and 40% in 2002 compared to 49% in 1997), a more detailed analysis reveals that the situation is changing in several respects: according to our calculations there has been a sizeable drop in the proportion of civil servants at the National Assembly who came from the senior branches of the civil service (4.5% in 2007, compared to 6% in 2002 but 10% in 1988 and 13.5% in 1968); joining the party apparatus before becoming a deputy is more common than in the past (35% in 2002 compared to about 20% in the 1960s); and deputies who had previously been civil servants have longer political career paths, which often start with them standing for office at the local level. Although in 1968 46% of former civil servants who became deputies made the switch directly, with no transition period, this figure dropped to 27% in 1986, and subsequently to as low as 16% in 1997 and 13% in 2002.

The specificity of the French case is that, in contrast to Great Britain and the Scandinavian countries, these shifts of alliances within the elites paved the way for criticism not of civil servants but of politicians; indeed the 2004 European Social Survey showed that, among all the European countries studied, the highest levels of trust in the probity of civil servants were to be found in France (table 8.2).

The Effects of European Integration

There is an extensive literature analyzing European integration, much of which has a clear ideological dimension, characterized by the arguments that Europe has replaced the nation state and that national elites have been sidelined. In fact, as political theory has given us no clear vision of future European integration which goes beyond the liberalization of public utilities and trade, there is clearly a need for more complex, balanced analysis, especially in view of the repeated affirmations of national sovereignty made at times of international tension and financial crisis. Three observations can be made.

First, the laying of the first foundations of European Union institutions in the 1950s was largely the work of senior French civil servants, especially the Finance Inspectors, under the supervision of Jean Monnet. Although the European project has developed into something very different from what was envisaged by its founding fathers, its influence does not necessarily conflict with the interests of the administrative elites. Europe has often been used to circumvent opposition from the trade unions, or even the political elites, in order to engineer reforms such as the liberalization of the banking and telecommunication sectors. Nevertheless, although surveys show that members of the senior branches of the French civil service do not feel particularly threatened by European construction, neither have they embraced it with much enthusiasm. Members of the great technical corps often prefer to play the internationalization card outside Europe by practicing *pantouflage*. The great administrative corps have also more or less taken a back seat in recent years. Until 1982, the Secretary General of European Affairs was an Inspector of Public Finances. Since then members of less prestigious corps have occupied this post. The work of European construction is largely carried out on a day-to-day basis by middle grade officials whose job it is to integrate legal norms and work on long term projects in co-operation with experts.

On the other hand, European integration is having a definite impact on professional strategies and cultures. European involvement in highly technical policy areas (health, environment, industry, finance) requires specialists, who are more likely to be found in the upper ranks of British-style civil services than in French-style corps, where generalists predominate. Each of the French great corps sought to meet European requirements by developing their particular expertise; the State Council in the legal domain, the Court of Accounts in the monitoring of public finances, and the prefects in the management of European funds. Nevertheless, the dominant culture of the European Union undoubtedly favors the middle classes and individuals with scientific or technical expertise. In strategic terms, it would appear that high levels of expertise and ability to handle multilateral negotiations are of greater importance than occupation of key posts. The administrative elite has frequently been happy to observe or supervise a process which is managed and monitored on a day-to-day basis by lower level officials.

So is there reason to believe that European elites are in the process of converging? This would require a harmonization of values and representations which still appears to be a long way off. A comparison of the degree of Europeanism of the elites and working classes of a number of European countries can be made using data from the *European Social Survey* (see table 8.3). Using a statistical scale which measures the preferred level of decision-making—Europe, the state, or local government—in six areas of public policy it can first be observed that commitment to Europe is, broadly speaking, an elite phenomenon.[29] On the basis of these results "Europe" could be said to be a creation of its elites which has failed to get its message across to the European working classes. A second point to note is the presence of wide discrepancies between the results for some of the countries in the survey: around 40 percentage points separate the German and British elites. The fact that France is the European country

Table 8.3 The proportion of committed pro-Europeans (%)

	GE	*SP*	*FR*	*UK*	*NL*	*SW*
Public sector elites	48	31	39	11	46	18
Private sector elites	50	36	54	10	49	24
Public sector working class	35	17	27	5	35	14
Private sector working class	28	19	27	5	30	12

Source: ESS, 2004.

with the biggest difference between its public and private sectors as regards attitudes to Europe is also noteworthy.

Elite systems are therefore made up of networks of complex alliances which vary from one country to the next. There is no large, perfectly integrated European elite, sharing a common culture and identical methods of socialization. Of course, globalization does contribute to the increased circulation of elites, as well as the creation of networks of individuals with similar lifestyles who form a kind of jet set. It would be a mistake, however, to think of such developments as unprecedented: similar phenomena could be observed within the world of the nineteenth century upper middle classes (think of Stendhal's trips to Italy). Furthermore, each national elite engages with internationalization differently.[30] Even though the common experience of privilege creates affinities between European elites, values and the consequences of rank differ greatly. So while a crude Marxist model might suggest that social class works as a passport for entry into the elites, other factors such as the career paths taken to gain access into the political and administrative elites, political choices, or the institutional order's need for legitimation may often be the determining factors. In France, the examples of high-ranking civil servants François Bloch-Lainé and Paul Delouvrier are particularly suggestive: although both sons of bankers they were also staunch defenders of state intervention and of an uncompromising conception of the administrative elite, formulating an ethics of the public entrepreneur which has disappeared from today's civil service.[31]

In Europe over the last twenty years there has been a tendency to steadily cut or privatize the public sector. Social elites who are interested in power and social recognition are increasingly drawn to careers in private companies or the media, rather than the civil service. On the other hand, the way the political and administrative elites are recruited has hardly changed, which could lead one to believe that these careers no longer attract the very best candidates. This paradox is certainly most apparent in France since the range of educational and career paths which can lead to membership of the elites are still limited: the introduction of an international dimension to higher education has further strengthened the position of the *grandes écoles*; although public action has diversified, the hard core of the grand corps has been left intact; stints as a ministerial advisor or in the upper ranks of the civil service are still stepping stones on the way to a ministerial career or even a senior position in a leading private firm.

The fact remains that a general lack of interest in democratic politics is now accompanied by a lack of trust in politicians, who are increasingly selected on the basis of their ability to come across well in the media. The way political elites can obtain legitimacy has changed. In the past it was based on their ability to modernize and transform society, which is now more the role of social elites in the broadest sense of the term. Today legitimacy is based more on an individual's perceived integrity. In France, a succession of financial scandals involving politicians at both national and local levels has demonstrated that the Gaullian spirit, present at the birth of the Fifth Republic, has evaporated, and that the elites have not been able to devise a new philosophy of public action to replace it. In this regard, modern politics remains marked by a need for exemplarity which cannot be satisfied by a largely prefabricated "democracy of opinion."

Notes

1. For more recent examples of broadsides in this tradition see Bentégeat, 1998; Minc, 2005.
2. Leridon, 2006.
3. For an analysis of the rise of the Extreme Right, see Pascal Perrineau's chapter (chapter 14).
4. See the studies of probity carried out as part of a major 2006 Cevipof project, under the supervision of Pierre Lascoumes.
5. Birnbaum, 1985.
6. Genieys, 2006.
7. Rouban, 2002b.
8. Charle, 2006.
9. Mills, 1956.
10. Bourdieu, 1989.
11. Dahl, 1961.
12. Rouban, 1998a.
13. Le Roy Ladurie, 1987; Dreyfus, 2000.
14. Antoine, 1989.
15. For a discussion about the "*esprit de corps*," see Derlien and Rouban, 2008.
16. Bodiguel, 1978.
17. Rouban, 2008.
18. Birbaum, 1994.
19. Distinctions between political parties and types of political post need to be made. As regards deputies, e.g., the alleged "takeover" by civil servants was far more striking on the Left of the political spectrum than on the Right. In 1978, 61% of left-wing deputies were civil servants, compared to 36% of right-wing deputies. Later the Left/Right gap became even wider: in 2002 the corresponding figures were 61% and 31%.
20. Page and Wright, 1999.
21. Knapp, 1995.
22. See chapter 4, by Janine Mossuz-Lavau, for a discussion of this topic.
23. Fougère and Pouget, 2004.
24. Rouban, 1998b.
25. Rouban, 2004.

26. Rouban, 2002a.
27. Revue française d'administration publique, 1998.
28. Rouban, 2004 and 2007.
29. The statistical definition of elites used here refers to those individuals, in both private and public sectors, who are in the top income bracket and have the highest educational qualifications.
30. Wagner, 1988.
31. Laurent and Roullier, 2005.

CHAPTER 9

The Media and Searching for Political Information

Arnaud Mercier

Using data from the European Social Survey (ESS), it is possible to examine the way in which the citizens of a number of European countries search for information, in particular information about politics. Attention will be drawn to several noteworthy features of these practices, using a systematic synthesis of the following three levels of analysis:

- a comparison of different attitudes toward the three different information media being studied (television, radio and the press), based on the survey's results regarding the amount of time participants in the survey spent using each medium (participants were asked to choose one of four options ranging from "never" to "a long time");
- a comparison of these practices between the seven countries chosen for the survey;
- an examination of the way age and educational level impacted on media consumption practices, as well as the relation between these practices and the following four political variables: the level of interest in politics the interviewee claimed to have, their degree of politicization,[1] whether they exercised their right to vote, and the ability to formulate a political opinion.

It should be noted that the ever-increasing use of the Internet as a source of information makes its exclusion from this survey highly regrettable. The results of a 2006 study, conducted by the Jupiter Research Consultancy, of more than 5,000 individuals in the United Kingdom, France, Germany, Italy, and Spain, and published in the *Financial Times* on October 9, 2006, revealed that Europeans were using the Internet more frequently than newspapers and magazines as a source of information. Television remained, and by a wide margin, the leading source of information: the citizens of these five countries still spent more than three times as much time watching TV news programs than they spent surfing the Internet for news. Nevertheless, they did spend an average of four hours a week on the Internet, compared to only three hours reading newspapers and magazines.

In the course of this chapter we will seek to answer the following two questions: first, are there significant differences between the behavior of the French and that of their European neighbors as regards searching for information, and second does any evidence of common European practices emerge? The data collected in the course of this survey is particularly valuable since it enables us to build a detailed picture of the way citizens access political information. The unavailability of such data until now has led to this aspect of relations between the media and politics to be neglected.

Some Links between Behavior, Political Attitudes, and Information Practices

The data gathered in this survey fall well short of settling the long-running debates over media influence on political behavior and attitudes. What the survey does do is shed light on the complexity of interactions between information practices, political behavior and political attitudes, which each simultaneously result from and influence the others. There are clear correlations between information practices and degrees of politicization. It is not possible, however, to produce a univocal explanatory diagram that would clearly show how politicization and searching for information are related, even though it is well established that searching regularly for information tends to politicize. Our analysis will therefore draw on the idea of an interactive loop, in which behaviors related to politics and information practices influence and stimulate one another. Each individual processes political information under the influence of their lived experience, personal prejudices, and expectations. As long ago as 1960 the work of Philip E. Converse showed that old information attracts new information. This process, which is closely linked to the phenomenon of selective attention, means that individuals tend to remember news concerning topics with which they are already relatively familiar, and that they also have less difficulty looking for and finding such information. "In short, people accumulate information to do with fields about which they are already relatively well informed."[2]

The possible effects of information received on political behaviors and attitudes can only be understood using an interactive diagram, in which the desire to look for information both provides an explanation for certain features of an individual's political behaviors and attitudes, and can also be caused by them. "The relationship between information and interest is undoubtedly complex and nonrecursive: while political interest increases the likelihood one will become politically informed, political information also stimulates interest."[3] "The general model of the causes and consequences of uses of the media" by William Miller[4] provides a good illustration of the multipolarity of the effects

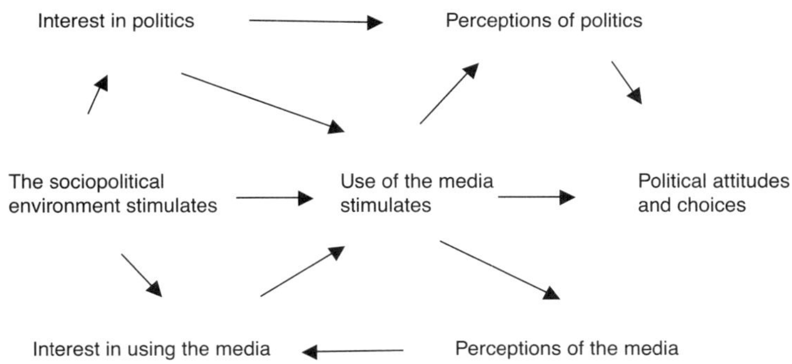

Figure 9.1 Influences between interest for information and interest in politics
Source: Miller, 1991.

of the media and the reciprocal influences between interest for information and interest in politics (figure 9.1).

As the work of Pippa Norris has shown, the results of surveys which examine the amount of time spent watching television programs (of all kinds) do not enable conclusions to be drawn about the impact of media consumption on political behaviors and representations. Norris's conclusions contrast sharply with those of Robert Putnam. Putnam regards the advent of television as a mass medium as being responsible for a significant and irreparable weakening of social ties, evidenced by the decline in active involvement in political parties and associations. In Pippa Norris's view, nothing could be further from the truth:

> Those who are tuning into network news and current affairs programs are also heavily engaged in modern life. Newspaper readership was even more heavily related to activism, although interestingly those who regularly tuned into talk shows on radio did not seem to be stimulated to participate in other forms of politics.[5]

The graph she uses to illustrate her argument demonstrates that the political activities under consideration are all, without exception, more frequently practiced by those who watch political news programs than those who do not. Similarly, her survey of the 1997 British general election revealed that:

> In the long term levels of political knowledge and participation are significantly associated with patterns of media consumption. The most attentive to news on television and in the press, and regular viewers and readers were significantly more knowledgeable than the average citizen about party politics, civics and the parliamentary candidates standing in their constituency.[6]

This runs counter to the hypothesis proposed by those critics who accuse the media of encouraging citizens to take a cynical and disillusioned view of politics, leading to their withdrawal of involvement in the public sphere.

While it is true that, by selecting certain images over others, and in their editorial choices, the media can fuel public disillusionment with politics, it is also the case that individuals who are most interested in politics tend to be heavy consumers of information. Using a multiple regression method, three researchers attempted to test the effect of high consumption of information during the 2000 U.S. presidential election campaign on the likelihood of a vote being cast based on the main campaign issues.[7] The data provided by the campaign polls indicates that electors who spent a lot of time following the media news coverage tended to have more definite opinions on the key issues of the campaign than those who did not. They were also more likely to base their opinions of the candidates on the candidates' stances on these issues. Knowing, however, that there is a correlation between information consumption and educational level, the researchers isolated this variable and compared low and high consumers of information, grouping individuals with similar educational levels into three categories. Having removed the education variable from the equation they observed that "the electors who follow the news (TV news, newspapers, radio) closely are more likely than those who do not to judge the election candidates according to their respective positions on the campaign issues." This statement holds true for electors of all three educational levels. Electors who follow the news most closely always have more clearly thought out opinions and a better knowledge of the candidates' positions, again irrespective of educational level. This study tends to support the analysis of Eveland,[8] according to which the news media help some electors to engage more fully with democracy, improving their knowledge of politics and helping them to form opinions.

There is one more idea that is worth mentioning: if citizens are ill-informed it may be because they believe that taking the trouble to become well-informed is not worth the effort. In fact, when seeking to minimize cognitive efforts, a cost-benefit analysis may lead an individual to be happy to make do with the bare minimum of information.

> Comparing the costs and benefits of attending to certain kinds of information can explain why people fail to take the opportunity to acquire political information. Even if people can obtain detailed information, the fact that the information is only valuable if it prevents them from making costly mistakes can dampen their enthusiasm to be well-informed. This explains voter decisions to attend to a candidate's party identification, work experience, involvement in scandals (if any), sound bites, interest group ratings or personal appearance instead of learning a candidate's complete legislative voting record, policy portfolio, or even their name. Electors have an incentive to attend to stimuli that promise high returns. When the opportunity costs are high for voters, they have an incentive to rely on the most effective and least cognitively costly indicators they can find.[9]

In such cases, voters often choose a candidate on the basis of which political party they represent.

Media Consumption and Searching for Political Information in Europe

Large Differences in Consumption between Media and Countries

Following a steady continuum, the proportion of Europeans who are very heavy consumers of a given media is highest for television, followed by radio, and last by the press (table 9.1). The European averages of heavy consumers of these media are 32.5%, 21%, and 12.5% respectively. The proportion of non-consumers follows the opposite trajectory: 26% of Europeans from the seven countries under consideration never read newspapers, 21.5% never listen to the radio, and only 8% never watch TV. When use of each medium in these countries is analyzed separately, significant differences between consumer habits becomes apparent. Variations between countries are lowest for television, which is clearly a genuine mass medium. The overall average of low television consumers (those individuals who watch TV for less than 30 minutes a day) is 8%, and only in France and Poland does this figure rise to 10%. The British, on the other hand, seem to be particularly dependent on television, since only 4% of them watch it for less than 30 minutes a day. Further evidence for this interpretation is provided by the results from the other end of the scale of consumption: the British are well above the average for heavy television consumers, since 50% of them watched television for more than two and a half hours a day, compared to the European average of 32.5%. Most of the other countries are close to the overall European average for heavy consumption (the figure for France is 34%), with the exception of Poland and, in particular, Sweden which,

Table 9.1 Daily media consumption and search for political information (%)

Daily consumption	*GE*	*SP*	*FR*	*UK*	*NL*	*PL*	*SW*	*Overall Average*
Less than 30m television	8	9	10	4	6	10	8	7.7
More than 2 hr 30 television	31	31	34	50	34	29	20	32.6
Never watch TV politics programs	7	10	12	10	5	8	5	8
More than an hour TV politics programs	17	17	24	25	28	18	21	21.3
Never listen to radio	15	31	20	23	25	21	21	21.5
More than 3h radio	21	18	16	25	22	31	16	21.3
Never listen to radio politics program	24	50	43	43	38	32	34	36.6
More than an hour radio politics program	5	10	7	9	7	10	8	7.7
Never read newspaper	20	48	39	25	19	31	8	26
More than an hour newspaper	14	6	9	20	16	9	13	12.6
Never read politics articles in newspaper	26	53	50	45	27	49	19	36.8
More than an hour reading politics articles in newspaper	4	3	3	5	5	2	4	3.8

with 29% and 21% of their populations respectively being heavy users, are well below the European average.

As regards the proportion of interviewees who never listen to the radio, five of the countries considered were close to the overall average of 21.5%. In Germany, on the other hand, there are far fewer non-listeners (15%) and Spain, at the other extreme, is clearly a country where radio listening is less widespread (31% of Spaniards never listen to the radio). There are fewer heavy consumers of radio programming (defined as more than 3 hours a day) than of television. Poland is the exception: it is the only country where there are more heavy consumers of radio than of television, and even there, only by a narrow margin (31% and 29%). In all the other countries in the survey, people spend considerably more time watching television than they do listening to the radio. Indeed, in both France and the United Kingdom there are twice as many individuals who are heavy consumers of television than of the radio.

Of the three media under consideration, consumption of newspapers varies the most among the seven countries. There is a seven point variation between the percentages for low television consumption. The equivalent figures for radio and newspapers are 16 and 40 respectively. The data reveals some striking contrasts between the various participant countries. The following proportions of European citizens never read a newspaper: half of Spaniards, almost two out of five French people, less than a third of Poles, a quarter of Britons, less than half of Germans and the Dutch, and only 8% of Swedes. There is less variation when it comes to big readers of newspapers, providing support for the theory than in all EU member states there is an educated elite who spend a lot of time reading newspapers. In countries where the popular press is well established, this can serve to boost the figures for high newspaper consumption, and explains why the United Kingdom has the highest proportion of big newspaper readers (20%). The other countries which had higher than average proportions of high consumers of newspapers were the Netherlands, Germany, and Sweden (16%, 14%, and 13% respectively).

Varied National Practices Regarding Information about Politics

As regards the consumption of TV programs covering politics, it should first be noted that only 29% of interviewees occupied the ends of the spectrum of consumption ("never" or "more than an hour"). Very few interviewees claimed to never watch television programs with political content (8% on average), leaving one-fifth who were heavy consumers. The vast majority of Europeans can be defined as average consumers of political television, which explains the relative lack of variation between countries. "Never" responses vary between 12% for France and 5% for Sweden and the Netherlands. There is slightly more variation within the "more than an hour" category of viewers, the highest figure being 28% for the Netherlands and the lowest 17% for Germany. Although television is a widely used source of information about politics, viewers generally neither avoid nor actively seek out programs with political content.

As regards radio, the situation is reversed. More than a third of the interviewees from the seven European countries covered by the survey claim that they never listen to radio programs about politics, compared with a small minority (8%) who are heavy consumers of this kind of program. Although there is a wide variation between countries regarding heavy consumption of political radio (from 5% in Germany to 10% in Spain), this category of consumer remains marginal in all the countries surveyed. Low consumption of radio programs about politics can therefore be observed throughout Europe. Focusing on the "nevers," there is again a great deal of variation between countries. Once more the highest percentage is twice that of the lowest but, given the greater proportions involved, these variations are considerably more significant. One out of two Spaniards and 43% of both the British and the French never listen to radio programs about politics. The Poles and the Germans (24%), on the other hand, are well below the European average. Consumption patterns in Germany indicated that there are a lot of "average" users of political radio programs, whereas in Poland radio is clearly the most commonly used source of political information. Only a very small minority of Europeans regularly dedicate a lot of time to reading newspaper articles about politics: just 4% do so for more than an hour a day.[10] While many Europeans may quickly read a couple of newspaper articles about politics every day, only a very few of them regularly consult the press at length for this kind of information: 5% of Britons, 3% of French, and 2% of Poles. The variations between the national percentages of "never read political articles in newspapers" are substantial and significant. Some countries' results depart quite strikingly from the overall European average, the number of "nevers" registered in Spain, where newspaper reading is low, being higher than the results for Sweden (19% of non-readers of newspapers) by a factor of 2.8. France has a similar level of non-readers of newspapers to Spain and Portugal (50%). By contrast, Germany and the Netherlands share a similar distribution of newspaper reader profiles: about a quarter of "nevers" and 4% to 5% of "more than an hours," the latter figure being close to the Swedish results. The only country whose results reveal an internal contrast is the United Kingdom, since despite having a lot of "nevers" (45%); it also has the highest proportion of regular high consumers of newspaper articles about politics (5%).

By way of summarizing the above analysis, individual profiles of the seven countries surveyed can be sketched.

The French are low consumers of the press (many "never," few "more than an hour"), and average consumers of both television and radio (not many "never," but not many "not more than an hour" either).

The case of the United Kingdom is interesting, since its results for "never" and "more than an hour" are consistently above the overall average, suggesting that the United Kingdom is a split society, at least in terms of media consumption.

Spain's profile is also remarkable. It always occupies first or second position in the "never" category and is below average for the number of "more than an hour" consumers two times out of three. These results demonstrate that Spaniards have relatively little enthusiasm for seeking information about politics.

Sweden's profile is the mirror image of Spain's. It is consistently below average in the "never" category and above average for "more than an hour" media consumers. These results reflect the continuation of a long tradition of public-spiritedness which encourages citizens to be well-informed about politics.

Germans spend close to the average amount of time using all three media. Germany is consistently below average for the "never" category, but also occupies last place for the number of "more than an hour" consumers for two out of the three media in the survey.

Finally, the Dutch and Polish profiles contrast sharply. It is clear that the Dutch obtain little political information from listening to the radio. Their preferred source is television. In Poland, on the other hand, radio is a major source of political information, in contrast to the press, which is regularly consulted at length by relatively few Poles.

The Impact of Age and Education on Looking for Information about Politics

The French profile reveals a general lack of interest in looking for information about politics. As regards the press, non-consumers form a majority or the largest group for every age group. They form an absolute majority of each age group from under 18 year olds to 44 year olds. There is hardly any perceptible variation between age groups and generations and there is no significant increase in the number of heavy consumers of the press among French people over the age of 55. The basic profile for over 55s is still characterized by a relative majority of "nevers," together with a high proportion of individuals who read the political press for "less than 30 minutes a day." The profile for listening to radio programs about politics follows broadly the same pattern. The distribution for 45- to 65-year-olds is similar to the distribution for the press, with a relative majority of "nevers" and a high proportion of "less than thirty minutes." The profile varies even less between age groups, with a relatively consistent degree of consumption of political information at medium to low levels. The younger generations use the television more for obtaining information. The profile for television is very different. While for those under the age of 18 the "nevers" are in first place, for the other age groups the most common response was 30 to 60 minutes, with the exception of 45- to 54-year-olds, who were most likely to reply that they watched television for "more than an hour." A high proportion of over 55s were also in the category of high consumers. Therefore for French people of all age groups obtaining political information from the media is not a priority, with the possible exception of those aged over 45 who follow politics on television.

Since we cannot make a detailed analysis of all media use by every age group in the seven countries surveyed, we will focus on the consumption of newspaper articles with a political content, where the contrasts between countries are the most striking. Three distinct profiles emerge. The Swedes are the biggest consumers of this type of information; a high proportion of Swedes over the age of 35 claim to read newspaper articles about politics for between 30 and 60 minutes a day, including 24% of 55- to 65-year-olds. Overall, a majority of Swedes from every age group read newspaper articles about politics for at least 30 minutes each day. The figure for 25- to 34-year-olds, for example, is 60%.

The second profile emerges from the data supplied by German and Dutch interviewees. There are a lot of big readers of political articles in Germany and in the Netherlands, although not as many as in Sweden. In both these countries a high proportion of those aged over 55 read from between 30 to 60 minutes daily. 60% of 45- to 54-year-olds read political articles for up to 30 minutes a day. Dutch people under the age of 35 are relatively high consumers of this kind of material. Like the Swedes, more than 50% of them read for up to 30 minutes daily. In Germany, the same phenomenon can be observed, although it first appears in the 25 to 34 age group. After the age of 55 the consumption patterns of these two countries are very similar.

The third and final profile groups together France, Spain, Poland, and the United Kingdom. In these four countries the proportion of individuals of all ages who read political articles for more than 30 minutes a day is low, and the vast majority of people either spend less than 30 minutes a day reading information about politics, or do not read this kind of material at all. It should be noted, however, that members of the older age groups do read a little more than the younger generations. In France, 91% of 25–34-year-olds never read or read for less than 30 minutes. 85% of British 18–24-year-olds, 95% of Polish 25–34-year-olds and 92% of Spanish 18 to 24 year olds have the same profile. A high proportion of the oldest individuals in the survey (the over 65s) also never read information about politics, or do so for less than 30 minutes a day: 79% of this age group in France, 84% in Spain, 90% in Poland, and "only" 72% in the United Kingdom.

Comparing the consumption of political programs between Europeans who have similar levels of education provides little evidence that a common European model is emerging (table 9.2). Among the countries involved in the survey, the patterns of consumption for television, the mass medium par excellence, vary the most. A few contrasting examples suffice to show how great the differences between countries can be. For those who have no qualifications or have just a primary school education the proportion who never watch programs about politics amounts to 9% in Sweden, and 15% in Germany. The corresponding figures for those with the highest educational qualifications—having completed at least two years of higher education—vary between 2% (Sweden) and 18% (France and the Netherlands). The proportion of participants without educational qualifications who never watch television programs about politics or watch for less than 30 minutes a day varies between 24% in France and 64% in Germany. As regards the other end of the spectrum of consumption, in some countries a significant proportion of unqualified individuals spend a lot of time watching this kind of television program (France 35%, closely followed by Sweden, the United Kingdom and the Netherlands), compared to only 11% in Germany. The results for the most highly qualified also vary a great deal: 32%

Table 9.2 Looking for political information and educational level (%)

	GE			*SP*			*FR*			*UK*			*NL*			*PL*			*SW*		
	1	2	3	1	2	3	1	2	3	1	2	3	1	2	3	1	2	3	1	2	3
Political TV program																					
Never	15	8	10	10	18	7	12	11	11	12	10	9	9	4	18	11	6	11	9	4	2
<30 m	49	41	14	22	34	25	30	37	33	30	27	26	30	29	18	34	39	32	25	31	32
>1 hr	11	16	35	24	17	32	21	15	22	28	23	23	29	29	18	17	19	11	27	18	19
Political radio program																					
Never	43	26	53	48	25	13	57	51	14	60	48	27	48	38	27	43	29	17	36	34	31
<30 m	40	48	26	31	39	52	23	26	52	21	30	38	34	38	46	34	39	46	34	38	44
>1 hr	3	5	6	6	10	9	7	11	9	7	7	15	6	7	9	8	12	8	10	6	7
Political newspaper articles																					
Never	49	28	55	53	39	8	66	52	44	48	48	38	42	28	18	69	48	22	25	21	6
<30 m	32	52	31	35	41	65	24	35	33	38	38	42	41	52	36	25	41	58	56	59	59
>1 hr	3	4	3	2	4	8	3	2	11	2	4	8	4	4	27	2	2	2	4	3	6

Key: column 1 indicates those individuals who have no qualifications or have only completed primary school; column 2 indicates those who have a secondary education; column 3 indicates those who have completed more than two years of university.

of Germans who fall into this category watch television programs with political content compared to 11% of Poles. The results for participants who have completed their secondary education show similar levels of variation. In other words, it is not possible to establish a relationship between educational level and levels of television consumption. The hypothesis that television programs with a political content have popular appeal among the least educated, and are somewhat looked down upon by those with the most educational qualifications could be advanced, but it is not borne out by the results of the survey. If a differential of percentage of consumption between those without qualifications and the most qualified is calculated, greatly contrasting results are obtained. A positive differential indicates that political programs on television are more popular with individuals without educational qualifications. On the other hand, a high negative differential means that this activity is favored by highly qualified individuals. As regards those who never watch this kind of program, France and the Netherlands both have negative scores, indicating that highly educated people in these countries tend not to rely on television for this kind of information, unlike those with fewer qualifications. Nevertheless, in all the other countries covered by the survey, there is a positive differential, ranging from + 0.5 in Spain to + 8 in Germany; very few of the most highly educated Germans do not watch television programs with a political content. If we turn our attention to high consumers of television, there are two countries which have a negative score: Spain and, most strikingly, Germany (-21). In these countries a highly educated person is likely to spend more time watching these kinds of television programs than a less educated individual. Nevertheless, the results show the opposite to be the case for the other countries in the survey. In Sweden the balance is + 9, and in France + 17. In these countries the proportion of those with relatively few educational qualifications who watch television programs with political content is higher than for their highly educated compatriots.

As regards the press a predictable and almost identical behavioral profile appeared across the board, with relatively minor variations between the seven countries. The fewer educational qualifications an individual possesses, the more likely they are to never read articles about politics, and the less likely they are to read such material for more than an hour a day. Although there is an appreciable difference between those without qualifications and those who finished secondary school, since members of the latter group are more likely to fall into the "read for less than 30 minutes" category than the "never" category, if the "nevers" and the "less than thirty minutes" are grouped together the results for those who completed primary school are the same as for those who completed secondary school. There are, however, considerable differences between the patterns of consumption of unqualified individuals and those people who are most highly qualified. The balance of consumption differentials clearly indicates an overall trend. The average balance is + 28 for those who never read articles about politics. This figure is halved if the "nevers" and "less than 30 minutes" are grouped together (+14) and becomes negative (–7) for the "more than an hours." The results show that, irrespective of the amount of educational qualifications that they have, the Europeans surveyed, with the notable exception of the Dutch, are unlikely to regularly spend a lot of time reading about politics in the press. While it is certainly the case that the proportion of high consumers among the most qualified can be up to double the figure for interviewees without qualifications, the numbers involved still only represent a small minority of interviewees: 11% of highly qualified Spaniards spend a long time engaged in this kind of reading, compared to 6% and only 2% of their Swedish and Polish counterparts, respectively. The differences between the number of "big readers" vary considerably in only two countries: the Netherlands (where the most highly qualified are 6.8 times more likely to read a lot than unqualified people), and Spain (4.4 times more likely). Elsewhere differences drop to much lower levels; the equivalent figure for France, for example, is 1.2 times. It is worth repeating that, in an effort to apply the same criteria to the press as was used for the audiovisual sector, the definition of a heavy consumer—"more than an hour"—probably covered too broad a spectrum of individuals.

If we turn to the profile for France, the variations between individuals with different educational backgrounds are relatively small, with the exception of the highest consumers of political television, since the most highly qualified French people, along with their Polish counterparts, are the lowest consumers of political programs, in sharp contrast with their least qualified compatriots, who watch this kind of program a lot. As regards the press, French people of all educational backgrounds are among the lowest consumers, since more than half of those without qualifications and as many as 39% of those with the most educational qualifications never read newspaper articles about politics. Only the Spaniards read less. When it comes to listening to the radio, unqualified French people tend to be below average consumers, while a relatively large proportion of highly qualified French people are high consumers of these kinds of radio programs. The operative word here is "relatively," since a "large proportion" here never exceeds 10%. The proportion of French people who never listen to radio programs about politics is often higher than in other countries, for all categories of individual from the least to the most educated. Overall, the French listen to the radio less than the other nationalities covered by the survey, and variations between consumption patterns of individuals with different educational levels are smaller than in most other countries. As a rule, the more years of study an individual has completed, the more time they are likely to spend listening to programs about politics, the exception being Sweden where those without qualifications listen to radio programs for twice as long as their most highly educated compatriots.

Involvement in Politics and Searching for Information about Politics

Among the three media, a clear hierarchy has established itself, with television in first place, followed by the radio, and finally, lagging well behind, newspapers. If interest in politics is factored into the equation, this ranking remains unaltered. For each medium, in every country, the proportion of those slightly or not at all interested in politics grows, depending on the medium. There is no clear correlation between not watching television programs about politics and not being interested in politics. 12% of interviewees who describe themselves as having no interest in politics never watch television programs about politics. The corresponding figures are higher for the other two media—44% for radio and 51% for the press—and suggest more of a correlation. Five of the countries in the survey display this kind of variation between the three media, with even higher levels of correlation. In France, the United Kingdom and Spain more than half of those who are not interested in politics do not search for such information on the radio and in newspapers, whereas only 12 to 14% do likewise among non-consumers of programs with political content on television. The hierarchy remains the same at the other end of the scale of consumption. On average 29% of those "interested" or "very interested" in politics watch television programs with political content for more than an hour a day; the corresponding proportions for the same groups' high consumption of radio and newspapers are 11% and 7% respectively. Citizens who are very interested in politics are not necessarily high consumers of media with political content, with the exception of television. French media consumption is slightly higher than average, though its dynamics are quite similar to those of the other countries in the survey. Regarding the behavior of those who are not interested in politics, the results for two countries stand out. In both Germany and Sweden no more than about a third of this category of citizen never look for information about politics on the radio or in newspapers, compared to a half or two thirds in the other countries involved in the survey. The Netherlands occupies a position half way between Germany and Sweden and the other countries on around 40%. The status of these three countries as relatively high consumers of information about politics is therefore partly due to the fact that even citizens of these countries who claim not to be interested in politics tend not to completely turn their backs on information related to politics.

When data for consumption of information about politics by those who claim to be interested in politics is analyzed, the correlations which emerge are exactly as one would expect (see table 9.3). If those who are interested or very interested in politics are grouped together, and individuals who are a little bit interested or not at all interested in politics are also grouped together, two opposing blocs emerge. The vast majority of those who never look for information about politics classify themselves as not interested in politics. The

Table 9.3 Proportion of various categories of media consumer who are interested and uninterested in politics (average of the seven countries expressed as a percentage)

	Interested in Politics	*Not Interested in Politics*
Never watch political television	24	76
Never listen political radio	36	64
Never read political articles	29	71
More than an hour of political television	64	36
More than an hour of political radio	64	36
More than an hour of political articles	80	20

highest consumers of political information, on the other hand, claim to be interested in politics. The two profiles which contrast most sharply are first the 76% of those who never watch television who are not interested in politics, and the 80% of citizens who read about politics for more than an hour daily who consider themselves to be interested in politics. Regarding the former group, there is a significant minority of individuals not interested in politics who still watch television programs about politics, no doubt because it is the only medium which presents political information in a way they find palatable. Consequently, those individuals who never watch political programs on television can be assumed to be quite uninterested in politics. On the other hand, since the press is the least "user-friendly" of the three media, one can safely assume that an individual who regularly spends a lot of time reading about politics in newspapers must have a real interest in politics.

These comparisons also show that even some of the minority who are very interested in politics are not necessarily high consumers of all media sources of political information: although only 5% of this category claim to never watch television programs which have this kind of content, as many as 15% of them never read newspaper articles about politics and 26% never listen to political radio (table 9.4).

Analysis of these results leads us to be cautious about drawing any definite conclusions about the political impact of the media, and in particular their influence on voting behavior. The value of speculating about the media's impact on the least politicized voters, potentially the most easily influenced and the most likely to switch party allegiance, must be limited by the fact that many of this type of voter simply abstain from consuming any information about politics.

As regards the press, there is a clear division between the three Northern European countries and the rest. Whereas around a fifth of Spanish, Polish, French, and British citizens see nothing unusual in an individual being very interested in politics and yet never reading articles with political content, for Germans, Dutch, and Swedes there would be something contradictory about these two responses. Be that as it may, the opposite profile—an individual who reads articles about politics despite being uninterested in politics—can be more easily explained. It can be argued that since each individual citizen can be said to have no rational incentive to vote, as no single vote can change the result of an election, by the same token neither do they have any incentive to seek information about politics. If our vote has no impact, why should we invest

Table 9.4 Proportion of those who are very interested in politics who are non-consumers of political information, for each of the three media under examination (%)

	GE	*SP*	*FR*	*UK*	*NL*	*PL*	*SW*	*Average*
No political television	4	4	9	6	6	1	2	4.5
No political radio	18	35	25	26	35	23	28	27
No political newspapers	14	22	22	21	11	22	7	17

cognitive and material resources in order to make our choice at the ballot box an informed one? Obtaining, analyzing and organizing the information used in one's decision making requires both time and effort. Furthermore, information can only be effectively used by those with a certain amount of knowledge and analytical ability, of the kind acquired during a relatively long period spent in the education system, or in the course of involvement in political activism. Morris Fiorina[11] has shown that the motivations behind an individual's gathering of political information does not necessary have anything to do with the political utility of that information. Some viewers obtain information about politics because they actively search for it, out of a sense of duty. They may be distinguished from the viewers of the kind of non-specialized television programs which Umberto Eco called "omnibus" programs, who can be exposed to political information without having really sought it out. Individuals may also use information for social self-definition (information about politics can be used as a conversation topic when interacting with family, friends, and colleagues. For some people their politics are part of the way they define themselves socially). Informed citizens during an election campaign can also be compared to racegoers or other sports fans. Campaign polls, though of questionable predictive value, receive extensive media coverage, heightening the resemblance between political campaigns and major sporting events.

The relation between looking for information about politics and the fact of having voted in the last election is close, where the citizen is a heavy consumer of political information. In fact the overall average proportion of heavy media consumers who voted in the last elections varied between 80% and 82%, depending on which medium they prefer to use. The two clearest indicators of likely political behavior are first the fact of never watching television programs about politics—the only category of media consumer for which non-voters (49%) are close to outnumbering voters (51%)—and second, big readers of the political press, who are the category of consumer with the highest proportion of voters (82%). In every country in the survey, members of the former category are the least likely to have voted, and in the following three countries voters in this group are actually outnumbered by non-voters: Sweden (where 49% of them voted), Poland (44%), the United Kingdom (40%). As regards heavy consumers, on the other hand, the highest proportions of voters were found among readers of the political press in Poland, France, and the Netherlands. 90% of heavy consumers of the Dutch press voted in the last elections. In the other countries in the survey, regular radio listeners were more likely to have voted than heavy consumers of the other media.

Research has shown that the extent to which individuals in Europe seek out information about politics correlates more closely with their level of politicization than with the amount of studies they have completed. "In each country, the more a citizen is politicised, the more likely they are to follow politics (for all the countries taken together the average value for Cramer's V is 0.30, and for each country the results are highly significant)."[12] Indeed, this coefficient, which measures the strength of association between two variables on a scale of 0 to 1, is considered to indicate a significant association when its value is

0.15 or above. Having said that, an individual's level of politicization is also strongly associated with the studies they have completed: the levels of educational achievement and interest in politics tend to rise together. As part of the 1999 survey of European values, Pierre Bréchon investigated the extent to which an individual's level of politicization and the amount of studies they had completed influenced how closely they followed politics. He found that:

> Where two individuals are equally politicised, but one of them has studied for longer than the other, it is not likely that there will be any difference between how closely they follow politics as a consequence of this discrepancy in educational levels. The consumption of political news therefore depends solely on the level of politicisation rather than on educational qualifications. Being educated provides no guarantee that an individual will follow political news. The people who take an interest in politics are those who attach some importance to politics.[13]

The ESS enabled us to make a more complex interpretation of these results, by combining the politicization indicator, on a scale of 0 to 7, with an indicator of consumption of political content from the news media. To do this, we focused on those individuals who spent more than 30 minutes a day either watching television programs or listening to radio programs with political content, or reading newspaper articles about politics. This indicator ranges from 0 to 3. The survey participants from each country were then split into two groups, one composed of individuals who had a secondary school education at best, and the second of individuals who had completed their secondary education and continued into higher education. As can be seen from figure 9.2, members of the latter group had a higher level of politicization. It can also be observed, however, that individuals with similar educational backgrounds and levels of politicization, such as German, French, and Swedish university graduates, can

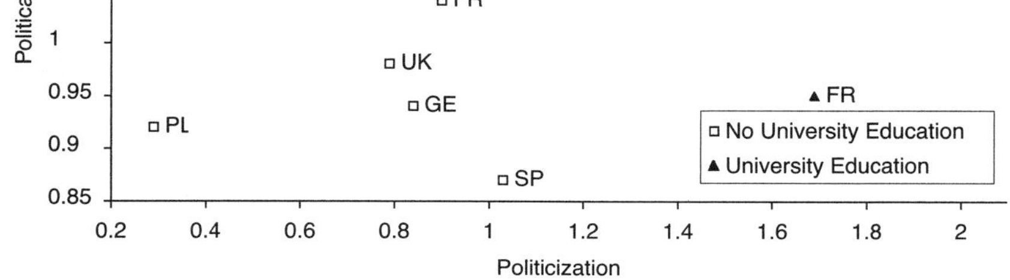

Figure 9.2 Politicization and consumption of political media

display very different patterns of consumption with regard to media with political content.

When these results are compared, significant differences between the various countries become apparent. When the responses to the other questions are taken into consideration, it is clear that for some countries their low consumption of political information provides an explanation for low participation in elections. In other countries the link is less clear. In the United Kingdom, where people watch more television than in any of the other countries in the survey, there is a significantly higher rate of electoral abstentionism among those who never watch television programs with a political content than among the public at large. In the United Kingdom, more than the other countries, if an individual watches no programs with a political content it is likely to be a clear indication that they are pursuing a strategy of actively avoiding politics, and are hence less likely to vote. This may be contrasted with the situation in Spain, where not searching for information about politics in the media is less of an indicator of probable electoral abstentionism than in its European neighbors. In the United Kingdom the electoral behavior of non-consumers of political information brings British levels of electoral abstentionism down to below the European average. The same can be said of Poland. The situation in France is less clear: it is not possible to establish any correlation between consumption of information about politics and electoral behavior. In France, however, consumers of different media do exhibit similar voting behavior to those of the other countries in the survey, insofar as big readers of the press are the most likely to vote, and individuals who do not watch television the least likely.

Information and Feelings about One's Ability to Understand Politics: A Strong but Variable Link

When the data on looking for information about politics is combined with the replies to the question which asks whether politics is regarded as being complicated, significant correlations are obtained. 39% of Europeans questioned stated that politics is too complicated. The results for three countries were below this average: the Netherlands (37%), Germany (32%), and Sweden (30%). A high proportion of citizens of Poland (47%), France (42%) and Spain (43%), on the other hand, considered that politics is overcomplex. The results reproduce the hierarchy of information consumption. The available data does not enable us to be sure about which of these phenomena causes the other. Certainly, where politicization is low or only present in isolated pockets, the world of politics seems strange, perplexing and difficult to fathom. It is understandable that in such a situation citizens lose interest in politics and avoid it, rather than seeking to use the available information to educate themselves and overcome feelings of inadequacy, so entering a virtuous circle where they acquire the tools required to interpret the world of politics, which gradually no longer seems alien to them. Recent research, drawing on cognitive science, has shown that citizens who strongly identify with a political party are more likely to retain political knowledge and discourse than those with no such affiliation.[14]

When Europeans are asked about their ability to form political opinions, the overall distribution between the three responses (difficult, easy, neither one nor the other) is as follows:

- 38.5% think that it is difficult, ranging from the French (59%) to the Germans (24%);
- 32.5% believe that it is neither easy nor difficult;
- 29% think that forming political opinions is easy.

Compared to this overall average, the same responses combined with information gathering practices reveal a clear correlation. The feeling that an opinion is difficult to form increases by ten points for television and 7 points for radio among those who never look for information about politics. For heavy consumers of information the variations are considerably smaller, with the exception of those who read a lot about politics. 47% of them believe that forming an opinion is easy, which is 17 points higher than the overall average. So big readers of the press tend to find it relatively easy to form political opinions (table 9.5).

Nevertheless, although comparisons between different media reveal little variation, numerous disparities between the various countries studied do exist. The results for the Netherlands, Poland and Sweden are similar, and close to the overall average. France distinguishes itself from its European neighbors by having well above average numbers of interviewees who claim to have difficulty in formulating political opinions. Particularly high proportions of those French participants in the survey who never seek information about politics in the media acknowledge having difficulty forming political opinions. 60% of French people who never watch television programs with political content fall into this category; the corresponding figures for non-consumers of politics on the radio and in the press are 65% and 63% respectively. Even more surprisingly, a high proportion of heavy consumers of politics in the media claim to experience the same kind of difficulties: 56% of regular television viewers, and 46% and 42% of the highest consumers of radio and newspapers fall into this category. All these percentages are well above the European average, and the French results for those who spend more than an hour reading newspaper articles with a political content are more than twice the European average, and fully five times the score for Spain. This shows that in France a high proportion of regular consumers of the medium which requires the highest levels of receptiveness and cultural capital nevertheless still have difficulty forming political opinions, in contrast to their German, Polish, and Spanish counterparts, of who 59% or more have no difficulty in accomplishing this task. The French results are no doubt symptomatic of a general feeling among the electorate of dissatisfaction, confusion and disenchantment with the range of political choices on offer.[15] In Spain, as in France, a consistently high proportion of low consumers of information about politics claim to have difficulty in forming

Table 9.5 Is forming an opinion of political issues difficult, easy, or neither one or the other? (%)

	GE	*SP*	*FR*	*K*	*NL*	*PL*	*SW*	*Overall Average*
Never watches political television								
difficult	42	56	60	40	46	49	47	48.8
Neither difficult nor easy	29	19	24	32	41	23	29	27.1
easy	29	26	16	29	13	28	24	24.1
>1hr of political TV								
difficult	16	36	56	29	34	31	45	34.9
Neither difficult nor easy	30	24	27	30	37	34	30	30.5
easy	55	41	17	41	29	36	25	34.6
Never listens to political radio								
difficult	32	52	65	39	40	45	44	45.5
Neither difficult nor easy	31	23	24	30	33	32	32	29
easy	37	26	11	31	27	24	24	25.5
>1hr of political radio								
difficult	14	33	46	24	36	33	43	32.2
Neither difficult nor easy	42	22	29	35	36	36	27	32.5
easy	44	45	25	41	28	31	31	35.3
Never reads political press								
difficult	35	54	63	41	49	46	52	48.5
Neither difficult nor easy	34	23	25	33	32	33	27	29.3
easy	31	23	13	26	20	21	22	22.2
>1hr of political press								
difficult	12	8	42	17	26	17	27	20.5
Neither difficult nor easy	29	25	32	44	33	23	35	33
easy	59	67	26	39	41	60	38	46.5

opinions about politics. Nevertheless in Spain—unlike France—the proportion of high consumers of information about politics who find it easy to form political opinions is consistently above the European average, rising to 67% for big readers of the Spanish press. This demonstrates that in Spain, where there are relatively few heavy consumers of information about politics in the media, the fact of being a high consumer is a clear differentiating factor, strongly correlating with confidence in one's ability to easily formulate political opinions. The United Kingdom and Germany are in line with this trend: relatively few high consumers of political media doubt their ability to form political views. The proportion of German interviewees who found such opinions easy to formulate was consistently above average, as was the corresponding percentage of Britons for two of the three media within the survey. Finally the exceptional nature of the results for Sweden should be noted. The proportion of Swedish heavy consumers of all three media who claim to have difficulty forming political opinions is well above the overall European average. This is surprising in the light of the fact that fewer Swedes than any other nationality in the survey consider politics to be too complicated (30%). The Swedes, who generally do not claim to find politics too complicated, are very interested in politics and are the most politicized nation in the survey, also pride themselves on avoiding making hasty political judgments, even when they are heavy consumers of information about politics.

* * *

We can offer a summary of the preceding in the form of a table that ranks the seven countries in the survey according to answers given (table 9.6) to the ten questions asked on table 9.5.

France emerges from these rankings as a country where there is a crisis of confidence in politics and in the political media. Although in France the level of involvement in political protest indicates a highly politicized nation, fewer French vote in elections than their neighbors and relatively few French people claim to be interested in politics. Furthermore, although consumption of television programs with a political content is relatively high, the corresponding results for both radio and the press are lower than the European average. The French positions in the rankings provide further evidence of a longstanding mistrust of the media, which is confirmed by the annual poll which measures the level of public trust in the media.

In 2007, this Sofres poll produced the following results: only 14% of French people claim to follow the news very closely. 49% think that newspaper coverage of the news provides a somewhat or totally inaccurate version of the events described. The corresponding figures for radio and television are 43% and 52% respectively.

If points are given for a country's various individual rankings—one point for being top and so on down to seven points for the lowest ranking—and then added up to produce an overall ranking, the country whose politicization indicators and proportion of heavy consumers are the highest overall will occupy the top of the rankings. The country with the fewest points, resulting from being repeatedly near the top of the rankings, will be the country having the most above average levels of politicization, the heaviest consumers of political information and the fewest non-consumers of such information.

In each column in the table a dividing line has been drawn between countries with above and below average results. Before establishing an overall general ranking, a number of preliminary observations can be made. Sweden is above this line in 9 categories out of 10, Germany in 8 out of 10, and the Netherlands 7 out of 10. None of the other countries have a majority of above average rankings. At the other end of the rankings, Poland is below average in 9 cases out of 10, and the United Kingdom and France in 7 out of 10. A clear divide between Northern European countries and the other countries is already apparent. The final rankings confirm the impression given by this initial observation. The distribution of points according to the ranking shown in table 9.6 is as follows (in some cases the order has been reversed): Sweden: 23 points; The Netherlands: 29 points; Germany: 36 points; The United Kingdom: 40 points; Poland: 50 points; Spain: 51 points; France: 51 points.

Table 9.6 Ranking of participating countries relating to politicization indicators and looking for information

Ranking 1 to 7	*Ranking 1 to 7*	*Ranking 1 to 7*	*Reversed ranking 7 to 1*	*Reversed ranking 7 to 1*	*Ranking 1 to 7*	*Reversed ranking 7 to 1*	*Ranking 1 to 7*	*Reversed ranking 7 to 1*	*Ranking 1 to 7*
Very interested in politics	***Level of politicization***	***Voted in last election***	***Politics is complicated***	***Political TV never***	***Political TV >1hr***	***Political radio never***	***Political radio >1hr***	***Political press never***	***Political press >1hr***
NL	Sweden	Sweden	Sweden	NL	NL	Germany	Poland	Sweden	UK
Sweden	France	NL	Germany	Sweden	UK	France	Spain	Germany	NL
Germany	Spain	Spain	NL	Germany	France	Sweden	UK	NL	Germany
UK	Germany	Germany	UK	Poland	Sweden	Poland	Sweden	UK	Sweden
Poland	UK	France	Spain	UK	Poland	UK	France	Poland	Spain
France	NL	UK	France	Spain	Spain	NL	NL	France	France
Spain	Poland	Poland	Poland	France	Germany	Spain	Germany	Spain	Poland

The seven countries can be put into three distinct groups. The first group consists of Sweden and the Netherlands, whose citizens are well informed and have a high level of politicization. Then, occupying the middle ground, Germany and the United Kingdom can be grouped together, although comparing their respective results to the average score for each question—Germany generally finishing above average and the United Kingdom below—gives Germany a profile closer to those of Sweden and the Netherlands. The third and final group is made up of Poland, Spain, and France, who have contrasting profiles: they are either relatively politicized countries who are nevertheless low consumers of information about politics (Spain, France), or are high consumers of political information from one medium but have a very low level of politicization (Poland).

These rankings show that within Europe different cultural heritages give rise to contrasting patterns of cultural consumption. The *Eurobarometer* special survey "The Participation of Europeans in Cultural Activities," which was published in April 2002,[16] showed that alongside massive convergence phenomena (89% of EU citizens watch the news and other topical television programs; 60% listen to the radio every day), certain cultural practices are very unevenly distributed across Europe. So, while 46% of Europeans read a newspaper every day, this figure rises to 77% in Finland and Sweden, and 65% in Germany, and drops to between 20 and 25% for Greece, Spain, and Portugal. Results for magazines and books read also vary widely.

> The citizens of most Northern European countries tend to read more than people in other regions of Europe: 71.8% of Swedes, 66.2% of Finns and 63.2% of British participants in the survey had read a book in the previous twelve months [...]. The exception is Belgium: 58.3% of Belgians claimed not to have read a book during the same period which puts them behind the Portuguese (67.3%) and ahead of Greece (54.3%) and Spain (52.7%) in the "non-reader" rankings.[17]

Even for a new medium like the Internet which has developed quickly outside any specific tradition, European user practices vary considerably. Scandinavians generally adopted new information technologies earlier and in greater numbers than the peoples of continental Europe, particularly those living in Southern Europe. As a consequence, the results published in the *Eurostat Yearbook 2005* reveal a clear North-South digital divide: the rankings for Internet use by private individuals were headed—by some margin—by Sweden and Iceland (83%), followed by Denmark, then Germany (61%), with, at the other end of the scale, Italy, Portugal, and Poland registering scores of around 30%. The European average was 48%.[18]

Our study's findings and the supplementary data mentioned above are congruent with the conclusions of the previous decennial study of European values (1999), which demonstrated that there are considerable variations between the extents to which citizens of the countries of Europe follow political news. Of those countries where citizens who regularly seek out information are in the minority, the United Kingdom was top of the list; only 23% of Britons take an interest in political news, followed by Spain (35%). Starting from the other end of the scale the first three positions were occupied by Sweden (72%), Germany (61%), and Denmark (63%). Behind them came France (57%), Austria (57%), and the Netherlands (53%). With the notable exception of the United Kingdom's last place, these results are in line with the results of the survey presented here, in which Spain was ranked bottom and Sweden top.

It is also worth pointing out that, according to this survey, in only two of the countries did the media enjoy a relatively high degree of trust: the Netherlands (55%) and Sweden (45%), compared to an overall European average of 34%. There seems to be no automatic link between media consumption and trust in the media: 40% of Spaniards interviewed said they trusted the media, despite the fact that in Spain consumption of political news is relatively low. It is therefore necessary to seek more general explanations linked, in particular, to a kind of "civic culture" often associated with Protestant countries. These countries tend to display a profile which includes the following features: few interviewees who failed to attempt to locate themselves on a Left-Right political axis; a level of politicization higher than the European average; a greater likelihood that citizens will discuss politics with their friends; a more widespread belief that politics is an important part of life; a greater faith in social institutions; above average rates of participation in elections; greater numbers of people who are members of one or more association. One aspect of this kind of culture is their members' commitment to searching for information. Henry Milner[19] calls this "civic competence" and in Chapter 12 of his book explains how Sweden is the society that corresponds most closely to this model. According to Milner such a context gives rise to a virtuous circle:

> Institutions and policies which nurture civic competence generate a virtuous circle, as increased civic competence leads to more informed political participation, which in turn leads to fairer socio-economic conditions. Such conditions encourage citizens to keep themselves well informed about government decisions, hence restarting the cycle.[20]

The 1999 European survey has enabled us to calculate an index of criticism of democracy which provides support for this thesis. The countries where there is most criticism of the way democracy functions are France, Belgium, and Portugal, and the highest levels of satisfaction are to be found in Austria, Germany, Sweden, and the Netherlands.

Although there are many forces in Europe which are working toward the creation of a common culture, it is clear that as regards many attitudes and behaviors, including information practices, national and cultural differences remain. French media habits are unlike those which prevail in the North of Europe. The French are relatively politicized and anti-establishment, but these values do not translate into high levels of active searching for information about politics: television and radio consumption in France are close to the average for the seven European countries in the survey, and low readership levels for material related to politics is symptomatic of the structural weakness of the French press culture.

Notes

1. Engaging, or not, in the following activities were taken as indicators of an individual's level of politicization: making contact with a politician or politicians over the preceding twelve months, working for a political party or an association, wearing or distributing political campaign badges, taking part in a political demonstration, boycotting a product for political reasons, signing a petition.
2. Iyengar, 1990, p.163.
3. Carpini and Kennamer, 1994, p. 453.
4. Miller, 1991.
5. Norris, 1996, p. 477.
6. Norris, 1999, p.113.
7. Kim, Scheufele, and Shanahn, 2005.
8. Eveland, 2002.
9. Lupia and McCubbins, 1998, p. 54.
10. This low figure may be the result of the use of the same time-based indicator ("more than an hour") for all three media. Indeed, which of us can say that they read "newspaper articles about politics or current affairs" for more than an hour a day?
11. Fiorina, 1990.
12. Bréchon, 2002b, p. 102.
13. Ibid., pp. 102–103.
14. Kuklinski and Quirk, 2001.
15. Perrineau, 2003.
16. *Eurobarometer*, 2002.
17. Ibid., p. 5.
18. *Eurostat Yearbook*, 2005.
19. Milner, 2004.
20. Ibid., p.15.

CHAPTER 10

What Remains of Class Voting?

Nonna Mayer

According to the thesis put forward by the sociologist Seymour M. Lipset in his book, *Political Man: The Social Bases of Politics*, the electoral game is essentially a reflection of the class struggle: "In virtually every economically developed country, the lower-income groups vote mainly for parties of the Left, while the higher-income groups vote mainly for parties of the right."[1] However, almost thirty years later he is one of the first people, along with Terry Clark, to predict the disappearance of social classes and of the privileged link between left-wing parties and people from working-class backgrounds.[2]

The stakes are high. Despite the rise of the middle classes, the so-called working classes continue today to represent the majority of the electorate. And these are the classes that the radical and populist Extreme-Rights developing in Europe today are trying to win over. Does the notion of a "class vote" still have meaning? If so, what are the theoretical and empirical bases for it? This chapter will address these questions from a comparative perspective, looking at France in a European context and paying particular attention to questions of definition and measurement. The Marxist approach stresses the position of individuals in the process of production, the relationship to capital and to work, domination, and conflict. It sees social classes as collective actors, equipped with a class conscience and with political representation. On the other hand, the Weberian approach stresses the unequal access of individuals to economic, social, and political resources without these latter being necessarily cumulative or producing a sense of class consciousness. Rather than classes, it identifies social strata according to their position on scales based on income, qualifications, and prestige. These two approaches will be combined here, taking both the relationship to the means of work and social position into account.

The Origins of Class Voting

The Sociological Model

Electoral sociology really came into its own in the United States after the Second World War with opinion polls and the groundbreaking work of Paul Lazarsfeld and his team at Columbia University.[3] They carried out a survey to measure the impact of the 1940 presidential election among a representative panel of inhabitants of Erie County in Ohio. The panel was questioned on seven different occasions and the results revealed, to their great surprise, that the electoral campaign had only a limited effect on the political choices made. The majority of voters had made their minds up well before the campaign started and remained faithful to their initial choices which corresponded to their social and professional background. Three variables played a key role: economic and social status,[4] religion, and place of residence. Three out of four rich protestant farmers voted for the Republican candidate and 90% of the urban Catholic labor force voted for the Democratic candidate: "People think, politically, as they are, socially. Social characteristics determine political characteristics," such is the main conclusion of their study.[5] This sociological model was nonetheless rapidly called into question first by researchers at the University of Michigan who placed the psychological mechanisms of "party identification" at the heart of their model and then by economic approaches to voting. In Europe, on the contrary, the idea that politics is the reflection of social structures imposed itself durably both under the influence of Marxism and because, unlike American parties,[6] European parties were built on the bases of class.

This is what Seymour M. Lipset and Stein Rokkan showed in their groundbreaking book, *Party Systems and Voter Alignments: Cross-National Perspectives*.[7] They link the genesis of European parties to four basic conflicts. The first two are the product of a "nation-building" process which saw the nation-state progressively impose itself against both local, regional, and linguistic particularities (the center-periphery cleavage) and the influence and privileges of the Church. The second two are the result of the industrial revolution which first opposed the rising bourgeois industrial class to landowners and then workers to capitalist owners. The sequential interaction between these four cleavages gave birth to the partisan and electoral cleavages of today (table 10.1). The political parties were seen as agents for the transformation of these social conflicts into long-lasting political divisions which they would then contribute to maintaining. The first three cleavages gave rise to parties which differed from one country to another as the building of the nation-state, the rate of industrialization, the shock of the Reformation and the Counter-Reformation did not occur at the same time or indeed at the same pace. However, the same cleavage along the lines of class was to be found everywhere with left-wing parties defending the working classes and conservative parties defending the middle and upper classes.

The Working-Class Vote

The English sociologist, Robert Alford measured this "class vote" with the help of a simple indicator named after him which was to be used worldwide.[8]

Table 10.1 The four stages in the formation of party systems

Cleavage	*Critical Period*	*Issue*
Center/periphery	Reformation—Counter-reformation: sixteenth–seventeenth centuries	National vs. supranational religion; national language vs. Latin
State/Church	National (French) Revolution: post-1789	Secular vs. religious control of mass education
Land/industry	Industrial Revolution: nineteenth century	Tariff levels for agricultural products; Control vs. freedom for industrial enterprise
Owner/worker	Russian Revolution: 1917	Integration into national polity vs. commitment to international revolutionary movement

Source: Lipset and Rokkan, 1967, p. 47.

He identified two classes: one made up of workers and one made up of non-workers. He also identified two types of vote: a left-wing vote (Labor) and a right-wing vote (Conservative). The indicator is calculated by subtracting the proportion of workers from non-workers who vote Left. If during a given election all the workers vote to the Left and none of the non-workers do, the indicator takes on the value of 100 (100%-0%) resulting in a perfect class vote. If the proportion of workers and non-workers who vote Left is identical, then the index falls to 0 and there is no class vote. Should the proportion of non-workers voting to the Left be higher than the number of workers voting Left, then there is a negative index or inverse class vote. He compared the results of 53 electoral surveys carried out between 1936 and 1962 in the United States, in Britain, in Canada, and in Australia and found that the British case, where the index went up to + 40 was the purest example of "class voting," whereas it fell to + 16 in the United States and was non-existent in Canada. In their analysis of British elections between 1963 and 1970, Butler and Stokes[9] confirm the privileged bond between British workers in the 1960s and the Labour Party, which was seen as the "defender of the workers."

A similar phenomenon can be observed in France. The non directive interviews carried out by Guy Michelat and Michel Simon at the end of the 1960s,[10] reveal two antagonistic sub-cultures: the Catholic sub-culture defined by religion on the one hand and a non-religious sub-culture of workers defined by class antagonism on the other. The latter defined themselves as workers, fighting against capitalist bosses, they believed in the virtues of collective action, they preferred left-wing parties and trade unions, above all the Communist Party (PC) which was seen as the natural ally of the working "class." The following interview extract demonstrates this clearly:

> It seems to me that any self-respecting worker has to have communist tendencies all the same, he has communist ideas—it goes without saying. He is a communist sympathiser, necessarily, because he works for a boss, he works for some guy who gets rich by the sweat of your brow, automatically you're a communist, you're a communist sympathiser, that's all there is to it."[11]

Their survey took these results further. The right-wing vote was higher among people who practiced a religion. The left-wing vote increased depending on the degree of integration in the working class as measured by the number of working-class connections or attributes possessed (being a worker oneself, having a working-class father or spouse, etc.). It went from 18% amongst women who were without any connection to 55% for workers whose fathers were also workers. The effects of "objective" social class were seen to combine with those of the "subjective" social class, i.e. the class individuals feel they belong to.[12] Identification with the working class increased with the number of working-class attributes. The communist vote was the most frequent amongst people who accumulated objective and subjective belonging to the working class (43%). But it was the subjective class which exercised decisive influence over political choice. Among the people surveyed, those who did not have any attachments to the working class but who identified with it nonetheless voted communist more often than the working-class sons of workers who did not share this feeling (31% as against 22%).

Using the same categories of cleavages—professional, religious, and territorial—as those highlighted by Lipset and Rokkan, a comparative survey carried out by Richard Rose in fifteen countries confirmed the determining influence of religion and social class on political choice.[13] Average variance explained by these three factors was 25% with a peak of more than 45% in Austria and more than 50% in the Netherlands. The religious variable was top of the list in "pillarised"[14] countries such as the Netherlands (50%), Belgium (23%), Austria (30%) and Catholic countries like Italy (22%) and France (28%). Social class had the strongest effect in the Scandinavian countries, with Sweden and Finland at 32% followed by Norway and Denmark. On first glance, the results seemed to confirm the thesis that cleavages were "frozen" and that the party system of the 1960s largely reflected the structure of cleavages in the 1920s.[15]

Death and Resurrection of Class Voting

From Cleavage Voting to Issue Voting?

And yet, at the same moment, the first signs that the model was losing impetus began to appear. The Alford index which until then supported the thesis of the "class vote" was only used from then on by those who announced its decline as shown in the diagram below which was printed in a great number of publications (figure 10.1). This phenomenon varied from one country to another. The fall of the index was particularly precocious and brutal in the United States, gradual in France and late and relatively limited in Sweden where in 1985 the Alford index still reached + 35. However, the shape of the curves in the graph was generally the same, seeming to prefigure the disappearance of class voting.

During the same period, electoral "volatility" seemed to be on the rise. This was true whether it was measured at the level of individuals by tracing their electoral itinerary through opinion polls or at a collective party level by calculating

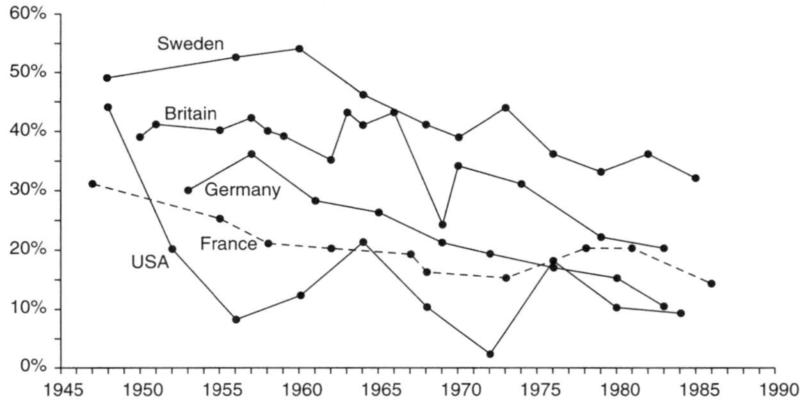

Figure 10.1 Changes in the Alford Index
Source: Clark et al., 1993.

the gains accumulated by all parties between two consecutive national elections.[16] The trend was toward electoral de-alignment,[17] and toward a questioning among voters of their usual habit of voting for the party assimilated to their class or religious preference.

This decline in the link between social and political cleavages is generally associated with changes brought about by the shift from the industrial to the postindustrial society that modified the balance between classes and the way people relate to politics. The fact that the economy became so much more service oriented reduced the number of workers to the benefit of the middle classes and white-collar workers. Economic growth, improvements in standards of living, and the fact that they could buy their own home made workers more individualistic and less concerned about solidarity. In parallel to their "embourgeoisement"[18] the "proletarisation" of routine non manual employees and a subsequent blurring of class borders could also be observed. More generally, the rising levels of education and particularly of higher education, the role of the media, the rise in "post-materialist" hedonistic and anti-authoritarian values theorized by the American sociologist, Ronald Inglehart,[19] are all factors which have encouraged the political emancipation of individuals. Better informed, more politically aware, they have become less dependent on political parties and better able to make up their minds depending on issues specific to the election and to the candidates presented. The individual has become "individualistic," "rational,"[20], "able to choose."[21] In the long run, "issue voting" would compete with the religious or socio-professional based "cleavage voting."[22] Finally, the political supply, the parties on offer changed. These same post-materialist values were shaking up the system of party alignment, giving rise to new demands which had not been taken into account and favoring the emergence of new left-wing parties (ecologists and alternatives). They also encouraged the emergence of Extreme-Right and populist parties[23] in reaction to a society judged to be too permissive and too open. The old parties themselves reinforced the decline of the class vote by changing their political discourse to widen their electoral base, thereby running the risk of losing their initial electorate. By opening up to the middle classes and by focusing on post-materialist issues, the working-class parties in particular blurred their image and lost some of their power of attraction among workers.

There are two variants of the thesis according to which class voting is declining. According to the first, socio-professional cleavages do not disappear: they change. Quite a lot of work has been done analyzing the fragmentation of the British working class, contrasting the old industrial working class of northern England and Scotland with a new class in the south of the country. This new class was better qualified, better off, worked in light industry, had developed a more instrumental and less collective vision of the trade unions and of politics and was more interested in the private sphere of activity. Dunleavy and Husbands[24] developed this distinction between public and private sector workers which also distinguished between consumers of public goods (social housing, public transport, and state health care) and consumers of private goods (car ownership, private housing, private health care). The first group tend to vote Labor and the second Conservative. Other authors pointed out the cleavages linked to education and the shift toward the Left of the new middle classes who had knowledge but not power and who were particularly sensitive to post-materialist issues, leaning toward the new left-wing parties.[25] The other variant argued that social and professional cleavages were declining. According to this view, political cleavages today are drawn only around post-materialist issues and values.[26] It argued that belonging to a given generation, gender, and ethnic identity have become increasingly important when deciding how to vote, transcending the barriers of class.

The Indicators Battle

However, these results were rapidly called into question because of weaknesses in their methodological bases. Results always depend of course on how the measures are taken. Having studied 300 elections in 12 European countries taking place over a century, Bartolini and Mair[27] support the opposite thesis: in the long term, it is electoral stability which dominates with the volatility observed being an optical illusion resulting from the fact that the period studied was too recent and also from the indicators used. If the notion of cleavage is studied with rigor, if one reasons in the long term starting with the end of the nineteenth century, if one retains only the volatility between blocks rather than movement within each camp then electoral mobility seems much stronger during the inter-war period.

The Alford index was the one to receive most criticism for a number of reasons. It doesn't take variations in numbers within each class over time and within the electorates considered into account. Nor does it take into account the complexity of social structure in postindustrial society which can not be reduced to two classes. Finally, it does not take account of the complexity of the political landscape and especially within multi-party systems. Using more sophisticated statistical methods together with more finely tuned and more subtle socio-professional and political divisions, other research has put the decline of the class vote into perspective. In England, Anthony Heath and his colleagues at Oxford[28] carried out research using loglinear models based on the calculation of odds ratios. The odds of workers having voted Left rather than Right (O_L/O_R) is related to the odds of non-workers having voted Left rather than Right ($\bar{O}_L/\bar{O}_R$). The further the value is from 1, the stronger the class effect is. Rather than confining themselves to the worker/non-worker dichotomy, the authors returned to the more elaborate classification put forward by John Goldthorpe and Robert Erikson.[29] This classification takes account of the degree of autonomy in the workplace, the level of expertise and the exercise of authority to distinguish the service class from routine non manual employees and manual workers. They conclude that, in England, there is no linear decline in class voting but rather "trendless fluctuations" where class voting decreased between 1964 and 1979 and then rose again. The specific context of each election must be taken into account, the decline in the working-class vote, for example, usually sanctions a long period of Labour government.

The most sophisticated model is the one proposed by Michael Hout, Jeff Manza, and Clem Brooks[30] in their analysis of class voting in the United States. Using presidential elections between 1948 and 1992 they measure what they call, "the total class vote" as opposed to the "traditional class vote" as measured by the Alford index. They take account of all possible electoral choices including abstention and ballots for independent candidates. They distinguish six socio-professional categories, based on Goldthorpe's classification and they use a synthetic indicator, the kappa index which summarizes a series of multinomial logistic regressions. They conclude that class voting has not disappeared in the United States. On the other hand, important realignments have taken place as workers have detached themselves form the Democratic Party, company owners have stressed their support for the Republicans and professionals and managers[31] have shifted toward the Democrats.

The controversy has not yet been settled as Geoffrey Evans' collective book illustrates,[32] bringing together fervent opponents and defenders of the class vote thesis, all of them camping on their own positions.[33] More recently, the major studies of Knutsen[34] and Thomassen[35] reassess transformations in cleavage voting in Europe and Jeroen Van de Waal, Peter Achterberg, and Dick Houtman even conclude that there has been a revival of class voting, drawing from the data of the International Social Mobility and Politics File.[36]

France in the European Mirror

In the light of these debates, the major electoral surveys carried out at the Cevipof enable an in-depth study of change in class voting in France from the presidential election of 1978 to the 2002[37] presidential election to be undertaken. During this period, social structure changed enormously.[38] The overall level of qualifications rose. From 1980 to 2002 the proportion of young people aged 20–24 in higher education increased from 18% to 43%. The proportion

Table 10.2 Correspondence between Goldthorpe's and the INSEE's classification

Goldthorpe and Erikson (1992)	*The INSEE's Socio-professional Groups*
Self-employed	*Agriculteurs, commerçants, artisans*
Upper service class	*Cadres, professions intellectuelles supérieures, chefs d'entreprise*
Lower service class	*Professions intermédiaires*
Routine non-manual employees	*Employés*
Skilled workers, unskilled workers	*Ouvriers*

Source: Cevipof post-electoral surveys and the French Electoral Panel, 2002.

of self-employed receded. Farmers represented 20% of the active population in 1954 and less than 5% in 2002 and the share of artisans and shopkeepers dropped from 12% to 5%. The proportion of workers fell from more than 30% to 25%, while the number of routine non-manual employees doubled to reach 30%. The number of people in the upper service class quadrupled and the lower service class doubled. Today, taken as a whole, professionals and managers make up one third of the workforce. Finally, mass unemployment, mostly affecting routine non manual employees and workers began in 1974 and varied between 8% and 12% throughout the period as against less than 2% in the 1960s. This was also a politically volatile period which witnessed the arrival of the Left in power followed by its defeat, the implantation of the *Front National* (FN) in the French political landscape, the return of the Left as a result of the surprise dissolution in 1997, three periods of cohabitation, and the return of the Right as a result of the political "earthquake" on the April 21, 2002, when Jean-Marie Le Pen beat the socialist candidate, Lionel Jospin in the first round of the presidential election thus qualifying for the second round.

Two indicators of social class were used. The first of these was the interviewee's occupation using the INSEE's nomenclature of six socio-professional groups (SPG) which is quite similar to Goldthorpe and Erikson's classification (table 10.2). The second indicator used was the socio-professional status which distinguishes between the self-employed and employees who work for a boss. This includes both public sector employees whose employer is the state and private sector employees. The unemployed, retirees and women who have given up paid employment were reclassified according to their last job, the effects of the professional background on electoral behavior being prolonged beyond the temporary or definitive cessation of activity. Lastly, on the political front, the emergence of the *Front National* was taken into account and a distinction was made between votes for the Left, the Center-Right, and the Extreme-Right.

Class Dealignments and Realignments

During the period studied, the privileged bonds between workers and left-wing parties were effectively eroded (table 10.3). In 1978, seven out of ten workers voted for them.

In 2002, only 43% of them did so. Although the left-wing vote remained the largest among them, the gap with non-worker employees practically disappeared.

The Alford index which was at 23 in 1978 was at zero in 2002. This receding of the Left was linked to transformations within the working-class landscape which was greatly affected by industrial restructuring and unemployment. This partly benefited the *Front National*. It obtained its highest score from workers in the 1995 presidential election or more precisely from those workers who did actually vote as the abstention rate was highest[39] amongst this section of the electorate. Between 1978 and 2002, the total number of votes cast by workers for the Extreme-Right increased from 1% to 26%. Harnessing the disappointment aroused by the arrival of the Socialists in power in 1981, the FN portrayed itself as the privileged defender of the little guy against the great and powerful, the people against the elites. Conversely, the salaried middle classes—a category with a high proportion of young people, urban dwellers, well-educated people, non church goers, and sensitive to post-1968 values—moved closer to the Left and in particular to the Socialist Party which had been renovated in 1971. This switching of political allegiances drew the new socio-professional cleavages.

The first of these distinguishes between employees and the self-employed. Four out of five of the latter prefer the right-wing to left-wing parties who, to their minds, defend employees against owners and reinforce state intervention in economic life. In 2002, the level of left-wing votes among the two groups was still separated by 23 points as against 32 in 1978 (table 10.3). A second cleavage has appeared between private and public sector employees. The latter are more likely to vote Left that has remained the dominant political force amongst them throughout the period studied. During the same period,

Table 10.3 The left-wing vote by socio-professional group and status (%)

	Leg. election 1978	*Pres. election 1988*	*Pres. election 1995*	*Leg. election 1997*	*Pres. election 2002*
Socio-professional group					
Farmers	26	29	20	27	18
Owners	31	32	19	31	20
Executives and Managers	45	41	46	46	43
Mid-level employees	57	48	45	51	50
Routine non manual employees	54	52	38	52	39
Workers	70	63	49	52	43
Alford Index	**23**	**18**	**11**	**5**	**0**
Status					
Self-employed	28	30	22	29	21
Salaried	60	54	44	51	44
Gap	**32**	**24**	**22**	**22**	**23**
Sector					
Private	58	52	40	47	39
Public	64	58	52	57	51
Gap	**6**	**6**	**12**	**10**	**12**
Total	53	49	41	48	43
Numbers	3,867	3,091	3,149	1,963	2,826

Source: Cevipof post-electoral surveys and the French Electoral Panel, 2002.

the Left receded among private sector employees who tend to be more receptive to either Le Pen type political messages (workers and routine non manual employees) or messages from the Center Right (managers and professionals). The gap between the two groups has risen from 6 points in 1978 to 12 points since 1995. The persistence of unemployment, which has affected private sector employees massively, has made them see public sector employees as privileged as they have guaranteed jobs and better pension schemes. In the meantime, the latter are fearful of the economic liberalism of the Right and the risks of deregulation associated with the building of the European Union. Socio-professional cleavages have shifted. However, they have not disappeared.

A correspondence factor analysis allows these transformations to be visualized more synthetically (figure 10.2). This is done by projecting the six socio-professional groups onto the political landscape and following their movements in time from one election to another.[40] Three phenomena clearly appear. Workers have progressively moved toward the center of the graph, shifting away from their initial anchoring on the Left. Managers and the upper service class, on the other hand, have moved away from the Right. A loglinear model of these different parameters[41] confirms the hypothesis of a transformation and not the disappearance of class voting. To the de-alignment of workers corresponds a realignment of mid-level employees toward the Left and of the self-employed toward the Right.

The Perturbing Effect of the Front National

The only exception to this rule is the vote for the *Front National* which brings yesterday's class enemies—workers and small business owners—into the same camp through their rejection of immigrants.[42] This blurring of boundaries

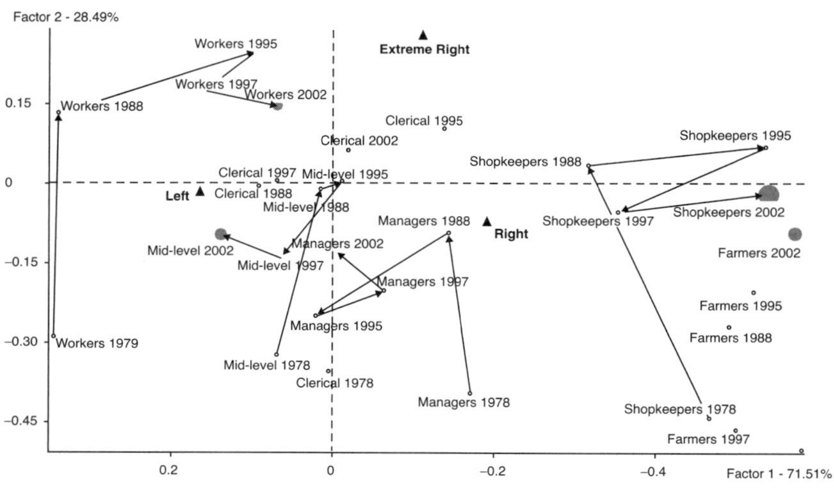

Figure 10.2 Changes in the vote by socio-professional group in France 1978–2002

Source: Cevipof post-electoral surveys and the French Electoral Panel, 2002 (Cautrès and Mayer, 2004, p. 154).

Table 10.4 The Le Pen vote by socio-professional group (%)

Socio-professional group	*1998*	*1995*	*2002*	*Gap*
Farmers	10	10	22	12
Owners	19	19	22	3
Executives and Managers	14	4	13	−1
Mid-level employees	15	14	11	−4
Routine non manual employees	14	18	22	8
Workers	17	21	23	6

Source: Cevipof post-electoral surveys and the *Panel électoral français*, 2002.

intensified again during the 2002 presidential election, when for the first time the FN leader made advances in rural and agricultural areas. The level of the Le Pen vote is identical among farmers, company owners, non manual employees and workers. The only categories to resist his influence are executives and managers (table 10.4). The specific nature of the Le Pen vote is confirmed by taking the different parameters likely to explain the vote into account.[43]

Religion and socio-professional status (self-employed, public sector employee, private sector employee) remain the best predictors of choice between left- and right-wing candidates in the first round. The same can not be said for the Extreme-Right. In this case, it is no longer the socio-professional status which counts but the level of education and the sex of the voter. Whatever their age, less well-educated voters gave their vote more often to Le Pen or Mégret on April 21, and men much more willingly than women. If women had been the only ones to vote on that day, Le Pen would have been in third position after Jospin and Chirac. If only men had voted, Le Pen would have taken first place, in front of Chirac and Jospin. The simplistic discourse of the *Front National* which makes immigrants the single cause of all problems in France today, and "national preference," the miracle remedy for unemployment, is more readily listened to among the less well educated. Added to this, the physical and verbal violence that surrounds Le Pen rebuffs female voters, as does the traditional image of the woman at home which he conveys.

The *Front National* therefore appears to be a perturbing element in the French political landscape, bringing together a composite electorate by means of the federating issue of immigration. Whatever the election, this is the problem which together with insecurity is the primary motivation for this electorate. This is quite clearly a cross-cleavage and cross-class issue vote.

European Electoral Tendencies

The first wave of the European social survey was carried out late 2002, early 2003 in around 20 countries including France. It provided an opportunity to compare the French situation to what was happening in other European countries. There already exist several comparative studies on electoral cleavages. The one which Jacques Thomassen directed recently on the European voter, using the European electoral survey data bank of the International Committee for

Research into Elections and Representative Democracy (ICORE),[44] confirms a general weakening of the relationship between party choice and class membership. However, he confines himself to the six countries for which comparable data since the 1960s are available: Denmark, (West) Germany, the Netherlands, Norway, Sweden and the United Kingdom. Oddjborn Knutsen's study,[45] using several *Eurobarometers* waves (1975–1997), includes France alongside Belgium, Denmark, Germany, Ireland, Italy, the Netherlands, and the United Kingdom. Knutsen keeps to the Left-Right dichotomy using the whole range of class vote indicators to show how it reached its highest level in Denmark and its lowest in Italy and Germany. During the period under study, it declined overall by 35% (Kappa index) to 47% (Alford index) on average. The decline was highest in Denmark and the Netherlands, insignificant in Germany and middling in France. Using the ESS survey, this analysis can be continued. Our socio-professional indicator comes close to John Goldthorpe and Robert Erikson's categorization (table 10.2), distinguishing four groups of employees from executives and managers to workers and classifying the self-employed separately.[46] The second indicator used is the status divided into three positions distinguishing between self-employed workers and public and private sector employees.[47] The electoral indicator used is the reconstitution of the votes in the last national election. The question was often asked several months after the election and is understood here essentially as an indicator of political position. It correlates to the position on a Left-Right scale and degree of party alignment. France is compared to two countries where class voting was particularly high, Sweden and the United Kingdom, to Germany where it was particularly low and to Spain, a southern country where industrialization is more recent.

In three of these five countries, it can be observed that the level of left-wing voting—the ecologists are included here—increases regularly as one goes down the social scale: from company owners to senior and mid-level executives, then to clerical and sales staff, reaching its maximum among workers. In Sweden and the United Kingdom in particular, almost three quarters of workers say they voted Left and 60% do so in Spain where the group is the largest[48] (table 10.5). In France, on the other hand, the working-class exception is no more. There is no longer any difference between the level of left-wing votes among workers, non manual employees and mid-level employees. Finally in Germany, the Alford index is negative. The left-wing vote is higher among mid-level employees and executives and managers than among workers as had been observed in France right after the 2002 presidential election (table 10.3). But if the relationship to the means of production is taken as an indicator contrasting employees as a whole to the self-employed, the class vote clearly remains. In all five countries, including Germany, the fact of being self-employed clearly decreases the likelihood of a left-wing vote.

Finally, the cleavage between public and private sector employees is really strong only in France (the gap in the level of left-wing voting among the two groups stands at 14 points) where debate on maintaining public service has been particularly intense and to a lesser extent in Germany. It is inexistent elsewhere.

Table 10.5 Left-wing vote by socio-professional group and by country (%)

	GE	*SP*	*FR*	*UK*	*SW*
Socio-professional group					
Self-employed	33	31	37	56	40
Executives and managers, Liberal professions	58	34	50	63	48
Mid-level employees	68	41	58	63	55
Routine non manual employees	55	53	58	63	65
Workers	55	60	57	74	74
Alford Index	**–1**	**18**	**4**	**12**	**18**
Status					
Self-employed	33	31	37	56	40
Salaried	59	54	56	66	62
Gap	**26**	**23**	**19**	**11**	**22**
Sector					
Private	57	54	51	66	61
Public	65	54	65	65	64
Gap	**9**	**0**	**14**	**–1**	**3**

Source: ESS survey, 2003.

These results are based on the reconstitution of past votes whose unreliability is well known and on a simplified socio-professional nomenclature which limits the comparison. They need to be completed by national electoral surveys using much more detailed social and political indicators and notably questions on feelings of belonging to a given class. They show nonetheless that "class voting" continues to exist but in other forms. The main cleavages highlighted by Lipset and Rokkan have not disappeared. They have softened and shifted as a result of change in socio-professional structures and in the party system. This has varied greatly from one country to another. Overall, the link between belonging to the working class and voting to the Left has declined everywhere though it nonetheless remains strong in Sweden and more generally in the Scandinavian countries and in Britain (Table 10.5). On the other hand, from an electoral point of view, the Left has made progress amongst non working-class employees and has broadened its base beyond its habitual electorate amongst clerical and sales staff and mid-level employees. This can be read in either of two ways, as a class de-alignment but also as a class realignment. It can also be read as a wider opposition between the self-employed, who answer only to themselves and employees who are dependant on a boss. In other words, the socio-professional category one belongs to continues to be a factor in determining whether one votes Left or Right and more so than income or level of qualification.[49]

However, it is equally obvious that mid-level employees do not make up a class in the same way that yesterday's workers did. Some of them at least—and in particular industrial workers who worked for large companies and lived in the same social housing areas—had a strong professional identity and a class culture which meant they leaned toward the left-wing unions and parties, and in particular the Communist Party. The world of non working-class employees seems much more fragmented and the notion of "middle" class less a mobilizing force. As for the parties, they refer less and less to the notion of class and in this way contribute themselves to untying the links between social classes and votes.

Notes

1. Lipset, 1981, 234.
2. Lipset and Clark, 1991; see also Clark and Lipset, 2001.
3. Lazarsfeld, Berelson, and Gaudet, 1944.
4. The socioeconomic status was identified by the interviewer who placed the people interviewed on a scale of 1–5, using a synthetic indicator narrowly correlated to the professional sector, level of education and the feeling of belonging to a particular class (Lazarsfeld, Berelson, and Gaudet, 1944, pp.17–21).
5. Ibid., p. 27.
6. Opposition between Republicans and Democrats was essentially built around the issues of slavery and the Civil War, although a class dimension was also present.
7. Lipset and Rokkan, 1967.
8. Alford, 1963.
9. Butler and Stokes, 1969.
10. Michelat and Simon, 1977.
11. Interviews with workers who declared they had no religion, carried out in 1966 (Michelat and Simon, 1977).
12. The indicator is the following: "Do you feel you belong to a social class? If yes, which one? (free answers)."
13. Rose, 1974.
14. The term comes from the Netherlands, from *verzuiling*: pillar. Society is segmented vertically into communities (religious, ideological, linguistic, ethnic, etc.) which rely on an associative network (schools, unions, sports clubs, cultural associations, etc.). These associations and clubs take the individual in hand from birth to death and shape his/her relationship to the world and to politics.
15. Lipset and Rokkan, 1967, pp. 50–56.
16. Pedersen, 1979.
17. Crewe and Denver, 1985.
18. Goldthorpe et al., 1969.
19. Inglehart, 1990.
20. Habert, 1996.
21. Rose and McAllister, 1986.
22. Franklin et al., 1992.
23. Kitschelt and McGann, 1995.
24. Dunleavy and Husbands, 1985.
25. Grunberg and Schweisguth, 1983.
26. Inglehart, 1990.
27. Bartolini and Mair, 1990.
28. Heath, Jowell, Curtice, 1985; Heath et al., 1991; Cautrès and Heath, 1996.
29. Goldthorpe and Erikson, 1992.
30. Hout, Manza, and Brooks, 1995b.
31. The "professionals" category includes self-employed people such as doctors and lawyers, etc.
32. Evans, 1999.

33. See also Hout, Brooks, and Manza, 1995a; Nieuwbeerta, 1996; Chauvel, 2002; Chopart and Martin, 2004; Brooks, Nieuwbeerta, and Manza, 2006.
34. Knutsen, 2006.
35. Thomassen, 2006.
36. Van de Waal, Achterberg, and Houtman, 2007.
37. These data are taken from the second wave of the French Electoral Panel 2002 carried out by telephone after the second round of the presidential election with a representative national sample of the metropolitan French registered voters (May 13–31, 2002, N = 4,017); three Cevipof post-electoral surveys run by the SOFRES as face to face interviews after the second round of the general election in 1978 (March 20–30, 1978, N = 4,507) and after the last two presidential elections (May 9–20, 1988, N = 4,032 and May 9–24, 1995, N = 4,078); and a survey carried out by the Cevipof, CRAPS, CIDSP, *Libération*, administered by the SOFRES by telephone between the two rounds of the 1997 general election (May 26–31, 1997, N = 3,010).
38. The following figures are based on the report on social and political change in French society drawn up by Galland and Lemel (2006).
39. If the percentages are recalculated on the basis of registered voters, on April 21 workers had the highest abstention rate at 31%, higher than votes for the Left (29%), the Right (22%) and the Extreme-Right (18%).
40. Cautrès and Mayer, 2004.
41. Ibid., p.153.
42. Perrineau, 1997; Mayer, 2002.
43. Logistic regressions on left-wing, moderate Right, and Extreme-Right votes in the first round of the 2002 presidential election. Apart from socio-professional status, explicative variables include the number of links to the working class, income and assets, gender, level of education checked against age (Cautrès and Mayer, 2004, pg. 175).
44. Thomassen, 2006.
45. Oddjborn Knutsen, 2006.
46. The recoding was done by Luc Rouban on the basis of the ISCO-88 classification in 9 positions: 1–2 = Executives and higher intellectual professions 3 = Mid-level employees; 4–5 = Clerical and sales staff; 6–9 = Workers. I created a fifth category extracting the self-employed (farmers, company owners, artisans, shopkeepers, doctors, lawyers). Police and military come under mid-level employees and farm laborers under workers.
47. The distinction between public and private sector employees was reconstituted by Luc Rouban (2005) on the basis of the ESS variable “nacer1.” Civil servants, teachers, health and social services employees were classified in the public sector.
48. 45% as against 31% in Germany and between 24% and 27% in the three other countries.
49. Cautrès and Mayer, 2004.

CHAPTER 11

The Green Movement

Daniel Boy

It is frequently claimed that the best electoral terrain for Green parties is to be found in Northern Europe. Germany is presented as the cradle of political ecology for several reasons: the *Grünen* had their first electoral successes there; this is where anti-nuclear movements succeeded in emerging onto political terrain with the programmed closure of German nuclear centers and finally, ecological civic-mindedness is thought to have a clear impact on the electoral behavior of German voters. In France, on the other hand, a country described as being impregnated with the chronic lack of civic spirit which characterizes the Latin countries, it is widely believed that ecology has not really become part of everyday mentalities. This is presented as the reason why the green party took root there only later and without managing to achieve the same degree of electoral success as it did in Germany. The critical comparison often goes further: the French *Verts* are said to be ecologists in name only as it is claimed that, in reality, they do not defend environmental values with sufficient fervor due to an overly exclusive attachment to Left and indeed Extreme-Left values. Whether rightly or wrongly, French ecologists are reproached with being more concerned with the traditional issues of the Left-Right struggle (equality of living conditions or refusal of discrimination, for example), than with environmental values. How true are these assertions? Does the history of ecological movements in Europe confirm that France has fallen behind on this issue? In comparison with their Belgian, German or Dutch counterparts are the French *Verts* less worthy of the name? Does a comparison of the values subscribed to by different Green electorates in Europe reveal a relative homogeneity among them or not? In France, where the anti-nuclear movement has not managed to oppose the setting in place of a gigantic nuclear power program, are people more attached to rationalist values and if so, is this difference noticeable even among French Green electorates? To put it briefly, is a French Green less critical of scientific and technical development than a German or

Swedish Green? Even though the amount of survey data available is not sufficient to provide a full answer to these questions, this research will nonetheless provide some kind of partial answer.

The Founding of the Green Parties: A Few Landmarks

The birth of the Green parties took place at more or less the same time in different European countries. The majority of them were founded in Western European democracies around the beginning or middle of the 1980s: in Germany, *Die Grünen* were founded in January1980, in Walloon Belgium, *Écolo* was founded at the beginning of 1980 and in Great Britain, the Green Party was founded in 1985. In parallel to their emergence on the political landscape, the Green parties began to present candidates at local or national elections around the same time: in Germany for the local elections in 1978 and the federal election in 1980, in Belgium in 1981.

Compared to these examples, the French case is not so different. Based on the presentation of candidates for election alone, the French ecologists can even be said to be ahead of their European counterparts. During the French presidential election of 1974, members of *Amis de la Terre* (Friends of the Earth) presented an "ecologist" (the term Green was not in use then) candidate for the first time. They chose René Dumont, an agronomist known for his pacifist views and for his books advocating a type of agriculture which would respect the environment in developing countries. The appearance on television of this pioneer of political ecology during the 1974 electoral campaign was probably the occasion when environmental themes were brought to the attention of the French public for the first time. René Dumont obtained a relatively low score of 1.32% of votes cast but he showed militants for the first time that an electoral campaign provides a favorable terrain for the spreading of ecologist ideas in that it provides a captive and exceptional audience. French ecologists were encouraged by this relative success and continued to present candidates at local and national elections with sometimes remarkable success. Thus, after the 1977 local election in Paris, candidates on the ecologist ticket obtained almost 10% of the votes cast. In the 1978 general election, the ecologists, who were present in roughly half the constituencies, obtained an average of 4.5% of votes cast. This was a low but encouraging figure for a movement which, at that moment in its history, had no lasting politically aligned organisation to lean on. Small committees were put together for each election. They brought the activists together, designated candidates, joined in the struggle for election and came to an end as an organisation once the election was over. In France, the merger between the different groups representing the various branches of political ecology took place only in 1984 during the Clichy Congress.

In the French case, these first successes were followed by quite a long "period in the desert" which contributed to confirming the stereotype of a chronic weakness within French political ecology. The arrival of the Left in power with the election of François Mitterrand in 1981, and the subsequent election of a parliament largely dominated by the Socialists marked the opening of a difficult period for the *Verts* at the very moment when Green parties in Northern Europe were beginning to obtain encouraging electoral results. In France, where the economic crisis was gathering strength, the Left put a Keynesian economic policy in place designed to relaunch the economy and put an end to the economic crisis of the time. The Left was convinced of the virtues of growth and as part of its creed focused on aggressive industrial policies, relaunching consumption and the development of scientific and technical research. One example of this conversion to new ways of thinking is that until 1981 when they came into power, the Socialists had advocated a moratorium on the building of nuclear power centers. Once they came into power they adopted a nuclear program identical to that of the outgoing Gaullist majority. In this production-oriented context which seemed to appeal to the Socialist Party electorate, it was very difficult for the *Verts* to get their point of view across: it was easier to preach moderation in economic growth, a halt to nuclear power and reasonable consumption in the context of the relative prosperity of the 1970s than during times of economic crisis in the 1980s. The *Verts* had been abandoned by a section of their electorate for the Socialist Party and struggled to obtain more than a few percentage points in general elections: 1.1% in 1981 and 2.5% in 1986.

These difficulties were the result of the external political context. However, a change in internal policy which would weigh on the electoral strategy of the *Verts* for a long time to come was added to this. Shortly after the Party was founded in 1986, the members discussed their political future during their annual general meeting. Led by Yves Cochet, some of them, (probably a majority), openly evoked the need to reach an agreement on program and electoral strategy with the Socialist Party. However, when a vote was taken, the position defended by the Alsatian environmentalist militant Antoine Waechter, won the confidence of the majority of those present. According to the winning motion, the *Verts* agreed to abstain from making any political agreement with anyone. In Waechter's terms, ecology was "not available for marriage" and would develop independently of any other political organisation of any kind. The "neither right nor left" policy was born and would remain in place until 1993. During this period, the *Verts* voluntarily forbade themselves from concluding any electoral agreement with another party. This, of course was a risky strategy in an electoral system dominated by a two-round majority system for national elections at least. However, the adoption of this strategy of political isolation did not prevent them from obtaining their first notable electoral successes at the end of the 1980s. This was in elections where the voting system was such that there was no need to find political alliances. In the 1989 European election, which used a PR type voting system, the list headed by Antoine Waechter totaled 10.7% of votes cast. This was only slightly less than half the score of the Socialist list (23.6%) and more than the Communist Party score (7.8%). In the local elections of the same year, the *Verts* obtained 8.1% of the votes in the 129 towns where they were present, but because of the lack of a second round agreement with the Left, this success was not transformed into actual local election. In the 1992 regional elections, the *Verts* obtained 7.5% of the votes, in spite of the presence of a rival ecologist party, *Génération écologie*, led by Brice Lalonde.[1]

For the Greens, the 1993 general election was a semi-success as by sharing constituencies with their competitor, *Génération écologie,* they scored 7.8% of the vote. However, in the 1994 European elections, the *Verts* scored only 5% of the vote—one of the worst scores among European countries: in Germany the *Grünen* scored twice as much (10.1%), in Walloon Belgium they scored 13%, and in Ireland 7.9%. Dominique Voynet, the new leader of the *Verts* was a candidate in the 1995 presidential election but was unsuccessful in his bid winning just 3.4% of the votes cast. This series of bad results convinced the *Verts* leaders of the urgent need to reach an agreement with a political party. Negotiations with the Socialist Party were accelerated when Jacques Chirac dissolved the National Assembly in 1997. Following their agreement on program and electoral strategy with the Socialist Party, a certain number of constituencies were reserved for the *Verts* in which a Green candidate represented the Left as a whole. As a result of this strategy, 5 *Verts* deputies were elected including Dominique Voynet. Following the Left's electoral win, the *Verts* entered a coalition government for the first time. Dominique Voynet was appointed Minister for the Environment in Lionel Jospin's government.

At the end of this somewhat chaotic period, the *Verts* seemed to be following the same route as their German and Belgian counterparts as they had also entered into government coalitions. Like them, they were now faced with the difficult problem of how to manage power at the national level.

Electoral Criteria: Northern Success, Southern Failure?

Given its relatively precocious appearance, the difficulties experienced by political ecology in France need to be explained. One hypothesis suggests that this relative failure is part of a rule observable throughout Europe that ecological concerns developed more easily in northern than in southern countries. This hypothesis needs to be evaluated and the results obtained by ecologists in different European elections provide a useful basis for comparison as they indicate the relative success of Green parties at regular intervals for elections of the same type. Moreover, European elections have always provided a favorable terrain for the Green parties: environmental issues have always been particularly prominent at this level because of Europe's trans-national character, and also because the European Union has been perceived to be one of the drivers of environmental policy for several years now.

Without going into detail on all observable changes since the first European elections, it is nonetheless possible to distinguish three groups of countries characterized by unequal levels of Green voting (see table 11.1):

- countries where the ecology vote has always obtained good scores: the first is Belgium (both Walloon and Flemish), Luxembourg, Germany and later, Austria and Finland;

- countries where ecology has almost never achieved electoral success include: the UK, Greece, Spain, Italy, Denmark, Norway, and a good number of Eastern European countries;
- finally, the third category includes countries where the ecology vote is always quite low or irregular: this is the case for France, Sweden, Ireland and the Netherlands.

Clearly, this division does not allow the conclusion to be drawn that the distribution of Green votes is directly related to the North-South dimension. The rule can probably be verified by cross-checking against voting patterns in Germany, Belgium and Finland (strong results in the North) as against the counter examples of Italy, Spain, and Greece (weak results in the South).

However, there are many dissonant cases: notably the irregularity of results in Sweden and the quasi-absence of electoral ecology in Denmark, Norway and the United Kingdom. Convincing explanations for these exceptions abound: in the UK, it is clear that, in spite of the presence of powerful organizations for the defense of the environment, the Green Party has not found a place for itself within the electoral landscape as a direct result of the first past the post system which makes the emergence of new political forces difficult. From this point of view, the relative 'openness' of the political system provides important criteria to explain the success or failure of Green movements in Europe. In France, the two-round majority vote system in place for legislative, cantonal, and presidential elections severely complicates the political expression of ecological issues. Moreover, its best results have always been obtained in local,

Table 11.1 Scores obtained by green parties in the 2004 European elections in decreasing order (%)

Country	*Party*	*Score (%)*
Luxembourg	Les Verts (VERTS)	15.02
Austria	Die Grünen—Die Grüne Alternative (GRÜNE)	12.75
Germany	Die Grünen/Bündnis 90 (GRÜNE)	11.94
Finland	Vihreät (VIHR)	10.43
Malta	Alternattiva Demokratika/The Green Party (AD)	9.33
Portugal	Partido Comunista Português (PCP) Partido Ecologista "Os Verdes" (PEV)	9.1
Belgium	Groen ! (ex-AGALEV) Ecolo	8.7
The Netherlands	Groen Links (GL)	7.39
France	Les Verts	7.38
United Kingdom	Green Party (GP)	6.25
Sweden	Miljpartiet de Gröna (MP)	5.91
Latvia	Latvijas Zaļo partiju	4.63
Ireland	Green Party (GP)	4.32
Czech Republic	Strana Zelenŷch	3.2
Italy	Federazione dei Verdi (VERDI)	2.46
Cyprus	Kinima Oikologon Perivallontiston (KOP)	0.86
Slovenia	Stranka Ekoloskih Gibanj Slovenije (SEG)	0.59
Greece	Ellines Oikologoi	0.5
Poland	Zieloni 2004	0.27

regional, or European elections where the system involved at least one proportional element. Similarly, the lack of public finance for political parties until the beginning of the 1990s, seriously handicapped the Green movement which had neither the ability not the desire to seek finance elsewhere—and notably in the private sector—which might be more or less legal.

The exception of Denmark, a country situated in Northern Europe where political ecology is totally absent from the electoral landscape, is also worthy of interest. Paradoxically, it is probably precisely because environmental policy is so important in the country that there exists no one party specialized in this area: the environmental question is so well covered by the traditional parties that there is no room on the political scene for an ecology party as such to develop. This scenario is probably the same for Norway.

However, apart from these exceptions, and indeed others which remain without a convincing explanation, the hypothesis that political ecology is more present in Northern Europe has been relatively well verified. How can this be explained? It is sometimes suggested that Northern European countries are culturally more disposed to take environmental issues into account or that the weight of the strong romantic tradition in countries such as Germany or Austria explain their tendency to respect and protect nature whereas, in accordance with Descartes' precept, the Cartesian tradition leads the French rather to "become the masters and owners of nature." Another factor might be the influence of religion. For example, one might wonder whether Protestantism is more likely to favor environmental civic-mindedness as within that tradition the role of individual responsibility is more important than in the Catholic and Latin tradition. Or perhaps these differences can be explained by the weight of economic factors: more economic success and more well-being also generate more environmental damage and therefore stronger social pressure to protect the environment. Or indeed, a higher average level of education in Northern European countries might be the cause of a stronger tendency to protect the environment. All of these hypotheses are interesting but difficult to test.

With regard to cultural disposition, surveys on what kind of relations science and technology are perceived to have with nature may reveal whether the differences between countries are perceptible and whether they seem to correspond to the levels of concern for ecological matters nationally observed. The surveys used in this text provide a good example. The following question was posed in the 2004 ESS survey: "Modern science can be relied on to solve our environmental problems" A comparison of answers, (where respondents indicated whether they agreed or disagreed with this question), in different countries present in the survey shows that the positive answers[2] occur much more frequently in Southern Europe (Greece 79%, Portugal 71%, Spain 65%) than in Northern Europe (Denmark 24%, Austria 27%, Germany 31%). France is in an intermediary position with 60%. This provides proof that the level of confidence in science to solve environmental problems is higher in countries where political ecology has succeeded less in imposing itself than in Northern European countries where an inverse configuration can be observed: the higher the rate of ecology, the less the level of confidence in science.[3]

With regard to difference of attitudes between Catholics and Protestants, the idea that this factor might contribute to explaining a tendency to vote ecologist in countries, for example, where the two religions are in competition, has never been highlighted. However, in the surveys used here, the question posed above ("*Modern science can be relied on to solve our environmental problems*") is answered slightly differently depending on religious belonging. Protestants disagree with this opinion more often than Catholics. This may be the sign of a stronger concern to defend the environment through personal deeds more than relying solely on scientific and technological development. However, as shall be seen later, among the five countries under study here, those who vote ecologist tend generally not to be very religious and can not be differentiated in any case according to Catholic as opposed to Protestant criteria.

Five Cases of Political Ecology: France, Belgium, Germany, the Netherlands, Sweden

The first step in providing a more precise analysis of those who declare that they vote for or are sympathizers of the Ecologists in the ESS surveys was to select appropriately representative countries. France, Belgium, Germany, the Netherlands, and Sweden are all countries where the ecologist vote has reached relatively strong levels therefore providing a sufficient number of individuals for the purposes of this study even if the levels observed are somewhat unequal. Second, the decision to use feelings of empathy with political ecology as criteria should be explained. The ESS surveys provide information both about how people voted in the last national election and about "the party you feel closest to."[4] In each country, all those who vote for and/or who describe themselves as ecologist sympathizers were taken into consideration to maximize the number of individuals available for the analysis. Using these criteria, the following numbers of individuals are obtained: Germany, 236; Belgium, 217; the Netherlands, 177; Sweden, 98; France 95. In each of the five countries, a comparison was made between Green and non-Green nationals based on a series of criteria aimed at indicating in what way there are differences between "ecologists"[5] from one country to another and within the same country (by comparing them to other voters).

A Sociology of Greens

It is often claimed that women are more attached to the defense of the environment that men, that they are more sensitive to the risks posed by industry and more anxious to see precautionary policies applied. Moreover, these differences seem to be confirmed irrespective of the individual's socio-cultural background.[6] This survey shows that women are a little less likely than men (34% of women, 44% of men) to hold with the idea of "trusting science to solve environmental problems." In the five countries considered, the Ecologists include a higher proportion of women. But although this gap is constant it is not always of the same size: the highest proportion of women is found among German and Swedish Greens (63% and 64% respectively); in France and Belgium, the percentages are lower at 55% and 58%.

Because it only came into being over the last 30 years, ecological thinking seems to find it easier to convince younger age groups. This is also confirmed by the results of this survey: on average, ecologists—understood in the sense of this research—are younger than the electorate as a whole. The gap is a minimum of 6.4 years in Germany (41.5 years old as opposed to 47.8 years old) and reaches a maximum of 9.4 years in Sweden (37.3 years old as opposed to 46.7 years old). Given these figures, two different possibilities arise: either the attachment to political ecology is a generational phenomenon which is likely to spread as the younger generation takes its place in society, or it is a young person's thing that decreases as the individual subscribing to these ideas gets older. The surveys used here do not allow a clear answer to this question to emerge as it is not possible to compare the attitudes of cohorts of voters over several waves.

Those who define themselves by their empathy with ecology are younger than the average age of voters in general and also have a better level of education. Indeed, this is often the most characteristic trait of this group and is always pointed out in comparative studies particularly when they concern Green party members as a population.[7] The ESS surveys provide a measure of educational levels which allows comparisons between different countries to be made: it shows the total number of years of study carried out. In the five countries chosen here, the average number of years in education for individuals who choose ecology is around twelve. This is the approximate equivalent in France of primary and secondary school. Among the "ecologists" in the national samples, the average number of years in education is about two years higher: 14.8 in Germany, 13.7 in France, 14.2 in the Netherlands, 13.5 in Sweden and 13.8 in Belgium. The supplementary studies are roughly equal in all the countries considered here thus corresponding to a regular pattern. These extra years in education among "ecologists" can probably be partly explained by the fact that on average this group is younger: we know that, given the considerable increase in the number of graduates over the past thirty years, the percentage of them among younger generations is relatively high. This provides proof that the gap in levels of education (in number of years) is higher among people who are at least 45 years old than among younger people (less than 45 years old). However, the gaps in level are nonetheless characteristic of those who empathize with the values of political ecology. There are several explanations for this. The first is undoubtedly that the values at the heart of political ecology (the environment, quality of life, support for democracy) are more firmly anchored within the educated middle classes. The second possible explanation is that taking into account and understanding the environmental question—which is a recent phenomenon in the history of ideas—might be more accessible to people with a fuller educational background.

Beyond educational level, socio-professional structure constitutes a second type of indicator (see table 11.2).

Table 11.2 Greens and Non-Greens according to sector (%)

	Private sector employees	*Public sector employees*	*Self-employed*
Germany			
non-Greens	68	22	10
Greens	51	36	13
France			
non-Greens	61	28	11
Greens	46	45	10
The Netherlands			
non-Greens	62	28	10
Greens	47	46	7
Sweden			
non-Greens	62	29	9
Greens	52	36	12
Belgium			
non-Greens	58	28	13
Greens	50	39	10
Overall	*62*	*27*	*11*

From this point of view, it should first be noted that, in all of the five countries chosen, the "ecologists" can be distinguished from other respondents by the fact that they are more likely to belong to the public sector: in France, for example, which has the maximum gap on this criteria, 45% of "Greens" work in the public sector as against 28% of "non-Greens." Undoubtedly, this professional specificity more generally characterizes proximity to parties on the Left—the political camp that the Greens in the countries considered here are clearly attached to. In the case of France, which is the only country where this comparison can be made, we noted that the number of *Verts* party members working in the public sector is even higher than the number of Socialist Party members doing so.[8]

To go further in characterizing the areas respondents work in, those close to the Greens belong much more often to two particular sectors in the public sector, Education and Health Here again, this characteristic of the "ecologists" is true in every country considered and the percentages observed are often quite close. In Germany, for example 32% of "ecologists" work in Education or in Health as against 14% among those who sympathize with other parties. In France, the same percentages are respectively 32% and 18%, in Belgium 30% and 17%. To use classical terminology, it could be said that the "ecologists" in our sample belong more often to the "social reproduction" sector than to the productive sector. It is possible that this distance from the corporate world, in other words from the values linked to the private sector and its production imperatives, may partly explain empathy with ecology. This hypothesis can be stated without inferring any particular meaning to this type of relation itself: do individuals feel closer to ecology and the environment because the sector they work in is relatively independent of the weight of production constraints or do individuals choose this type of profession because of an early attachment to ecological values?

Ecology and Politics

Turning now to the nature of the links between ecology and politics, one might wonder whether empathy with political ecology fosters more active political commitment and whether this differs in the five countries under study or not. Two different indexes were reviewed. The first measures politicization in terms of the respondent expressing a strong interest in politics, considering that politics is important in life, and discussing politics frequently with friends and family. The second shows whether, over the previous 12 months the respondent has worked in a political campaign, (worn a badge, put up posters, etc.), signed a petition, participated in a demonstration or indeed boycotted certain consumer products for political or moral reasons or in defense of the environment.

With regard to the first point, politicization, in each of the five countries, respondents sympathetic to ecological matters are characterized by a higher level of politicization (see table 11.3). The gap is highest in Germany (58% for the Greens as against 47% for non-Greens). In the Netherlands and in Sweden, there is a 9 point difference whereas in France and in Belgium it is only 5 points.

With regard to the second point, commitment, the differences are even greater. Depending on the country, there are 20 to 30 points of difference in the degree of commitment as measured by this index (see table 11.4). To a certain extent, we are looking here at measures designed to protect the environment (boycotting certain consumer products) and therefore at behavior obviously linked to sympathy for ecological questions. However, the

Table 11.3 Index of politicization (%)

	–	+
Germany		
non-Greens	53	47
Greens	42	58
France		
non-Greens	73	27
Greens	68	32
The Netherlands		
non-Greens	58	42
Greens	49	51
Sweden		
non-Greens	65	35
Greens	56	44
Belgium		
non-Greens	74	26
Greens	69	31
Overall	*62*	*38*

Table 11.4 Index of commitment (%)

	–	+
Germany		
non-Greens	77	23
Greens	42	58
France		
non-Greens	72	28
Greens	45	55
The Netherlands		
non-Greens	86	14
Greens	68	32
Sweden		
non-Greens	68	32
Greens	47	53
Belgium		
non-Greens	80	20
Greens	53	47
Overall	75	25

differences are nonetheless important and the conclusion can effectively be drawn that there is a higher degree of "non conventional" commitment among Green sympathizers.

The Left, the Right, and Religion

Apart from a few rare exceptions, the European Green parties are aligned with left-wing parties and some have even made electoral alliances or indeed have taken part in coalition governments[9] with them. It is nonetheless more difficult to decide whether attitudes toward the environment necessarily include commitment to the Left or not. It has been argued that a preoccupation with protecting nature can be adapted just as easily to right-wing as to left-wing sympathies. For the population studied here two indicators will be analyzed. The first is a classic Left-Right scale with 11 possible positions (from 0 to 10)[10]; the second is made up of answers to two questions on left-wing values. Finally, a comparison will be made of the positions of different groups on questions measuring religious attachment (see table 11.5).

In table 11.5, the positions of Greens and non-Greens in each of the five countries have been brought together on a Left-Right scale. This time national differences are worth noting and in particular the fact that the French *a fortiori* when they are sympathetic to the Greens, are more frequently located in the Extreme-Left boxes. Apart from that, it is regularly observed that respondents who are Green sympathizers always position themselves further to the Left than their non-Green counterparts in the same country. Looking at the total to the Left, that is, 0–4 on the scale there is a gap of 42 percentage points between Greens and non-Greens in Germany, 33 in France, 48 in the Netherlands, 19 in Sweden and 32 in Belgium.

Table 11.5 Aggregate positions on a Left-Right scale in ten positions (%)

	0 + 1	*2 + 3 + 4*	*5*	*6 + 7 + 8*	*9 + 10*
Germany					
non-Greens	4	32	40	22	2
Greens	6	72	19	2	0
France					
non-Greens	10	29	29	26	7
Greens	19	52	20	9	0
The Netherlands					
non-Greens	3	24	28	41	5
Greens	8	67	18	7	1
Sweden					
non-Greens	8	32	22	33	5
Greens	7	51	28	14	0
Belgium					
non-Greens	6	23	40	27	4
Greens	9	53	23	15	1
Overall	*6*	*31*	*31*	*28*	*4*

In order to confirm this anchorage to the Left of those who declare themselves to be sympathetic to the ecologists, a comparison was made of the degrees of agreement with two propositions clearly appropriate to the Left-Right dimension:

- "*the government should take measures to reduce inequalities in income*" and,
- "*employees need strong unions to defend their conditions at work and their salaries.*"

For the first of these two questions, the results show that effectively a large number of Green movement sympathizers tend to choose egalitarian government measures with the French tending to be the most likely to make this choice (followed very closely by French non-Greens), and then Swedish, Belgian, and Dutch Greens. The German Greens are an exception to the rule here and are ranked in the final position.

On the second point, it is again the French Greens who subscribe most to left-wing values but here again in each country Green sympathizers frequently give the answer corresponding to a left-wing value.

The final indicator of position on Left-Right values is the question of religion. It is widely known that, traditionally, quite a narrow link between religious attitudes or behavior and attachment to the Left or Right exists. An analysis using several indicators of the religious positions of the national groups of Greens and non-Greens reveals different phenomena depending on the country.

In France, the Netherlands and Belgium, the Greens are noticeably less religious than their non-Green counterparts (see table 11.6). Thus, 76% of French "ecologists" say they are of "no religion" as against 48% of non-ecologists. In Germany and in Sweden, there is no marked religious difference between Greens and non-Greens.

Table 11.6 Three indicators of irreligiosity (%)

	No Declared Religion	*Never Attends Religious Ceremonies*	*Never Prays*
Germany			
non-Greens	45	42	43
Greens	47	41	44
France			
non-Greens	48	48	52
Greens	76	63	60
The Netherlands			
non-Greens	55	50	45
Greens	71	60	54
Sweden			
non-Greens	70	38	54
Greens	74	36	43
Belgium			
non-Greens	49	46	43
Greens	65	54	52
Overall	*54*	*45*	*47*

Cultural Liberalism

"Cultural liberalism" sometimes called "universalism" designates a series of opinions and attitudes considered to be more tolerant with regard to individual liberty, respect for each individual's values and a refusal of authoritarian processes. Over the past few years, this heading has often included values such as: the acceptance of foreigners, the refusal of racism, the promotion of values designed to fulfill the child rather than impose authority in schools, tolerance vis-à-vis sexuality, and so on. As a general rule, it would appear that this set of values forms a dimension which is easily just as revealing of difference in values as the traditional Left-Right cleavage is. It has been shown that the higher the level of education, the more these values are adopted. Given the social and cultural characteristics of Green voters and/or sympathizers, it can be expected that they in particular adhere to these types of values.

Two indicators can be used here to test the distribution of cultural liberalism within our different groups. The first is supplied by responses to the statement: "Male and female homosexuals should be free to live their lives as they see fit." The second is supplied by the answers to a series of three judgments centered on the role of immigrants in society in economic and cultural terms and in terms of quality of life.[11]

For the first of these two indicators it seems that, if the "strongly agree" answer is considered in each country, Green respondents display a more tolerant attitude toward homosexuals: the gaps observed go from a minimum of 16 percentage points (in the case of Sweden) to 23 in the case of Belgium.

With regard to the figures which express opinions on immigrants using the three questions taken into account, it would appear that they are indeed higher, i.e. that attitudes are more tolerant in each country amongst those who declare themselves to empathize with the Green parties (table 11.7).

Table 11.7 Opinions on immigrants

	Level of Appreciation of Immigrants (0 to 30)
Germany non-Greens	15.9
Germany Greens	19.9
France non-Greens	14.6
France Greens	17.9
The Netherlands non-Greens	15.3
The Netherlands Greens	18.1
Sweden non-Greens	18.7
Sweden Greens	20.9
Belgium non-Greens	14.4
Belgium Greens	17.4
Overall	*16.1*

Science and the Environment

To conclude this panorama of attitudes, we shall now turn to what constitutes the heart of ecological protest: the problem of scientific and technological developments and the protection of the environment. There are only two questions on this theme in the questionnaire: "*Economic growth always ends up harming the environment*" and "*Modern science can be relied on to solve our environmental problems.*"

For the first of these two opinions, the differences in attitudes are quite striking: in the sample as a whole, 36% of the people questioned "strongly agree" or "agree." Amongst French ecologists the percentage of those who agree is higher at 56% but there is no notable difference here with non-Greens (55%). Here, the differences observed seem to correspond to national tendencies in attitude more than the impact of political culture.

For the second question, on the other hand, the attitudes detected seem to be linked both to adherence to the Green project and to nationality: in the sample, 39% of people "trust science to solve environmental problems." This proportion is higher among French and Belgian non-ecologists, and in higher proportions than are found among the ecologists of these countries (for example respectively 56% and 42% in the case of France). Finally, agreement with this opinion is weakest among Swedish and German ecologists (23% and 18% respectively).

* * *

Ecology movements were born at roughly the same time and under equivalent conditions throughout Europe. They were carried by a wave of protest against the deterioration of the environment which first saw the light of day at the beginning of the 1970s. Initially, they were organized in small local pressure groups, then associations and finally in electoral committees. Little by little they became involved in politics by regularly presenting candidates at every kind of election.

In many European countries, they now score significant percentages in national elections. In four cases, they have taken part in wining electoral coalitions and have participated in the management of power. France is often seen to be a case apart and it is frequently argued that ecology has not found as favorable a terrain there as in Northern European democracies. However, a historical analysis shows this not to be entirely true: the ecological parties were created in France at more or less the same time as in the majority of other European countries. French political ecology certainly spent a period of time in the doldrums when the Left arrived in power. It also suffered as a result of Malthusian electoral tactics by confining itself for a time to the slogan "neither right nor left." However, since the middle of the 1990s, it has obtained more than respectable scores in local elections and regularly presents itself as a necessary partner within left-wing government coalitions.

The study of five countries where political ecology realizes scores higher than the European average shows furthermore, that beyond national differences, voters or sympathizers with the ecological movement form a fairly homogenous population. They are younger than the average voter, they are better educated and often work in Health or Education. The "ecologists" are distinguished by a real ideological unity: they tend to be more rallied than others by the political struggle and are anchored to the political Left. They support environmental values but also this "universalism" which rejects intolerance and racism.

Notes

1. Lalonde was one of the administrators of Amis de la Terre. He participated in several election battles with members of the Verts, but became ill at ease within the organisation and founded his own movement in 1991.
2. The total number of "agree strongly" and "agree" answers are included here.
3. However, some notable exceptions can be observed, Belgium, for example where the ecologists have always had excellent electoral results and where there is an average level (59%) of confidence in science.
4. "Is there a political party you feel closer to than all the other parties? If so, which one?"
5. For the purposes of clarity, those answering to the criteria selected (votes and/or is close to the Greens), will be called "ecologists" or "Greens," and all others will be called "non-Greens" or "non Ecologists."
6. See Bord and O'Connor, 1997.
7. See, e.g., Boy, et al., 2003, p. 29.
8. Ibid., p. 31.
9. E.g., recently in France, Germany, Belgium, Sweden, and Italy, Müller-Rommel and Poguntke, 2002.
10. In the French questionnaire the following question is asked:

    French people are usually ranked on a scale of this type which goes from left to right. Where would you personally situate yourself on this scale? 0 means you are to the left, 10 means you are to the right, and the intermediary marks means you are somewhere in between.

11. The texts of these questions are the following:
—"*Overall, would you say it is good or bad for the economy of the country that foreigners come to live in (name of country)? 0 means it is bad for the economy, 10 means it is good for the economy and the numbers in between will allow you to nuance your opinion*";—"*Would you say that (country) culture is more threatened or more enriched by the presence of immigrants? 0 means that (country) culture is threatened, 10 means it is enriched, and the numbers in between will allow you to nuance your opinion*";—"*Would you say that the presence of immigrants in (name of country) makes life more pleasant or less pleasant? 0 means life it less pleasant, 10 means it is more pleasant, and the numbers in between will allow you to nuance your opinion.*" An overall grade was calculated using the answers supplied, it goes from a minimum of 0 to a maximum of 30 for the most positive answers on immigrants.

CHAPTER 12

French Socialism: An Exception in Europe?

Henri Rey

At the end of 2006, just a few months before the French presidential election was due to be held, observers of the French Socialist Party were presented with a paradox. While a year earlier, more than a half of electors who declared themselves to be close to the party chose to ignore the advice of the majority of the party's leadership and membership and voted against the ratification of the European Constitutional Treaty, some opinion polls suggested that a majority of French people intended to vote for Ségolène Royal in the presidential election. The ambivalence of this situation indicates certain specific features of French socialism, as well as the PS's influence as a governing party and the fragility of its political and organizational base.

These specificities can only be understood by reference to the history of socialism in France, the long-standing influence of communism on the French political scene, the relations between socialism and communism and socialism and trade unionism, the late adoption of a culture of government, and the articulation of domestic and European issues. French socialism displays a number of similarities with other European socialist and social democratic parties, regarding the way power is exercised, the importance of the functions exercised within the framework of representative democracy and, to a greater extent than may be at first apparent, the profound nature of the ideological shifts which have been discreetly effectuated.

This presentation of French socialism will be organized in two main parts: first, the historical roots and ideological and political particularities of socialism in France will be outlined, and then the party's organizational model, the distribution of its support bases throughout French society and its reaction to the crisis of traditional party activism will be discussed.

The Uncertain Identity of French Socialism

Social Democracy, Laborism, and Socialism: French Socialism's Diverse Origins

The European socialist movement, which established itself during the nineteenth century with the extension of the right to vote and the rapid growth of the industrial working class, developed in different ways and at different rates from country to country. Depending on the nature of their relations with trade unions and other organizations—such as co-operatives, mutual benefit societies and charities which assisted the poor—mass parties fell into one of three main categories: social democratic parties, labor parties, and socialist parties.[1]

Social Democratic Parties, of which the German Social Democratic Party is the archetype, are characterized by a large working class base and close links with a powerful trade union movement. Originally greatly inspired by orthodox Marxism, their struggle is both economic—for better pay and conditions in the short term—and organized by the trade unions, and political—for the extension of their democratic Rights—which is under the control of the party. In the short term, such parties campaign to have their representatives elected to political office with a view to achieving reforms, but their long term goal is to establish a new kind of regime, socialism. At the same time, a profusion of initiatives instigated by party members—consumer cooperatives, collective leisure pursuits, education projects, mutual aid . . . —led to the creation of an alternative workers' society "a place to live, setting itself up *ipso facto* as a rival and challenger to mainstream society."[2] From 1875 to 1914, social democratic parties, which were formed in Scandinavia, Austria and the Netherlands as well as in Germany, experienced rapid growth, both in terms of their membership and their share of the electorate: in the 1912 parliamentary elections the SPD obtained 34.8% of the vote nationally—peaking at 55% in Saxony—and by 1914 had more than a million members, most of whom were skilled laborers.[3] Most of the other European social democratic parties regularly captured over 20% of the vote.

Labor Parties, notably the British Labour Party, which was founded in 1906, grew out of the trade union movement. Originally, these parties were simply parliamentary arms of the trade unions, and the vast majority of new members were already trade unionists when they joined the party. The founding members of the British Labour Party hesitated for a while before creating an independent party, instead of continuing, as previously, to rely on entering into alliances with the Liberal Party or, less frequently, the Tories. The party was given the name Labour, in preference to a name which contained the word socialism, and its contingent of Marxists was relatively small. The Belgian Workers' Party resembled the British Labour Party, both regarding the origins of its membership—almost all its members were already trade unionists or members of mutual benefit societies or co-operatives—and the fact that these organizations were represented throughout the party hierarchy.

Socialist Parties formed a composite group which included the French Socialist Party (SFIO). In the countries of Southern Europe, which experienced industrialization later than the North of Europe, the socialist movement was numerically weak—when it was founded in 1905 the SFIO had 35,000 members, by 1914 its membership has grown to 93,000—and had limited influence among the working class. It was split into various factions that did not unite into a single party until 30 years after the formation of the SPD. Marxism, which was often distorted in translation, as was the case in France with Guesdism, was influential but not hegemonic, and constituted one component in an attempt at creating a "Jauresian synthesis," which was a mixture of Marxism and Republican Humanism.[4] The trade union movement, which was also relatively weak, was determined to retain a high degree of independence from political parties. A year after the founding of the SFIO, the CGT adopted the Charter of Amiens (1906), which opposed the idea that trade unions and political parties should work together, except at election time, and asserted the absolute right of the trade union movement to define its own strategies and orientation and to independently struggle for the emancipation of the workers. Nevertheless, when the socialists obtained over a million votes in the 1910 and 1914 elections they became an influential force in the French parliament. French socialism, in its local, administrative, and independent variations, outgrew the SFIO which, despite its revolutionary rhetoric and several proletarian strongholds in the North of France, did not solely rely on the working class for support. Thus, before the shock of the First World War, French socialism was marked by two great disparities, first between its performances in elections and the location of its supporters, and second between its claims to represent a certain social class and the social backgrounds of its members and leadership. The characteristics a party displays when it first appears on the political landscape can have lasting effect: the forms of the party will be perennially differentiated, depending on the power structure of the party, which was defined in an ideal-typical way by Panebianco[5] as "the dominant coalition." The degree of internal cohesion of this coalition (which is not restricted to the party's official leadership), its degree of stability, and the organization of the links between its various constituent bodies and to external organizations are part of the party's "genetic code."

Communism and Socialism

The First World War and the Russian Revolution presented the various European socialist parties with a series of dilemmas. Faced with the logic of a conflict between nations, internationalism and pacifism, which were core principles in socialist programs, had to be discarded. Only a minority of socialists refused to enter the patriotic pact, which in both Germany and France was based on the notion of the necessary defense of one's country when it found itself under attack.

The war reopened divisions within the socialist and trade union movements between pacifists on the one hand and more or less reluctant supporters of national union on the other. The 1917 Bolshevik Revolution, which precipitated Russia's withdrawal from the First World War, immediate generated a lot of sympathy across Europe. Similar insurrections which broke out in Germany, Austria, and Hungary were quickly put down. Nothing of this kind happened in France, and as a consequence the revolution was viewed in a positive light, and not only by members of the socialist party. The first flouting of fundamental freedoms by revolutionaries were compared to similar incidents in the 1789 French Revolution, and failed to provoke the same levels of criticism and disapproval which characterized British reactions to the revolution.

The growing influence of the Bolshevik Revolution in France may be partly explained as a reaction to the heavy casualties sustained in the war, and the feelings of suspicion toward socialist and left-wing Republican leaders who were held partly responsible for the course the war had taken. It was in this context that the socialist movement made spectacular gains in popularity with 100,000 new members joining in 1919 alone. At the Congress of Tours the vast majority of these new members voted to join the Comintern on the terms imposed by the Bolsheviks, while the remaining minority refused. The division between "communists" and "socialists" may appear somewhat arbitrary—joining the Comintern seeming to be largely an emotional choice made by individuals lacking in experience and motivated by dissatisfaction with the former leadership—but this situation gave rise to what would prove to be one of the most lasting, fundamental splits in the French political landscape. Despite the fact that for a short period immediately after the war some socialists and trade unionists gave their support to the Russian Revolution, the situation in France was rather different from the circumstances that prevailed in other parts of Western Europe: in some countries there had been unsuccessful uprisings, in others a large majority of party leaders and members had opposed the revolution on ideological grounds, and elsewhere parties of the Left refused to accept the preconditions for joining which the Comintern sought to impose. As Annie Kriegel observed,[6] if the Congress of Tours had been held a few months later, a quite different majority could have emerged.

The minority of delegates at the Congress of Tours who refused, with Léon Blum, to join the Comintern set about the painstaking task of rebuilding the SFIO (the "old house" to which Blum appealed everyone to return). The party was now essentially made up of a network of elected members and party leaders, a majority of who had remained loyal, and an increasing number of former members who had gone back on their original decision to join the communists. Their change of heart was largely precipitated by the fact that the PCF had been placed under the direct control of Comintern cadres during the "bolchevisation" period, resulting in the mass defection from the PCF of all but its core working class support. In 1925 the SFIO regained most of its pre-Tours Congress militant base. Between the wars the SFIO, whose left-wing support was eroded by the Communist Party, increasingly relied upon the support of the middle classes and civil servants, especially members of the teaching profession. During the Popular Front period, however, the temporary coalition between the communists and the socialists increased support for both parties.

The unprecedented levels of support for left-wing parties among the French lower classes was undermined by the fall of the Popular Front—just months after the introduction of the major reforms for which it is famous (which included the introduction of the 40 hour week and annual paid holidays)—and the Communists' unquestioning acceptance of Soviet foreign policy positions. Nevertheless, in the aftermath of the Second World War the Left's fortunes would turn again. Thanks to the heroic involvement of many communists in the Resistance, and the communist participation in coalition governments under the leadership of De Gaulle, the PCF enjoyed unprecedented levels of prestige and influence. Today, this is perhaps difficult for us to imagine. This peak in their popularity had a class dimension—the PC was the party of the workers—and a national dimension, which had already begun to emerge during the Popular Front period. In January 1945 the PCF already had 380,000 members, and by the end of 1946 membership had jumped to 800,000, making it the "biggest party in France," a position it held for an extended period. The party dominated the main workers' union, the CGT, and regularly won over 5 million votes—amounting to over a quarter of the votes cast—throughout most of the duration of the Forth Republic. By winning half the blue collar vote and over a quarter of the white collar vote in the 1951 elections, the CGT established itself as the main representative of working class people, way ahead of the SFIO (who, although they only managed to win 15% of the blue collar vote and 11% of the white collar vote, did attract the votes of 33% of civil servants).

For more than thirty years the Communist Party exercised hegemony over large parts of the French working classes. At no time in this period did the Socialist Party even approach this kind of dominance. Paradoxically, the SFIO was under political and ideological pressure from communism, even though socialist leaders openly proclaimed their anti-communism—echoing Guy Mollet for whom communists were "not of the left but from the East." Socialists, being "of the left," were obliged to remain true to certain principles and doctrines.

A Strange Attachment to Doctrine

Since it was competing with a powerful communist party and had only weak or indirect links with working class trade unions, the French socialists continued to rely on rhetoric and doctrine which seemed outdated and ill-suited to contemporary French society in general, and the social and political reality of the party in particular. From the time of the radical reform of the SFIO, just after the Congress of Tours, to the aftermath of the Second World War, and even on into the early years of the Fifth Republic, certain Marxist definitions and precepts were regularly referred to. The continued use of notions such as "the dictatorship of the proletariat" (up until the Cold War period) and, until much later, "class struggle" or "collective appropriation of the means of production" may, on the face of it, seem surprising coming from a party which had no qualms about forming coalitions with centrist or even Right of Center parties. The distinctions for example between "maximum programmes" and "minimum programmes," between winning power and exercising it, between reform and reformism, which were made in an effort to legitimate socialist participation in government, provided the rationale, in the immediate postwar period, for both the compromises made in government and parliament with moderate and conservative parties, and the continuing uncompromising adherence to party doctrine in speeches made at party conferences.

Repeated attempts within the party to revise declarations of principle, aimed at reconciling the party's theoretical positions with actual policy, all ended in failure. This seemingly schizophrenic attitude also extended to the party's internal regulation, revealing a desire to remain loyal to both the past—the socialist and revolutionary tradition—and the long term ideal of achieving a truly socialist society, which the party is unwilling to abandon. The present, and its inevitable compromises, is viewed as a kind of parenthesis. In the immediate postwar period Northern European social democratic parties acknowledged the impact of the expansion of the service sector on national economies, and began to define themselves as the representatives of not just the working class but of all wage-earners. This evolution may be contrasted with the stance of the SFIO which, while in power in 1956, escalated military involvement in Algeria, but refused to make compromises regarding doctrine. In Germany at around the same time (November 1959) the Bad Godesberg congress was held, at which the SPD made a radical break from established party doctrine, with a view to obtaining an electoral majority. Casting aside Marxism, the SPD cited the party's historical roots in "Christian ethics, humanism and classical philosophy." The SPD, which had previously defined itself as the party of the working classes, announced that it was now the "party of all the people"[7] and, by embracing a socially oriented market model, made itself more appealing to middle class voters.

Although post-1968 the SFIO underwent major upheavals, transforming itself in 1971 at the Congress of Epinay into the Socialist Party (the PS), the doctrinal particularity of French socialism survived intact. Although François Mitterrand, on his election as the leader of the newly formed PS, expressed a willingness to enter into a tactical alliance with the Communists, he drew the line at campaigning with the PC with a shared ideological stance. He opted instead for an empirical approach based on a joint policy manifesto and electoral alliances at all levels of government. The strategy he set out before the Socialist International aimed at uniting with the Communist Party, which at the time was much more powerful than the PS, with a view to later replacing it as the dominant force on the Left. Nevertheless Mitterrand, though a Republican of the Left, was by no means averse to the use of Marxist rhetoric, as the following perhaps surprising quotation demonstrates:

> I concede that Sweden is not sufficiently socialist insofar as, despite an unprecedented level of wealth distribution among social groups and individuals, it has failed to strike at the heart of capitalism, the heart of capitalism's power, namely the ownership of the principal means of production.[8]

In 1981 Mitterrand invited Jean-Pierre Chevènement to draft the party's election manifesto, which was entitled "Changer la vie" (Change Life). Chevènement was the founder and a prominent member of Ceres—the Centre of Socialist Studies, Research and Education—a group situated on the Left of the party, whose credo drew on an original synthesis of Marxism, Sorelian anarcho-syndicalism and nationalism. Lionel Jospin, who took over the leadership of the PS after the party's successful 1981 election campaigns, did not accept the use of the term *social democrat* until 1985—it had previously been considered to have negative connotations—and the term only featured prominently in the party's declaration of principle in 1991.

Despite these changes, no attempt was made to theorize the identity of French socialism with relation to European social democracy. Meanwhile the socialist government had, as promised, initially carried out important structural reforms (nationalizations, decentralization). They quickly became aware, however, of the economic risks their policies entailed and reverted, with the 1982–1983 austerity plan, to a more traditional way of managing public affairs, although they never openly admitted that this had been a policy U-turn. Moreover the Left, once back in power, failed to oppose the privatizations carried out by the right-wing government between 1986 and 1988, preferring to avoid the issue by making vague noises about their support for a "mixed economy." Failures to openly discuss its changes in values and policy and acknowledge that some of its historic goals were now illusory became a characteristic feature of contemporary French socialism. The spectacle of a party in denial invited comparison with the SFIO's earlier stubborn refusal to abandon its attachment to doctrine, and is evidence of the remorse that must have been felt in the party. As Alain Bergounioux said, "Culturally, French socialism has never had its social democratic moment." As the 2007 Presidential elections approached, the gap between practice and rhetoric became so wide that when Dominique Strauss-Kahn declared that he was a social democrat it was clearly an attempt to differentiate himself from the party's other two prospective candidates for the presidency.

An Idiosyncratic Party

The PS may be characterized not only ideologically, but also in terms of a number of social and organizational features. Among these characteristics are a small number of members for such an electorally successful party, a tendency to recruit among relatively privileged social groups, fewer links with associations and the trade union movement than in the past, an internal pluralism, highly autonomous local organizations, and a high concentration of power in the hands of deputies and other elected officials. It may also be defined in terms of its standing in the party system, in which it occupies a prominent position as a party of government. The party is well integrated into the various levels of public policymaking, and receives most of its funding from the state, making it a *cartel party*.[9] Although, in common with others parties of government, it is often described as a "catch-all" party,[10] the PS does not share many of the commonest defining characteristics typical of political parties. A good starting point for beginning to understand the organizational structure of the PS is the four "circles of participation" defined by Maurice Duverger[11]: voters, supporters, party members and party activists who together constitute a system that operates from the center outward. The outermost circle, occupied by the PS's electorate, is both the most important and the most difficult to understand.

The Electors

The PS, like most other French political parties, can no longer take for granted the consistent support of a loyal section of the electorate. Furthermore, for the different types of election it is possible to differentiate between first round and second round PS voters. Over the past twenty-five years the PS has obtained, on average, 29% of the votes cast in the first round of legislative elections, and 40% in the second round. In the four Presidential elections held during this period the party won, on average, 25% of the vote in the first round, and 51% in the second round polls in which a PS candidate featured. Behind these averages, there was a great deal of variation in the party's performances in each type of election.[12]

Most European socialist parties are more electorally consistent than the PS (table 12.1): from 1986 to 2006, during which time the PS's best score was almost double its worst (19%–37%), SPD scores fluctuated within a range of 7 points (33.5%–40.9%), the British Labour Party's varied by 12 points (30.8%–43.2%), the PSOE by 10 points (34.2%–44%) and the Swedish SAP's vote remained within a range of 7 percentage points (36.4%–43.2%).

These variations show that the electoral potential of the PS at this point in their thirty-odd year history is marked by both strength and fragility. In loosening the Communist Party's grip on electors of the Left from the time of the Epinay Congress (1971) to its electoral successes in 1981, the PS showed itself capable of attracting the votes of both the working classes and middle class employees. Over this period France experienced rapid urbanization and an explosion in the service sector, and the Socialist party—by championing the permissive values and liberalization of mores which had been demanded during the 1968 protests—showed itself to be in tune with the profound social and cultural transformations that were taking place. The party also managed to capture a part of the working class vote in sectors and parts of the country

Table 12.1 PS results for each round of legislative elections from 1981 to 2007 (percentage of votes cast)

	First round	*Second round*
1981 Legislative elections	37.9	50.1
1986 Legislative elections	32.8	single round
1988 Legislative elections	37.2	45.7
1993 Legislative elections	19	30.8
1997 Legislative elections	25.7	38.6
2002 Legislative elections	24.1	35.8
2007 Legislative elections	24.7	42.2

where the communists were weakest and then, around 1981, also began to make inroads into the traditional communist vote. For ten years these successes ensured that the socialist vote remained relatively stable, thanks to the consistent support of salaried employees, and despite the disillusionment of working class voters from around 1983 onward. When Mitterrand was reelected in 1988 he still enjoyed the support of large sections of the working class (41% in the first round, 63% in the second) and employees (37% and 55%), but in the course of his second term the defection of working class voters, who had already been abstaining in ever greater numbers, gathered momentum.

In the 1993 legislative elections this cycle was broken. The PS was routed as its vote was almost halved, with working class voters deserting it in even greater numbers than the rest of the electorate. This downward trend continued in the next two elections (the 1994 European elections and the 1995 Presidential election). As Guy Michelat and Michel Simon have noted,[13] this was when the working class vote really turned their backs on the PS. From then on large sections of the working class and other categories of employees only voted socialist in the second round of elections, and then only *faute de mieux*.

While the PS vote went into decline among the working classes, the party managed to retain the support of middle class employees and even make up some ground on the Right among senior managers. The intermediary professions (technicians, schoolteachers, nurses etc.,) have consistently voted for the Socialist Party in greater numbers than the rest of the electorate. As a result of working class defections and increased support from the managerial class, the center of gravity of the socialist electorate became even more firmly located in the middle classes, in particular among middle class public sector employees. This shift happened, however, at a time when members of these social categories, which were highly heterogeneous, began to be increasingly exposed to various kinds of social insecurity (lower job security, difficulty obtaining suitable housing, devaluation of university degrees) which were likely to influence their political views.[14]

Young electors (18–24-year-olds), who helped Mitterrand to victory in the second round of the 1981 presidential elections, and again when he was reelected in 1988, deserted the PS in large numbers in the 1993 legislative elections, contributing significantly to the defeat of the Left. On April 21, 2002, Lionel Jospin only managed to obtain 13% of the youth vote and 16% of all the votes cast. The reduction of the PS's youth vote compared to 1988 was as great as their drop in support among working class electors. Gender is not a significant variable. In the 2002 election equal numbers of men and women voted for Jospin, whereas in 1981 the PS candidate obtained more support from male voters, and in 1988 a majority of his voters were women.[15]

In future elections one of the Socialist Party's main objectives will be to recapture the votes of working class people who may be tempted to abstain or to cast a protest vote. This concern is shared by many other socialist and social democratic parties in Europe.

By comparing the make-up of the PS electorate with that of seven other European socialist and social democratic parties (see table 12.2), the French

Table 12.2 The electorate of Social Democrat and Socialist parties in eight European countries: Sociodemographic variables and replies to a number of questions (%)

	GE	*SP*	*FR*	*UK*	*IT*	*NL*	*PL*	*SW*
Women	51	55	51	53	53	55	47	48
18–34-year-olds	19	18	21	20	21	18	24	20
Over 55s	35	40	33	40	35	39	33	42
University educated	25	14	32	21	12	25	18	25
Without religion	44	23	58	49	28	68	12	73
Self-evaluation:								
Left wing	57	79	80	36	78	64	60	65
Centrist	30	11	16	39	12	19	26	23
Unionized	19	13	11	23	25	30	12	72
Working	41	33	50	45	49	28	34	57
Interested in politics	68	27	52	58	53	66	54	60
Satisfied with democracy	35	39	23	50	22	42	16	58
Immigration bad for job market	44	39	25	36	34	17	49	11
Gays free to live as they wish*	32	40	57	21	35	53	10	24

Note: * In complete agreement.
Source: ESS, 2003.

socialist party's current idiosyncrasies can be both highlighted and put in perspective.

Indeed, the most important variations are due to differences between countries. So, for example, the proportion of socialist electors who are aged between 18 and 34 varies between 18 and 24% (21% for the PS), whereas for the electorate as a whole it varies between 19% in the United Kingdom and 32% in Poland. The comparatively high proportion of university graduates among the PS electorate can be partly explained by the fact that there are more graduates in France than in Spain, Italy, or Poland. Examining, for example, the penetration of parties in different social milieus, several important differences can be identified (see table 12.3).

New Labour in Britain and the Swedish Social Democrats are the only parties in the survey whose highest scores were among the working class electorate. The PS, on the other hand, like the SPD and the Italian "democrats of the left," obtained a relatively high level of support from members of the intermediate professions, and provoked less disillusionment among the managerial class than their Swedish, Italian, and Spanish counterparts.

In countries covered by the survey which have a Catholic tradition, PS voters stand out (table 12.2) because of their irreligiosity, in sharp contrast to the socialist electorates of Italy, Spain and, in particular, Poland. PS voters are also less likely to be members of a trade union than socialist voters in neighboring European countries, reflecting the weakness of the French trade union movement. PS voters are also the most likely, with their Spanish counterparts and Italian ex-communists, to locate themselves on the Left of the political spectrum, reflecting the party's clear self-positioning in the French political landscape. As supporters of a party which has been in opposition

Table 12.3 Penetration of Socialist and Social Democratic parties among various categories of working voters in eight European countries (percentage of votes cast)

	GE	*SP*	*FR*	*UK*	*IT*	*NL*	*PL*	*SW*
Workers	29	24	36	52	25	13	21	34
Intermediate professions	38	24	40	37	37	13	41	29
Managers	30	14	34	43	19	15	36	24
Overall	31	23	36	48	27	13	26	31

since their electoral defeats of 2002, they take a much more negative view of the way democracy functions in their country than supporters of the British Labour Party or the SAP in Sweden. The fact that Le Pen made it through to the second round of the 2002 Presidential election indicated that in France, as in the Netherlands, immigration has been near the top of the political agenda. This despite the fact that in these two countries, as well as in Sweden, traditions of openness to other people and the integration of immigrants are relatively well-established, with socialist voters being the least likely to think of immigrants as individuals who may "steal" their jobs. Finally, to round up this brief overview of the similarities and differences between PS voters and their European counterparts, the levels of cultural liberalism of French socialist voters—a large proportion of whom are, as we have seen, university graduates—are closely comparable with those found in the Netherlands with regard to the right of gays to choose their own lifestyles. The proportion of French socialist voters who unreservedly support such freedoms is the highest of all the European social democratic and socialist electorates covered by the survey.

Links between the party proper and socialist voters are maintained by a system of networks which partially compensate for the lack of organic links between the PS and trade unions and associations.[16] By studying several PS departmental federations Frédéric Sawicki was able to identify the range of interactions which constitute a "milieu of socialist sympathisers." Thus *laïcité* was one issue which mobilized a grouping of secular associations, teaching unions and political clubs, whose main orientation shifted from radicalism to socialism. The PS recruits not only voters, but also over a quarter of its membership from these milieus, each of which are jealous of their independence. Other significant sources of socialist support include left-wing Catholics, who contributed to the rise of the PS in the early 1970s, and helped the party make inroads into former conservative strongholds in the West and East of France (Brittany, non-coastal areas of western France, Alsace, and Lorraine), and among wine producers in Languedoc-Roussillon... Although changes in the recruitment and training of teachers and the decline in support for the PS among left-leaning Catholics have diminished the effectiveness of the above-mentioned networks, common ground, complicity and tacit agreement—as well as internal bickering—are still very much in evidence in Socialist Party circles, particularly at the local level.

The Inner Circles

Following Maurice Duverger's model, we come next to the inner circles. Moving from the fringes to the center of the organization, party supporters, members, and activists constitute circles which, though more or less difficult to clearly distinguish between themselves, all differ from mere voters in that they have an explicit and relatively long-term commitment to the party.

Party supporters strictly speaking play no role in the functioning of the party and consequently have none of the rights or obligations of party members. They can, however, be asked to choose the party's candidate, as was the case in Italy in 2005, and, more routinely, are influential actors insofar as they give the party material and financial support, participate in party rituals (party festivals, meetings, and demonstrations), provide assistance during election campaigns and, more generally, help to spread the party's message. When the party launches a recruitment campaign it naturally targets individuals who are already PS supporters, including former members who, for whatever reason, have at some point ceased to be politically active without, however, having changed their political allegiances. The category of party supporters, thus defined, is smaller than that used by polling organizations, who regard interviewees as PS supporters if they designate the PS as the party they feel closest to, or least distant from. For polling organizations, an individual is regarded as a supporter if they express an abstract preference for a party, even if they do nothing to act upon that preference.

Some citizens who are interested in politics decide to become a member of the Socialist Party. When new members join they are given a party card, and are required to make a regular financial payments to the party—their party dues—the size of which depends on their income. Membership confers a number of rights: the rights to elect party officials (including the party leader); to choose the party's election candidates; to debate, amend and vote on policy documents; and to participate in major decisions (regarding the referendum for the European Constitutional Treaty, for example). The number of members is limited though, partly due to the PS's long-standing practice of screening membership applications in order to preserve balance between the various factions of the party and maintain the party's existing power structure. The PS leadership broke with this tradition when, in the run-up to the 2007 Presidential election, they launched an Internet recruitment campaign where new members, admitted to the party for a reduced annual subscription of 20 euros, were offered the opportunity to participate in the selection of the party's candidate for the Presidency. This campaign, similar to earlier recruitment drives undertaken by the UMP in France and New Labour in Britain (which invited new members to join for 10 pounds), was a great success: 80,000 new members—10% of whom were individuals who rejoined the party—signed up in a matter of months, swelling total PS membership from 130,000 to 210,000. Despite the success of this campaign, and falling membership of left-wing parties elsewhere in Europe, PS membership is still much lower than that of other European socialist and social democratic parties: the SPD has more than 500,000 members and the British Labour Party 450,000.

The social and demographic profile of PS members is very different from both the French population as a whole and the party's electorate. According to the available data, these differences are becoming more pronounced: two surveys of party members carried out in 1985[17] and 1998[18] revealed a party whose membership is ageing. In 1998, the average age of PS members was 55, compared to 48 in 1985, and declining recruitment among the younger generations gave grounds for concern about the party's future. The internet recruitment drive helped to reverse this trend: the average age of new recruits (43) and the proportion of new young members (those aged less than 30) were very close to the corresponding averages for the population as a whole. An increase in the number of highly educated upper class and upper middle class party members and a simultaneous abandonment of the party by the vast majority of its working class members are the two main features of recent trends in party recruitment. The social and cultural make-up of Socialist Party membership tend to make the party a preserve of the relatively privileged, cut off from the wider society.

PS members are expected to devote a certain amount of time and effort to the party. Many participate in a very limited way. Party *activists* are members who actively contribute to the party's cause over an extended period. An activist is an individual who works for a collective cause on a relatively long term basis. An activist is an active member of a party, a trade union, or an association.[19] As Jean Maîtron, the author of the French Biographical Dictionary of the Workers' Movement, put it: "An individual who occasionally participates in a movement or agrees to make a one-off commitment to a well-established organisation cannot be regarded as an activist." Activism entails not simply a long term commitment to party activities, but also the fact that, over an extended period of involvement in party work, individuals become integrated in a social group whose symbolic systems they gradually appropriate. Activism is an imperfectly understood form of political participation. The fact that activists are unpaid volunteers who often willingly take on thankless tasks begs the question: is their generosity as disinterested as it seems? Researchers have sought to identify "the rewards of militantism,"[20] rewards which may be material or symbolic, direct or indirect, explicit or unacknowledged (particularly to the activists themselves). The most obvious reward militantism can offer is the possibility of access to elected office and related employment opportunities, especially in an organization like the PS, where in 1998 a third of party members had been elected to some kind of official post, albeit often in the lower ranks of the hierarchy. Active participation in a political party, or trade union, can also offer members a way of educating themselves, by developing skills such as writing or public speaking. Many activists also take advantage of networking opportunities. Such possibilities for personal advancement must qualify any presumption of lack of self-interestedness on the part of political activists. Active participation in politics also involves the individual in making emotional and psychological investments and can become an important part of their identity, as the party becomes "a good thing,"[21] coming to share some characteristics of other entities which are "bigger than the individual" such as family, church and community. Notwithstanding this range of possible motivations for becoming deeply involved in party politics, party activism has been on the wane for some time. Symptoms of the crisis include the drop in party recruitment figures, an ageing party membership, a discrepancy between the social and educational backgrounds of party members and that of the population as a whole, a decline in party activities, and growing dissatisfaction with the internal organization of the party. Traditional activism, classically characterized in working class movements by disinterested devotion to the party, faith in progress, an urge to proselytize, and a lasting commitment to political activism and self-abnegation, is becoming a thing of the past. The heroic figure of the activist has failed to survive the collapse of communism, the institutionalization of trade unionism and the extended period in office of governments of the Left. Party activism in today's Socialist Party is going through a period of transition where traditional models are being abandoned in favor of newly emerging forms of political participation and activism. In the absence of well-established new models, the state of activism tends to be defined in a negative way, in terms of the decline of traditional practices. This decline was highlighted when the party leadership was shocked, disappointed and puzzled, having twice failed to predict the voting behavior of the French electorate, in the Presidential vote of April 2002 and the referendum on the European Constitutional Treaty in 2005. The party's modus operandi and the party leadership's way of communicating with the electorate, which had both operated more or less successfully over several decades, now seem to be increasingly ineffective. In a sense, the drop in the level of internal party activity is a reflection of this: members are now much less willing to give up their time to working for the party than in the past. In 1998 only 10% of PS members spent more than two hours a week helping the party, and more than a quarter of party members were virtually inactive, spending less than an hour a month engaged in party activities. These levels of commitment compare unfavorably with thirteen years previously, when four times as many members spent more than two hours a week doing party work. Now, a substantial amount of the time—sometimes all of the time—many activists dedicate to the PS is spent attending party meetings. These relatively low levels of involvement in party activities indicate that the amount of satisfaction members derive from involvement in party work is rather limited. Do rank and file members feel that they have the ear of the leadership? Do they feel as if they are genuinely participating in party life? And do they approve of the way their organization functions? In a 1998 survey[22] we interviewed a group of PS members and asked them whether they agreed with the following statements: (1) "The party leadership does not pay much heed to the opinions of rank and file party members"; (2) "The work members do for the party often goes unacknowledged"; (3) "Political parties in general are more interested in representing electors than party members." 73% of the 12,000 participants in the survey were totally or substantially in agreement with the first statement, 81% with the second, and 77% with the third. Many party members are acutely aware that their influence on party policy is limited to the point of being almost negligible and feel that rank and file members live in a different world from the party leadership. Members struggle to locate themselves, between the leadership and the potential electors, who are the main focus of the leaders' attentions. Nevertheless, although large sections of the membership feel that they lack influence and that their contributions go largely unrecognized, only a minority (35%) regard the way that the party functions as undemocratic, and there is a general appreciation of the fact that the PS party members can air their views freely, and that a variety of views are tolerated, which is not the case in more authoritarian political parties.

The organization of the party, based on the separation of the leadership, local party structures and the rank and file membership—giving each level of the hierarchy a high degree of autonomy—means that the PS can be described as a "stratarchic" party, as defined by Eldersveld[23] and Kesselman.[24] The relative autonomy between levels in the party does not mean that internal tensions and contradictions have been avoided. Indeed, sections of the leadership regard the composition and culture of the grass roots as major obstacles to the development and modernization of the party. They are concerned about the narrow sociodemographic profile of the membership, and, in particular, about the activist habituses—in which new arrivals are greeted with suspicion, posts within the party are allocated among its various factions, and in which a vocal minority display a weakness for verbal jousting. These problems are acknowledged as representing major obstacles to the development and modernization of the party. What is envisaged is a transformation of the PS through the redefinition of the role of the party members mentioned above, involving both the regeneration of the grass roots and a radical change in the relationship between the grass roots and the party leadership. Party members' traditional obligation to offer a substantial long term commitment to involvement in party activities, an obligation honored in recent years by a declining proportion of the membership, would be replaced by the requirement for members to participate at certain key moments in the internal decision-making processes, such as the choice of election candidates or the endorsement of the party manifesto. Also, while certain forms of internal decision-making would be abandoned, relations between the grass roots and the party leadership would be formalized through the introduction of a set of democratic regulations, which would provide for the direct election by party members of the party leader, the party's candidate for the Presidency, and most of its candidates for legislative elections, as well as the use of internal referendums. The lack of party unity has made the use of more formal procedures to regulate the internal functioning of the party all the more necessary.

These changes must be viewed in the context of two major trends, which are not confined to the world of political parties: first, the profound transformation of all kinds of activism—in trade unions and associations as well as political parties—and second increasing calls for wider participation. Regarding the first trend, the work of Jacques Ion is enlightening.[25] He points to the rise in à la carte activism, which reveals a profoundly modified representation of time. "It is no longer a case of preparing for a better tomorrow. The risk is that tomorrow could well be worse than today. The idea of risk has become a central preoccupation . . . " The weakening of collective identities and the preoccupation with the short term at the expense of medium and long term strategies, coupled with the decline of grand narratives, have impacted on the goals and methods of political activism. The old formula—of long term commitment to a cause (reflecting social status), the firm belief in a better future and the acceptance of a hierarchy and party discipline—seems to have been replaced by *à la carte* commitment, fear of the future and the development of more egalitarian organizational structures.

After the success of its membership recruitment campaign, which paved the way for the "primaries" and the subsequent nomination of its candidate for the 2007 Presidential election, the Socialist Party finds itself at a crossroads. One option is to transform the way it does politics, by further swelling the ranks of its membership, encouraging its supporters to be more directly involved in the party's election campaigns, and facilitating exchanges between the leadership and the party's rank and file. The choice of this path would entail a radical departure from traditional party doctrine, a more inclusive approach, a rejection of ideology and an attempt to reconcile party theory and practice. The way the party debates and deliberates on policy would also need to be reformed. The alternative is for the party to abandon the experiments to welcome grassroots input, undertaken during the 2007 Presidential campaign, and revert to its former practice of leaving internal regulation and exchange in the hands of the party's large network of deputies and elected officials.

Notes

1. The two books by Bergounioux and Grunberg [1996 and 2005] are the standard texts in this field, particularly as historical approaches to French socialism.
2. Kriegel, quoted by Bergounioux and Grunberg, 1996.
3. Gougeon, 1996.
4. Bergounioux and Grunberg, 2005.
5. Panebianco, 1982.
6. Kriegel, 1970.
7. Gougeon, 1996.
8. Mitterrand, 1977.
9. Katz and Mair, 1995.
10. Kirchheimer, 1996.
11. Duverger, 1981.
12. Perrineau, 2006.
13. Michelat and Simon, 2004.
14. Chauvel, 2006.
15. Perrineau, 2007.
16. Sawicki, 1997.
17. Rey and Subileau, 1991.
18. Rey, Subileau, and Ysmal, 1999.

19. Mouriaux, 1983.
20. Gaxie, 1977.
21. Ansart, 1987.
22. Rey, Subileau, and Ysmal, 1999.
23. Eldersveld, 1964.
24. Kesselman, 1972.
25. Ion, Franguiadakis, and Viot, 2005.

CHAPTER 13

Right-wing Parties in France and in Europe

Florence Haegel

Political parties to the Right of the political spectrum in France have changed considerably since 2002. The UMP (Union pour un mouvement populaire), was created from what was the RPR (Rassemblement pour la République). It has become the uncontested leader of the right-wing camp, renewed its leadership with the election of Nicolas Sarkozy as its president in November 2004, and has shown a clear desire to break with the Chirac years. In parallel, the UDF (Union pour la démocratie française), has jettisoned its radical and liberal components, affirmed its autonomous strategy and centered itself on the promotion of François Bayrou's candidacy for the Presidency. The UDF claim to be a centrist party that is a dangerous position to adopt in a bipolar system. It has been suggested that these changes signify the end of the specific character of the French Right. Starting with the postwar period, this specificity essentially stemmed from the central role played within it by Gaullism and its affiliated organizations. The hypothesis that a kind of European convergence is taking place can be justified if one considers that in France, a clearly dominant conservative strand has progressively come into being on the Right. This strand has been nurtured by the fading of Gaullism and the emergence of a "new" UDF makes it more easily identifiable within the current of Christian democracy which is solidly implanted in the history of right-wing parties in Europe. In order to test such a hypothesis, a comparison between the French Right and its European counterparts is needed. This comparison will be undertaken successively at an organizational and an ideological level both from the point of view of how these parties are structured and how they have changed.

Organizational Change

The organizational approach to political parties transgresses ideological classifications and provides a framework for an understanding of the partisan phenomenon. Although this approach is not content to merely describe the Right (or the Left) as a certain type of organization, it has always suggested the existence of affinities between a social, ideological, or cultural positioning and a type of partisan structure. The question therefore arises as to whether the European Right has a common partisan shape and if so, whether the French case is in some way specific or different. In organizational studies, the French Right is frequently seen as having a slightly different status. This is often attributed to the fact that the French parties have such a loose structure and also to the characteristics of a type of partisan structure engendered by Gaullism. However, it is also attributed to a weakness in the ability of right-wing parties in France to galvanize supporters as they are less well implanted throughout society than their European counterparts are. Finally, it may also be linked to the particularities of the institutional system in which these organizations operate. There are several questions to be answered here:

- How does the institutional structure of French right-wing parties compare to that of their European counterparts?
- Do these parties continue to have low rates of membership?
- Can their specific nature be attributed to the fact that they are subject to the institutional constraint of presidentialization?

Toward a Strengthening of Partisan Structures

In comparative studies on European parties,[1] right-wing parties and more precisely those who follow in the footsteps of Gaullism are usually seen as having a particular status (although this varies somewhat depending on the period). For example in Panebianco's work,[2] the Gaullist party is distinguished from other major European right-wing parties to the extent that it is assimilated to charismatic type parties. This notion is inspired by a Weberian analysis which describes a type of foundation built up around an exceptional personality together with the presence of mechanisms for identification with and loyalty to the leader. But above all the analysis associates this type of foundation with a type of structural organization which continues to exist long after the party was first founded. According to Pannebianco, such a party links strong centralization (central recruitment of party elites) with a weak institutional structure and the absence of factions. The pertinence of such an analysis today can be questioned to the extent that these parties have a stronger bureaucratic structure than they did a few years ago and furthermore, they can no longer be said to be completely devoid of any real pluralism.

In comparison with other organizations on the European Right, the Gaullist parties (including the ex-RPR) were traditionally characterized by a weak institutional structure. This was revealed by the weakness of their bureaucracy and was measurable by the amateurism and lack of professionalism of their "central organisation" as it was called. The absence of a clear division of labor among party activists within the management team together with the lack of expertise among those with official posts underlines this. On top of that, the official party decision-making entities were short-circuited more often than not. In the case of the ex-RPR, they were not consulted about major strategic choices. The decision to approve the Maastricht treaty, for example, was taken by a small steering committee which didn't even exist in the statutes. Similarly, the way in which these parties functioned showed a very relaxed attitude toward the rules as demonstrated by the rarity of sanctions or of exclusions. Exclusions take place mainly with dissident candidacies or following a refusal to respect official electoral strategies. Even in these cases, the individual excluded from the party was often re-admitted after a time. Thus, a comparison with other parties on the European political Right shows how flexible the RPR were with the management of disputes. For example, in the Spanish *Partido Popular*, the duty to be loyal and disciplined with regard to party ideology is written into the statutes. Both of these elements are protected by sanctions when they are transgressed. Moreover, these types of disciplinary sanctions, which are often the result of ideological oppositions, are not rare.[3]

At first glance, this assessment of the RPR as having a weak institutional structure seems to go against the image of the party as a centralized organization. However, institutional structure is not synonymous with centralization which can be incarnated in the authority of a leader rather than in the weight of rules and bureaucracy. Furthermore, a distinction has to be made between the way a party organizes itself and the way in which it legitimizes itself. The Gaullist Right did indeed legitimate itself by drawing on charismatic leadership. It shared a system of representations and beliefs which promoted authority and cultivated mechanisms for delegation to the leader. But this was not an entirely faithful reflection of actual practices and relations with the leader within the party. In reality, throughout the history of the RPR, the authority of the leader was contested quite vigorously in particular as a result of competition for the presidency from among Gaullist ranks: Michel Debré and Marie-France Garaud in 1981 and Edouard Balladur in 1995. When the UMP was set up in place of the RPR, this was accompanied by a shift toward a stronger institutional and bureaucratic structure together with increased professionalization. This began with Alain Juppé and has been carried on and amplified by Nicolas Sarkozy. This change includes a strategy to increase the number of administrative staff. It also involves a form of professionalization by recruitment on the basis of qualification and also by subcontracting to private sector companies. These are used particularly for communications such as by internet, the management of televised images, etc. Finally, this movement toward a stronger institutional structure can also be measured by the fact that a whole set of internal rules and regulations have recently been elaborated (see infra).

The absence of factions and the resistance to pluralism[4] are presented as the other characteristic traits of the "charismatic model" as applied to Gaullist right-wing parties. Pluralism within partisan organizations includes debate about tendencies, structure, functions, and indeed legitimacy. While the struggle between tendencies within both the Italian and the British Right have been analyzed,[5] there has been no real study of how pluralism functions within the French Right. In this type of party, the mechanisms for displaying loyalty and the personalization of the leader together with the celebration of unity make any public expression of diversity illegitimate. Of course, clans, teams, and subleaders do exist but there are no instruments available to organize this diversity. The internal functioning of these parties is ruled neither by the principle of competition nor by the principle of deliberation. In other words competitive and open elections are entirely exceptional and single or uncontested candidacies are most often the rule. It is just as rare that internal disagreement be made public through debate. As Charles Pasqua said "debate is not our cup of tea."[6] The party provided a setting for the expression of pluralism on two occasions. The first time was in February 1990 after specific channels had been set up such as voting on certain motions during party congresses and the relative success of the Pasqua-Séguin faction. The second time was in 1999 with the very open competition which characterized the election of the party president, Michèle Alliot-Marie.[7] In 2002, the main change made to the statutes of the UMP specifically concerned the organization of pluralism by the creation of a Right for different tendencies to exist. But because of resistance to this and because the main subleaders refused to become involved in this new plan, the creation of "factions" was postponed. Instead of this, a contract was put in place based on private and non transparent negotiations and giving rise to particular and revisable agreements. In such an opaque system, party management retains control at all times and is in a position to establish client type relations with others in that it can deal differently with different people as it chooses. The hypothesis can now be put forward that with respect to both institutional structure and pluralism, the French Right is in the process of losing some of its specific characteristics. This is true even though resistance to this process still exists.

Toward Change in Types of Partisan Mobilization

Maurice Duverger[8] draws a distinction between a *parti de cadre* and a *parti de masse*. The first type includes parties created from within parliamentary circles which actively promote elected representatives and especially those with social status from the upper echelons of society. The second group is made up of parties who encourage wide membership and who attribute a central role to their members within the party while ensuring the necessary measures are in place to support them. According to Duverger, Center-Right parties in Europe have most often signed up for the *parti de cadre* model. However, on a European scale, this is too simple a comparison between parties.[9] The notion of a *parti de cadre* does apply generally to liberal parties. However, it doesn't account for the major parties on the European political Right. These are parties which not only promote membership—many of them are also very integrated in society. This is often accomplished through professional associations, as is the case of the CDU in Germany or social clubs and societies as is the case of the British Conservative party.

In terms of numbers of members, the French Right has never equaled these major Conservative or Christian-Democrat parties. The UDF, which today has some 30,000 members, is characterized by a form of membership which is often discrete, distant, informal, and intermittent. The parties openly admit that they prefer "quality" to "quantity" and even occasionally operate a kind of selection process of members. Although the partisan infrastructure is clearly connected to committed Catholicism and although many senior party members come from parochial and associative networks linked to the Catholic social and educational movement,[10] the party can not be totally assimilated to the Christian-Democrat model because of the narrowness of its base. The RPR in the past and the UMP today are different from the UDF in terms of numbers of members and also in terms of the roles ascribed to them. In keeping with the practices of Gaullist type organizations, the UMP seeks out and celebrates active party membership. It claims to have more than 320,000 members following an intense campaign implemented to consolidate Nicolas Sarkozy's authority within the party. It does not yet rival the major parties on the European Right but it has (momentarily?) made up for the party's late start.

This recent development within the French Right echoes the movement to place more emphasis on the role of members together with the introduction of measures designed to achieve internal democracy—a term which designates the increasing power of members within the parties—observable at European level. Indeed, in reaction to obvious changes,[11] a certain number of European Conservative parties[12] have recently discovered the value of recruiting and of mobilizing members from time to time. In imitation of the Left, though proceeding less transparently than them, most of these parties have changed their internal rules to give more say to members in the selection of candidates for senior party positions, political candidates and programs. The object of the exercise is to reinforce the sense of satisfaction members derive from active participation and also to improve the image of the party among the electorate. For party members, being involved in the choice of the future candidate for the party presidency is very motivating indeed. It is also a great mobilizing factor because of the media value of the issue and because competition is involved. The survey of new UMP[13] members provides an idea of how important this motivation is. Fully 85% of them took part in the designation of the candidate for the presidential election and more precisely to support Nicolas Sarkozy, (78% joined as a result of the personality and political message of Nicolas Sarkozy[14]). This movement goes hand in hand with a greater flexibility in types of membership. Within the UMP, as within other right-wing parties in Europe, (the British Conservative Party for example), flexibility in the work carried out by party members is now accepted and a variety of membership types (ordinary member, partner, volunteer, etc.) is now catered to.

Although it might seem paradoxical to those who expected these reforms to lead to a shift of power toward local entities, they were in fact accompanied by a movement toward centralization.[15] This was particularly visible in the previously more decentralized organizations.[16] It is nonetheless true that the keystone of these reforms is the election of the leader by the membership at large and that this is mainly done by plebiscite.

Toward Full Presidentialization

In many comparative studies,[17] the specific nature of the regime under the Fifth Republic justifies the characteristics of the French parties as a consequence of the imperative of presidentialization. In reality, the notion of a "presidential party"[18] is not so clear and it is unsure whether this notion allows a distinction to be made between French parties and their European counterparts. The parties remain at the heart of the selection process for the presidency in parliamentary regimes. This is true both in France and throughout Europe where media promotion of politics in all these countries has entailed a strong personalization of party-aligned leadership. Furthermore, the political system under the Fifth Republic is in reality a mixed or hybrid system to the extent that it combines two principles which are generally considered to be antagonistic: the election of the president by universal suffrage and the power of the Parliament to overthrow the government. The hybrid character of the Fifth Republic forces the parties to establish a dual system of cooperation, both legislative and presidential, and leaves the question of the link between each of these levels open. The introduction of the presidential logic, in any case, created a degree of uncertainty about the role attributed to the parties and also about the type of party expected to emerge. Initially, and in keeping with Gaullist perceptions, presidentialization was expected to develop outside of the parties' spheres of influence and even contribute to weakening them. However, an examination of change within the French Right reveals the complex effects of the move toward presidentialization on the parties themselves. Overall, the logic of presidentialization has strengthened right-wing organizations as they have concentrated on exerting control over the process and have restructured around the issue.

The history of the French Right clearly shows the difficulty it has had in integrating a presidential logic into the partisan framework. Moreover, compared to the Left, the French right-wing parties seem to have found it difficult to adapt to this way of thinking. The non-Gaullist Right, which was federated under the UDF from 1978, was initially hostile to the movement toward presidentialization. After 1981, it did not manage to agree on a candidate chosen directly and clearly from within its ranks. Of course, this situation was not the same for the section of the right wing that claimed to be Gaullist but contrary to what might have been predicted, it adapted only with great difficulty. Given the privileged link between Gaullism and the Constitution of the Fifth Republic and specifically with the institution of the presidency, the so-called Gaullist party took a long time to become more presidential in the sense that they strongly resisted the adoption of rules for the selection of a presidential candidate. Their attachment to the Gaullist interpretation—nonetheless countered by the increasing number of candidacies on the Right—and the assimilation of the presidential election to a supra-partisan vote doubtless go a long way to explaining this resistance.

Since the 2007 presidential election the French right-wing parties could rightly be considered to have become presidentialized or, to put it another way, they have regained a form of control over this election which might otherwise have partially escaped them. Since 2002, the UDF has not only adapted to the presidential election but has adopted it wholeheartedly. Its strategy is entirely centered on the promotion of its candidate, François Bayrou, and since this decision was taken it seems to have been playing a game of double or nothing. The strategies and negotiations used for the general election were therefore largely indexed to the results of the presidential election (reduction of the length of the presidential mandate and inversion of the calendar imposing this chronological framework). The party, which has been known in the past for the weakness of its bureaucracy and for its flexibility was reorganized to facilitate these strategies. In spite of much procrastination, the UMP has moved to a new stage by including rules for the selection of candidates in the statues. The decision to do this was taken by the political committee on December 6, 2005. Although the candidate is "supported" rather than "invested" by the party and the procedure remains flexible rather than fixed, it nonetheless seems certain that the UMP, which is dominant on the French Right, will not go back on these decisions. It should also be noted that the party continues not to punish dissident candidates. In the case of both the UDF and the UMP, the important point is that presidentialization has not taken place outside of the parties and furthermore that the parties have been strengthened by it. Indeed, Nicolas Sarkozy's strategy to conquer the party—and on another level François Bayrou's—has ratified the necessary balance between partisan authority, in other words control over the party, and the presidential candidacy. On this point, changes within the French right-wing parties are fairly similar to changes in other European right-wing parties.

Ideological Transformations

Generally speaking, research carried out on "political families" distinguishes between three types of right wing in Europe.[19] The liberal Right came into being in the nineteenth century in response to the interests of the rising bourgeoisie mobilized against landowners. It was the fruit of industrialization and is historically characterized by the defense of different kinds of liberties—economic liberty (defense of commercial and manufacturing interests), political liberty (the fight against absolutism) and religious liberty (rationalist distance from religion). The conservative Right took a position against the affirmation of political liberty and the extension of universal suffrage and in defense of landowners and rural society. It remains attached to tradition and favorable to the respecting of social hierarchy. Finally, the Christian-Democrat Right was born in the nineteenth century but only became a veritable political force on a European scale after the Second World War when it played a full role in the establishment of the Welfare State and the building of Europe. In reality, it combined more conservative ideas on the defense of the Catholic Church with other strands focusing on the promotion of a third way between capitalism and collectivism. Today, it has a clearly expressed desire to be multi-denominational. In France, this triptych was blurred historically by the emergence of what René Rémond[20] called the Bonapartist tradition, traces of which he finds in Gaullism. On a European scale and more contemporarily, this classification can also be questioned given the convergence between Christian-Democrats and Conservatives,[21] and indeed the adoption by many European right-wing parties of liberal economic positions. To compare the French Right with its European counterparts from an ideological rather than from an organizational point of view, two questions will be dealt with successively here.[22] The first of these deals with questions posed by liberalism from an economic and a cultural point of view. The second will deal more specifically with issues relative to religious and ethnic diversity. For each of these four dimensions, an attempt will be made to look firstly at the positions held by the parties themselves on a European level. Secondly, the ideological structuring of right-wing European electorates will be measured with the help of indicators available in the European Social Survey 2003 wave.[23] A distinction will not be made between conservative, democratic, and liberal tendencies within the different parties which make up the European right-wing. This distinction is pertinent in certain countries but is difficult to measure in the French context given the weakness of democratic and liberal tendencies in France as their respective small size in the survey[24] shows.

Economic Liberalism and Cultural Liberalism

The ideological structuring of European right-wing parties can generally be understood to have two main dimensions. The first of these is economic liberalism. The second is cultural liberalism which refers to the whole range of issues covered by the liberalization of morals. Opinions on abortion and on homosexuals are generally the most reliable indicators used. Diversity in ideological structuring according to country can be perceived by looking at the positions of right-wing European parties on these two questions and above all by situating their electorate's positions on these questions.

If the positions adopted by right-wing parties on issues relative to economic liberalism are taken into account, the basic shift since the 1980s is toward the adherence of the majority of European right-wing parties to the principles of neoliberalism. Toward the end of the 1980s, a survey[25] measuring the programs within the different parties was carried out. It was based on evaluations of the parties by national specialists and established the proximity of their positions with respect to economic liberalism.[26] At that time, the liberal parties obtained an average of 15.3, the conservative parties 15.8 and the Christian-Democrat parties, 13.9. This shift had therefore reduced the differences between the liberal and conservative Right. It had also diminished the gap between these parties and a number of major parties of Christian-Democrat tradition (such as the Austrian ÖVP or the Dutch CDA), or indeed Gaullist parties (such as the French Ex-RPR). This rapprochement had also contributed to blurring the original Christian-Democrat identity of the European Popular Party (EPP). The EPP's strategy to absorb a large range of right-wing parties (*Forza Italia*, the Spanish *Partido Popular*, the British Conservative Party and the French ex-RPR) while ensuring parliamentary hegemony partly diminished its specific identity.[27] A certain amount of tension exists between a small number of minority representatives such as Belgium, the Netherlands, and Ireland who sought to affirm the social Christian-Democrat aspect and parties from the Christian-Democrat tradition who clearly adhere to the principles of privatization and the questioning of the Welfare State such as the CDA in Belgium and the ÖVP in Austria. However, in spite of these tensions, there does exist a kind of bipolarization within the European Parliament on economic and social questions such as the establishment of a minimum European salary and the limitation of mandatory work time for example.

If an attempt is made to measure the positions of right-wing electorates on economic liberalism using a simple question on whether the government should intervene to reduce differences in salary (table 13.1), three types of observation can be made:

- Among the countries selected[28] the degree of adherence to economic liberalism as measured by this indicator varies greatly: there is a 53-point gap between Danish right-wing voters who are the most liberal and Spanish right-wing voters who are the most interventionist. These differences provide a good illustration of the gap which continues to exist on the question of economic liberalism between different European right-wing electorates but also perhaps more accurately between certain parties and their electorates;
- The countries with the most liberal right-wing voters are all Northern European (Denmark, Germany, the Netherlands, and the United Kingdom). Sweden and Belgium are exceptions to this. These are also the countries where polarization is strongest or in other words where the gap with the Left is the widest;
- French right-wing voters are situated somewhere in the middle.

On this last point, it should be remembered that the French Right has been involved in an ideological transformation since 1981 essentially rallying to the liberal vision of politics. Moreover, with regard to the level of adherence to liberalism, the ex-RPR, which has become the UMP, and the UDF share a common vision. They are both clearly in favor of giving more freedom to private sector companies as the figures show. In 2002, 72% of Chirac voters were in favor of this and 76% of Bayrou's supporters were also.[29] Generally speaking, since

Table 13.1 Economic liberalism among European right-wing parties in 2003 (%)

	BE	*GE*	*DK*	*SP*	*FR*	*UK*	*IT*	*NL*	*PL*	*SW*
Disagree* with the idea that the government should reduce differences in income	20	39	60	7	18	39	9	35	20	27
Gap between the right and the left	+7	+15	+26	+3	+13	+22	+1	+19	+12	+20

Note: * People who disagree or strongly disagree with this statement.

1981, economic liberalism clearly seems to be the common ideological cement of the moderate Right. This is true even if, from time to time, depending on prevailing attitudes and public opinion, certain representatives advance the idea of protection for the country or for individual citizens against the effects of competition. The values of autonomy, liberty and merit are well entrenched in the vision of society proposed by the French Right.

On questions relating to society, the one thing right-wing European parties usually have in common is a form of resistance toward changing values. There are nonetheless differences between them as debates within the European parliamentary group reveal. In its declaration of principle, "A union of values" which was adopted in January 2001, the EEP did reaffirm its reserves about abortion. However, there are real distinctions between parties classed as Christian-Democrat which tend not to be permissive and the other parties. And perhaps more precisely there are visible gaps in position between parties in multi-denominational countries such as the German CDU or the Dutch CDA and the exclusively Protestant parties of the Scandinavian countries which are far more conservative on questions related to moral issues.[30] On a European scale, this internal tension among the Right expressed itself through the Rocco Buttiglione affair. When the Barroso commission was set up in October 2004, he was auditioned for the post of Commissioner for Justice, Liberty, and Security. On this occasion, Buttiglione, who is a member of the Catholic movement "Communion and Liberation," and the former Minister for European Affairs in Silvio Berlusconi's government, publicly expressed very traditional opinions on marriage and homosexuality. When this affair erupted, divergences between the German Right, a strong supporter of the moral order, and the French Right became apparent. An examination of the structure of their respective electorates shows that these divergences are still firmly in place.

The question on homosexuality in the ESS survey allows a measure to be taken of the degree of approval for the liberalization of morals among right-wing electorates. The way the question is formulated "gay men and lesbians should be free to live their own life as they wish" makes it more of a tolerance indicator (each individual should be free to live as they see fit in their private life) than a measure of recognition for the rights of homosexuals. If the question had been about "rights" as expressed in current debate, the opinions of right-wing voters would probably have been less favorable. Whatever the case may be, table 13.2 reveals three essential elements:

- deviation between right-wing electorates is significant (31 points between the most permissive and the most puritanical of them) but far less contrasted than deviation on economic liberalism;
- the level of adherence to cultural liberalism is not directly linked to the degree to which the issue is polarized. Thus, in Denmark and France, where in both countries the right-wing electorate seems to be more tolerant of homosexuality, the situation is different. In Denmark, antagonism has softened; in France, it continues just like in the Netherlands where the question of tolerance became a political issue, in particular within

the debate on Europe and in Spain where the Right is particularly virulent against recognition of homosexual marriage. In other countries, the homosexual question has not become a political question and has not led to a Left-Right polarization.

- finally, the attachment of the British and German right-wing electorates to moral conservatism should be underlined. In the United Kingdom, within the Conservative Party, there is visible tension between a minority of "cultural liberals" in favor of homosexuality and multiculturalism on the one hand and the traditionalists on the other.[31] In Germany, the CDU—and even more so the CSU—hold very conservative positions on questions of moral interest.

Figure 13.1 provides an overall view of this ideological structure and allows the French Right to be situated on a European scale. On these two ideological dimensions, it seems less to the Right than many of its European counterparts. It is less favorable to economic liberalism than the majority of right-wing parties in Northern Europe and significantly less puritanical on social questions than any other right-wing party with the exception of Danish groups. Obviously, the position of European right-wing electorates on these two dimensions can not be interpreted without reference to the existence or not of an Extreme-Right electorate. The fact that the British Conservative electorate seems to be furthest to the Right ideologically (it allies a strong adherence to the principles of economic liberalism with a form of moral order) is partially because it includes voters who in other European countries vote for the Extreme-Right. However, as will be seen with regard to xenophobia, the presence of an Extreme-Right is not enough to relieve right-wing movements of their more traditional or xenophobic attitudes.

Acceptance of Religious and Ethnic Diversity

Two further dimensions should be taken into account to complete this comparative analysis of the French Right. Both of these concern what might be termed as attachment to or acceptance of religious and ethnic diversity. With regard to the first of these, it should be specified that this is not about religious belonging as such which is analyzed elsewhere in this book. What follows is rather an examination of the rejection or promotion of religious diversity—a subject which is and has been a controversial issue at European level.

Table 13.2 Cultural liberalism among the European Right in 2003 (%)

	BE	*GE*	*DK*	*SP*	*FR*	*UK*	*IT*	*NL*	*PL*	*SW*
Agreement* with the idea according to which gays and lesbians should be free to live as they wish	31	18	40	20	40	9	27	32	8	24
Deviation between right and left	–18	–17	–7	–20	–19	–12	–4	–21	0	–1

Note: * Individuals who declare that they strongly agree with this proposition.

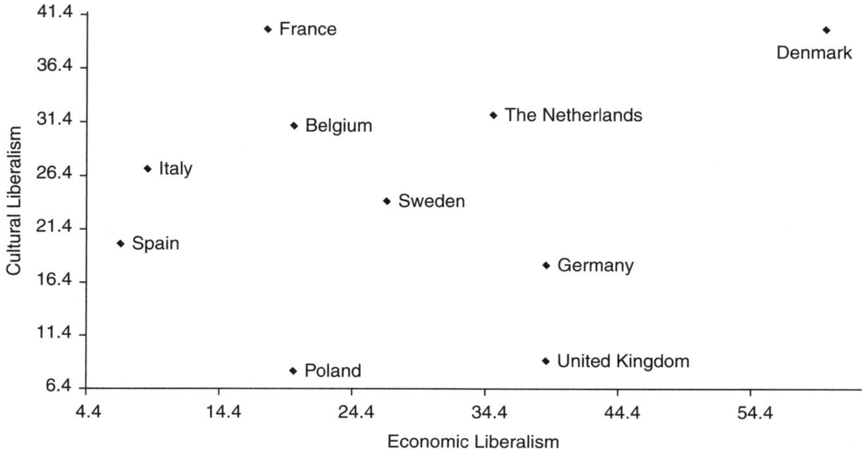

Figure 13.1 Economic and cultural liberalism within the European Right

Indeed, the religious issue was at the heart of public debate recently and particularly within the very ranks of the European Right when the question of whether reference to Christian values should be included in the Constitutional Treaty and the recognition of legal guarantees to the Churches was hotly debated in the European Parliament. It is not necessary here to give full details of the debate but the main point was that a cleavage appeared within the EEP between those against the inclusion of any reference to religion and those who militated for the explicit recognition of the Christian heritage. This included those in favor of a text containing the exact terms of the Preamble to the Polish Constitution as proposed by right-wing German, Danish, and Italian parliamentarians. This debate clearly revealed the Vatican's desire to exercise its influence on the building of Europe. It also showed how well the German, Italian, Polish, and Spanish Right could mobilize. Further, the cleavage was personified through the opposition of Jacques Chirac, the leader of the French State who spoke in the name of the principle of secularism embedded in the French constitution and the leader of the Spanish state, José Maria Aznar who called for the Christian reference. It would be simplistic to claim that this opposition was a faithful translation of the current state of positions within national groups in the European Parliament. A certain number of French right-wing parliamentarians in particular seem less hostile than their leader to the inclusion of a reference to Christianity. However, it does reveal the diversity of ideological structures among right-wing electorates.

An analysis of the degree of acceptance or rejection of religious pluralism within European right-wing electorates (table 13.3), allows three observations to be made:

- overall (and apart from the two cases pointed out below), the extent of national differences seems less significant than for the other dimensions;

- difference of opinion between Left and Right is also small;
- only two national cases are clearly distinct: the Polish right-wing electorate is, unsurprisingly the least favorable to religious diversity and the French right-wing is the most favorable to religious pluralism: there is a 40 point difference between them.

The first observation shows why the inclusion of the Christian reference on the European agenda was of such interest to the CDU-CSU which is the biggest party in the EEP in terms of numbers. This issue brought European right-wing parties together who, as shown above, remain divided on many other questions. The second observation suggests that in most European countries, the acceptance or rejection of religious pluralism is more of a cultural than a political question. Finally, the third observation allows the specific nature of the French Right to be measured. Historically, the religious question in France has always been right at the heart of political debate. It remains one of the cleavages opposing the Left to the Right both from the point of view of electoral behavior and the commitment of voters to one party or another.[32] However, the Right rarely makes a political issue of it since 1984 when they reacted against Mitterand's controversial proposal on the public financing of private schools From this point of view, the promotion of religious identification undertaken by Nicolas Sarkozy in his book *La République, les religions, l'espérance*[33] seems both novel and risky. What's more, this position was less clearly enunciated in the 2007 presidential campaign.

Together with attitudes toward religious diversity, attitudes toward ethnic diversity complete this table on the ideological structuring of the European Right. Immigration constitutes a political cleavage in the majority of European countries, it is often a subject of debate and calls for the development of public policies around it. And in all European countries, right-wing electorates are clearly more hostile to immigrants that left-wing electorates. The parties which represent these right-wing electorates tend to be in favor of more control over migratory movement. It is nonetheless true that in spite of varying forms of rapprochement, the way in which immigrant populations are hosted and integrated differs from one country to another.[34]

The way in which immigration is handled has been a decisive and sensitive question for the French Right since the arrival of the *Front National* on the French political landscape. Depending on the circumstances and on the

Table 13.3 Rejection of religious pluralism within the European Right in 2003 (%)

	BE	*GE*	*DK*	*SP*	*FR*	*UK*	*IT*	*NL*	*PL*	*SW*
Disagreement* with the idea that: «it is better for a country to have a variety of different religions»	32	35	45	35	11	30	37	20	51	34
Deviation between the right and the left	+12	+12	+10	+12	0	+12	+10	+4	+2	+3

Note: * Individuals who declare that they disagree or strongly disagree with this proposition.

Table 13.4 Xenophobia within the European Right in 2003 (%)

	BE	*GE*	*DK*	*SP*	*FR*	*UK*	*IT*	*NL*	*PL*	*SW*
Xenophobia	42	48	41	34	41	58	27	34	35	24
Deviation between the right and the left	+5	+14	+14	+7	+16	+18	+6	+6	–5	+2

leaders, the aim of winning over *Front National* voters is more or less brought to the fore and the visibility and content of discourse on immigration varies considerably. Between 1986 and 1993, right-wing electoral programs showed themselves to be concerned that the preoccupations of FN voters be taken into account and in particular their concerns about immigration. For example, in 1998, the RPR affirmed that "the limits of tolerance have been transgressed," advocated "expulsion without leniency" of illegal immigrants, stigmatized "polygamy," announced that "certain aspects of our system of social solidarity should be reconsidered" and that the body of law on nationality should be reformed. Conversely, Jacques Chirac's presidential program in 1995 reversed the order of priorities by relegating themes of security and immigration to the last position.

Even though any evaluation of the degree of xenophobia and hostility toward immigrants partially depends on the indicators chosen, the French Right generally appears to be one of the most hostile on this issue. If the degree of xenophobia is analyzed using an index drawn from questions on the "costs" and "advantages" of immigration,[35] the following points can be made (table 13.4):

- With the exception of Poland which is a country of emigration, there is a strongly negative perception of immigration amongst the majority of European right-wing electorates;
- The British Conservative Party's electorate is the most hostile to immigration and—as indicated above—includes voters who would vote Extreme-Right in other countries;
- However, in countries where the Right faces competition from "its right," the right-wing electorate is also characterized by high levels of xenophobia.

Figure 13.2 provides an overall vision of the position of European right-wing electorates on this double rejection of religious and ethnic diversity.

It is thus clear that there is very little connection between these two dimensions. This illustrates the fact that the French right-wing electorate is an exception with regard to religious pluralism, thus recalling the entrenchment of the secular norm in French political culture but that in spite of the presence of an Extreme-Right electorate, this electorate shares a high level of xenophobia with Belgium, Denmark, and also Germany and the United Kingdom.

At the end of this portrait of organizational and ideological transformations in the French Right as compared to its European counterparts, it becomes

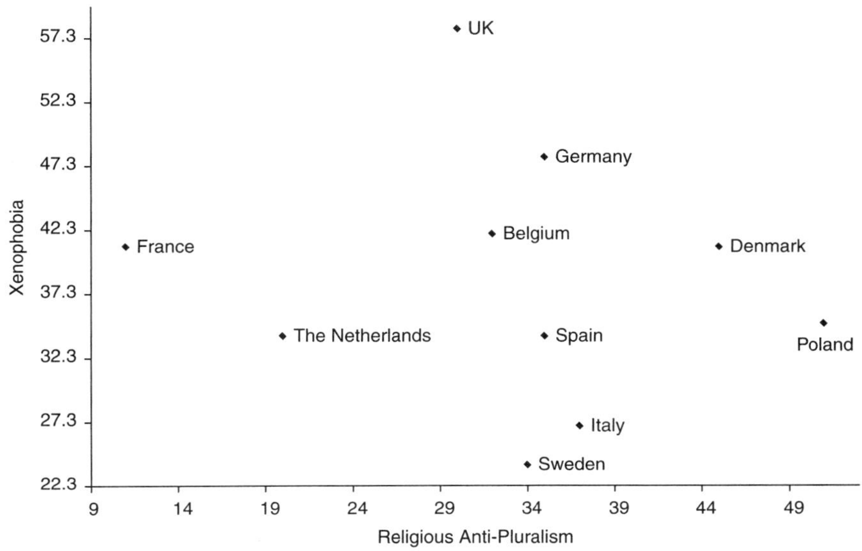

Figure 13.2 Rejection of religious pluralism and xenophobia within the European Right

apparent that the supposed specific character of the French Right is less obvious than it used to be. From an organizational point of view, the strengthening of its internal structures and its ability to galvanize its supporters has reduced the gap with other right-wing organizations. The charismatic model which was formerly used to analyze it, for example, has become less pertinent today. In the same way, the impact of presidentialization has not led to a radical distinction of the French Right on a European scale. From an ideological point of view, the right-wing electorate seems generally less to the Right than electorates in the majority of other European countries with regard to economic and cultural liberalism and religious pluralism. It is much less out of step with regard to xenophobia. However, with the exception of the religious dimension which does give it a certain type of specificity, the other variants are not sufficient for it to be given the status of exceptionality.

Notes

1. Charlot, 1967 and 1983.
2. Panebianco, 1988.
3. Chadel, 2000.
4. Cf. Haegel, 2007.
5. Gamble, 1974; Zuckerman, 1979.
6. Quoted in *Le Monde*, February 7, 1990.
7. Haegel, Pütz, and Sauger, 2003.
8. Duverger, 1981.
9. Alexandre-Collier and Jardin, 2004.
10. Fretel, 2004a and 2004b.

11. Dalton and Wattenberg, 2000.
12. Scarrow, 1996.
13. Survey: "The new members of the UMP," Ipsos, carried out on September 21 and 22, 2005, sample size: 604 new members, quota method, phone interviews.
14. In the Socialist Party, 65% justify their membership by the fact that it gives them the chance to "have a say in the choice of the Party's candidate." Internet survey of new Socialist Party members, May 2006, (sample: 18,000 new members).
15. Katz and Mair, 1994 and 1995.
16. It is interesting to note that the UDF and the British Conservative Party files that were administered at local level before the advent of these changes have now been centralized.
17. Elgie, 1998.
18. Pütz, 2007.
19. Van Beyme, 1985; Ware, 1996; Wilson, 1998.
20. Rémond, 1982 and 2005.
21. Delwit, 2003.
22. This chapter does not include an analysis of French and European right-wing parties' attitudes to European integration.
23. My thanks to Vivianne Lehay for her help in processing the data.
24. Because the number of *Démocracie libérale* and UDF voters is so small (n = 4 and n = 50 respectively), in the samples used in this survey, it is impossible to know whether the small number of ideological differences between the three electorates is the result of these low numbers or the result of a movement towards convergence.
25. This survey was carried out among experts in the different countries concerned. They were asked to classify the official position of the different parties on a scale of economic liberalism going from 1 (positions favorable to state control) to 20 (the most liberal positions).
26. Laver and Hunt, 1992.
27. The liberals, who were witnessing the triumph of their ideology, became marginalized from an organizational point of view.
28. For each country considered, the right-wing electorate is made up of voters having voted for a conservative, liberal, or Christian-Democrat party, depending on what is available in each country.
29. The French electoral panel survey, CEVIPOF, 2002.
30. The abovementioned survey [Laver and Hunt, 1992], based on expert opinions on the official ideological positions of the parties measured the diversity of European right-wing parties on societal questions (abortion, homosexuality, etc.) at the end of the 1980s: the liberal parties obtained an average grade for moral rigor of 7.9, the conservative parties, 12.2, the Christian-Democrat parties 15.5, and the protestant Scandinavian parties were still less permissive with an average grade of 18.4.
31. E.g., at the end of October 2003, the selection of the Conservative leader gave rise to competition between Ian Duncan Smith (supported moreover by Margaret Thatcher) and Michael Portillo. The former incarnated traditional conservatism, (favorable to the return of corporal punishment), while the latter wanted to promote "tolerant Conservatism," particularly with regard to homosexuality.
32. The importance of the religious variable as an explication for electoral behavior is well known. It should also be noted that it is more effective than socio-professional categories or levels of education in distinguishing between Socialist Party and UMP members: 47% of Socialist Party members declare themselves to be of no religion (survey carried out in 1998, cf. Boy et al. [2003]) as against 11% of UMP members

(survey carried out by Florence Faucher-King, Florence Haegel and Nicolas Sauger for the Cevipof at the UMP party conference on the November 28, 2004).

33. Sarkozy, 2004.
34. Guiraudon, 2000.
35. This indicator was drawn from the following questions:
    - "Would you say that people from other countries who come to live here take the work of (nationality of country) people or that they contribute to creating new jobs?";
    - "Most people who have come to live here work and pay their taxes. They also use social and health services. Overall, do you think that these people benefit from this more than they contribute or that they contribute more than they benefit";
    - "Would you say it is generally bad or good for the (nationality of country) economy that people come to live here from other countries?";
    - "Using this card, would you say that cultural life in (name of country) is generally undermined or enriched by people coming to live here from other countries?."

    For each of these questions a scale from 1 to 10 was proposed. The three most negative answers on immigrants were considered, arbitrarily to be xenophobic.

CHAPTER 14

The Extreme-Right in Europe

Pascal Perrineau

Recent general and presidential elections have shown a strong level of dynamism among populist, nationalist, and sometimes Extreme-Right parties in a number of European[1] countries. Several of these have ended up in government: in Austria where Jorg Haider's FPÖ joined with the conservative *ÖVP* in the government led by Wolfgang Schüssel (2000–2005); in Italy where Umberto Bossi's Lega Nord joined with the National Alliance and with Forza Italia in the government led by Silvio Berlusconi (2001–2006 and from 2008); in Poland where the Liga Polskich Rodzin (LPR) and Samoobrona governed side by side with the traditional right-wing party, the *PiS* from October 2005 to October 2007; in the Netherlands where Pim Fortuyn's (LPF) list joined forces with the Christian Democrats of the *CDA* and with the liberals in the *VVD* in a government led by Jan Peter Balkenende (2002–2003); in Slovakia where the national Slovak party (the *SNS*) has been part of a government led by the Left since 2006 and finally in Switzerland where the leader of the *UDC-SVP*, Christoph Blöcher, was Minister for Justice and for the Police within the Conseil Fédéral from December 10, 2003 to December 12, 2007. Electoral advances made by these parties have been noticeable in Western Europe and particularly in Austria (26.9% for the *FPÖ* in 1999, followed by a noticeable decline in 2002 when the party only obtained 10%; it then managed a slight increase in 2006 with respectively: 11% for the *FPÖ* without Haider and 4.1% for the Bündnis Zukunft Österreich). Both of these parties then recovered and gained a very strong position in the 2008 general election with 17.5% for the FPÖ and 10.7% for the BZÖ. The Extreme-Right also made progress in Belgium (12% for the Vlaams Belang and 2% for the *Front National* in 2007), in Denmark (13.8% for the Dansk Folkeparti—DF—in 2007), in France (16.9% for Jean-Marie Le Pen and 2.3% for Bruno Mégret during the presidential election of April 2002; 11.3% for the FN and 1.1% for the *MNR* in the general election in June; this was followed by a decline in 2007: 10.4%

for Jean-Marie Le Pen and 4.3% for the FN in the general election) and in the Netherlands (17% for the Pim Fortuyn List in 2002, followed by a sharp decline in 2003 which saw the LPF fall as low as 5.7% and then 0.2% in 2006).

Outside of the European Union, similar movements were recorded in Norway where Carl Hagen's Fremskrittspartiet (Progress Party) obtained 22.1% of the vote in the 2005 general election, and in Switzerland where Christoph Blöcher's *UDC-SVP* reached 22.5% of the vote in the 1999 general election followed by 26.6% in 2003 and 29% in 2007 thus becoming the undisputed leading party in Switzerland. The same phenomenon as in the West can be observed in Central and Eastern Europe among countries which have recently joined the European Union.[2] The growth in ultra-nationalist forces there can be explained by many factors including: concerns about integrating the European Union and the efforts made to do so, a certain amount of nostalgia for national-Communism, the prickly questions of national minorities, etc. Examples include the Romanian, Corneliu Tudor (his party, *Romania Mare*, scored 19.5% of the vote in the 2000 general election and then 12.9% in the 2004 election, the party leader himself obtained 12.6% of the vote in the first round of the 2004 presidential election), Volen Siderov, leader of the Ataka party in Bulgaria (he obtained 21.5% in the first round of the October 2006 presidential election and 24.1% in the second round) or indeed the Polish agitator Andrzej Lepper (who scored 15.1% of first round votes in the October 2005 presidential election and whose agrarian and populist movement, Samoobrona, received 11.4% of the vote in the general election of June 2005; the *LPR*, an Extreme-Right Catholic movement, obtained 8%: both of these experienced a strong decrease in 2007: 1.5% for Samoobrona and 1.3% for the *LPR*).

There can be no doubt that what is taking place here is a rise—albeit a sometimes irregular rise—in national-populism. This political formula of national-populism can be defined as a nationalist movement ideologically centered on the defense of national identity which is conceived of in both historical and ethnic terms and which functions as a populist movement where the charismatic leader multiplies appeals to a people who are supposedly "healthy," lucid and "virtuous."[3] Over the past twenty years, this national-populism which is both a protest (in the name of the "little man" against the "great and powerful") and identity-centered (reference to the "pure" ethnic nation) has met with a great response in Europe.

Nonetheless, certain European countries have remained sheltered from this upsurge and have only experienced marginal Extreme-Right movements (for example, Spain, Germany, Finland, Ireland, or indeed Sweden). During the European elections in June 2004, the Extreme-Right or nationalist Right obtained significant results in Latvia (29.8% for the *TB-LNNK* list), in Poland (15.7 for the *LPR*, 10.1% for *Samoobrona*), in Slovakia (16.7 for the *LZ-HZDS* list), in Belgium (14.3% for the Vlaams Blok—which became the *Vlaams Belang* in November 2004—and 3.2% for the Walloon *Front National*), in France (10.1%), in Italy (7% divided between four parties), in Denmark (6.8% for the *DF*) and in Austria (6.3%), in Lithuania (5.7% for the *LLRALRS* list), in Slovenia (5% for Slovenska Nacionalna Stranka). Everywhere else, the

Extreme-Right has remained under 5%: Germany, Spain, Finland, Greece, Ireland, Luxembourg, Portugal, Great Britain, Sweden, the Czech Republic, Cyprus, Hungary, and Malta.[4]

The Diversity of Extreme-Right Movements

These Extreme-Right movements, all of which vehicle populist and nationalist messages, are very diverse. The Italian Umberto Bossi, the Frenchman Jean-Marie Le Pen, the Dutchman Pim Fortuyn or indeed the Norwegian Carl Hagen or other Extreme-Right leaders, do not all share the same political *credo* nor indeed do they all have the same origins.

Umberto Bossi's *Lega Nord* is the political arm of a well-off regional area (the Lombardy region) which asserted itself by opposing Roman centralism and a centralized State accused of being overly generous to the *Mezzogiorno* regions. Jean-Marie Le Pen, on the other hand, draws greatly on the theme of French unity and nostalgia for "central" nationalism by opposing centrifugal movements in peripheral regions. The Polish leaders of the *Liga Polskich Rodzin* defend values of a moral and authoritative order which are close to those of fundamentalist Catholicism. These have very little to do with the Pim Fortuyn List created by a man whose overt homosexuality was perfectly in line with Dutch cultural liberalism. Anti-Communism has often been part and parcel of the European Extreme-Right but in former East Germany, one of the main German Extreme-Right organizations, the *NPD*, finds virtue in the ex-Communist regime of the "German Democratic Republic" and claims that "East Germany was a better Germany" than West Germany. Finally, like many Scandinavian Progress Parties, Carl Hagen's *Fremskrittspartiet* was born as a reaction to the development of the Welfare State in a number of Northern European countries whereas other leaders such as those of the *NPD* in Germany boast of the merits of "national socialism."

All of these movements are different and one of the clearest manifestations of this diversity is the difficulty they encounter in working together at European level. Over three terms of office there was no European group of Extreme-Right parties in the Strasburg Parliament. From 1979 to 1984, the Extreme-Right was too weak to contemplate forming a group. In 1984, Jean-Marie Le Pen had managed to head a small group (the Group of the European Right) organized around the French *FN* and the Italian *MSI*. He renewed the experience in 1989, but separated from the *MSI* which was opposed to the German Republikaner on the question of Upper Adige (a region in Northern Italy, with around one million inhabitants, which separated from Austria following the Saint-Germain treaty in 1919). He presided over the fate of a group which included 10 FN representatives, six Republikaner and one representative from the Vlaams Blok. Between 1994 and 2007, the Extreme-Right did not manage to constitute a group and remained scattered between several groups within the European Parliament. These included the Union for Europe of the Nations which brought "sovereignists" together, including a representative from the *Dansk Folkeparti*, four Latvian representatives from *TB-LNNK* and four representatives from *Samoobrona*; the Independence and Democracy Group which brought together "sovereignists," six representatives from the Polish *LPR*, four representatives from the *Lega Nord* and a Greek extremist from *LAOS*; and finally a group for non-registered representatives including, amongst others, the seven *FN* representatives, the three *Vlaams Blok* representatives, three Polish representatives from the Polish *LPR*, three Slovakian representatives from the *HZDS*, two Italian neo-fascists (*MSI-FT* and Alternativa Sociale), a Unionist representative from Northern Ireland (DUP) and a representative from the Austrian *FPÖ*. It was only in January 2007 that a new Extreme-Right group called "Identity, Tradition, Sovereignty," brought 20 representatives together (7 *FN* representatives, 3 *Vlaams Belang* representatives, 1 *FPÖ* representative, 2 Italian representatives from *Alternativa Sociale* and from the Movimento Sociale *Fiamma*, 1 independent British representative, 5 Romanian representatives from the Partidul România *Mare* (PRM) and 1 from *Ataka*, the Bulgarian party). The group was dissolved on November 14, 2007 after the resignation of five MEPs from the Partidul România Mare. They resigned following a speech made by Alessandra Mussolini (Mussolini's granddaughter) from *Alternativa Sociale* complaining about the behavior of a group of Romanys in Italy and describing them as Romanians. In spite of their differences and in spite of the nationalists' eternal difficulty in arousing international solidarity, these forces do share some common features.[5]

A Few Invariants

Independently of heterogeneous and sometimes quite fuzzy doctrinal references and in spite of varied political itineraries, these diverse political groupings are all characterized by a centralized partisan organizational structure under the authority of a charismatic leader, by frequent use of popularity-seeking electioneering and finally by a number of central and recurring themes in their political lines of argument.[6] One of the most frequent of these is a strong xenophobic sensitivity which is expressed by frequent recourse to "anti-immigration" themes, an affirmed authoritarian component which is particularly explicit in the domain of "law and order," a composite economic program that amalgamates 1980s neoliberalism and 1990s protectionism and finally an immoderate use of "anti-system" discourse denouncing the "elites from above." Of course, a number of these themes have been used in other times by political forces with little regard for democracy. A direct and general amalgamation with the Fascism of the inter-war period would nonetheless be ambiguous and indeed incorrect. The Fascist parties of the 1920s and 1930s were born in the context of a very profound economic and social crisis—the great depression of 1929—which has no equivalent in the last 25 years. They also developed because of frustrations resulting directly from the First World War: the frustration of Germany which had been humiliated in defeat and equally the frustrations of Italy which became the neglected victor. Today, neither economic or social misery nor the traumatisms of a long and bloody conflict are present in Europe. These Fascist parties were also totalitarian in that their aim was that one single party would dominate the whole of society and organize it from top to bottom. Neither the Austrian *FPÖ*, nor the French *FN*, the German *Republikaner*, the Dutch *LPF* or even the *Lega Nord* in Italy favor such an exit from the pluralist democratic regime. The inter-wars parties practiced Führerprinzip or the "cult of the Duce." The central role played by the leaders of the national-populist parties of today falls far short of this. Finally, no organization today recommends either massive state intervention in the economy—as the Nazis and Fascists did—or a corporatist organization of society. Today's reality cannot be viewed through yesterday's glasses as to do so would run the risk of missing the element of modernity which characterizes these contemporary Extreme-Right movements. By focusing only on filiations, there is a danger of missing what constitutes the scope and the originality of a new political phenomenon. Moreover, it is interesting to note that the old Fascist type extreme right-wing movements which continue to exist in Europe are somewhat drained and lifeless.[7] Neither the Spanish Extreme-Right (only 0.17% for the four Extreme-Right lists present in the last European elections of June 2004), which spends most of its time mired in nostalgia for a long-defunct Francoism,[8] nor Italian neo-fascism (2.08% for the three neo-fascist parties in the last European elections), the inheritor of Mussolini type Fascism, not the Greek Extreme-Right, which has not yet forgotten the Regime of the Colonels (0.42% for the two nostalgic Extreme-Right lists during the last European elections), nor the Portuguese Extreme-Right which continues to be filled with the memory of Salazarism (the Partido Nacional Renovador obtained 0.24% of the vote during the European elections), meet with a great response among the electorate. All of these movements are languishing in electoral marginality. On the other hand however, when these more or less distant inheritors of the old movements take today's problems on board, their successes are sometimes spectacular. In terms of votes, the *FPÖ* in Austria, the *FN* in France, the *Dansk Folkeparti* in Denmark, the *Fremskrittspartiet* in Norway and indeed the Pim Fortuyn List in the Netherlands have all gone way beyond the 10% mark and in the case of Austria have even gone beyond the 20% mark.

Discontentment with Modernity

In a remarkable work first published in 1930, Sigmund Freud showed how "Civilisation and its Discontents"[9] was the cause of a collective outburst of death-wish ideologies in Europe. European culture, which like any culture was built on a renouncing of primitive impulses seemed to him to be in the grips of a deep discontentment and was no longer capable of preventing the development of a veritable "aggressive impulse" and even a death wish. More than 70 years later, the analysis made by the father of psycho-analysis remains valid. However, a sociological explanation rooted in a profound discontentment with modernity must be added to this psychological explanation. This explanation is at one and the same time economic, socio-cultural and political.

On an economic level, whole sections of industrial capitalism have disappeared leaving a postindustrial type of capitalism in their wake. In modern

European economies, the decline of the industrial society has paved the way for the explosion of a service economy, a fractured labor market, the appearance of a "dual society" where precarious and marginal jobs requiring few qualifications are assigned to "people at the bottom of the social heap."[10] For these people, the dual society means the disappearance of everything that made sense in the industrial society. Industrial capitalism characterized by strong state regulation had given birth to a society of homogenous classes which created lasting feelings of belonging to social backgrounds, (the working class, the peasant/rural class, the bourgeoisie), ideologies (the Right, the Left) and political families (the Communist Party, social democracy, Christian democracy, the conservative block). This world where strong allegiances were continually reproduced no longer exists. For example, in the French case, the two universes of Left and Right—one structured around the Communist Party and the "Communist counter-society" and the other around the Catholic Church and its network organizations—have both disappeared leaving a tremendous sense of abandonment behind them. A great deal of anxiety and nostalgia have flourished and grown out of the ruins of the old world. Le Pen in France, Jorg Haider in Austria, Filip Dewinter in Belgium, and others elsewhere have succeeded in picking up on these feelings, fostering them, giving voice to them and finding an electoral outlet for them.

This is particularly strong amongst the working-class group which used to be a central actor in the development of industrial capitalism. Since the beginning of the 1990s, electoral advances made by the Extreme-Right among the working-classes, which until then had been the protected hunting ground of the social-democrat and Communist Left, have been general throughout Europe. The *FN* in France, the Norwegian *FrP*, the Flemish *Vlaams Blok*, the German Extreme-Right (*Republikaner*, *DVU*, *NPD*) and the Austrian *FPÖ* have all experienced a pronounced proletarianisation of their electorate. Thus, the anxieties generated by the falling apart of industrial capitalism have supplied the European Extreme-Right with contingents of working class voters who have added their support to the traditional and less numerous electorate made up by the lower middle class (artisans, shopkeepers, small entrepreneurs, the self-employed). In 2004, working class voters made up three quarters of the Extreme-Right electorate as a whole (in the seven countries studied as a whole, these working class voters only make up 56% of the overall electorate). Among this electorate the level of education is of course low: 84% of Extreme-Right voters do not have an educational qualification or have only a primary or secondary school diploma (table 14.1). The clear overrepresentation of men in the Extreme-Right electorate should also be noted. This is the reflection of a masculine discontentment and a confused search for authority in a society which is ever less capable of generating jobs and a meaningful sense of identity for all its members.[11]

This "alliance between the shop and the workshop" is at the heart of the winning formulas developed by European Extreme-Right parties.[12] During the 1990s, they were well aware of how to design their programs and ideological orientations in order to appeal to these two clienteles. The working class was

Table 14.1 Profiles of Extreme-Right electorates in Europe

		Sex		*Qualification*		*Social class*		
		Men	*Women*	*No qualification, Primary, Secondary*	*Post secondary, higher education*	*Upper + middle*	*Working class*	*Numbers*
Austria	Extreme-Right	71	29	94	6	25	75	(51)
	Electorate as a whole	49	51	84	16	33	67	(1038)
Belgium	Extreme-Right	60	40	94	6	23	77	(149)
	Electorate as a whole	48	52	70	30	43	57	(1296)
Denmark	Extreme-Right	58	42	77	23	25	75	(97)
	Electorate as a whole	46	54	54	46	45	55	(757)
France	Extreme-Right	51	49	77	23	35	65	(83)
	Electorate as a whole	48	52	53	47	51	49	(1045)
Norway	Extreme-Right	67	33	65	35	31	69	(196)
	Electorate as a whole	50	50	51	49	44	56	(1310)
Poland	Extreme-Right	57	43	92	8	12	88	(140)
	Electorate as a whole	54	46	79	21	31	69	(739)
Switzerland	Extreme-Right	55	45	80	20	36	64	(281)
	Electorate as a whole	51	49	69	31	47	53	(1018)
Seven countries average (*)	Extreme-Right	56	44	84	16	25	75	(719)
	Electorate as a whole	50	50	63	37	44	56	(5910)

Note: * For the seven countries as a whole where the extreme-right has a significant number of followers, the averages were balanced in function of the demographic weight of each country.

Source: European Social Survey, 2004.

bathed in nostalgia for a national and industrial capitalism which also offered assistance to those in need. They felt threatened by a postindustrial type of capitalism that was more transnational, economically liberal, and individualist. The extreme right-wing parties stepped in to offer a protective state, which would organize the redistribution of wealth and the reduction of inequality and which would reserve the advantages of the Welfare State for nationals alone. This "Welfare State chauvinism"[13] was often very well received amongst a working class which had been destabilized by competition with foreign workers in the labor market and the whittling away of Welfare State resources. More traditionally, the Extreme-Right offers the self-employed lower middle class a state recentered on its role as figure of authority, the purveyor of "law and order," together with an anti-fiscal and frequently demagogical program.

In social and cultural terms, modernity is characterized above all by the ever stronger affirmation of what might be called an "open society."[14] This spirit of openness which is present in all European societies and many others besides, is essentially economic in nature and is linked to many different factors. These include, the globalization of economic and financial exchanges, a political open-mindedness resulting from the building of Europe, the development of the supranational level of inter-State international relations, and finally, a cultural and social spirit of openness with the increase of migration, the growing mobility of populations and the more and more pluricultural nature of our societies. There have been two types of reaction to this triple opening. A great many people from the upper and middle classes see only the positive aspects of this more open society or believe that in the long run they will benefit from it. On the other hand, many individuals with a lower level of education at the bottom of the social scale do not have the necessary tools to fully understand what is changing and anxiously observe as the world which serves as their reference—the stable and relatively self-contained society of preceding generations—disintegrates. This explains why they gather so easily behind the leaders of the modern Extreme-Right parties who are the champions of the "closed society." These leaders know better than anyone else how to exploit these anxieties and concerns. Jorg Haider's *FPÖ* leads the charge against the Hungarian, Slovenian, or Czech "invaders." Le Pen denounces "Euroglobalism," "cosmopolitanism," calling for an exit from Europe and from the Euro. Pia Kjaersgaard, leader of the *Dansk Folkeparti*, glorifies Danish homogeneity "which has never been and which must never become a land of immigration." As Tor Bjorklund and Jorgen Goul Andersen point out, the anti-immigration dimension has never ceased to make headway in these parties' programs.[15]

Of Extreme-Right voters 67% believe that their country should only authorize the admittance of "few" or even "no" immigrants (as against an average of 44% for the electorate as a whole). This rejection of immigration reaches particularly high levels in Denmark, France, Austria, Belgium and Norway (see table 14.2).

All the European Extreme-Right leaders agree on the "detrimental effects" of the open society, on the need to halt the process and to move back toward more "closed" or self-sustaining societies. A new cleavage which has little to do with the traditional Right-Left cleavage has thus emerged in a number of European countries. It appeared for the first time in France during the 1992 referendum on approval of the Maastricht Treaty dividing the electorate into two more or less equal parts. This cleavage separates those who have adapted to globalization, to the building of Europe and to the multi-cultural society from those who believe they can protect themselves from these changes by closing borders and by advocating models of more or less "closed" societies. Forty-three % of European Extreme-Right voters believe that "European unification has gone too far" (as against only 30% of the electorate as a whole), only 32% believe that unification "should go further" (as against 46% of the electorate as a whole) (see table 14.3). In Austria, Denmark, Belgium, France and Switzerland (which does not belong to the European Union) between 54% and 67% of Extreme-Right voters believe that "European unification has gone too far." Only Poland, which was not yet part of the European Union when the survey took place and Norway, which refused to join the Union in 1994,

Table 14.2 The hostility of Extreme-Right voters toward migratory influx (%) "The country should allow immigrants in"

		"A lot" or "some"	*"Few" or "none"*	*"Don't know"*
Austria	Extreme Right	22	76	2
	Electorate as a whole	49	48	3
Belgium	Extreme-Right	27	71	2
	Electorate as a whole	53	46	1
Denmark	Extreme-Right	12	87	1
	Electorate as a whole	51	48	1
France	Extreme-Right	19	81	0
	Electorate as a whole	52	47	1
Norway	Extreme-Right	35	65	0
	Electorate as a whole	58	42	0
Poland	Extreme-Right	42	56	2
	Electorate as a whole	64	35	1
Switzerland	Extreme-Right	42	57	1
	Electorate as a whole	63	36	1
Seven countries average (*)	Extreme-Right	31	67	2
	Electorate as a whole	54	44	2

Note: * For the seven countries as a whole where the extreme-right has a significant number of followers, the averages were balanced in function of the demographic weight of each country.

Source: ESS survey, 2004.

Table 14.3 The attitude of Extreme-Right voters toward Europe (%)

		European Unification			
		Has gone too far (0 to 4)	*Central position (5)*	*Should go further (6 to 10)*	*Don't know*
Austria	Extreme-Right	67	14	17	2
	Electorate as a whole	42	21	34	3
Belgium	Extreme-Right	56	22	20	2
	Electorate as a whole	37	19	42	2
Denmark	Extreme-Right	58	17	22	3
	Electorate as a whole	32	17	48	3
France	Extreme-Right	55	25	19	1
	Electorate as a whole	34	24	40	2
Norway	Extreme-Right	33	27	36	4
	Electorate as a whole	36	27	33	4
Poland	Extreme-Right	23	18	52	7
	Electorate as a whole	14	17	65	4
Switzerland	Extreme-Right	54	25	19	2
	Electorate as a whole	30	21	48	1
Seven countries average (*)	Extreme-Right	43	22	32	3
	Electorate as a whole	30	22	46	2

Note: * For the seven countries as a whole where the extreme-right has a significant number of followers, the averages were balanced in function of the demographic weight of each country.

Source: ESS survey, 2004.

remain more sheltered from the stigmatization engendered by the process of European unification.

With its long tradition of "inward-looking nationalism" the Extreme-Right has well understood that it is far better placed than other political families to exploit all the anxieties aroused by the "open society."

Lastly, the final element of the crisis in modernity to nourish the Extreme-Right dynamic: discontent with democracy. In his illuminating political history of religion, Marcel Gauchet showed how "disenchantment with the world" affected more than just the religious sphere. More generally, it has affected all systems of representation which provide an account of how the collective ought-to-be evolves over time and therefore of political ideologies.[16] This toppling of the systems of representation claiming a knowledge of and control over the future has brought about a loss of political references and a profound crisis vis-à-vis political representation. This is general throughout Europe but the crisis has been deeper in certain countries because political representation is no longer seen to represent the diversity, novelty and complexity of the cleavages running through our modern societies. As Marcel Gauchet wrote in *Disenchantment with the World*, as an axial form of the relationship to politics, "conflict must potentially involve the totality of collective action and be embedded in civil discord, whether it represents a disagreement on the political stage or involves relations formed between individuals and groups."[17] However, voters today and particularly (though not only) Extreme-Right voters, relate very little to the conflicts and cleavages present on the political scene.

Of Extreme-Right voters 59% (as against 49% of the electorate as a whole) have no confidence in politicians and 71% are not satisfied with the way democracy functions (as against 56% of the electorate as a whole). Denmark and Switzerland are the only countries to have experienced more modest political discontent and an Extreme-Right electorate which is less critical of the political system (see table 14.4).

In a situation where citizens think: "society is changing but the system for the sharing-out of power and the elites themselves never-change," the populists, who appeal both by protesting and by creating a strong sense of identity, are taken to be the only true opponents to the system. In France, it was after a long *cohabitation* (when the President and the government come from opposite sides of the political spectrum) of five years duration between Left and Right that Jean-Marie Le Pen, the herald of a radical opposition to the "system" and to the "Establishment," was propelled by voters to the second round of the 2002 presidential election. Thus, Extreme-Right movements from "outside the system" can reach record levels, although these tend to decrease again as soon as they integrate the system. This was the case for the *FPÖ* after it became part of the government in February 2000, with the conservatives from the *ÖVP* or, in another example, the *LPF* in the Netherlands following its alliance with the Christian Democrats of the *CDA* and the conservative liberals of the *VVD*.

The rise of Extreme-Right parties in Europe is not an inevitable phenomenon. Admittedly, at a time when Politics is becoming desecrated and disenchanted, there are those who nourish a certain amount of nostalgia for the

Table 14.4 Political discontent among Extreme-Right voters (%)

		No trust in politicians	*Low level of satisfaction with the functioning of democracy*
Austria	Extreme-Right	61	51
	Electorate as a whole	53	38
Belgium	Extrem- Right	53	73
	Electorate as a whole	33	45
Denmark	Extreme-Right	28	25
	Electorate as a whole	13	18
France	Extreme-Right	58	80
	Electorate as a whole	45	57
Norway	Extreme-Right	52	47
	Electorate as a whole	33	33
Poland	Extreme-Right	75	84
	Electorate as a whole	76	78
Switzerland	Extreme-Right	29	33
	Electorate as a whole	23	29
Seven countries average (*)	Extreme-Right	59	71
	Electorate as a whole	49	56

Note: * For the seven countries as a whole where the extreme-right has a significant number of followers, the averages were balanced in function of the demographic weight of each country.

Source: ESS Survey, 2004.

revolutionary or ultra-reactionary passions of yore which just a few decades ago enlivened the political arena. But, as Marcel Gauchet recalled recently, "enchantment with politics was the nightmare of the 20th century."[18] The resurgence, here and there of right- or left-wing extremisms is often merely the echo of an unsuccessfully completed disenchantment and the difficulty of accepting a political landscape which is "disenchanted," "modest" but also and above all modern.

Notes

1. Unlike in other chapters, Germany, Spain, Italy, Britain, the Netherlands, and Sweden will not be referred to in the comparative analysis here as the number of Extreme-Right voters in these countries is low or inexistent. On the other hand, Austria (*FPÖ* voters), Belgium (*Vlaams Blok*, which became the *Vlaams Belang* in November 2004 and *Front National* voters), Denmark (Dansk Folkeparti and Fremskridtspartiet voters), Norway (*Fremskrittspartiet* voters), and Switzerland (*SVP* voters) have been included alongside France (*Front National* voters) and Poland (Samoobrona and Liga Polkskich Rodzin voters).
2. Minkenberg, 2002.
3. Taguieff, 2002.
4. Minkenberg and Perrineau, 2007.
5. Evans and Ivaldi, 2002.
6. Mudde, 1995.
7. Ignazi, 2003.

8. Casals, 2005.
9. Freud, 1995.
10. Betz, 2004.
11. Perrineau, 1997.
12. Kitschelt and McGann, 1995.
13. Andersen and Björklund, 1990.
14. Perrineau, 2001.
15. Blaise and Moreau, 2004.
16. Gauchet, 1985.
17. Ibid., p. 194.
18. Gauchet, 2002.

CONCLUSION

France in Europe

Luc Rouban

How can we situate France within the European context? The preceding chapters of this book reveal a country where political "normality" is in crisis, politicization manifesting itself more in protest on the margins rather than in engagement in the processes of democracy. This contrasts with the dynamics of politicization in the countries of Northern Europe, for example. Several factors contribute to a growing disconnection between the state of society—both in its evolution and its involution—and the arguments and policy ideas which politicians have to offer. This disconnection may have its origins in two related trends.

The first concerns the inability of politicians to address the actual concerns of their various constituents. Symptoms of this dissatisfaction with a stagnating status quo include the shift of working-class votes from the Left to the Far Right, leaving the French Socialist Party more reliant on the votes of senior managers than those of the working classes; the mistrust of politicians and the media, even among the most highly educated citizens, who are skeptical about the accuracy of available information; the fact that trade unions are still largely preoccupied with political protest at a time when workers are more interested in obtaining actual improvements in their working conditions; and the underrepresentation of women in key political positions. The policy options formulated within the party political apparatuses fail to satisfactorily address the concerns provoked by recent transformations within society; these include the emergence of "postmaterialist" values, such as environmental protection, and the impact of the economic downturn on the standard of living of not only the poorest sections of society, but the middle classes as well.

On the other hand, policies aimed at liberalizing the French economy meet fierce resistance from well-established social structures which have been central to politics in the Fifth Republic. The electorate is unprepared for and unconvinced by what politicians have to offer, which fails to engage with their principal concerns. The reluctance of French employees to embrace economic liberalization constitutes a major obstacle to European political integration. Even after a succession of privatization programs, introduced by both left- and right-wing governments, the public sector has retained its political specificity. Besides, a career in the civil service still offers the most reliable route to take for individuals who have ambitions to make a career in politics. The vision of a pluralist society offered by the elites, who are now obliged to negotiate with ever-increasing numbers of pressure groups, is at odds with the French attachment to a statist model which prioritizes social solidarity. This is not a narrow nationalistic model, of the kind that can be observed in Great Britain. It reflects concern for social solidarity, which does not seem to be high in the list of the priorities of the European project.

It remains to be seen whether this national situation is symptomatic of a general transformation of politics in Europe, or whether France presents an anomaly or even an archaism. An investigation of French specificity can begin with two questions.

The first thing to ask is whether Europe is witnessing a convergence of national situations. After the rejection by referendum of the 2005 European Constitutional Treaty, much has been written about France's distancing itself from the rest of Europe. It has also been suggested that France constitutes a special case which is not susceptible to reform. Does France constitute a uniquely special case, or are all the countries involved in the European project special cases looking for a lowest common denominator? To properly analyze the dynamics at play we would need to be able to consult a series of historical surveys of a variety of European countries. Since no such surveys exist we have had to rely on the European Social Survey to obtain a picture of national situations and so attempt to assess the current state of Europe in the middle of the first decade of the twenty-first century.[1] Another way of putting this question would be to ask ourselves if France should be seen as one of a sub-group of rich European countries, or rather as a member of a sub-group of Mediterranean or "Latin" countries, which could be compared to the more liberal, 'Atlanticist' countries of Northern Europe.

Second, we could focus on the internal homogeneity of European countries. In all European societies there is a division between on the one hand well-qualified individuals and on the other hand those who, because of their lack of qualifications, are under a greater threat of unemployment and social exclusion, and more likely to vote for extremist candidates. Is the division between those with and without qualifications greater in France than elsewhere in Europe?

Therefore we can endeavor to discover the degree of external and internal homogeneity of France, comparing it to a number of other European countries, who themselves present a variety of sociopolitical and cultural characteristics.[2]

In order to reply to this two-part question an analysis of two fundamental dimensions which structure political behavior and attitudes is required. These dimensions touch on fundamental values which operate on a deeper level than such conjectural phenomena as the electoral ascendance of the Right or the

Left, which of course vary from one year to the next and can depend on domestic issues which are beyond the scope of an international survey.

The first of these dimensions concerns self-positioning of Europeans on two issues: first Europe, and second the rise of economic liberalism. These two questions are closely linked, given that European construction is a free market project, a fact that the positions of the European Commission, the decisions of the European Court in Luxemburg, and the terms of the European Constitutional Treaty have made abundantly clear.

In order to measure attitudes toward Europe, an index was calculated using replies to six questions regarding the appropriate level for decisions to be taken in several areas of public policy.[3] Interviewees were asked whether the main decision-making powers in these policy areas should be in the hands of international, European, state or local governing bodies.

An index for measuring attitudes to liberal economics was calculated using replies to two questions, one concerning state intervention ("is state intervention beneficial, in principle, for the country's economy?") and the other regarding the need for state intervention to reduce disparities in income. This index gives an indication of attitudes toward the appropriate extent of state involvement in the economy, and has nothing to do with attitudes toward freedom to do business or placing restrictions on companies.

The ESS is instructive on these two matters in the following ways. First, the average level of acceptance of economic liberalism across Europe is very low, even when the replies of the self-employed and not just salaried employees are taken into account. If the replies of salaried employees are singled out, they show an even less favorable attitude to liberalism. Denmark and the United Kingdom stand out as the two countries that take a more positive view of liberalism: they produced averages of 0.66 and 0.5 respectively, while the overall average of the group of European countries surveyed was 0.45.[4] The least liberal countries are Portugal (0.22), Spain (0.29), and Greece (0.30).

The overall score for France was 0.37 and, uniquely among the countries in the survey, the level of liberalism for people with qualifications was lower (0.33). These results can be explained by the fact that in the large French public sector there is a high proportion of qualified individuals. Variation with the replies to questions regarding liberalism is very low. This enables us to conclude that French people generally reject economic liberalism, understood as the philosophy that considers that regulation of economic life is best left the market.

The ESS also provides useful data regarding levels of Europeanization. When the survey goes beyond questioning participants about their general attitude to the construction of a European community and focuses on European integration of specific policy areas the general level of Europeanization is relatively low. Nevertheless, the range of replies is much wider here, and there are appreciable differences between countries. Whereas the Europe average is 1.3, the national results vary between a minimum of 0.72 in the United Kingdom to a maximum of 1.77 in Germany. France is one of the most pro-European countries, with an average score of 1.53.

These two sets of results demonstrate that the combination of liberalism and Europeanism, a prerequisite of the successful completion of the current phase of European construction, is rarely found in the countries that participated in the survey. There are either high levels of Europeanism and low levels of liberalism, as is broadly the case in France and Italy, or higher levels of liberalism in countries where an attachment to politics being conducted on a national level still predominates, such as Denmark or the United Kingdom. Furthermore, the difference between the two indices is widest in Belgium, the Netherlands, and France, providing a clear indication of the tension that exists between two political dimensions that need to be harmonized in European Union political theory and practice. It is worth reiterating at this point that France and the Netherlands were the two countries where referenda on the European Constitutional Treaty resulted in victories for the "no" vote.

The combination of these two indicators enables the attitudes of European citizens toward Europeanization and economic liberalism to be represented graphically (figure conclusion.1).

What emerges is that there is no clear division of European countries into "Northern countries" and "Southern countries." What does become apparent, though, is that when each national population is divided into those with and without educational qualifications, the European project has the support of educated citizens in Germany, Belgium, Italy, and the Netherlands and, to a lesser extent, Denmark and France. Educated British and Polish people on the other hand, are far more Euroskeptic. We can therefore note that divisions over Europe within the countries in the survey are not uniform, and that levels of international homogeneity vary greatly. While the United Kingdom has a high degree of internal homogeneity, attitudes to Europe displayed by educated Germans, Danes, Italians, and Portuguese vary considerably from those of their less educated compatriots.

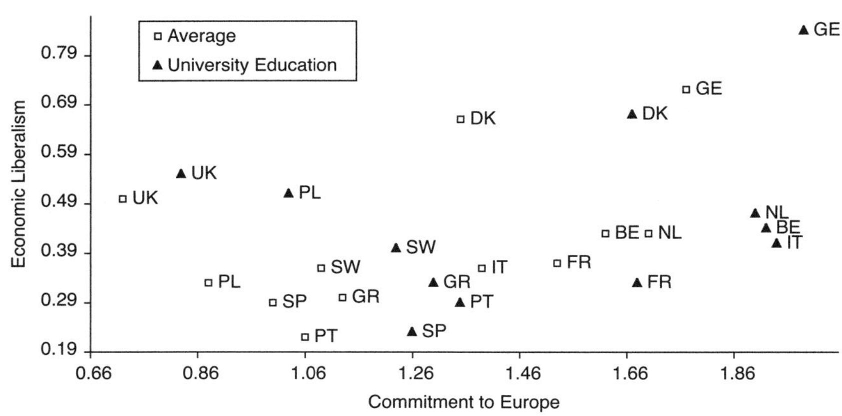

Figure Conclusion.1 Europeanization and economic liberalism

Another dimension of political life which is worth considering in the context of European integration is the degree of openness to the outside world and the capacity to accept other people, including foreigners. France arguably has a reputation for being inward-looking, suspicious of multiethnicity, and afraid of globalization and international exchange. To test whether these characterizations of French people are accurate, two indicators can be combined, the first measuring the level of xenophobia of interviewees, the second the degree of interpersonal trust, defined as the extent to which in our social relations we spontaneously tend to trust other people. These indicators provide two complementary perspectives, the first reflecting openness to foreigners, the second expressing a more general acceptance of social otherness.

The xenophobia indicator was calculated using replies to a series of questions eliciting the interviewee's opinions on the impact of immigration.[5] Interpersonal trust was measured using a question which asked interviewees to locate themselves on a scale of trustfulness.

Xenophobia is the indicator with the largest standard deviation, due to a wide variation of national scores. The average index for the countries studied is 1.95, ranging from a minimum of 1.47 in Sweden to a maximum of 3.03 in Greece. France emerges from this study as a country with a low average level of xenophobia (1.76). Together with Italy and Sweden, France is one of the least xenophobic countries in Europe. The most xenophobic European countries, apart from Greece, are the United Kingdom (2.17) and Belgium (2.13).

Although French people, in general, are not very xenophobic, when establishing social relations with others they are not particularly trusting. Their average level of interpersonal trust is 0.85, compared to the Europe average of 0.93. As regards trustfulness, French interviewees can be grouped together with the Greeks (0.57), who have the lowest indicator, the Poles (0.59), and the Portuguese (0.71). We can observe a split between countries with high jobless figures and countries where the employment situation is more favorable; in the latter group levels of interpersonal trust are higher: Denmark scored 1.64, Sweden 1.4, and the Netherlands 1.35.

When these two indicators are combined, educated Danes, Dutch, and Swedes are shown to have the highest degree of openness to others. In every country there is a close link between educational levels and levels of xenophobia. The largest differences between qualified and unqualified interviewees were observed in Italy, Poland, and Portugal (see figure conclusion.2).

These results seem to indicate that the problematic relationship the French have with politics has less to do with their attitudes toward foreigners or to Europe, and more to do with France's domestic situation. The source of France's political "malaise" appears to be located in French people's mistrust of their fellow citizens rather than in nationalistic or xenophobic sentiments.

It becomes necessary, therefore, to study the extent to which French people are politically integrated. Political integration can be represented by putting the level of politicization on one axis, and the level of trust in political institutions on the other. The politicization indicator is calculated using three variables: level of interest in politics, the frequency with which the interviewee

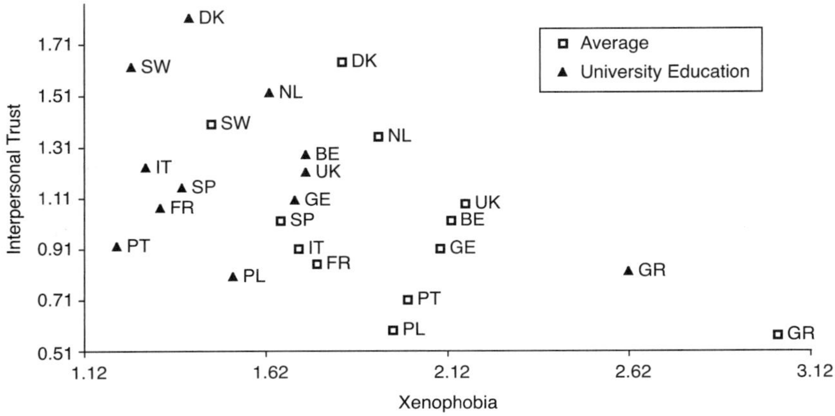

Figure Conclusion.2 Personal openness

discusses politics with family and acquaintances, and the amount of importance attached to politics. The second indicator is calculated using replies to questions about levels of trust in elected representatives, the national parliament, the judicial system, and the police.

We can advance the hypothesis that the higher each of these two indicators are, the greater the level of political integration, since high scores are obtained by individuals who take a keen interest in politics and have a high degree of trust in the way their country's institutions operate.

Generally speaking, political integration in France is weak. This weakness derives from a combination of relative lack of interest in politics and low levels of trust in political institutions. France scores 0.92 for politicization, compared to an overall average of 1 for the countries surveyed. Interest in politics in France is higher than in Southern European countries (both Greece and Portugal scored 0.8), but considerably lower than in Northern European countries such as Germany (1.4), Denmark (1.3), and the Netherlands (1.3). As regards confidence in institutions, France's results are the worst among the founding members of the EU, with a score of 0.95, compared to an overall average of 1.05 for all the countries in the survey. The lowest levels registered were in Poland (0.59), Portugal (0.61), and Spain (0.78), and the highest, once again, in Denmark (2.1) and Sweden (1.62).

Figure Conclusion.3 shows that the average levels of political integration for all the citizens of Germany, Denmark and the Netherlands of all levels of education are higher than the levels of political integration among the most highly educated French people. On the other hand, the gap between levels of integration of the population as a whole and those of the most highly educated sections of society is narrower in France than in Germany, Denmark, Italy, the Netherlands, and Sweden, countries in which there appears to be a clear division between the upper classes and the rest of the people. The European

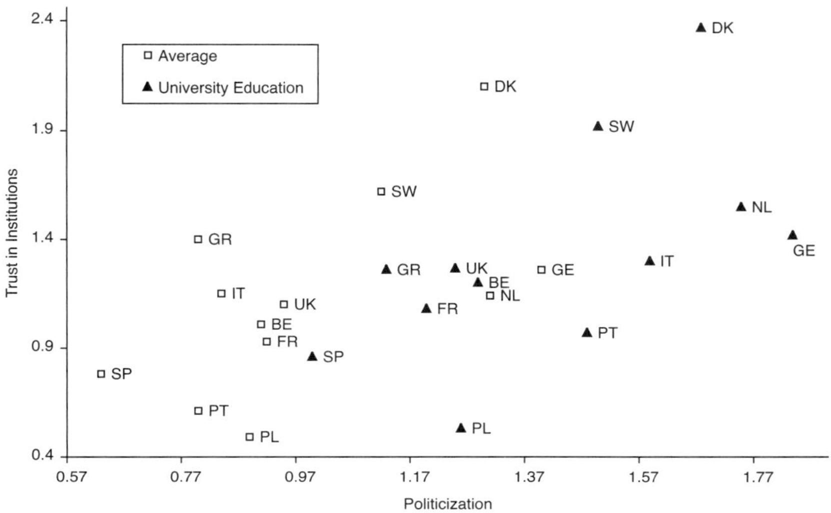

Figure Conclusion.3 Political integration

project seems to be an elite-led phenomenon in these countries as well (see figure conclusion.1).

Therefore the factors which are most likely to determine both political integration and the degree of openness to others need to be established. Xenophobia—as well as interpersonal trust—is directly related to educational level and social background. On the other hand, likely level of interest in politics, in the widest sense, depends on a combination of factors: level of job satisfaction, profession, job sector, and country of origin. An individual's position in society gives no automatic indication of his or her level of politicization. It is true that independent professionals as well as private and public sector managers are *on average* much more interested in politics than members of the working classes. But that is only true within individual countries, or in an average group of Europeans, an average group which clearly has no sociological or even political meaning. The results obtained are very different if the various dividing lines which cross Europe are taken into account. For example, German or Dutch workers who are unhappy in their jobs are more politicized than Greek or Portuguese managers who are also unhappy in their jobs, and have similar levels of politicization to French managers who dislike their jobs. Furthermore, among those who enjoy a certain amount of job satisfaction, there is no statistically significant difference in levels of politicization between public sector managers and workers. The only determining factor is nationality. In the private sector, on the other hand, the difference between managers and workers is the only discriminating factor and is far more significant than nationality.

As can be seen from table conclusion.1, the wide statistical variations in degree of politicization can be explained by the interplay of several discriminating

Table Conclusion.1 Politicization in Europe and its discriminating factors—Percentage of highly politicized citizens

Low Job Satisfaction		*High Job Satisfaction*	
Managers, senior professionals		**Public sector**	
Average	50	*Average*	44
Germany, Denmark, Netherlands	58	Germany	65
Spain, France, United Kingdom, Italy	47	Spain, France, United Kingdom	30
Greece, Portugal	38	**Private sector**	
Workers		*Average*	36
Average	28	Managers	53
Germany, Netherlands	41	Workers	27
Belgium, France, United Kingdom	26		
Spain, Greece, Italy, Portugal	17		

factors. The fact remains, nonetheless, that an individual's attitude to their work seems to constitute the "latent variable" which structures the results as a whole. This emerged from an analysis of segmentation measured by the CHAID algorithm. This latent variable removes the national framework, which is generally the main limitation of comparative studies, and brings to light sociopolitical configurations which would otherwise have remained undiscovered. Future research will no doubt build on these findings, so avoiding a purely commonsensical or 'political' approach.

The diversity of situations in Europe can therefore not be explained using simple sociological indicators, which are unable to take account of the complexity of sociopolitical realities. Neither an individual's socio-professional standing, nor their nationality, or the part of the economy they work in are overdetermining factors. There is no such thing as a European employee, any more than there is a European civil servant. This is not to say, however, that a British person will always be different from a French person, or that Northern Europe is and will always be a completely different world from Southern Europe. Complex cross-border groupings of citizens appear, each simultaneously belonging to a variety of interacting worlds. Here, complexity should not be confused with chaos. Attitudes to politics are influenced by a range of factors that, though undoubtedly complex, are identifiable and susceptible to classification. Voters may be only dimly aware of these factors which nevertheless ultimately have a great bearing on their electoral behavior.

Recent major economic trends, such as the globalization of finance, cannot therefore have direct and immediate consequences on the sociopolitical situation of each country. Their effects are mediatized and translated in the internal order of social arrangements which apply to both the world of politics and the world of work. The political dimension of social phenomena must therefore not be ignored since it leads us to ask whether the internal social order needs to be changed and if so to what end. The results of the ESS clearly show that "Europe" remains a mythical figure which struggles to propose a social model and certainly cannot be said to have a political philosophy other than a utilitarian and ill-defined social liberalism. Europe cannot solve France's domestic problems, which include the decline of the French trade union movement, the fondness of trade unions for militant gestures, the growing influence of pressure groups, the rift between France's citizens and its political elites, the discontent of employees in both the private and public sectors, and the underrepresentation of women in the highest levels of government. In this sense, there is no perfect social and political system, no "model" to imitate. The construction of a country's socio-political system is always a matter of domestic politics.

It is nevertheless a fact that characterizing France within the context of Europe, once care has been taken to reify neither Europe nor national societies, leads us to a somewhat paradoxical conclusion. France, which has always been presented as the very model of uniformity and the centralized state, now appears from the vantage point of other European countries to be a country where numerous norms and normalities are in competition. Various social visions promoted by trade unions, associations, private enterprise and elites have regularly forced political parties and governments to abandon important policy measures. This uncomfortable coexistence of a host of seemingly incompatible visions for France is the major obstacle to the emergence of social democracy, since social democracy requires the kind of long term social consensus which, however desirable, shows no signs of emerging in the foreseeable future.

Notes

1. We have used data from the first wave of the ESS, which was collected in 2003. This choice was made for technical reasons connected with the great diversity of questions related to politics in this survey. The variables we use are structural variables which change little from year to year. An empirical verification carried out on the second wave of the survey, which used data gathered in 2004, which are for the moment the most recent data available, show that the national situations are stable, according to the main indicators used, providing a guarantee of quality.
2. The countries under consideration here are Germany, Belgium, Denmark, Spain, France, Greece, Italy, the Netherlands, Poland, Portugal, Sweden, and the United Kingdom.
3. Agriculture policy, defense policy, the fixing of interest rates, immigration policy, environmental protection, social policy.
4. It should be pointed out that these indicators are calculated using weighted results that take the distribution of age groups into consideration. The average indicators for the 12 countries surveyed are calculated using multiple weighting which combines the relative size of the population of each country with age groups.
5. These questions asked interviewees whether they thought immigration was good or bad for their national economy, impoverished or enriched their national culture, did or did not cause an increase in crime, had a positive or negative impact on the employment situation and, finally, whether immigrants as a group were net beneficiaries or contributors of taxation and social services. Interviewees were asked to reply on a scale of 0 to 10. Statistically, the five questions showed a high degree of internal consistency (Cronbach's alpha = 0.7).

Bibliography

Achin (Catherine), *Le mystère de la chambre basse. Comparaison des processus d'entrée des femmes au Parlement. France-Allemagne, 1945–2000*, Paris, Dalloz, 2005.

Achin (Catherine), Levêque (Sandrine), *Femmes en politique*, Paris, La Découverte, 2006.

Alexandre-Collier (Agnès), Jardin (Xavier), *Anatomie des droites européennes*, Paris, Armand Colin, 2004.

Alford (Robert R.), *Party and society: The Anglo American democracies*, Chicago (IL), Rand McNally, 1963.

Amadieu (Jean-François), Groux (Guy), "Entre l'entreprise et l'État: les nouveaux systèmes de règles," in Jacques Commaille, Bruno Jobert (eds.), *Les métamorphoses de la régulation politique*, Paris, LGDJ & Maison des Sciences de l'Homme, 1998, pp. 241–255.

Andersen (Jorgen Goul), Björklund (Tor), "Structural change and new cleavages: The Progress parties in Denmark and Norway," *Acta Sociologica*, 33(3), 1990, pp.195–218.

Ansart (Pierre), *La gestion des passions politiques*, Lausanne, L'Age d'Homme, 1987.

Antoine (Michel), *Louis XV*, Paris, Fayard, 1989.

Ballmer-Cao (Thanh-Huyen), Mottier (Véronique), and Sgier (Lea) (eds)., *Genre et politique: débats et perspectives*, Paris, Gallimard, 2000.

Bard (Christine), Baudelot (Christian), and Mossuz-Lavau (Janine), *Quand les femmes s'en mêlent. Genre et pouvoir*, Paris, Éditions de la Martinière, 2004.

Barthélémy (Martine), *Associations: un nouvel âge de la participation?* Paris, Presses de Sciences Po, 2000.

Bartolini (Stefano), Mair (Peter), *Identity, competition, and electoral availability: The stabilization of European electorates, 1885–1985*, Cambridge, Cambridge University Press, 1990.

Bataille (Philippe), Gaspard (Françoise), *Comment les femmes changent la politique et pourquoi les hommes résistent*, Paris, La Découverte, 1999.

Becquet (Valérie), de Linares (Chantal) (eds.), *Quand les jeunes s'engagent. Entre expérimentations et constructions identitaires,* Paris, L'Harmattan, 2005.

Bentégeat (Hervé), *Les nouveaux rois de France*, Paris, Ramsay, 1998.

Berger (Peter) (ed.), *Le Réenchantement du monde,* trad. fr., Paris, Bayard, 2001 (1st ed. 1999).

Bergounioux (Alain), Grunberg (Gérard), *L'Ambition et le remords. Les socialistes français et le pouvoir (1905–2005)*, Paris, Fayard, 2005.

———, *L'Utopie à l'épreuve. Histoire du socialisme européen*, Paris, Bernard de Fallois, 1996.

Betz (Hans-Georg), *La droite populiste en Europe. Extrême et démocrate?*, Paris, Autrement, coll. "Cevipof/Autrement," 2004.
Birnbaum (Pierre), *La fin du politique*, Paris, Le Seuil, 1975.
——— (ed.), *Les élites socialistes au pouvoir*, Paris, PUF, 1985.
———, *Les sommets de l'État: essai sur l'élite du pouvoir en France*, Paris, Seuil, 1994, [2nd ed.].
Blaise (Pierre), Moreau (Patrick) (eds.), *Extrême-droite et national-populisme en Europe de l'Ouest*, Bruxelles, Centre de recherche et d'information socio-politiques, 2004.
Blom-Hansen (Jens) "Still corporatism in Scandinavia? A survey of empirical findings," *Scandinavian Political Studies*, 23(1), 2000, pp. 85–106.
Bodiguel (Jean-Luc), *Les anciens élèves de l'ENA*, Presses de Sciences Po, Paris, 1978.
Boissonnat (Jean), *Le travail dans vingt ans*, Paris, Odile Jacob, 1995.
Bord (Richard), O'Connor (Robert), "The gender gap in environmental attitudes: The case of perceived vulnerability to risk," *Social Science Quarterly*, 78(4), 1997, pp. 830–840.
Bourdieu (Pierre), *La noblesse d'État: grandes écoles et esprit de corps*, Paris, Minuit, 1989.
Boy (Daniel), Chiche (Jean), "La gauche radicale et les Verts, des contestations hétérogènes," in Pascal Perrineau (ed.), *Le vote européen 2004–2005*, Paris, Presses de Sciences Po, 2005, pp. 205–228.
Boy (Daniel), Platone (François), Rey (Henri), Subileau (Françoise), and Ysmal (Colette), *C'était la gauche plurielle*, Paris, Presses de Sciences Po, 2003.
Boyer (Robert), "Rapport salarial, croissance et crise: une dialectique cachée. Introduction à une comparaison de sept pays européens," in Robert Boyer (ed.), *La flexibilité du travail en Europe*, Paris, La Découverte, 1986.
Bréchon (Pierre), "Les valeurs politiques en Europe: effet du contexte national et des attitudes religieuses," *Archives de sciences sociales des religions*, 93, January–March 1996, pp. 99–128.
———, "L'évolution du religieux," *Futuribles*, 260, January 2001, pp. 39–48.
———, "Influence de l'intégration religieuse sur les attitudes: analyse comparative européenne," *Revue française de sociologie*, 43(3), 2002a, pp. 461–483.
———, "Des valeurs politiques entre pérennité et changement," *Futuribles*, Les valeurs des Européens, 277, July–August 2002b, pp. 95–128.
———, "Générations et politique en Europe occidentale," dans Olivier Galland, Bernard Roudet (ed.), *Les jeunes Européens et leurs valeurs*, Paris, La Découverte, 2005, pp. 93–116.
Bréchon (Pierre), Denni (Bernard), "L'univers politique des catholiques pratiquants. Enquête par questionnaire dans huit assemblées dominicales grenobloises," *Revue française de sociologie*, 24(3), 1983, pp. 505–534.
Bréchon (Pierre), Tchernia (Jean-François), "L'évolution des valeurs des Français," *Futuribles*, 253, May–June 2000, pp. 5–20.
Brooks (Clem), Nieuwbeerta (Paul), and Manza (Jeff), "Cleavage-based voting behavior in cross-national perspective: Evidence from six post-war democracies," *Social Science Research*, 35(1), 2006, pp. 88–128.
Burnham (James), *The managerial revolution or what is happening in the world now*, Harmondsworth, Pelican Book, 1945.
Butler (David), Stokes (Daniel), *Electoral change in Britain: The evolution of electoral choice*, New York, Saint Martin's Press, 1969.
Casals (Xavier) (ed.), *Political survival on the Extreme Right. European movements between the inherited past and the need to adapt to the future*, Barcelona, Institut de Ciències Politiques I Socials, 2005.

Cautrès (Bruno), Heath (Antony), "Le déclin du vote de classe? Une analyse comparative en France et en Grande Bretagne," *Revue internationale de politique comparée*, 3(3), 1996, pp. 541–568.

Cautrès (Bruno), Mayer (Nonna), "Les métamorphoses du vote de classe," in Bruno Cautrès and Nonna Mayer (eds.), *Le nouveau désordre électoral. Les leçons du 21 avril 2002*, Paris, Presses de Sciences Po, 2004, pp. 145–160.

Certeau (Michel de), *La faiblesse de croire,* Paris, Seuil, 1987.

Chadel (Frédérique), *Étude comparative du leadership au sein des partis politiques: le Rassemblement pour la République et le Partido Popular*, Political Science thesis, Université d'Aix-Marseille/Université Autonome de Barcleone, 2000.

Charle (Christophe), *Les élites de la république 1880–1900*, Paris, Fayard, 2006 (2nd ed.).

Charlot (Jean), *L'UNR. Étude du pouvoir au sein d'un parti politique*, Paris, Armand Colin 1967.

———, *Le Gaullisme d'opposition, 1946–1958*, Paris, Fayard, 1983.

Chauvel (Louis), "Pouvons nous encore parler de classes sociales? "*Revue politique et parlementaire*, 1017–1018, March–April 2002, pp. 147–154.

———, *Les classes moyennes à la dérive*, Paris, Seuil, 2006.

Chopart (Jean-Noël), Martin (Claude) (eds.), *Que reste-t-il des classes sociales?* Paris, Editions ENSP, 2004.

Clark (Terry), Lipset (Seymour M.), *The breakdown of class politics*, Chicago (IL), University of Chicago Press, 2001.

Clark (Terry), Lipset (Seymour M.), and Rempel (Michael), "The declining political significance of social class," *International Sociology*, 8(3), September 1993, pp. 293–316.

Commaille (Jacques), Jobert (Bruno) (eds.), *Les métamorphoses de la régulation politique*, Paris, LGDJ, 1999.

Constant (Benjamin), *Principes de politique,* in *Œuvres,* Paris, Gallimard, coll. "La Pléiade," 1957.

Constantelos (John), "Europeanization and the Italian political system: Politics and policy," *Journal of European Public Policy*, 11(6), 2004, pp. 941–1127.

Coxall (William N.), *Pressure Groups in British Politics*, Harlow, Longman, 2001.

Crête (Jean), Favre (Pierre), *Générations et politique*, Paris, Economica, 1989.

Crewe (Ivor), Denver (David) (eds.), *Electoral change in Western democracies*, London, Croom Helm, 1985.

Dahl (Robert), *Who governs? Democracy and power in an American city*, New Haven (CT), Yale University Press, 1961 (Fr. ed.: *Qui gouverne?* Paris, Armand Colin, 1971).

Dalton (Russell J.), Kuechler (M.) (eds.), *Challenging the political order*, Cambridge, Polity Press, 1990.

Dalton (Russell J.), Wattenberg (Martin. P) (eds.), *Parties without partisans. Political change in advanced industrial democracies*, Oxford, Oxford University Press, 2000.

Davie (Grace), "Believing without belonging. Is this the future of religion in Britain," *Social Compass,* 37, 1990, pp. 456–469.

De Singly (François), *Le soi, le couple, la famille*, Paris, Nathan, 1996.

Delli Carpini (Michael X.), Kennamer (D.J.), "Effects of the news media environment on citizen knowledge of state politics and government," *Journalism Quarterly*, 71(2), Summer 1994, pp. 443–456.

Delwit (Pascal), *Démocraties chrétiennes et conservatismes en Europe. Une nouvelle convergence?*, Bruxelles, Editions de Bruxelles, 2003.

Delwit (Pascal) and De Waele (Jean-Michel), *Les Partis verts en Europe*, Paris, Editions Complexe, 1999.
Delwit (Pascal), Poirier (Philippe) (eds.), *Parlement puissant, électeurs absents? Les élections européennes de juin 2004*, Brussels, Editions de l'Université de Bruxelles, 2005.
Derlien (Hans-Ulrich), Rouban (Luc), "Societal links and social differentiation of the public service" in H-U. Derlien, B. G. Peters (eds.), *The state at work, comparative public service systems*, vol. II, Cheltenham, Edward Elgar, 2008, pp. 146–191.
Donegani (Jean-Marie), *La liberté de choisir. Pluralisme religieux et pluralisme politique dans le catholicisme français contemporain,* Paris, Presses de Sciences Po, 1993.
Donegani (Jean-Marie), Sadoun (Marc), *La Démocratie imparfaite,* Paris, Gallimard, Folio, 1994.
Dreyfus (Françoise), *L'invention de la bureaucratie*, Paris, La Découverte, 2000.
Drouin (Vincent), *Enquête sur les générations et la politique, 1958–1995*, Paris, L'Harmattan, 1995.
Dumazedier (Joffre), *Vers une civilisation du loisir?* Paris, Le Seuil, 1962.
Dunleavy (Patrick), Husbands (Christopher T.), *British democracy at the crossroads*, London, Allen and Unwin, 1985.
Dunleavy (Patrick), O'Leary (Brenda), *Theories of the state. The politics of liberal democracy*, Basingstoke, Macmillan, 1987.
Dunlop (John T.), *Industrial relations systems*, Boston (MA), Harvard Business School, 1993 (1st ed.: 1958).
Duverger (Maurice), *Les partis politiques*, Paris, Armand Colin, 1976, and Seuil, 1981 (1st ed.: 1951).
Eldersveld (S.J.), *Political parties, a behavioral analysis*, Chicago (IL), Rand McNally, 1964.
Elgie (Robert),"The classification of democratic regime types: Conceptual ambiguity and contestable assumptions," *European Journal of Political Research*, 33(2), 1998, pp. 219–238.
Esping-Andersen (Gøsta), *The three worlds of welfare capitalism*, Cambridge, Polity Press, 1990.
Eurobarometer, "The Participation of Europeans in Cultural Activities," Brussels, Commission of the European Union, April 2002.
Eurostat Yearbook, Brussels, Commission of the European Union, 2005, http://epp.eurostat.ec.europa.eu.
Evans (Geoffrey) (eds.), *The decline of class politics? Class voting in a comparative context*, Oxford, Oxford University Press, 1999.
Evans (Jocelyn A.J.), Ivaldi (Gilles), "Les dynamiques électorales de l'extrême-droite européenne," *Revue Politique et Parlementaire*, 1019, May–June/July–August 2002, pp. 67–83.
Eveland (W.P.), "News information processing as mediator of the relationship between motivations and political knowledge," *Journalism & Mass Communication Quarterly*, 79, 2002, pp. 26–40.
Falkner (Gerda) "Corporatist governance and Europeanisation: No future in the multi-level game," *European Integration online Papers (EIoP)*, 1997, (http://eiop.or.at/eiop/texte/1997–011a.htm).
Fink-Hafner (Danica), "Organized interests in the policy-making process in Slovenia," *Journal of European public policy*, 5(2), 1998, pp. 285–302.
Fiorina (Morris P.), "Information and rationality in elections," in J.A. Ferejohn and J.H. Kuklinski (eds.), *Information and democratic processes*, Urbana, University of Illinois Press, 1990, pp. 329–342.

Flautre (Anne), *Les remaniements temporels. Le cas du Compte Épargne Temps*, Doctoral Thesis in Sociology, Université Toulouse-Le Mirail, 2002.

Fougère (Denis), Pouget (Julien), "L'emploi public s'est-il diversifié? Sexe, niveau d'étude, origine sociale et origine nationale des salariés de la fonction publique," Complément au rapport sur *La diversité dans la fonction publique* remis par Mme Dominique Versini au Ministre de la Fonction Publique et de la Réforme de l'État, La Documentation Française, Paris, 2004.

Franklin (Mark), Mackie (Thomas), and Valen (Henry), *Electoral change: response to evolving social and attitudinal structures in Western countries*, Cambridge, Cambridge University Press, 1992.

Fretel (Julien), "Le parti comme fabrique de notables. Réflexions sur les pratiques notabiliaires des élus de l'UDF," *Politix*, 17(65), 2004a, pp. 45–72.

———, "Quand des catholiques vont au parti. De la constitution d'une illusion paradoxale et du passage à l'acte chez les "militants" de l'UDF," *Actes de la recherche en sciences sociales*, 155, 2004b, pp. 76–89.

Freud (Sigmund), *Le malaise dans la culture*, Paris, Coll. Quadrige, PUF, 1995 (1st ed. in German: Vienne, Internationaler Psychoanalytischer Verlag, 1930).

Galbraith (John K.), *The new industrial state*, Boston (MA), Houghton Mifflin, 1967.

Galland (Olivier), Lemel (Yannick) (eds.), *La société française. Pesanteurs et mutations: le bilan*, Paris, Armand Colin, 2006.

Gamble (Andrew), *The conservative nation*, London, Routledge and Paul, 1974.

Gauchet (Marcel), *Le désenchantement du monde, Une histoire politique de la religion*, Paris, NRF, Gallimard, 1985.

———, "Pacification démocratique, désertion civique," *Le Débat*, 60, May–August 1990, pp. 87–98.

———, Le double refus du religieux et du politique, *Le Figaro*, 29 July 2002, p. 23.

———, "La droite, la gauche un an après," *Le Débat*, 126, September–October 2003, p. 25–37.

Gavini (Christine), *Emploi et régulation. Les nouvelles pratiques de l'entreprise*, Paris, CNRS Éditions, collection "CNRS Sociologie," 1998.

Gaxie (Daniel), "Economie des partis et rétributions du militantisme," *Revue française de science politique*, 27(1), February 1977, pp. 123–154.

Gehler (Michael), Kaiser (Wolfram), *Christian democracy in Europe since 1945*, London and New York, Routledge, 2004.

Genieys (William), "Nouveaux regards sur les élites du politique," *Revue française de science politique*, 56(1), February 2006, pp.121–147.

Goldthorpe (John H.), Erikson (Robert), *The constant flux: A study of class mobility in industrial societies*, Oxford, Clarendon Press, 1992.

Goldthorpe (John), Lockwood (David), Bechhofer (Frank), and Prat (Jenny), *The affluent worker in the class structure*, Cambridge, Cambridge University Press, 1969.

Gougeon (Jean-Pierre), *La social-démocratie allemande*, Paris, Aubier, 1996.

Grant (Wyn), *Pressure groups and British politics*, Basingstoke, Macmillan, 2000.

Grossman (Emiliano), "Les groupes d'intérêt économiques face à l'intégration européenne: le cas du secteur bancaire," *Revue française de Science politique*, 53(5), 2003, pp. 737–760.

———, "Lobbying et vie politique." *Problèmes politiques et sociaux*, 918, 2005, p. 120.

Grossman (Emiliano), Saurugger (Sabine), "Les groupes d'intérêt français entre l'exception française, l'Europe et le monde," *Revue internationale de politique comparée*, 11(4), 2004, pp. 507–529.

Groux (Guy), "L'entreprise publique et la négociation collective: du statut au contrat," in Luc Rouban (ed.), *Le service public en devenir*, Paris, L'Harmattan, collection "Logiques politiques," 2000, pp. 177–197.

Groux (Guy), Mouriaux (René), *La CFDT*, Paris, Économica, 1989.

Groux (Guy), Pernot (Jean-Marie), *La grève*, Paris, Presses de Sciences Po, coll. "Contester," 2008.

Grunberg (Gérard), Mayer (Nonna), "Démocratie représentative, démocratie participative" in Pascal Perrineau (ed.), *Le désenchantement démocratique*, La Tour d'Aigues, Editions de l'Aube, 2003, pp. 215–230.

Grunberg (Gérard), Muxel (Anne), "La dynamique des générations," in Gérard Grunberg, Nonna Mayer, and Paul Sniderman (eds.), *La démocratie à l'épreuve. Une nouvelle approche de l'opinion des Français*, Paris, Presses de Sciences Po, 2002, pp. 135–170.

Grunberg (Gérard), Schweisguth (Etienne), "Le virage à gauche des classes moyennes salariées," in Georges Lavau, Gérard Grunberg, Nonna Mayer (eds.), *L'univers politique des classes moyennes*, Paris, Presses de Sciences Po, 1983, pp. 351–377.

———, "Recompositions idéologiques," in Daniel Boy, Nonna Mayer (eds.), *L'électeur a ses raisons*, Paris, Presses de Sciences Po, 1997a, p. 139–178.

———, "Vers une tripartition de l'espace politique," in Daniel Boy, Nonna Mayer (eds.), *L'électeur a ses raisons*, Paris, Presses de Sciences Po, 1997b, pp.179–218.

———, "La tripartition de l'espace politique," in Pascal Perrineau and Colette Ysmal (eds.), *Le vote de tous les refus*, Paris, Presses de Sciences Po, 2003, pp. 341–362.

Guiraudon (Virginie), *Les politiques d'immigration en Europe: Allemagne, France, Pays-Bas*, Paris, L'Harmattan, 2000.

Habert (Philippe), *L'électeur rationnel*, Paris, Vinci, 1996.

Haegel (Florence), "Faire l'union. La refondation des partis de droite après les élections de 2002," *Revue française de science politique*, 52(5–6), October–December 2002, pp. 561–576.

———, "Le pluralisme à l'UMP. Structuration idéologique et compétition interne," in Florence Haegel (ed.), *Partis politiques et système partisans français*, Paris, Presses de Sciences Po, 2007, pp. 219–254.

Haegel (Florence), Pütz (Christine), and Sauger (Nicolas), "Les transformations de la démocratie dans et par les partis: l'exemple de l'UDF et du RPR," in Pascal Perrineau (ed.), *Le désenchantement démocratique*, Editions de l'Aube, La Tour d'Aigues, 2003, pp. 175–198.

Hastings (Michel), Strudel (Sylvie), "Gauche indivise et gauches singulières," in Pierre Bréchon, Annie Laurent, and Pascal Perrineau (eds.), *Les cultures politiques des Français*, Paris, Presses de Sciences Po, 2000, pp.165–188.

Heath (Anthony), Jowell (Roger), and Curtice (John), *How Britain votes*, Oxford, Pergamon Press, 1985.

Heath (Anthony), Jowell (Roger), and Curtice (John), Evans (George), *Understanding political change. The British Voter, 1964–1987*, Oxford, Pergamon Press, 1991.

Hervieu-Léger (Danièle), *Religion et écologie*, Paris, Le Cerf, 1993.

Hirschman (Albert O.), *Bonheur privé, action publique*, Paris, Fayard, 1983 (Oxford, M. Robertson, 1982).

Hopkin (Jonathan), Mastropaolo (Alfio), "From patronage to clientelism: Comparing the Italian and Spanish experiences" in Simona Piattoni (ed.), *Clientelism, interests and democratic representation*, Cambridge, Cambridge University Press, 2001, pp. 152–171.

Hout (Michael), Brooks (Clem), and Manza (Jeff), "Class voting in capitalist democracies since World War two: de-alignment, realignment or trendless fluctuations?" *Annual Review of Sociology*, 21, 1995a, pp. 137–163.

———, "The democratic class struggle in the United States, 1948–1992," *American Sociological Review*, 60, December 1995b, pp. 805–828.
Hyman (Richard), *Understanding European trade unionism. Between market, class and society*, London, Sage, 2001.
Ignazi (Piero), *Extreme Right parties in Western Europe*, Oxford, Oxford University Press, 2003.
Inglehart (Ronald), *Culture shift in advanced industrial society*, Princeton (NJ), Princeton University Press, 1990.
Institut français de l'environnement, *La sensibilité écologique des Français*, Orléans, Institut français de l'environnement, 2000.
Ion (Jacques), Franguiadakis (Spyros), and Viot (Pascal), *Militer aujourd'hui*, Paris, Autrement, 2005.
Iyengar (Shanto), "Shortcuts to political knowledge: The role of selective attention and accessibility," in J.A. Ferejohn, J.H. Kuklinski (eds.), *Information and democratic processes*, Urbana, University of Illinois Press, 1990, pp. 160–185.
Jacquier (Jean-Paul), "Le dialogue social français au regard de l'Europe," Ronéo, Le Bourg par Boudou, 2006.
Janssen (Jacques), Prins (Maerten), "The abstract image of God: The case of Dutch youth," *Archives de sciences sociales des religions*, 109, January–March 2000, pp. 31–48.
Jocou (Pierre), Meyer (Pierre), *La logique de la valeur*, Paris, Dunod, 1996.
Jordan (A.G.) and Richardson (Jeremy), *Governing under pressure. The policy process in a post-parliamentary democracy*, Oxford, Robertson, 1979.
Julliard (Jacques), *Contre la politique professionnelle*, Paris, Le Seuil, 1977.
———, *Autonomie ouvrière. Études sur le syndicalisme d'action directe*, Paris, Hautes Études, Gallimard-Seuil, 1988.
Katz (Richard.S.), Mair (Peter), *How parties organize*, London, Sage, 1994.
———, "Changing models of party organization and party democracy," *Party Politics*, 1995, 1(1), pp. 5–28.
Katzenstein (Peter), *Small states in world markets. Industrial policy in Europe*, Ithaca (NY), Cornell University Press, 1985.
Kesselman (Mark), "Système de pouvoir et cultures politiques au sein des partis politiques français," *Revue française de sociologie*, 16(4), October–December 1972, pp. 485–515.
Kim (S-H.), Scheufele (D.A.), and Shanahn (J.), "Who cares about the issues? Issue voting and the role of news media during the 2000 US presidential election," *Journal of Communication*, 55(1), 2005, pp. 103–121.
Kirchheimer (Otto), "The transformation of the European party systems" in Joseph LaPalombara, Myron Weiner (eds.), *Political parties and political development*, Princeton (NJ), Princeton University Press, 1966, p. 177–200.
Kitschelt (Herbert), Mc Gann (Anthony), *The radical Right in Western Europe: A comparative analysis*, Ann Arbor, University of Michigan Press, 1995.
Knapp (Andrew), "Vers un gouvernement d'inconnus? Hommes politiques et hauts fonctionnaires en Grande-Bretagne," in Henri Mendras, Ezra Suleiman (eds.), *Le recrutement des élites en Europe*, Paris, La Découverte, 1995, p. 128–157.
Knutsen (Oddbjørn), *Class voting in Western Europe: A comparative longitudinal study*, Lanham (MD), Rowman and Littlefield, 2006.
Kochan (Thomas), Katz (Harry C.), and McKersie (Robert B.), *The Transformation of American Industrial Relations*, New York, Basic Books, 1986.
Kriegel (Annie), *Aux origines du communisme français*, Paris, Flammarion, 1970.

Kuklinski (James H.), Quirk (Paul), "Conceptual foundations of citizen competence," *Political behavior*, 23(3), September 2001, pp. 285–311.

Lambert (Yves), "Vers un monothéisme des valeurs," *Le Débat*, 59, March–April 1990, pp. 90–105.

———, "L'Europe à un tournant," in *Futuribles*, Les valeurs des Européens, 277, July–August 2002, pp. 129–159.

L'Année politique, Paris, Editions du Grand Siècle, 1944–1945.

Laurent (Sébastien), Roullier (Jean-Eudes) (eds.), *Paul Delouvrier, un grand commis de l'État*, Paris, Presses de Sciences Po, 2005.

Laver (Michael), Hunt (William B), *Policy and party competition*, London, Routledge, 1992.

Lazarsfeld (Paul F.), Berelson (Bernard), and Gaudet (Hazel), *The people's choice: How the voter makes up his mind in a presidential campaign*, New York, Columbia University Press, 1944.

Le Galès (Patrick), "Gouvernance" in Laurie Boussaguet, Sylvie Jacquot, and Pauline Ravinet (eds.), *Dictionnaire des politiques publiques*, Paris, Presses de Sciences Po, 2004.

Le Galès (Patrick), Thatcher (Mark) (eds.), *Les réseaux de politique publique: débat autour des policy networks*, Paris, L'Harmattan, 1995.

Le Goff (Jean-Pierre), "Hypothèses pour comprendre le chaos ambiant," *Le Débat*, 126, September–October 2003, pp. 4–24.

Le Monde, *Entretien avec José Luis Rodriguez Zapatero*, Paris, July 29, 2004.

Le Roy Ladurie (Emmanuel), *L'État royal 1460–1610*, Paris, Hachette, coll. "Pluriel," 1987.

Lefranc (Georges), *Le mouvement syndical sous la Troisième République*, Paris, Payot, 1967.

Lehmbruch (Gerhard), "Neo-corporatism in comparative perspective," in Gerhard Lehmbruch, Philippe C. Schmitter (eds.) *Patterns of corporatist policy-making*, London, Sage, 1982, pp. 3–27.

Leridon (Matthias), "France 2006: où sont passées les élites?" dans TNS-SOFRES, *L'Etat de l'opinion 2006*, Seuil, Paris, 2006, p. 121–139.

Lévy (Jacques), "Un nouvel espace légitime," *Europolis The Newsletter—La Lettre*, 3, 1993.

Lichtenberger (Yves), "Comprendre le travail pour questionner le syndicalisme," *La Revue*, 15, 1998, pp. 3–10.

Lijphart (Arend), *Patterns of democracy. Government forms and performance in thirty-six countries*, New Haven (CT), Yale University Press, 1999.

Lipset (Seymour M.), *Political man: The social bases of politics*, Baltimore (MD), John Hopkins University Press, 1981 (1959, 1963).

Lipset (Seymour M.), Clark (Terry N.), "Are social classes dying?" *International Sociology*, 6(4), 1991, pp. 397–410.

Lipset (Seymour M.), Rokkan (Stein), "Cleavage structures, party systems, and voter alignments: An introduction," in S.M. Lipset and S. Rokkan (eds.), *Party systems and voter alignments: Cross-national perspectives*, New York, Free Press, 1967, pp. 1–64.

Lupia (Arthur), McCubbins (Mathew D.), *The democratic dilemma. Can citizens learn what they need to know?* Cambridge, Cambridge University Press, 1998.

Maire (Edmond), "Interrogations sur l'entreprise et l'anticapitalisme: l'individu et l'action syndicale," *CFDT Aujourd'hui*, March–April 1986.

Majone (Giandomenico), *La Communauté européenne: un État régulateur*, Paris, Monchrestien, 1996.

Manheim (Karl), *Le problème des générations*, Paris, Nathan, 1990.

Manoilescu (Mihail), *Le Siècle du corporatisme. Doctrine du corporatisme intégral et pur*, Paris, Felix Alcan-PUF, 1934.

Marques-Pereira (Bérangère), *La citoyenneté politique des femmes*, Paris, Armand Colin, 2003.

Marques-Pereira (Bérangère), Meier (Petra) (eds.), *Genre et politique en Belgique et en Francophonie*, Louvain-la-Neuve, Bruylant-Academia, 2005.

Marsh (David), Rhodes (R.A.W.), "Policy communities and issue networks. Beyond typology," in David Marsh, R.A.W. Rhodes (eds.), *Policy networks in British government*, Oxford, Clarendon, 1992.

Mayer (Nonna), *Ces Français qui votent Le Pen*, Paris, Flammarion, 2002.

Michelat (Guy), Simon (Michel), *Classe, religion et comportement politique*, Paris, Presses de Sciences-Po-Editions sociales, 1977.

———, *Les ouvriers et la politique*, Presses de Sciences Po, 2004.

Miller (William), *Media and voters*, Oxford, Clarendon Press, 1991.

Mills (Charles Wright), *The Power Elite*, New York, Oxford University Press, 1956 (Fr. ed.: *L'élite du pouvoir*, Paris, Maspero, 1969).

Milner (Henry), *La compétence civique. Comment les citoyens informés contribuent au bon fonctionnement de la démocratie*, Saint Nicolas, Presses de l'Université Laval, 2004.

Minc (Alain), *Le crépuscule des petits dieux*, Paris, Grasset, 2005.

Minkenberg (Michael), "The radical Right in post-socialist Central and Eastern Europe: Comparative observations and interpretations," *East European Politics and Societies*, Vol. 16(2), 2002, pp. 335–363.

Minkenberg (Michael), Perrineau (Pascal), "The radical Right in the European elections 2004," *International Political Science Review*, 28(1), 2007, pp. 29–55.

Missika (Jean-Louis), Les faux-semblants de la dépolitisation, *Le Débat*, 68, January–February 1992, pp. 14–19.

Mitterrand (François), *Politique*, Paris, Fayard, 1977.

Mossuz-Lavau (Janine), *Femmes/Hommes. Pour la parité*, Paris, Presses de Sciences Po, 1998.

———, "Parité: la nouvelle exception française," in Margaret Maruani (ed.), *Femmes, genre et sociétés*, Paris, La Découverte, 2005, pp. 307–314.

Mossuz-Lavau (Janine), Sineau (Mariette), *Enquête sur les femmes et la politique en France*, Paris, PUF, 1983.

———, *Les femmes dans le personnel politique en Europe*, Strasbourg, Conseil de l'Europe, 1984.

Mouriaux (René), *Les syndicats dans la société française*, Paris, Presses de Sciences Po, 1983.

Mudde (Cas), "Right-wing extremism analyzed. A comparative analysis of the ideologies of three alleged right-wing extremist parties (NPD, NDP, CP'86)," *European Journal of Political Research*, 27, 1995, pp. 203–224.

Müller-Rommel (Ferdinand), Poguntke (Thomas), *Green parties in national governments*, London, Frank Cass, 2002.

Muxel (Anne), *L'expérience politique des jeunes*, Paris, Presses de Sciences Po, 2001.

———, "La participation politique des jeunes: soubresauts, fractures, ajustements," *Revue française de science politique*, 52(5–6), October–December 2002, pp. 521–544.

Nieuwbeerta (Paul), "The democratic class struggle in post-war societies: Class voting in twenty countries, 1945–1990," *Acta sociologica*, 39(4), 1996, pp. 345–383.

Nora (Pierre), "Génération," in Pierre Nora (ed.), *Les lieux de mémoire*, Tome III, Les France, Volume 1, *Conflits et partages*, Paris, Gallimard, 1992.
Norris (Pippa), "Does television erode social capital? A reply to Putnam," *Political Science and Politics*, 29(3), September 1996, pp. 474–480.
———, *Critical citizen, global support for democratic governance*, Oxford, Oxford University Press, 1999.
———, *Democratic pheonix: Reinventing political activism*, Cambridge, Cambridge University Press, 2002.
Norris (Pippa), Curtice (John), Sanders (David), Scammell (Margaret), and Semetko (Holli A.), *On message. Communicating the campaign*, London, Sage, 1999.
Oakley (Ann), *Sex, gender and society*, London, Temple Smith, 1972.
Offe (Claus), "The attribution of public status to interest groups: Observations on the West German case" in Suzanne Berger (ed.), *Organizing interests in Western Europe: Pluralism, corporatism and the transformation of politics*, Cambridge, Cambridge University Press, 1981, pp. 123–158.
Ost (David), "Illusory corporatism in Eastern Europe: neo-liberal tripartism and post-communist class identities," *Politics and Society*, 28(4), 2000, pp. 503–530.
Page (Edward C.), Wright (Vincent) (eds.), *Bureaucratic elites in Western European states*, Oxford, Oxford University Press, 1999.
Palier (Bruno), *Gouverner la sécurité sociale: les réformes du système français de protection sociale depuis 1945*, Paris, PUF, 2002.
Panebianco (Angelo), *Political parties: Organization and power*, Cambridge, Cambridge University Press, 1982 (1988).
Pedersen (Mogens N.), "The dynamics of European party systems: Changing patterns of electoral volatility," *European Journal of Political Research*, 7(1), 1979, pp. 1–26.
Percheron (Annick), "Age, cycle de vie, génération et comportement électoral," in Daniel Gaxie (ed.), *Explication du vote. Un bilan des études électorales en France*, Paris, Presses de Sciences Po, 1985, pp. 228–262
———, "La mémoire des générations: la guerre d'Algérie—Mai 68," in SOFRES. *L'Etat de l'opinion 1991,* Paris, Seuil, 1991, pp. 39–57
———, *La socialisation politique,* Paris, Armand Colin, 1993.
Pérez-Solorzano (Nieves), "Organized interest in Central and Eastern Europe: Towards gradual Europeanisation," *Politique européenne*, 3, 2001, pp. 61–85.
Pernot (Jean-Marie), *Syndicats: lendemains de crise?* Paris, Folio-Gallimard, coll. "Actuel," 2005.
Perrineau (Pascal), *Le symptôme Le Pen. Radiographie des électeurs du Front national*, Paris, Fayard, 1997.
——— (ed.), *Les croisés de la société fermée, L'Europe des extrêmes droites*, La Tour-d'Aigues, Editions de l'Aube, 2001.
——— (ed.), *Le désenchantement démocratique*, La Tour-d'Aigues, Editions de l'Aube, 2003.
——— (ed.), *Le vote européen 2004–2005. De l'élargissement au référendum français*, Paris, Presses de Sciences Po, 2005a.
———, "La société française: un état de la recherche. Le rapport à la politique: une crise de la démocratie représentative?" *Les Cahiers Français*, Comprendre la société, 326, May–June 2005b, pp. 48–53.
——— (ed.), *Atlas électoral 2007*, Paris, Presses de Sciences Po, 2007.
Pütz (Christine), "La présidentialisation des partis français," in Florence Haegel (ed.), *Partis politiques et système partisans français*, Paris, Presses de Sciences Po, 2007, pp. 321–357.

Rémond (René), *Les droites en France*, Paris, Aubier, 1982.
———, *Religion et société en Europe,* Paris, Seuil, 1998.
———, *Les droites aujourd'hui,* Paris, Audibert, 2005.
Revue française d'administration publique, *Les fonctionnaires et la politique dans les pays de l'Union européenne*, 86, 1998, Paris, La Documentation française.
Rey (Henri), Subileau (Françoise), *Les militants socialistes à l'épreuve du pouvoir*, Paris, Presses de la Fondation nationale des sciences politiques, 2001.
Rey (Henri), Subileau (Françoise), Ysmal (Colette), *Les adhérents socialistes en 1998*, Paris, Cahiers du CEVIPOF n° 23, 1999.
Reynaud (Jean-Daniel), *Les règles du jeu. L'action collective et la régulation sociale*, Paris, Armand Colin, 1997 (1st ed. 1989).
Richardson (Dick), Roots (Chris), *The Green challenge, the development of Green parties in Europe*, London, Routledge, 1995.
Risse (Thomas), Cowles (Maria G.), "Europeanization and domestic change: Introduction," in Thomas Risse, Maria G. Cowles, and James Caporaso (eds.), *Transforming Europe: Europeanization and domestic change*, Ithaca (NY), Cornell University Press, 2001, pp. 1–21.
Roblain (Olivier), *Le bricolage comme mode de régulation dans une organisation en mouvement. Le cas des gestionnaires des ressources humaines à La Poste*, Doctoral Thesis in Sociology, Université Paris Dauphine, 2006.
Rosanvallon (Pierre), *L'âge de l'autogestion*, Paris, Le Seuil, 1976.
———, *Le peuple introuvable, Histoire de la représentation démocratique en France*, Paris, Gallimard, 1998.
Rose (Richard), *Electoral behavior: A comparative handbook*, New York, Free Press, 1974.
Rose (Richard), McAllister (Ian), *Voters begin to choose: From closed-class to open elections in Britain*, London, Sage, 1986.
Rouban (Luc), "Les entourages de l'Elysée et de Matignon 1974–1997," La *Revue Administrative*, 302, March–April 1998a, pp. 317–324; 303, May–June 1998a, pp. 420–426; 304, July–August 1998a, pp. 530–538.
———, *La fin des technocrates?* Paris, Presses de Sciences Po, 1998b.
———, *L'Inspection générale des Finances 1958–2000. Quarante ans de pantouflage*, Cahier du Cevipof, 31, Paris, http://www.cevipof.msh-paris.fr/publications/cahiers.html, 2002a.
———, "Les hauts fonctionnaires sous la Ve République: idées reçues et perspectives analytiques," *Revue française d'administration publique*, 104, 2002b, pp. 657–675.
———, "Politicization of the civil service in France: From structural to strategic politicization," in B. Guy Peters, Jon Pierre (eds.), *Politicization of the civil service in comparative perspective*, London and New York, Routledge, 2004, pp. 81–100.
———, *Public-privé: la culture sociopolitique des salariés en Europe*, Cahier du Cevipof, 40, Paris, http://www.cevipof.msh-paris.fr/publications/cahiers.html, 2005.
———, "Public management and politics: Senior bureaucrats in France," *Public Administration*, 85(2), 2007, pp. 473–501.
———, "Reform without doctrine: Public management in France," *International Journal of Public Sector Management*, 21(2), 2008, pp. 133–149.
Sainteny (Guillaume), *Les Verts*, Paris, PUF, 1997.
Sarkozy (Nicolas), *La République, les religions*, l'espérance, Paris, Le Cerf, 2004.
Sawicki (Frédéric), *Les réseaux du Parti socialiste*, Paris, Belin, 1997.
Scarrow (Susan), *Parties and their members. Organizing for victory in Britain and Germany*, Oxford, Oxford University Press, 1996.

Schmidt (Vivien), *From state to market? The transformation of French business and government*, Cambridge, Cambridge University Press, 1996.

———, "National patterns of governance under siege. The impact of European integration," in Reiner Eising, Beate Kohler-Koch (eds.), *The transformation of governance in the European Union*, London, Routledge, 1999, pp. 155–172.

———, *The futures of European capitalism,* Oxford, Oxford University Press, 2002.

———, "French capitalism transformed, yet a third variety of capitalism," *Economy and Society*, 32(4), 2003, pp. 526–554.

Schmitter (Philippe), "Still the century of corporatism?," *Review of Politics*, 36(1), 1974, pp. 86–131.

Schmitter (Philippe), Grote (Jürgen), "The corporatist Sisyphus: Past, present and future," *EUI Working Paper SPS*, 97(4), 1997, p. 1–22.

Schmitter (Philippe), Streeck (Wolfgang), "From national corporatism to trans-national pluralism—organized interests in the single European market," *Politics and Society*, 19 (2), 1991, pp. 133–164.

Schweisguth (Etienne), "La montée des valeurs individualistes," *Futuribles*, "Les valeurs des Européens," 277, July–August 1995, pp. 131–160.

———, "Le mythe du néo-conservatisme français," *Futuribles*, 227, January 1998, pp. 21–34.

———, "La dépolitisation en questions," in Gérard Grunberg, Nonna Mayer, and Paul Sniderman (eds.), *La démocratie à l'épreuve*, Paris, Presses de Sciences Po, 2002, pp. 51–86.

Scott (Joan W.), *Parité ! L'universel et la différence des sexes*, Paris, Albin Michel, 2005.

Sebaldt (Martin), *Organisierter pluralismus. Selbstverständnis und politische arbeit deutscher interessengruppen*, Opladen, Westdeutscher Verlag, 1997.

Shonfield (Andrew), *Modern capitalism. The changing balance of public and private power*, London, William Pickering, 1994.

Sineau (Mariette), *Profession femme politique. Sexe et pouvoir sous la Cinquième République*, Paris, Presses de Sciences Po, 2001.

Stigler (George), "The theory of economic regulation," *Bell Journal of Economics and Management*, 2, 1971, pp. 3–21.

Stoller (Robert), *Sex and gender*, New York, Science House Edition, 1968.

Taguieff (Pierre-André), *L'illusion populiste*, Paris, Berg International, 2002.

Tajfel (Henri), *Differentiation between social groups*, London, Academic Press, 1978.

Talin (Kristoff), "Les amants maudits: heurs et malheurs du couple religion et politique en Europe à l'aube du troisième millénaire," *Cahiers de recherches sociologiques,* 1999, 33, pp. 119–147.

Terssac (Gilbert de) (ed.), *La théorie de la régulation sociale de Jean-Daniel Reynaud*, Paris, La Découverte, coll. "Recherches," 2003.

Thébaud Françoise, *Écrire l'histoire des femmes*, Paris, ENS Éditions, 1998.

Thomassen (Jacques) (ed.), *The European voter. A comparative study of Modern Democracies*, New York, Oxford University Press-ECPR, 2006.

Tocqueville (Alexis de), *De la démocratie en Amérique,* Paris, Garnier-Flammarion, 1981.

Topf (Richard), "Beyond electoral participation," in Dieter Fuchs, Hans-Dieter Klingeman (eds.), *Citizens and the state*, Oxford, Oxford University Press, 1995, pp. 52–91.

Tournier (Vincent), "Générations politiques," in Bruno Cautrès, Nonna Mayer (eds.), *Le nouveau désordre électoral*, Paris, Presses de Sciences Po, 2004, pp. 229–252.

Tremblay (Manon) (ed.), *Femmes et parlements.* Un regard international, Montréal, Éditions du Remue-ménage, 2005.

Truman (David), *The governmental process. Political interests and public opinion*, New York, Alfred Knopf-Borzoi Books, 1951.

Van Beyme (Klaus), *Political parties in Western democracies*, Aldershot, Gower, 1985.

Van der Waal (Jeroen), Achterberg (Peter), and Houtman (Dick), "Class is not dead—it has been buried alive: Class voting and cultural voting in postwar Western societies (1956–1990)," *Politics and Society*, 2007, 35(3), pp. 403–426.

Vatta (Alessia), "Concertation and employers' organizations in Italy: The case of Confindustria," *South European Society and Politics*, 6(3), 2001, pp. 103–22.

Verley (Patrick), *L'échelle du monde. Essai sur l'industrialisation de l'Occident*, Paris, Gallimard, coll. "NRF Essais," 1997.

Vialatte (Jérôme), *Les partis Verts en Europe occidentale*, Paris Economica, 1996.

Visser (Jelle), "Two cheers for corporatism, one for the market: Industrial relations, wage moderation and job growth in the Netherlands," *British Journal of Industrial Relations*, 36(2), 1998, pp. 269–292.

———, "Union membership statistics in 24 countries," *Monthly Labor Review*, January 2006, pp. 38–49.

Vogel (David), *Kindred strangers: The uneasy relationship between politics and business in America*, Princeton (NJ), Princeton University Press, 1996a.

———, *Freer markets, more rules: Regulatory reform in advanced industrial countries,* Ithaca (NY), Cornell University Press, 1996b.

Wagner (Anne-Catherine), *Les nouvelles élites de la mondialisation*, Paris, PUF, 1998.

Ware (Alan), *Political parties and party systems*, Oxford, Oxford University Press, 1996.

Webb (Sydney and Beatrice), *Industrial democracy*, New York, Augustus M. Kelley, 1965 (1897).

Wilson (Frank) (ed.), *The European Centre Right at the end of the twentieth century*, New York, St Martin Press, 1998.

Zimmermann (Marie-Jo), *Effets directs et indirects de la loi du 6 juin 2000: un bilan contrasté*, Rapport de l'Observatoire de la parité entre les hommes et les femmes, Paris, March 2005.

Zuckerman (Alan S). *The politics of faction. Christian Democratic rule in Italy*, New Haven (CT), Yale University Press, 1979.

Index